The Language of New Media

Lev Manovich

The MIT Press Cambridge, Massachusetts London, England

This book was set in Bell Gothic and Garamond 3 by Graphic Composition, Inc.

Printed and bound in the United States of America.

Library of Congress Cataloging-in-Publication Data
Manovich, Lev.
  The language of new media / Lev Manovich.
      p. cm. — (Leonardo)
  Includes bibliographical references and index.
  ISBN 0-262-13374-1 (hc : alk. paper), 0-262-63255-1 (pb)
  1. Mass media—Technological innovations. I. Title. II. Leonardo
(Series) Cambridge, Mass.)

  P96.T42 M35   2000
  302.2—dc21   00-057882
10 9 8 7 6 5

To Norman Klein/Peter Lunenfeld/Vivian Sobchack

Contents

Contents

Contents

Contents

Foreword

I first encountered Lev Manovich three years ago, when he posted a message to the Rhizome e-mail list. The subject line was "On Totalitarian Interactivity." One passage in particular caught my attention: "A Western artist sees the Internet as a perfect tool to break down all hierarchies and bring art to the people. In contrast, as a post-communist subject, I cannot but see the Internet as a communal apartment of the Stalin era: no privacy, everybody spies on everybody else, always present are lines for common areas such as the toilet or the kitchen." Manovich's image of the Internet as a Russian apartment was made more vivid by the fact that I had recently spent a month living with an artist in Moscow. I had also just moved to New York from Berlin, where I had worked as a web designer. While in a material sense, the Internet is a globally homogeneous network with common tools and protocols, and while it is contributing, perhaps more than any other technology, to the globalization of economies and cultures, my experience in Berlin taught me that it nonetheless means very different things in different parts of the world. The perspective Manovich brought to the subject was a bracing reminder that the zeal with which most Americans (myself included) embraced computers and networks in the mid-1990s was not a global condition.

When Manovich wrote "On Totalitarian Interactivity," a debate was raging on the Rhizome e-mail list. The Europeans—who may have lagged technologically but had an edge when it came to theory—were on the attack, criticizing Americans for our "California ideology" (a deadly cocktail of naive optimism, techno-utopianism, and new-libertarian politics popularized by *Wired* magazine). In the midst of this highly polarized debate,

Manovich's displaced voice, the voice of someone who had "lived experience" of both ideological extremes, was refreshing indeed. His trajectory had taken him from the surreal world of Leonid Brezhnev's Russia to the hyperreal world of Walt Disney's California. Having grown up in Russia, completed his higher education in the United States, and lived and worked here ever since, he sees the world through the eyes of what he calls a "postcommunist subject," but one might say with equal accuracy that he wears a set of new-world glasses as well.

Having studied film theory, art history, and literary theory, and having worked in new media himself as artist, commercial designer, animator, and programmer, Manovich approaches new media in a way that is both theoretical and practical. This multilevel hybridity—simultaneously postcommunist and late-capitalist, at once academic and applied—lends his ideas a richness and complexity that is more than a little unusual in a field dominated on the one hand by techno-utopians and on the other by ivory-tower theory wonks. My own interest in new media has been focused on the Internet and its potential as a tool and a space for art making. Art has always been bound up with technology, and artists have always been among the first to adopt new technologies as they emerge. We monkey around with new technologies in an effort to see what they can do, to make them do things the engineers never intended, to understand what they might mean, to reflect on their effects, to push them beyond their limits, to break them. But some technologies seem to hold considerably more promise for artists than others. The Internet is particularly ripe with the potential to enable new kinds of collaborative production, democratic distribution, and participatory experience.

It is precisely this newness that makes new media an interesting place for cultural producers to work. New media represents a constantly shifting frontier for experimentation and exploration. While new media are understood in terms of the older media that precede them, they are nonetheless freed, at least to some extent, from traditional constraints. Having to figure out how new tools work necessitates innovation and encourages a kind of beginner's mind. New media attract innovators, iconoclasts, and risk-takers. As a result, some of the hottest creative minds spend their time hacking around with new technologies that we barely understand. In this sense the new media artists of today have much in common with the video artists of the early 1970s. Manovich has made significant contributions to new media art as well, with his net-based projects "Little Movies" and "Freud-Lissitzky Navigator." Because of their very newness, new media are slightly beyond the effective reach of established institutions and their bureaucracies. Net art is a case in point. While museums started to catch on to the net as an art medium in the last years of the 1990s and began to collect, commission, and exhibit net-based work, most of the artists who interest them made their names outside the gallery-museum matrix. The net art community of the late 1990s possessed an anarchic quality of entrepreneurial meritocracy strikingly different from the rest of the art world, where gallery schmoozing and the ability to produce marketable objects have remained primary determinants of success.

But this freedom comes at a cost. Sluggish as they may seem, galleries and museums serve an important interpretive function. They focus the attention of critics and audiences, situate work in historical context, and allocate time and space for us to experience and reflect on the work itself. On the technological frontiers of art making, where museums fear to tread, critical dialogue becomes all the more important. But the newness of new media makes it particularly difficult to write about, or at least to say anything useful. Most writers lapse into futurology, or remain mired in ungrounded theory. That makes this book by Lev Manovich all the more unusual and important. The first detailed and encompassing analysis of the visual aesthetics of new media, the book locates new media within the history of visual culture, articulating connections and differences among new media and older forms. Finding the origins of new media aesthetics in painting, photography, cinema, and television, Manovich looks at digital imaging, human-computer interface, hypermedia, computer games, compositing, animation, telepresence, and virtual worlds. In doing so, he eclectically and imaginatively draws on film theory, literary theory, and social theory. Just as important, he draws on his own working experience with new media technologies and computer science to lay out the fundamental principles that distinguish new media from old. In his analysis, he offers detailed readings of particular objects in art and popular culture. Unique in their depth and scope, the chapters that follow will be of interest not only to academics, but also to artists and designers who seek a better understanding of the history and theory of their practice.

At a recent conference on the theory and culture of computer games, a panelist asked this provocative question: "If in the early years of cinema we already had seminal works that defined the language of the medium, why haven't we seen the computer-game equivalent of D. W. Griffith's *Birth of a Nation?*" The answer, of course, is that we have. The question is how to recognize it. To do so, we need to build a history and theory of the language of new media. In this groundbreaking work, Lev Manovich has done a great deal of the fundamental conceptual work toward that end.

Mark Tribe
Founder, Rhizome.org
New York City

Prologue: Vertov's Dataset

The avant-garde masterpiece *Man with a Movie Camera,* completed by Russian director Dziga Vertov in 1929, will serve as our guide to the language of new media. This prologue consists of a number of stills from the film. Each still is accompanied by a quote from the text summarizing a particular principle of new media. The number in brackets indicates the page from which the quote is taken. The prologue thus acts as a visual index to some of the book's major ideas.

[78–79] A hundred years after cinema's birth, cinematic ways of seeing the world, of structuring time, of narrating a story, of linking one experience to the next, have become the basic means by which computer users access and interact with all cultural data. In this respect, the computer fulfills the promise of cinema as a visual Esperanto—a goal that preoccupied many film artists and critics in the 1920s, from Griffith to Vertov. Indeed, today millions of computer users communicate with each other through the same computer interface. And in contrast to cinema, where most "users" are able to "understand" cinematic language but not "speak" it (i.e., make films), all computer users can "speak" the language of the interface. They are active users of the interface, employing it to perform many tasks: send e-mail, organize files, run various applications, and so on.

[84–85] The incorporation of virtual camera controls into the very hardware of game consoles is truly a historic event. Directing the virtual camera becomes as important as controlling the hero's actions. . . . [In computer games], cinematic perception functions as the subject in its own right, suggesting the return of "New Vision" movement of the 1920s (Moholy-Nagy, Rodchenko, Vertov, and others), which foregrounded the new mobility of the photo and film camera, and made unconventional points of view a key part of its poetics.

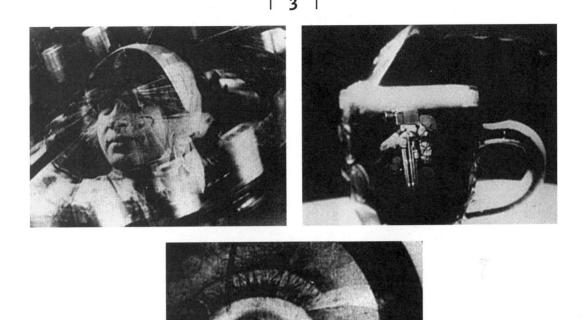

[148] Editing, or montage, is the key twentieth-century technology for creating fake realities. Theoreticians of cinema have distinguished between many kinds of montage, but for the purpose of sketching an archeology of the technologies of simulation that led to digital compositing, I will distinguish between two basic techniques. The first technique is temporal montage: Separate realities form consecutive moments in time. The second technique is montage within a shot. It is the opposite of the first: separate realities form contingent parts of a single image. . . . Examples include the . . . superimposition of images and multiple screens by avant-garde filmmakers in the 1920s (for instance, the superimposed images in Vertov's *Man with a Movie Camera* and the three-part screen in Abel Gance's 1927 *Napoléon*).

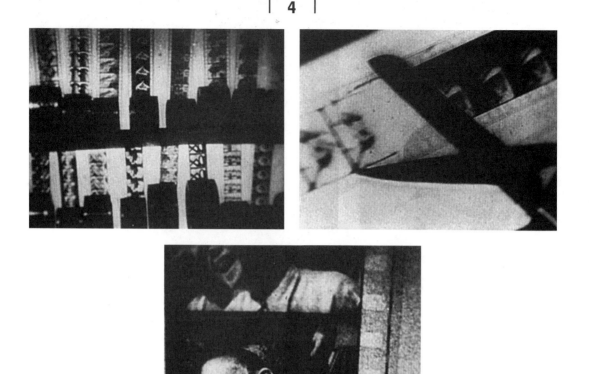

[149] As theorized by Vertov, film can overcome its indexical nature through montage, by presenting a viewer with objects that never existed in reality.

[158] Although digital compositing is usually used to create a seamless virtual space, this does not have to be its only goal. Borders between different worlds do not have to be erased; different spaces do not have to be matched in perspective, scale, and lighting; individual layers can retain their separate identities rather than being merged into a single space; different worlds can clash semantically rather than form a single universe.

[172] The cameraman, whom Benjamin compares to a surgeon, "penetrates deeply into its [reality's] web"; his camera zooms in order to "pry an object from its shell." Due to its new mobility, glorified in such films as *Man with a Movie Camera,* the camera can be anywhere, and with its superhuman vision it can obtain a close-up of any object. . . .

When photographs are brought together within a single magazine or newreel, both the scale and unique locations of the objects are discarded—thus answering the demand of mass society for a "universal equality of things."

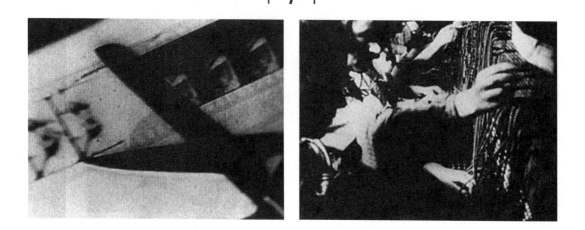

[173–174] Modernization is accompanied by a disruption of physical space and matter, a process that privileges interchangeable and mobile signs over original objects and relations. . . . The concept of modernization fits equally well with Benjamin's account of film and Virilio's account of telecommunication, the latter but a more advanced stage in the continual process of turning objects into mobile signs. Before, different physical locations met within a single magazine spread or film newsreel; now they meet within a single electronic screen.

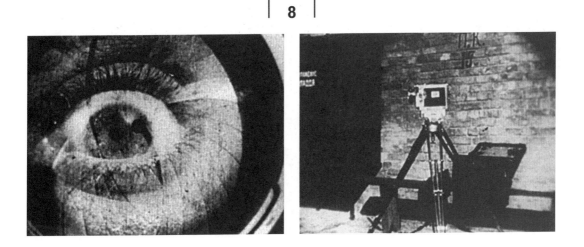

[202] Whose vision is it? It is the vision of a computer, a cyborg, an automatic missile. It is a realistic representation of human vision in the future, when it will be augmented by computer graphics and cleansed from noise. It is the vision of a digital grid. Synthetic computer-generated imagery is not an inferior representation of our reality, but a realistic representation of a different reality.

[239] Along with Greenaway, Dziga Vertov can be thought of as a major "database filmmaker" of the twentieth century. *Man with a Movie Camera* is perhaps the most important example of a database imagination in modern media art.

[241] Just as new media objects contain a hierarchy of levels (interface—content; operating system—application; Web page—HTML code; high-level programming language—assembly language—machine language), Vertov's film contains at least three levels. One level is the story of a camera-man shooting material for the film. The second level consists of shots of the audience watching the finished film in a movie theater. The third level is the film itself, which consists of footage recorded in Moscow, Kiev, and Riga, arranged according to the progression of a single day: waking up—work—leisure activities. If this third level is a text, the other two can be thought of as its metatexts.

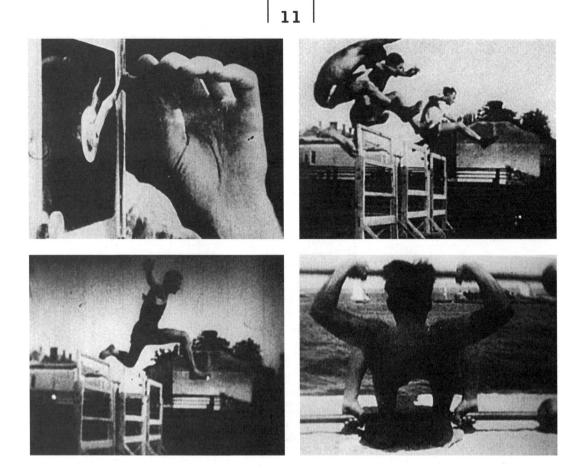

[242] If a "normal" avant-garde film still proposes a coherent language different from the language of mainstream cinema, that is, a small set of techniques that are repeated, *Man with a Movie Camera* never arrives at anything like a well-defined language.

Rather, it proposes an untamed, and apparently endless, unwinding of techniques, or, to use contemporary language, "effects," as cinema's new way of speaking.

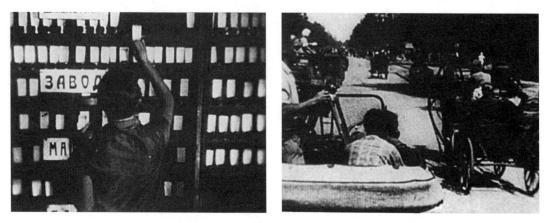

[243] "And this is why Vertov's film has particular relevance to new media. It proves that it is possible to turn "effects" into a meaningful artistic language. Why is it that in Witney's computer films and music videos effects are just effects, whereas in the hands of Vertov they acquire meaning? Because in Vertov's film they are motivated by a particular argument, which is that the new techniques of obtaining images and manipulating them, summed up by Vertov in his term "kino-eye," can be used to decode the world. As the film progresses, straight footage gives way to manipulated footage; newer techniques appear one after another, reaching a roller-coaster intensity by the film's end—a true orgy of cinematography. It is as though Vertov restages his discovery of the kino-eye for us, and along with him, we gradually realize the full range of possibilities offered by the camera. Vertov's goal is to seduce us into his way of seeing and thinking, to make us share his excitement, as he discovers a new language for film. This gradual process of discovery is film's main narrative, and it is told through a catalog of discoveries. Thus, in the hands of Vertov, the database, this normally static and "objective" form, becomes dynamic and subjective. More important, Vertov is able to achieve something that new media designers and artists still have to learn—how to merge database and narrative into a new form.

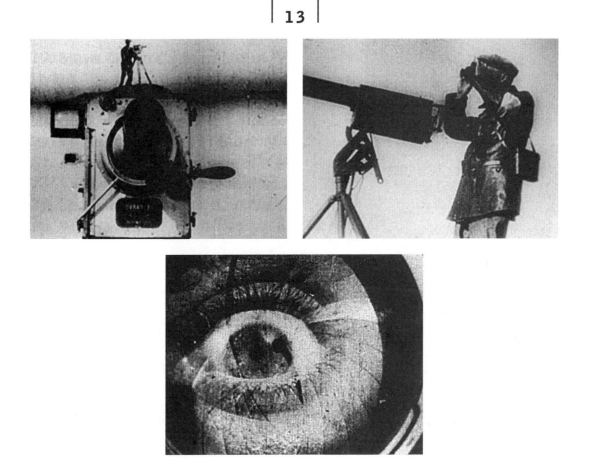

[262] If modern visual culture exemplified by MTV can be thought of as a Mannerist stage of cinema, its perfected techniques of cinematography, mise-en-scène and editing self-consciously displayed and paraded for its own sake, Waliczky's film presents an alternative response to cinema's classical age, which is now behind us. In this metafilm, the camera, part of cinema's apparatus, becomes the main character (and in this respect, we can connect *The Forest* to another metafilm, *Man with a Movie Camera*).

[275–276] . . . Vertov stands halfway between Baudelaire's flâneur and to-day's computer user: no longer just a pedestrian walking down a street, but not yet Gibson's data cowboy who zooms through pure data armed with data-mining algorithms. In his research on what can be called "kino-eye interface," Vertov systematically tried different ways to overcome what he thought were the limits of human vision. He mounted cameras on the roof of a building and a moving automobile; he slowed and sped up film speed; he superimposed a number of images together in time and space (temporal montage and montage within a shot). *Man with a Movie Camera* is not only a database of city life in the 1920s, a database of film techniques, and a database of new operations of visual epistemology, but also a database of new interface operations that together aim to go beyond simple human navigation through physical space.

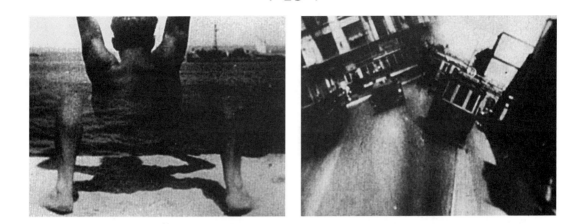

[306–307] One general effect of the digital revolution is that avant-garde
aesthetic strategies came to be embedded in the commands and interface
metaphors of computer software. In short, the avant-garde became materialized in a computer. Digital cinema technology is a case in point. The avant-
garde strategy of collage reemerged as the "cut-and-paste" command, the
most basic operation one can perform on digital data. The idea of painting
on film became embedded in paint functions of film-editing software. The
avant-garde move to combine animation, printed texts, and live-action
footage is repeated in the convergence of animation, title generation, paint,
compositing, and editing systems into all-in-one packages.

[316] Cinema's birth from a loop form was reenacted at least once during its history. In one of the sequences of *Man with a Movie Camera,* Vertov shows us a cameraman standing in the back of a moving automobile. As he is being carried forward by the automobile, he cranks the handle of his camera. A loop, a repetition, created by the circular movement of the handle, gives birth to a progression of events—a very basic narrative that is also quintessentially modern—a camera moving through space recording whatever is in its way.

[317] Can the loop be a new narrative form appropriate for the computer age? It is relevant to recall that the loop gave birth not only to cinema but also to computer programming. Programming involves altering the linear flow of data through control structures, such as "if/then" and "repeat/while"; the loop is the most elementary of these control structures. . . . As the practice of computer programming illustrates, the loop and the sequential progression do not have to be considered mutually exclusive. A computer program progresses from start to end by executing a series of loops.

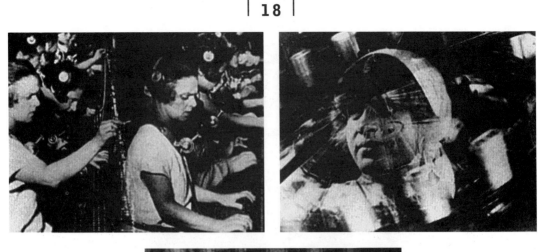

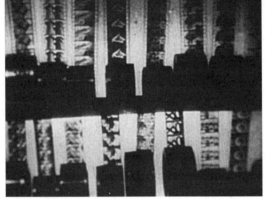

[322] Spatial montage represents an alternative to traditional cinematic temporal montage, replacing its traditional sequential mode with a spatial one. Ford's assembly line relied on the separation of the production process into sets of simple, repetitive, and sequential activities. The same principle made computer programming possible: A computer program breaks a task into a series of elemental operations to be executed one at a time. Cinema followed this logic of industrial production as well. It replaced all other modes of narration with a sequential narrative, an assembly line of shots that appear on the screen one at a time. This type of narrative turned out to be particularly incompatible with the spatial narrative that had played a prominent role in European visual culture for centuries.

[324] Since the development of the Xerox PARC Alto workstation, the Graphical User Interface (GUI) has used multiple windows. It would be logical to expect that cultural forms based on moving images will eventually adopt similar conventions. . . . We may expect that computer-based cinema will eventually go in the same direction—especially once the limitations of communication bandwidth disappear while the resolution of displays significantly increases, from the typical 1–2K in 2000 to 4K, 8K, or beyond. I believe that the next generation of cinema—*broadband* or *macrocinema*—will add multiple windows to its language.

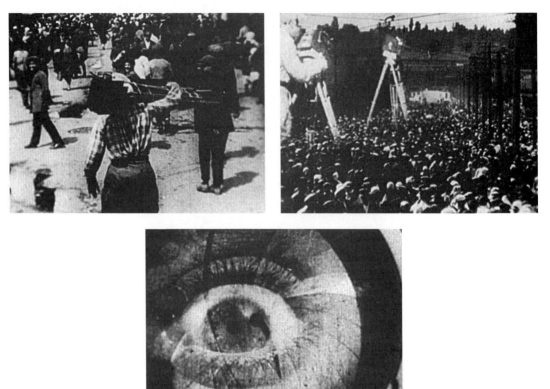

[326–327] If the Human Computer Interface (HCI) is an interface to computer data, and a book is an interface to text, cinema can be thought of as an interface to events taking place in 3-D space. Just as painting before it, cinema presents us with familiar images of visible reality—interiors, landscapes, human characters—arranged within a rectangular frame. The aesthetics of these arrangements ranges from extreme scarcity to extreme density. . . . It would take only a small leap to relate this density of "pictorial displays" to the density of contemporary information displays such as Web portals, which may contain a few dozen hyperlinked elements, or the interfaces of popular software packages, which similarly present the user with dozens of commands at once.

Acknowledgments

Special thanks: Doug Sery, my editor at MIT Press, whose support and continuous encouragement made this book possible; everybody else at MIT Press who brought their expertise and passion to this project; Mark Tribe, who read the manuscript in its entirety and offered numerous suggestions; Tarleton Gillespie, who offered invaluable help with editing at the last moment; Alla Efimova, for everything; Rochelle Feinstein, who served as my muse.

This book would not exist without all the friends, colleagues, and institutions committed to new media art and theory. I am grateful to all of them for ongoing exchange and intellectual and emotional support.

For providing inspiring places to work: Mondrian Hotel (West Hollywood, Los Angeles), The Standard (West Hollywood, Los Angeles), Fred Segal (West Hollywood, Los Angeles), Del Mar Plaza (Del Mar, CA), Gitano (NoLita, NYC), Space Untitled (Soho, New York), The Royal Library (Stockholm), De Jaren (Amsterdam).

Administrative support: Department of Visual Arts, University of California, San Diego; Department of Cinema Studies, Stockholm University; Center for User-Centered Interface Design, Royal Institute of Technology, Stockholm.

Word processor: Microsoft Word.
Web browser: Netscape Navigator, Internet Explorer.
Favorite search engine: www.hotbot.com.
Favorite moving image format: QuickTime.
HTML editor: Netscape Communicator, Macromedia Dreamweaver.
OS: Windows 98.

Hardware: SONY PCG505FX laptop.
Mobile phone: Nokia.

The principal editing of this book was done between July 1998 and November 1999 in La Jolla and Del Mar, California; Los Angeles; New York; Stockholm; Helsinki; and Amsterdam.

Although significant parts of this book have been written anew, I have drawn on material from a number of previously published articles. Sometimes only part of an article made it into the final manuscript; in other cases, parts ended up in different chapters of the book; in yet other cases, a whole article became the basis for one of the sections. In the following list, I cite the articles that were used as material for the book. Many of them were reprinted and translated into other languages; here I list the first instance of publication in English. Also, it has been my practice for a number of years to post any new writing I do to Nettime[1] and Rhizome,[2] two important Internet e-mail lists devoted to discussions of new media art, criticism, and politics. This practice enabled me to receive immediate feedback on my work and also provided me with a community interested in my work. Most articles, accordingly, appeared on these two e-mail lists before being published in more traditional print venues such as journals and anthologies or in Internet journals.

"Assembling Reality: Myths of Computer Graphics." In *Afterimage* 20, no. 2 (September 1992): 12–14.

"Paradoxes of Digital Photography." In *Photography after Photography,* edited by Hubertus v. Amelunxen, Stefan Iglhaut, Florian Rötzer, 58–66 (Munich: Verlag der Kunst, 1995).

"To Lie and to Act: Potemkin's Villages, Cinema, and Telepresence." In *Mythos Information—Welcome to the Wired World. Ars Electronica 95,* edited by Karl Gebel and Peter Weibel, 343–353 (Vienna and New York: Springler-Verlag, 1995).

"Reading Media Art." (In German translation) in *Mediagramm* 20 (ZKM / Zentrum für Kunst und Medientechnologie Karlsruhe, 1995): 4–5.

---

1. http://www.nettime.org.
2. http://www.rhizome.org.

"Archeology of a Computer Screen." In *NewMediaLogia* (Moscow: Soros Center for Contemporary Art, 1996).

"Distance and Aura." In_SPEED_: Technology, Media, Society 1.4 (http://www.arts.ucsb.edu/~speed/1.4 /), 1996.

"Cinema and Digital Media." In *Perspektiven der Medienkunst / Perspectives of Media Art,* edited by Jeffrey Shaw and Hans Peter Schwarz (Stuttgart: Cantz Verlag Ostfildern, 1996).

"What Is Digital Cinema?" In *Telepolis* (www.ix.de/tp) (Munich: Verlag Heinz Heise, 1996).

"The Aesthetics of Virtual Worlds: Report from Los Angeles." In *Telepolis* (www.ix.de/tp) (Munich: Verlag Heinz Heise, 1996).

"On Totalitarian Interactivity." In RHIZOME (http://www.rhizome.com), 1996.

"Behind the Screen / Russian New Media." In *art / text* 58 (August–October 1997): 40–43.

"Cinema as a Cultural Interface." In W3LAB (http://gsa.rutgers.edu/ maldoror/techne/w3lab-entry.html), 1998.

"Database as a Symbolic Form." In RHIZOME (www.rhizome.com), 1998.

"Navigable Space." (In German translation) in *ONSCREEN/OFFSCREEN— Grenzen, Übergänge und Wandel des filmischen Raumes,* edited by Hans Beller, Martin Emele and Michael Schuster (Stuttgart: Cantz Verlag, 1999).

"Cinema by Numbers: ASCII Films by Vuk Cosic." In *Vuk Cosic: Contemporary ASCII* (Ljubljana, Slovenia: Galerija Š.O.U. Kapelica, 2000). (http://www. vuk.org/ascii /)

"New Media: A User's Guide." In *NET.CONDITION* (ZKM / Zentrum für Kunst und Medientechnologie Karlsruhe and The MIT Press, forthcoming).

The Language of
New Media

Introduction

A Personal Chronology

Moscow, 1975. Although my ambition is to become a painter, I enroll in the mathematical ("matematicheskaya") high school, which in addition to a regular curriculum has courses in calculus and computer programming. The programming course lasts two years, during which we never see a computer. Our teacher uses a blackboard to explain the concepts of computer programming. First we learn a computer language invented in the Soviet Union in the late 1950s. The language has a wonderful Cold War name: "Peace-1" ("MiR-1"). Later we learn a more standard high-level language: ALGOL-60. For two years, we write computer programs in our notebooks. Our teacher grades them and returns them with corrections: missed end of the loop statement, undeclared variable, forgotten semicolon. At the end of the two-year course, we are taken—just once—to a data-processing center, which normally requires clearance to enter. I enter my program into a computer, but it does not run: Because I had never seen a computer keyboard before, I used the letter *O* whenever I need to input zero.

Also in 1975, I start taking private lessons in classical drawing, lessons that also last two years. The Moscow Architectural Institute entrance exams include a test in which the applicants have to complete a drawing of an antique bust in eight hours. To get the top grade, one has to produce a drawing that not only looks like the cast and has perfect perspective, but also has perfect shading. This means that all shadows and surfaces are defined completely through shading, so all the lines originally used to define them disappear. Hundreds of hours spent in front of a drawing board pay off: I get an A on the exam, even though out of eight possible casts I am assigned the most difficult one: the head of Venera. It is more difficult because, in contrast to casts of male heads such as Socrates', it does not have well-defined facets; the surfaces join smoothly together as though constructed with a spline modeling program. Later I learn that, during the 1970s, computer scientists were working on the same problem, that is, how to produce smoothly shaded images of 3-D objects on a computer. The standard rendering algorithm still used today was invented at the University of Utah in 1975—the same year I started my drawing lessons.[1]

---

1. B. T. Phong, "Illumination for Computer Generated Pictures," *Communication of the ACM* 18, no. 6 (June 1975): 311–317.

New York, 1985. It is early morning, and I am sitting in front of a Tetronics terminal in midtown Manhattan. I have just finished my night shift at Digital Effects, one of the first companies in the world devoted to producing 3-D computer animation for film and television. (The company worked on *Tron* and produced computer animation for all of the major television networks.) My job is to operate the Harris-500 mainframe, used to compute animations, and also the PDP-11, which controls the Dicomed film recorder, used to output animation on 35mm film. After a few months I am able to figure out the company's proprietary computer-graphics software written in APL (a high level programming language), and begin work on my first images. I would like to produce a synthetic image of an antique bust, but the task turns out to be impossible. The software is able to create 3-D objects only out of primitive geometric forms such as cubes, cylinders, and spheres—so I am forced to settle for a composition made out of these primitive forms. Tetronics is a vector rather than raster terminal, which means that it does not update its screen in real time. Each time I make a change in my program or simply change a point of view, I hit the enter key and wait while the computer redraws the lines, one by one. I wonder why I had to spend years learning to draw images in perspective when a computer could do it in seconds. A few of the images I create are exhibited in shows of computer art in New York. But this is the heyday of postmodernism: The art market is hot, paintings by young New York artists are selling for tens of thousands of dollars, and the art world has little interest in computer art.

Linz, Austria, 1995. I am at Ars Electronica, the world's most prestigious annual computer-art festival. This year it drops the "computer graphics" category, replacing it with the new "net art" category, signaling a new stage in the evolution of modern culture and media. The computer, which since the early 1960s has been used as a production tool, has now become a universal media machine—a tool used not only for production, but also for storage and distribution. The World Wide Web crystallizes this new condition; on the level of language, this fact is recognized around 1990 when the term "digital media" comes to be used along with "computer graphics." At the same time, along with existing cultural forms, computers begin to host an array of new forms: Web sites and computer games, hypermedia CD-ROMs and interactive installations—in short, "new media." And if in 1985 I had to write a long computer program in a specialized computer language just to put a picture of a shaded cube on a computer screen, ten years later I can choose from a number of inexpensive, menu-based 3-D software tools that run on ordinary PCs and come with numerous ready-made 3-D models, including detailed human figures and heads.

What else can be said about 1995? The Soviet Union, where I was born, no longer exists. With its demise, the tensions that for decades animated creative imaginations both in the East and the West—between freedom and confinement, interactivity and predetermination, consumerism in the West and "spirituality" in the East—disappear. What takes their place? A triumph of consumerism, commercial culture (based on stereotypes and limited clichés), megacorporations that lay claim to such basic categories as space, time, and the future ("Where Do You Want to Go Today?" ads by Microsoft; "Internet Time" by Swatch, which breaks twenty-four hours into 1,000 Swatch "beats"; "You will" ads by AT&T), and "globalization" (a term at least as elusive as "spirituality").

When I visit St. Petersburg in 1995 to participate in a small computer art festival called "In Search of a Third Reality," I see a curious performance, which may be a good parable of globalization. Like the rest of the festival, the performance takes place in the planetarium. Its Director, forced like everyone else to make his own living in the new Russian economic order (or lack thereof), had rented the planetarium to conference organizers. Under the black hemispherical ceiling with mandatory models of planets and stars, a young artist methodically paints an abstract painting. Probably trained in the same classical style as I had been, he is no Pollock; cautiously and systematically, he makes careful brushstrokes on the canvas in front of him. On his hand he wears a Nintendo Dataglove, which in 1995 is a common media object in the West but a rare sight in St. Petersburg. The Dataglove transmits the movements of his hand to a small electronic synthesizer, assembled in the laboratory of some Moscow institute. The music from the synthesizer serves as an accompaniment to two dancers, a male and a female. Dressed in Isadora Duncan–like clothing, they improvise a "modern dance" in front of an older and, apparently, completely puzzled audience. Classical art, abstraction, and a Nintendo Dataglove; electronic music and early twentieth-century modernism; discussions of virtual reality (VR) in the planetarium of a classical city that, like Venice, is obsessed with its past—what for me, coming from the West, are incompatible historical and conceptual layers are composited together, with the Nintendo Dataglove being just one layer in the mix.

What also arrives by 1995 is the Internet—the most material and visible sign of globalization. And by the end of the decade it will also become clear that the gradual computerization of culture will eventually transform all of it. So, invoking the old Marxist model of base and superstructure, we can say that if the economic base of modern society from the 1950s onward starts to shift toward a service and information economy, becoming by the 1970s a so-called post-industrial society (Daniel Bell), and then later a "network society" (Manual Castells), by the 1990s the superstructure starts to feel the full impact of this change.[2] If the postmodernism of the 1980s is the first sign of this shift still to come—still weak, still possible to ignore—the 1990s' rapid transformation of culture into e-culture, of computers into universal culture carriers, of media into new media, demands that we rethink our categories and models.

The year is 2005. . . .

Theory of the Present

I wish that someone in 1895, 1897, or at least 1903, had realized the fundamental significance of the emergence of the new medium of cinema and produced a comprehensive record: interviews with audiences; a systematic account of narrative strategies, scenography, and camera positions as they developed year by year; an analysis of the connections between the emerging language of cinema and different forms of popular entertainment that co-existed with it. Unfortunately, such records do not exist. Instead we are left with newspaper reports, diaries of cinema's inventors, programs of film showings, and other bits and pieces—a set of random and unevenly distributed historical samples.

Today we are witnessing the emergence of a new medium—the meta-medium of the digital computer. In contrast to a hundred years ago, when cinema was coming into being, we are fully aware of the significance of this new media revolution. Yet I am afraid that future theorists and historians of computer media will be left with not much more than the equivalents of the newspaper reports and film programs from cinema's first decades. They will find that analytical texts from our era recognize the significance of the com-

---

2. Daniel Bell, *The Coming of Post-industrial Society* (New York: Basic Books, 1973); Manuel Castells, *The Rise of the Network Society* (Cambridge, Mass.: Blackwell Publishers, 1996).

puter's takeover of culture yet, by and large, contain speculations about the future rather than a record and theory of the present. Future researchers will wonder why the theoreticians, who had plenty of experience analyzing older cultural forms, did not try to describe computer media's semiotic codes, modes of address, and audience reception patterns. Having painstakingly reconstructed how cinema emerged out of preceding cultural forms (panorama, optical toys, peep shows), one might ask why they didn't attempt to construct a similar genealogy for the language of computer media at the moment when it was just coming into being, that is, when the elements of previous cultural forms shaping it were still clearly visible and recognizable, before melting into a coherent language? Where were the theoreticians at the moment when the icons and buttons of multimedia interfaces were like wet paint on a just-completed painting, before they became universal conventions and thus slipped into invisibility? Where were they at the moment when the designers of *Myst* were debugging their code, converting graphics to 8-bit, and massaging QuickTime clips? Or at the historical moment when a twenty-something programmer at Netscape took the chewing gum out of his mouth, sipped warm Coke out of the can—he had been at a computer for sixteen hours straight, trying to meet a marketing deadline—and, finally satisfied with its small file size, saved a short animation of stars moving across the night sky? This animation would appear in the upper right corner of Netscape Navigator, and become the most widely seen moving image sequence ever—until the next release of the software.

What follows is an attempt at both a record and a theory of the present. Just as film historians traced the development of film language during cinema's first decades, I aim to describe and understand the logic driving the development of the language of new media. (I am not claiming that there is a single language of new media. I use "language" as an umbrella term to refer to a number of various conventions used by designers of new media objects to organize data and structure the user's experience.) It is tempting to extend this parallel a little further and speculate whether this new language is already drawing closer to acquiring its final and stable form, just as film language acquired its "classical" form during the 1910s. Or it may be that the 1990s are more like the 1890s, in the sense that the computer-media language of the future will be entirely different from the one used today.

Does it make sense to theorize the present when it seems to be changing so fast? It is a hedged bet. If subsequent developments prove my theoretical projections correct, I win. But even if the language of computer media develops in a different direction than the one suggested by the present analysis, this book will become a record of possibilities heretofore unrealized, of a horizon visible to us today but later unimaginable.

We no longer think of the history of cinema as a linear march toward a single possible language, or as a progression toward perfect verisimilitude. On the contrary, we have come to see its history as a succession of distinct and equally expressive languages, each with its own aesthetic variables, and each closing off some of the possibilities of its predecessor (a cultural logic not dissimilar to Thomas Kuhn's analysis of scientific paradigms.)[3] Similarly, every stage in the history of computer media offers its own aesthetic opportunities, as well as its own vision of the future: in short, its own "research paradigm." In this book I want to record the "research paradigm" of new media during its first decade, before it slips into invisibility.

Mapping New Media: The Method

I analyze the language of new media by placing it within the history of modern visual and media cultures. What are the ways in which new media relies on older cultural forms and languages, and what are the ways in which it breaks with them? What is unique about how new media objects create the illusion of reality, address the viewer, and represent space and time? How do conventions and techniques of old media—such as the rectangular frame, mobile viewpoint, and montage—operate in new media? If we construct an archeology connecting new computer-based techniques of media creation with previous techniques of representation and simulation, where should we locate the essential historical breaks?

To answer these questions, I look at all areas of new media: Web sites, virtual worlds,[4] virtual reality (VR), multimedia, computer games, interactive instal-

---

3. Thomas S. Kuhn, *The Structure of Scientific Revolutions,* 2d ed. (Chicago: University of Chicago Press, 1970).

4. By virtual worlds I mean 3-D computer-generated interactive environments. This definition fits a whole range of 3-D computer environments already in existence—high-end VR works that feature head-mounted displays and photo realistic graphics, arcade, CD-ROM and on-line multi-player computer games, QuickTime VR movies, VRML (Virtual Reality Modeling Language) scenes, and graphical chat environments such as The Palace and Active Worlds.

Virtual worlds represent an important trend across computer culture, consistently promising to become a new standard in human-computer interfaces and computer networks. (For a

lations, computer animation, digital video, cinema, and human-computer interfaces. Although the book's main emphasis is on theoretical and historical arguments, I also analyze many key new-media objects, from American commercial classics such as *Myst* and *Doom, Jurassic Park* and *Titanic,* to the work of international new media artists and collectives such as ART+COM, antirom, jodi.org, George Legrady, Olga Lialina, Jeffrey Shaw, and Tamas Waliczky.

The computerization of culture not only leads to the emergence of new cultural forms such as computer games and virtual worlds; it redefines existing ones such as photography and cinema. I therefore also investigate the effects of the computer revolution on visual culture at large. How does the shift to computer-based media redefine the nature of static and moving images? What is the effect of computerization on the visual languages used by our culture? What new aesthetic possibilities become available to us?

In answering these questions, I draw upon the histories of art, photography, video, telecommunication, design, and, last but not least, the key cultural form of the twentieth century—cinema. The theory and history of cinema serve as the key conceptual lens though which I look at new media. The book explores the following topics:

- the parallels between cinema history and the history of new media;
- the identity of digital cinema;
- the relations between the language of multimedia and nineteenth century pro-cinematic cultural forms;
- the functions of screen, mobile camera, and montage in new media as compared to cinema;
- the historical ties between new media and avant-garde film.

---

discussion of why this promise may never be fulfilled, see the "Navigable Space" section.) For example, Silicon Graphics developed a 3-D file system that was showcased in the movie *Jurassic Park*. Sony used a picture of a room as an interface in its MagicLink personal communicator. Apple's short-lived E-World greeted its users with a drawing of a city. Web designers often use pictures of buildings, aerial views of cities, and maps as interface metaphors. In the words of the scientists from Sony's The Virtual Society Project (www.csl.sony.co.jp/project/VS/), "It is our belief that future online systems will be characterized by a high degree of interaction, support for multi-media and most importantly the ability to support shared 3-D spaces. In our vision, users will not simply access textual based chat forums, but will enter into 3-D worlds where they will be able to interact with the world and with other users in that world."

Along with film theory, this book draws theoretical tools from both the humanities (art history, literary theory, media studies, social theory) and computer science. Its overall method could be called "digital materialism." Rather than imposing some a priori theory from above, I build a theory of new media from the ground up. I scrutinize the principles of computer hardware and software and the operations involved in creating cultural objects on a computer to uncover a new cultural logic at work.

Most writings on new media are full of speculation about the future. This book, in contrast, analyses new media as it has actually developed until the present moment, while pointing to directions for new media artists and designers that have yet to be explored. It is my hope that the theory of new media developed here can act not only as an aid to understanding the present, but also as a grid for practical experimentation. For example, the "Theory of Cultural Interfaces" section analyzes how the interfaces of new media objects are being shaped by three cultural traditions: print, cinema, and human-computer interface. By describing elements in these traditions that are already being used in new media, I point toward other elements and their combinations still awaiting experimentation. The "Compositing" section provides another set of directions for experiments by outlining a number of new types of montage. Yet another direction is discussed in "Database," where I suggest that new media narratives can explore the new compositional and aesthetic possibilities offered by a computer database.

Although this book does not speculate about the future, it does contain an implicit theory of how new media will develop. The advantage of placing new media within a larger historical perspective is that we begin to see the long trajectories that lead to new media in its present state, and we can extrapolate these trajectories into the future. The section "Principles of New Media" describes four key trends that, in my view, are shaping the development of new media over time: modularity, automation, variability, and transcoding.

Of course we don't have to accept these trends blindly. Understanding the logic that is shaping the evolution of new media language allows us to develop different alternatives. Just as avant-garde filmmakers have offered alternatives to cinema's particular narrative audio-visual regime throughout the medium's history, the task of avant-garde new media artists today is to offer alternatives to the existing language of computer media. This can be better accomplished if we have a theory of how "mainstream" language is now structured and how it might evolve over time.

Mapping New Media: Organization

This book aims to contribute to the emerging field of new media studies (sometimes called "digital studies") by providing one potential map of what the field can be. Just as a literary theory textbook might feature chapters on narrative and voice, and a textbook of film studies might discuss cinematography and editing, this book calls for the definition and refinement of the new categories specific to new media theory.

I have divided the book into a number of chapters, each of which covers one key concept or problem. Concepts developed in earlier chapters become building blocks for analyses in later chapters. In determining the sequence of the chapters, I considered textbooks on various established fields relevant to new media, such as film studies, literary theory, and art history; much as a textbook on film may begin with film technology and end up with film genres, this book progresses from the material foundations of new media to its forms.

One could also draw an analogy between the "bottom-up" approach I use here and the organization of computer software. A computer program written by a programmer undergoes a series of translations: high-level computer language is compiled into executable code, which is then converted by an assembler into binary code. I follow this order in reverse, advancing from the level of binary code to the level of a computer program, and then move on to consider the logic of new media objects driven by these programs:

1. "What Is New Media?"—the digital medium itself, its material and logical organization.
2. "The Interface"—the human-computer interface; the operating system (OS).
3. "The Operations"—software applications that run on top of the OS, their interfaces, and typical operations.
4. "The Illusions"—appearance, and the new logic of digital images created using software applications.
5. "The Forms"—commonly used conventions for organizing a new media object as a whole.

The last chapter "What Is Cinema?" mirrors the book's beginning. Chapter 1 points out that many of the allegedly unique principles of new media can already be found in cinema. Subsequent chapters continue to employ film history and theory as a means of analyzing new media. Having discussed different levels of new media—interface, operations, illusion, and forms—I then reverse my conceptual lens to look at how computerization changes cinema. I analyze the identity of digital cinema by placing it within the history of the moving image and discuss how computerization offers new opportunities for developing the language of film.

At the same time, the last chapter continues the "bottom-up" trajectory of the book as a whole. If chapter 5 looks at the organization of new cultural objects, such as Web sites, hypermedia CD-ROMs, and virtual worlds, all "children" of the computer, chapter 6 considers the effects of computerization on an older cultural form that exists, so to speak, "outside" computer culture proper—cinema.

Each chapter begins with a short introduction that discusses a concept and summarizes the arguments developed in individual sections. For example, chapter 2, "The Interface," begins with a general discussion of the importance of the concept of the interface in new media. The two sections of chapter 2 then look at different aspects of new media interfaces: their reliance on the conventions of other media and the relationship between the body of the user and the interface.

The Terms: Language, Object, Representation

In putting the word *language* into the title of the book, I do not want to suggest that we need to return to the structuralist phase of semiotics in understanding new media. However, given that most studies of new media and cyberculture focus on their sociological, economic, and political dimensions, it was important for me to use the word *language* to signal the different focus of this work: the emergent conventions, recurrent design patterns, and key forms of new media. I considered using the words *aesthetics* and *poetics* instead of *language,* eventually deciding against them. *Aesthetics* implies a set of oppositions that I would like to avoid—between art and mass culture, the beautiful and the ugly, the valuable and the unimportant. *Poetics* also bears undesirable connotations. Continuing the project of the Russian formalists of the 1910s, theoreticians in the 1960s defined *poetics* as the study of the specific properties of particular arts, such as narrative literature. In his *Introduction to Poetics* (1968), literary scholar Tzvetan Todorov, for instance, writes:

In contradistinction to the interpretation of particular works, it [poetics] does seek to name meaning, but aims at a knowledge of the general laws that preside over the birth of each work. But in contradistinction to such sciences as psychology, sociology, etc., it seeks these laws within literature itself. Poetics is therefore an approach to literature at once 'abstract' and 'internal.'[5]

In contrast to such an "internal" approach, I neither claim that the conventions, elements, and forms of new media are unique, nor do I consider it useful to look at them in isolation. On the contrary, this book aims to situate new media in relation to a number of other areas of culture, both past and present:

• other arts and media traditions: their visual languages and their strategies for organizing information and structuring the viewer's experience;
• computer technology: the material properties of the computer, the ways in which it is used in modern society; the structure of its interface, and key software applications;
• contemporary *visual culture:* the internal organization, iconography, iconology, and viewer experience of various visual sites in our culture—fashion and advertising, supermarkets and fine art objects, television programs and publicity banners, offices and techno-clubs;
• contemporary *information culture.*

The concept "information culture," which is my term, can be thought of as a parallel to another, already familiar concept—visual culture. It includes the ways in which information is presented in different cultural sites and objects—road signs; displays in airports and train stations; television on-screen menus; graphic layouts of television news; the layouts of books, newspapers, and magazines; the interior designs of banks, hotels, and other commercial and leisure spaces; the interfaces of planes and cars; and, last but not least, the interfaces of computer operating systems (Windows, Mac OS, UNIX) and software applications (Word, Excel, PowerPoint, Eudora, Navigator, RealPlayer, Filemaker, Photoshop, etc.). Extending the parallels with visual culture, information culture also includes historical methods for

---

5. Tzevan Todorov, *Introduction to Poetics,* trans. Richard Howard (Minneapolis: University of Minnesota Press, 1981), 6.

organizing and retrieving information (analogs of iconography) as well as patterns of user interaction with information objects and displays.

Another word deserving comment is *object.* Throughout the book, I use the term *new media object,* rather than *product, artwork, interactive media* or other possible terms. A new media object may be a digital still, digitally composited film, virtual 3-D environment, computer game, self-contained hypermedia DVD, hypermedia Web site, or the Web as a whole. The term thus fits with my aim of describing the general principles of new media that hold true across all media types, all forms of organization, and all scales. I also use *object* to emphasize that my concern is with the culture at large rather than with new media art alone. Moreover, *object* is a standard term in the computer science and computer industry, where it is used to emphasize the modular nature of object-oriented programming languages such as C++ and Java, object-oriented databases, and the Object Linking and Embedding (OLE) technology used in Microsoft Office products. Thus it also serves my purpose to adopt the terms and paradigms of computer science for a theory of computerized culture.

In addition, I hope to activate connotations that accompanied the use of the word *object* by the Russian avant-garde artists of the 1920s. Russian Constructivists and Productivists commonly referred to their creations as *objects* (*vesh, construktsia, predmet*) rather than works of art. Like their Bauhaus counterparts, they wanted to take on the roles of industrial designers, graphic designers, architects, and clothing designers, rather than remain fine artists producing one-of-a-kind works for museums or private collections. *Object* pointed toward the factory and industrial mass production rather than the traditional artist's studio, and it implied the ideals of rational organization of labor and engineering efficiency that artists wanted to bring into their own work.

In the case of new media objects, all these connotations are worth invoking. In the world of new media, the boundary between art and design is fuzzy at best. On the one hand, many artists make a living as commercial designers; on the other hand, professional designers are typically the ones who really push forward the language of new media by being engaged in systematic experimentation and also by creating new standards and conventions. The second connotation, that of industrial production, also holds true for new media. Many new media projects are put together by large teams (although, in contrast to the studio system of the classical Hollywood era, single producers or small teams are also common). Many new media objects, such as popular games or software applications, sell millions of copies. Yet another feature of the new media field that unites it with big industry is the strict adherence to various hardware and software standards.[6]

Finally, and most important, I use the word *object* to reactivate the concept of laboratory experimentation practiced by the avant-garde of the 1920s. Today, as more artists are turning to new media, few are willing to undertake systematic, laboratory-like research into its elements and basic compositional, expressive, and generative strategies. Yet this is exactly the kind of research undertaken by Russian and German avant-garde artists of the 1920s in places like Vkhutemas[7] and Bauhaus, as they explored the new media of their time: photography, film, new print technologies, telephony. Today, those few who are able to resist the immediate temptation to create an "interactive CD-ROM," or make a feature-length "digital film," and instead focus on determining the new-media equivalent of a shot, sentence, word, or even letter, are rewarded with amazing findings.

A third term that is used throughout the book and needs comment is *representation.* In using this term, I want to invoke the complex and nuanced understanding of the functioning of cultural objects as developed in the humanities over the last decades. New media objects are cultural objects; thus, any new media object—whether a Web site, computer game, or digital image—can be said to represent, as well as help construct, some outside referent: a physically existing object, historical information presented in other documents, a system of categories currently employed by culture as a whole or by particular social groups. As is the case with all cultural representations, new media representations are also inevitably biased. They represent/construct some features of physical reality at the expense of others,

---

6. Examples of software standards include operating systems such as UNIX, Windows, and MAC OS; file formats (JPEG, MPEG, DV, QuickTime, RTF, WAV); scripting languages (HTML, Javascript); programming languages (C++, Java); communication protocols (TCP-IP); the conventions of HCI (e.g., dialog boxes, copy and paste commands, the help pointer); and also unwritten conventions, such as the 640-by-480 pixel image size that was used for more than a decade. Hardware standards include storage media formats (ZIP, JAZ, CD-ROM, DVD), port types (serial, USB, Firewire), bus architectures (PCI), and RAM types.

7. Vkhutemas was a Moscow art and design school in the 1920s that united most leftist avant-garde artists; it functioned as a counterpart of the Bauhaus in Germany.

one worldview among many, one possible system of categories among numerous others. In this book I will take this argument one step further by suggesting that software interfaces—both those of operating systems and of software applications—also act as representations. That is, by organizing data in particular ways, they privilege particular models of the world and the human subject. For instance, the two key ways to organize computer data commonly used today—a hierarchical file system (Graphical User Interface from the 1984 Macintosh onward) and a "flat," nonhierarchical network of hyperlinks (1990s World Wide Web)—represent the world in two fundamentally different and in fact opposing ways. A hierarchical file system assumes that the world can be reduced to a logical and hierarchical order, where every object has a distinct and well-defined place. The World Wide Web model assumes that every object has the same importance as any other, and that everything is, or can be, connected to everything else. Interfaces also privilege particular modes of data access traditionally associated with particular arts and media technologies. For instance, the World Wide Web of the 1990s foregrounded the page as a basic unit of data organization (regardless of which media types it contained), while Acrobat software applied the metaphor of "video playback" to text-based documents. Thus interfaces act as "representations" of older cultural forms and media, privileging some at the expense of others.

In describing the language of new media, I have found it useful to use the term *representation* in opposition to other terms. Depending on which term it is opposed to, the meaning of *representation* changes. Since these oppositions are introduced in different sections of the book, I will summarize them here:

1. *Representation—simulation* ("Screen" section). Here, *representation* refers to various screen technologies such as post-Renaissance painting, film, radar, and television. I define *screen* as a rectangular surface that frames a virtual world and that exists within the physical world of a viewer without completely blocking her visual field. *Simulation* refers to technologies that aim to immerse the viewer completely within a virtual universe—Baroque Jesuit churches, nineteenth-century panorama, twentieth-century movie theaters.

2. *Representation—control* ("Cultural Interfaces" section). Here I oppose the image as a representation of an illusionary fictional universe and the image as a simulation of a control panel (for instance, GUI with its different icons and menus) that allows the user to control a computer. This new type of im-

age can be called *image-interface.* The opposition representation—control corresponds to an opposition between depth and surface: a computer screen as window into illusionistic space versus computer screen as flat control panel.

3. *Representation—action* ("Teleaction" section). This is the opposition between technologies used to create illusions (fashion, realist paintings, dioramas, military decoys, film montage, digital compositing) and representational technologies used to enable action, that is, to allow the viewer to manipulate reality through representations (maps, architectural drawings, x-rays, telepresence). I refer to images produced by later technologies as *image-instruments.*

4. *Representation—communication* ("Teleaction" section). This is the opposition between representational technologies (film, audio, and video magnetic tape, digital storage formats) and real-time communication technologies, that is, everything that begins with *tele-* (telegraph, telephone, telex, television, telepresence). Representational technologies allow for the creation of traditional aesthetic objects, that is, objects that are fixed in space or time and refer to some referent(s) outside themselves. By foregrounding the importance of person-to-person telecommunication, and *telecultural* forms in general that do not produce any objects, new media force us to reconsider the traditional equation between culture and objects.

5. *Visual illusionism—simulation* (introduction to "Illusions" chapter). *Illusionism* here refers both to representation and simulation as these terms are used in the "Screen" section. Thus illusionism combines traditional techniques and technologies that aim to create a visual resemblance of reality—perspectival painting, cinema, panorama, etc. *Simulation* refers to various computer methods for modeling other aspects of reality beyond visual appearance—movement of physical objects, shape changes occurring over time in natural phenomena (water surface, smoke), motivations, behavior, speech and language comprehension in human beings.

6. *Representation—information* (introduction to "Forms" chapter). This opposition refers to two opposing goals of new media design: immersing users in an imaginary fictional universe similar to traditional fiction and giving users efficient access to a body of information (for instance, a search engine, Web site, or on-line encyclopedia).

1

What Is New Media?

What is new media? We may begin answering this question by listing the categories commonly discussed under this topic in the popular press: the Internet, Web sites, computer multimedia, computer games, CD-ROMs and DVD, virtual reality. Is this all there is to new media? What about television programs shot on digital video and edited on computer workstations? Or feature films that use 3-D animation and digital compositing? Shall we also count these as new media? What about images and text-image compositions—photographs, illustrations, layouts, ads—created on computers and then printed on paper? Where shall we stop?

As can be seen from these examples, the popular understanding of new media identifies it with the use of a computer for distribution and exhibition rather than production. Accordingly, texts distributed on a computer (Web sites and electronic books) are considered to be new media, whereas texts distributed on paper are not. Similarly, photographs that are put on a CD-ROM and require a computer to be viewed are considered new media; the same photographs printed in a book are not.

Shall we accept this definition? If we want to understand the effects of computerization on culture as a whole, I think it is too limiting. There is no reason to privilege the computer as a machine for the exhibition and distribution of media over the computer as a tool for media production or as a media storage device. All have the same potential to change existing cultural languages. And all have the same potential to leave culture as it is.

The last scenario is unlikely, however. What is more likely is that just as the printing press in the fourteenth century and photography in the nineteenth century had a revolutionary impact on the development of modern society and culture, today we are in the middle of a new media revolution—the shift of all culture to computer-mediated forms of production, distribution, and communication. This new revolution is arguably more profound than the previous ones, and we are just beginning to register its initial effects. Indeed, the introduction of the printing press affected only one stage of cultural communication—the distribution of media. Similarly, the introduction of photography affected only one type of cultural communication—still images. In contrast, the computer media revolution affects all stages of communication, including acquisition, manipulation, storage, and distribution; it also affects all types of media—texts, still images, moving images, sound, and spatial constructions.

How shall we begin to map out the effects of this fundamental shift? What are the ways in which the use of computers to record, store, create, and distribute media makes it "new"?

In the section "Media and Computation," I show that new media represents a convergence of two separate historical trajectories: computing and media technologies. Both begin in the 1830s with Babbage's Analytical Engine and Daguerre's daguerreotype. Eventually, in the middle of the twentieth century, a modern digital computer is developed to perform calculations on numerical data more efficiently; it takes over from numerous mechanical tabulators and calculators widely employed by companies and governments since the turn of the century. In a parallel movement, we witness the rise of modern media technologies that allow the storage of images, image sequences, sounds, and text using different material forms—photographic plates, film stocks, gramophone records, etc. The synthesis of these two histories? The translation of all existing media into numerical data accessible through computers. The result is new media—graphics, moving images, sounds, shapes, spaces, and texts that have become computable; that is, they comprise simply another set of computer data. In "Principles of New Media," I look at the key consequences of this new status of media. Rather than focusing on familiar categories such as interactivity or hypermedia, I suggest a different list. This list reduces all principles of new media to five—numerical representation, modularity, automation, variability, and cultural transcoding. In the last section, "What New Media Is Not," I address other principles that are often attributed to new media. I show that these principles can already be found at work in older cultural forms and media technologies such as cinema, and therefore in and of themselves are in sufficient to distinguish new media from old.

How Media Became New

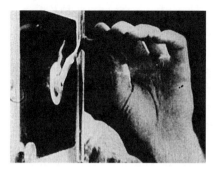

On August 19, 1839, the Palace of the Institute in Paris was filled with curious Parisians who had come to hear the formal description of the new reproduction process invented by Louis Daguerre. Daguerre, already well known for his Diorama, called the new process *daguerreotype.* According to a contemporary, "a few days later, opticians' shops were crowded with amateurs panting for daguerreotype apparatus, and everywhere cameras were trained on buildings. Everyone wanted to record the view from his window, and he was lucky who at first trial got a silhouette of roof tops against the sky."[1] The media frenzy had begun. Within five months more than thirty different descriptions of the technique had been published around the world— Barcelona, Edinburgh, Naples, Philadelphia, St. Petersburg, Stockholm. At first, daguerreotypes of architecture and landscapes dominated the public's imagination; two years later, after various technical improvements to the process had been made, portrait galleries had opened everywhere—and everyone rushed to have her picture taken by the new media machine.[2]

In 1833 Charles Babbage began designing a device he called "the Analytical Engine." The Engine contained most of the key features of the modern digital computer. Punch cards were used to enter both data and instructions. This information was stored in the Engine's memory. A processing unit,

---

1. Quoted in Beaumont Newhall, *The History of Photography from 1839 to the Present Day,* 4th ed. (New York: Museum of Modern Art, 1964), 18.

2. Newhall, *The History of Photography,* 17–22.

which Babbage referred to as a "mill," performed operations on the data and wrote the results to memory; final results were to be printed out on a printer. The Engine was designed to be capable of doing any mathematical operation; not only would it follow the program fed into it by cards, but it would also decide which instructions to execute next, based on intermediate results. However, in contrast to the daguerreotype, not a single copy of the Engine was completed. While the invention of the daguerreotype, a modern media tool for the reproduction of reality, impacted society immediately, the impact of the computer was yet to be seen.

Interestingly, Babbage borrowed the idea of using punch cards to store information from an earlier programmed machine. Around 1800, J. M. Jacquard invented a loom that was automatically controlled by punched paper cards. The loom was used to weave intricate figurative images, including Jacquard's portrait. This specialized graphics computer, so to speak, inspired Babbage in his work on the Analytical Engine, a general computer for numerical calculations. As Ada Augusta, Babbage's supporter and the first computer programmer, put it, "The Analytical Engine weaves algebraical patterns just as the Jacquard loom weaves flowers and leaves."[3] Thus a programmed machine was already synthesizing images even before it was put to processing numbers. The connection between the Jacquard loom and the Analytical Engine is not something historians of computers make much of, since for them computer image synthesis represents just one application of the modern digital computer among thousands of others, but for a historian of new media, it is full of significance.

We should not be surprised that both trajectories—the development of modern media and the development of computers—begin around the same time. Both media machines and computing machines were absolutely necessary for the functioning of modern mass societies. The ability to disseminate the same texts, images, and sounds to millions of citizens—thus assuring the same ideological beliefs—was as essential as the ability to keep track of their birth records, employment records, medical records, and police records. Photography, film, the offset printing press, radio, and television

---

3. Charles Eames, *A Computer Perspective: Background to the Computer Age* (Cambridge, Mass: Harvard University Press, 1990), 18.

made the former possible while computers made possible the latter. Mass media and data processing are complementary technologies; they appear together and develop side by side, making modern mass society possible.

For a long time the two trajectories ran in parallel without ever crossing paths. Throughout the nineteenth and the early twentieth centuries, numerous mechanical and electrical tabulators and calculators were developed; they gradually became faster and their use more widespread. In a parallel movement, we witness the rise of modern media that allow the storage of images, image sequences, sounds, and texts in different material forms— photographic plates, film stock, gramophone records, etc.

Let us continue tracing this joint history. In the 1890s modern media took another step forward as still photographs were put in motion. In January 1893, the first movie studio—Edison's "Black Maria"—started producing twenty-second shorts that were shown in special Kinetoscope parlors. Two years later the Lumière brothers showed their new Cinématographie camera/projection hybrid, first to a scientific audience and later, in December 1895, to the paying public. Within a year, audiences in Johannesburg, Bombay, Rio de Janeiro, Melbourne, Mexico City, and Osaka were subjected to the new media machine, and they found it irresistible.[4] Gradually scenes grew longer, the staging of reality before the camera and the subsequent editing of samples became more intricate, and copies multiplied. In Chicago and Calcutta, London and St. Petersburg, Tokyo and Berlin, and thousands of smaller places, film images would soothe movie audiences, who were facing an increasingly dense information environment outside the theater, an environment that no longer could be adequately handled by their own sampling and data processing systems (i.e., their brains). Periodic trips into the dark relaxation chambers of movie theaters became a routine survival technique for the subjects of modern society.

The 1890s was the crucial decade not only for the development of media, but also for computing. If individual brains were overwhelmed by the amount of information they had to process, the same was true of corporations and of governments. In 1887, the U.S. Census Bureau was still

---

4. David Bordwell and Kristin Thompson, *Film Art: An Introduction,* 5th ed. (New York: McGraw-Hill), 15.

interpreting figures from the 1880 census. For the 1890 census, the Census Bureau adopted electric tabulating machines designed by Herman Hollerith. The data collected on every person was punched into cards; 46,804 enumerators completed forms for a total population of 62,979,766. The Hollerith tabulator opened the door for the adoption of calculating machines by business; during the next decade electric tabulators became standard equipment in insurance companies, public utility companies, railroad offices, and accounting departments. In 1911, Hollerith's Tabulating Machine Company was merged with three other companies to form the Computing-Tabulating-Recording Company; in 1914, Thomas J. Watson was chosen as its head. Ten years later its business tripled, and Watson renamed the company the "International Business Machines Corporation," or IBM.[5]

Moving into the twentieth century, the key year for the history of media and computing is 1936. British mathematician Alan Turing wrote a seminal paper entitled "On Computable Numbers." In it he provided a theoretical description of a general-purpose computer later named after its inventor: "the Universal Turing Machine." Even though it was capable of only four operations, the machine could perform any calculation that could be done by a human and could also imitate any other computing machine. The machine operated by reading and writing numbers on an endless tape. At every step the tape would be advanced to retrieve the next command, read the data, or write the result. Its diagram looks suspiciously like a film projector. Is this a coincidence?

If we believe the word *cinematograph,* which means "writing movement," the essence of cinema is recording and storing visible data in a material form. A film camera records data on film; a film projector reads it off. This cinematic apparatus is similar to a computer in one key respect: A computer's program and data also have to be stored in some medium. This is why the Universal Turing Machine looks like a film projector. It is a kind of film camera and film projector at once, reading instructions and data stored on endless tape and writing them in other locations on this tape. In fact, the development of a suitable storage medium and a method for coding data represent important parts of the prehistory of both cinema and the com-

---

5. Eames, *A Computer Perspective,* 22–27, 46–51, 90–91.

puter. As we know, the inventors of cinema eventually settled on using discrete images recorded on a strip of celluloid; the inventors of the computer—which needed much greater speed of access as well as the ability to quickly read and write data—eventually decided to store it electronically in a binary code.

The histories of media and computing became further entwined when German engineer Konrad Zuse began building a computer in the living room of his parents' apartment in Berlin—the same year that Turing wrote his seminal paper. Zuse's computer was the first working digital computer. One of his innovations was using punched tape to control computer programs. The tape Zuse used was actually discarded 35mm movie film.[6]

One of the surviving pieces of this film shows binary code punched over the original frames of an interior shot. A typical movie scene—two people in a room involved in some action—becomes a support for a set of computer commands. Whatever meaning and emotion was contained in this movie scene has been wiped out by its new function as data carrier. The pretense of modern media to create simulations of sensible reality is similarly canceled; media are reduced to their original condition as information carrier, nothing less, nothing more. In a technological remake of the Oedipal complex, a son murders his father. The iconic code of cinema is discarded in favor of the more efficient binary one. Cinema becomes a slave to the computer.

But this is not yet the end of the story. Our story has a new twist—a happy one. Zuse's film, with its strange superimposition of binary over iconic code, anticipates the convergence that will follow half a century later. The two separate historical trajectories finally meet. Media and computer—Daguerre's daguerreotype and Babbage's Analytical Engine, the Lumière Cinématographie and Hollerith's tabulator—merge into one. All existing media are translated into numerical data accessible for the computer. The result: graphics, moving images, sounds, shapes, spaces, and texts become computable, that is, simply sets of computer data. In short, media become new media.

This meeting changes the identity of both media and the computer itself. No longer just a calculator, control mechanism, or communication device,

---

6. Ibid., 120.

the computer becomes a media processor. Before, the computer could read a row of numbers, outputting a statistical result or a gun trajectory. Now it can read pixel values, blurring the image, adjusting its contrast, or checking whether it contains an outline of an object. Building on these lower-level operations, it can also perform more ambitious ones—searching image databases for images similar in composition or content to an input image, detecting shot changes in a movie, or synthesizing the movie shot itself, complete with setting and actors. In a historical loop, the computer has returned to its origins. No longer just an Analytical Engine, suitable only for crunching numbers, it has become Jacquard's loom—a media synthesizer and manipulator.

Principles of New Media

The identity of media has changed even more dramatically than that of the computer. Below I summarize some of the key differences between old and new media. In compiling this list of differences, I tried to arrange them in a logical order. That is, the last three principles are dependent on the first two. This is not dissimilar to axiomatic logic, in which certain axioms are taken as starting points and further theorems are proved on their basis.

Not every new media object obeys these principles. They should be considered not as absolute laws but rather as general tendencies of a culture undergoing computerization. As computerization affects deeper and deeper layers of culture, these tendencies will increasingly manifest themselves.

1. Numerical Representation

All new media objects, whether created from scratch on computers or converted from analog media sources, are composed of digital code; they are numerical representations. This fact has two key consequences:

1. A new media object can be described formally (mathematically). For instance, an image or a shape can be described using a mathematical function.

2. A new media object is subject to algorithmic manipulation. For instance, by applying appropriate algorithms, we can automatically remove "noise" from a photograph, improve its contrast, locate the edges of the shapes, or change its proportions. In short, *media becomes programmable.*

When new media objects are created on computers, they originate in numerical form. But many new media objects are converted from various forms of old media. Although most readers understand the difference between analog and digital media, a few notes should be added on the terminology and the conversion process itself. This process assumes that data is originally *continuous,* that is, "the axis or dimension that is measured has no apparent indivisible unit from which it is composed."[7] Converting continuous data into a numerical representation is called *digitization.* Digitization consists of two steps: sampling and quantization. First, data is *sampled,* most often at regular intervals, such as the grid of pixels used to represent a digital image. The frequency of sampling is referred to as *resolution.* Sampling turns continuous data into *discrete* data, that is, data occurring in distinct units: people, the pages of a book, pixels. Second, each sample is *quantified,* that is, it is assigned a numerical value drawn from a defined range (such as 0–255 in the case of an 8-bit greyscale image).[8]

While some old media such as photography and sculpture are truly continuous, most involve the combination of continuous and discrete coding. One example is motion picture film: each frame is a continuous photograph, but time is broken into a number of samples (frames). Video goes one step further by sampling the frame along the vertical dimension (scan lines). Similarly, a photograph printed using a halftone process combines discrete and continuous representations. Such a photograph consists of a number of orderly dots (i.e., samples), although the diameters and areas of dots vary continuously.

As the last example demonstrates, while modern media contain levels of discrete representation, the samples are never quantified. This quantification of samples is the crucial step accomplished by digitization. But why, we may ask, are modern media technologies often in part discrete? The key assumption of modern semiotics is that communication requires discrete units. Without discrete units, there is no language. As Roland Barthes put it, "Language is, as it were, that which divides reality (for instance, the contin-

---

7. Isaac Victor Kerlov and Judson Rosebush, *Computer Graphics for Designers and Artists* (New York: Van Nostrand Reinhold, 1986), 14.

8. Ibid., 21.

uous spectrum of the colors is verbally reduced to a series of discontinuous terms)."[9] In assuming that any form of communication requires a discrete representation, semioticians took human language as the prototypical example of a communication system. A human language is discrete on most scales: We speak in sentences; a sentence is made from words; a word consists of morphemes, and so on. If we follow this assumption, we may expect that media used in cultural communication will have discrete levels. At first this theory seems to work. Indeed, a film samples the continuous time of human existence into discrete frames; a drawing samples visible reality into discrete lines; and a printed photograph samples it into discrete dots. This assumption does not universally work, however: Photographs, for instance, do not have any apparent units. (Indeed, in the 1970s semiotics was criticized for its linguistic bias, and most semioticians came to recognize that a language-based model of distinct units of meaning cannot be applied to many kinds of cultural communication.) More important, the discrete units of modern media are usually not units of meanings in the way morphemes are. Neither film frames nor halftone dots have any relation to how a film or photograph affects the viewer (except in modern art and avant-garde film—think of paintings by Roy Lichtenstein and films of Paul Sharits—which often make the "material" units of media into units of meaning).

The most likely reason modern media has discrete levels is because it emerged during the Industrial Revolution. In the nineteenth century, a new organization of production known as the factory system gradually replaced artisan labor. It reached its classical form when Henry Ford installed the first assembly line in his factory in 1913. The assembly line relied on two principles. The first was standardization of parts, already employed in the production of military uniforms in the nineteenth century. The second, newer principle was the separation of the production process into a set of simple, repetitive, and sequential activities that could be executed by workers who did not have to master the entire process and could be easily replaced.

Not surprisingly, modern media follows the logic of the factory, not only in terms of division of labor as witnessed in Hollywood film studios, animation

---

9. Roland Barthes, *Elements of Semiology,* trans. Annette Lavers and Colin Smith (New York: Hill and Wang, 1968), 64.

studios, and television production, but also on the level of material organization. The invention of typesetting machines in the 1880s industrial-
ized publishing while leading to a standardization of both type design and
fonts (number and types). In the 1890s cinema combined automatically produced images (via photography) with a mechanical projector. This required
standardization of both image dimensions (size, frame ratio, contrast) and
temporal sampling rate. Even earlier, in the 1880s, the first television systems already involved standardization of sampling both in time and space.
These modern media systems also followed factory logic in that, once a new
"model" (a film, a photograph, an audio recording) was introduced, numerous identical media copies would be produced from this master. As I will
show, new media follows, or actually runs ahead of, a quite different logic of
post-industrial society—that of individual customization, rather than mass
standardization.

2. Modularity

This principle can be called the "fractal structure of new media." Just as a
fractal has the same structure on different scales, a new media object has
the same modular structure throughout. Media elements, be they images, sounds, shapes, or behaviors, are represented as collections of discrete
samples (pixels, polygons, voxels, characters, scripts). These elements are assembled into larger-scale objects but continue to maintain their separate
identities. The objects themselves can be combined into even larger objects—again, without losing their independence. For example, a multimedia "movie" authored in popular Macromedia Director software may consist
of hundreds of still images, QuickTime movies, and sounds that are stored
separately and loaded at run time. Because all elements are stored independently, they can be modified at any time without having to change the Director "movie" itself. These "movies" can be assembled into a larger "movie," and
so on. Another example of modularity is the concept of "object" used in Microsoft Office applications. When an "object" is inserted into a document (for
instance, a media clip inserted into a Word document), it continues to maintain
its independence and can always be edited with the program originally used to
create it. Yet another example of modularity is the structure of an HTML document: With the exemption of text, it consists of a number of separate objects—
GIF and JPEG images, media clips, Virtual Reality Modeling Language (VRML)
scenes, Shockwave and Flash movies—which are all stored independently,

locally, and/or on a network. In short, a new media object consists of independent parts, each of which consists of smaller independent parts, and so on, down to the level of the smallest "atoms"—pixels, 3-D points, or text characters.

The World Wide Web as a whole is also completely modular. It consists of numerous Web pages, each in its turn consisting of separate media elements. Every element can always be accessed on its own. Normally we think of elements as belonging to their corresponding Web sites, but this is just a convention, reinforced by commercial Web browsers. The Netomat browser by artist Maciej Wisnewski, which extracts elements of a particular media type from different Web pages (for instance, images only) and displays them together without identifying the Web sites from which they are drawn, highlights for us this fundamentally discrete and nonhierarchical organization of the Web.

In addition to using the metaphor of a fractal, we can also make an analogy between the modularity of new media and structured computer programming. Structural computer programming, which became standard in the 1970s, involves writing small and self-sufficient modules (called in different computer languages *subroutines, functions, procedures, scripts*), which are then assembled into larger programs. Many new media objects are in fact computer programs that follow structural programming style. For example, most interactive multimedia applications are written in Macromedia Director's Lingo. A Lingo program defines scripts that control various repeated actions, such as clicking on a button; these scripts are assembled into larger scripts. In the case of new media objects that are not computer programs, an analogy with structural programming still can be made because their parts can be accessed, modified, or substituted without affecting the overall structure of an object. This analogy, however, has its limits. If a particular module of a computer program is deleted, the program will not run. In contrast, as with traditional media, deleting parts of a new media object does not render it meaningless. In fact, the modular structure of new media makes such deletion and substitution of parts particularly easy. For example, since an HTML document consists of a number of separate objects each represented by a line of HTML code, it is very easy to delete, substitute, or add new objects. Similarly, since in Photoshop the parts of a digital image usually kept placed on separate layers, these parts can be deleted and substituted with a click of a button.

3. Automation

The numerical coding of media (principle 1) and the modular structure of a media object (principle 2) allow for the automation of many operations involved in media creation, manipulation, and access. Thus human intentionality can be removed from the creative process, at least in part.[10]

Following are some examples of what can be called "low-level" automation of media creation, in which the computer user modifies or creates from scratch a media object using templates or simple algorithms. These techniques are robust enough so that they are included in most commercial software for image editing, 3-D graphics, word processing, graphics layout, and so forth. Image-editing programs such as Photoshop can automatically correct scanned images, improving contrast range and removing noise. They also come with filters that can automatically modify an image, from creating simple variations of color to changing the whole image as though it were painted by Van Gogh, Seurat, or another brand-name artist. Other computer programs can automatically generate 3-D objects such as trees, landscapes, and human figures as well as detailed ready-to-use animations of complex natural phenomena such as fire and waterfalls. In Hollywood films, flocks of birds, ant colonies, and crowds of people are automatically created by AL (artificial life) software. Word processing, page layout, presentation, and Web creation programs come with "agents" that can automatically create the layout of a document. Writing software helps the user to create literary narratives using highly formalized genre conventions. Finally, in what may be the most familiar experience of automated media generation, many Web sites automatically generate Web pages on the fly when the user reaches the site. They assemble the information from databases and format it using generic templates and scripts.

Researchers are also working on what can be called "high-level" automation of media creation, which requires a computer to understand, to a certain degree, the meanings embedded in the objects being generated, that is, their

---

10. I discuss particular cases of computer automation of visual communication in more detail in "Automation of Sight from Photography to Computer Vision," *Electronic Culture: Technology and Visual Representation,* ed. by Timothy Druckrey and Michael Sand (New York: Aperture, 1996), 229–239; and in "Mapping Space: Perspective, Radar, and Computer Graphics," *SIGGRAPH '93 Visual Proceedings,* ed. by Thomas Linehan (New York: ACM, 1993), 143–147.

semantics. This research can be seen as part of a larger project of artificial intelligence (AI). As is well known, the AI project has achieved only limited success since its beginnings in the 1950s. Correspondingly, work on media generation that requires an understanding of semantics is also in the research stage and is rarely included in commercial software. Beginning in the 1970s, computers were often used to generate poetry and fiction. In the 1990s, frequenters of Internet chat rooms became familiar with "bots"—computer programs that simulate human conversation. Researchers at New York University designed a "virtual theater" composed of a few "virtual actors" who adjusted their behavior in real-time in response to a user's actions.[11] The MIT Media Lab developed a number of different projects devoted to "high-level" automation of media creation and use: a "smart camera" that, when given a script, automatically follows the action and frames the shots;[12] ALIVE, a virtual environment where the user interacts with animated characters;[13] and a new kind of human-computer interface where the computer presents itself to a user as an animated talking character. The character, generated by a computer in real-time, communicates with the through user natural language; it also tries to guess the user's emotional state and to adjust the style of interaction accordingly.[14]

The area of new media where the average computer user encountered AI in the 1990s was not, however, the human-computer interface, but computer games. Almost every commercial game included a component called an "AI engine," which stands for the part of the game's computer code that controls its characters—car drivers in a car race simulation, enemy forces in a strategy game such as *Command and Conquer,* single attackers in first-person shooters such as *Quake.* AI engines use a variety of approaches to simulate human intelligence, from rule-based systems to neural networks. Like AI expert systems, the characters in computer games have expertise in some well-defined but narrow area such as attacking the user. But because computer games are

---

11. http://www.mrl.nyu.edu/improv/.

12. http://www-white.media.mit.edu/vismod/demos/smartcam/.

13. http://pattie.www.media.mit.edu/people/pattie/CACM-95/alife-cacm95.html.

14. This research was pursued at different groups at the MIT lab. See, for instance, the home page of the Gesture and Narrative Language Group, http://gn.www.media.mit.edu/groups/gn/.

highly codified and rule-based, these characters function very effectively; that is, they effectively respond to the few things the user is allowed to ask them to do: run forward, shoot, pick up an object. They cannot do anything else, but then the game does not provide the opportunity for the user to test this. For instance, in a martial arts fighting game, I can't ask questions of my opponent, nor do I expect him or her to start a conversation with me. All I can do is "attack" my opponent by pressing a few buttons, and within this highly codified situation the computer can "fight" me back very effectively. In short, computer characters can display intelligence and skills only because programs place severe limits on our possible interactions with them. Put differently, computers can pretend to be intelligent only by tricking us into using a very small part of who we are when we communicate with them. At the 1997 SIGGRAPH (Special Interest Group on Computer Graphics of the Association for Computing Machinery) convention, for example, I played against both human and computer-controlled characters in a VR simulation of a nonexistent sports game. All my opponents appeared as simple blobs covering a few pixels of my VR display; at this resolution, it made absolutely no difference who was human and who was not.

Along with "low-level" and "high-level" automation of media creation, another area of media use subjected to increasing automation is media access. The switch to computers as a means of storing and accessing enormous amounts of media material, exemplified by the "media assets" stored in the databases of stock agencies and global entertainment conglomerates, as well as public "media assets" distributed across numerous Web sites, created the need to find more efficient ways to classify and search media objects. Word processors and other text-management software has long provided the capacity to search for specific strings of text and automatically index documents. The UNIX operating system also included powerful commands to search and filter text files. In the 1990s software designers started to provide media users with similar abilities. Virage introduced Virage VIR Image Engine, which allows one to search for visually similar image content among millions of images as well as a set of video search tools to allow indexing and searching video files.[15] By the end of the 1990s, the key Web search engines

---

15. See http://www.virage.com/products.

already included the option to search the Internet by specific media such as images, video, and audio.

The Internet, which can be thought of as one huge distributed media database, also crystallized the basic condition of the new information society: overabundance of information of all kinds. One response was the popular idea of software "agents" designed to automate searching for relevant information. Some agents act as filters that deliver small amounts of information given the user's criteria. Others allow users to tap into the expertise of other users, following their selections and choices. For example, the MIT Software Agents Group developed such agents as BUZZwatch, which "distills and tracks trends, themes, and topics within collections of texts across time" such as Internet discussions and Web pages; Letizia, "a user interface agent that assists a user browsing the World Wide Web by . . . scouting ahead from the user's current position to find Web pages of possible interest"; and Footprints, which "uses information left by other people to help you find your way around."[16]

By the end of the twentieth century, the problem was no longer how to create a new media object such as an image; the new problem was how to find an object that already exists somewhere. If you want a particular image, chances are it already exists—but it may be easier to create one from scratch than to find an existing one. Beginning in the nineteenth century, modern society developed technologies that automated media creation—the photo camera, film camera, tape recorder, videorecorder, etc. These technologies allowed us, over the course of 150 years, to accumulate an unprecedented amount of media materials—photo archives, film libraries, audio archives. This led to the next stage in media evolution—the need for new technologies to store, organize, and efficiently access these materials. The new technologies are all computer-based—media databases; hypermedia and other ways of organizing media material such as the hierarchical file system itself; text management software; programs for content-based search and retrieval. Thus automation of media access became the next logical stage of the process that had been put into motion when the first photograph was taken. The emergence of new media coincides with this second stage of a

---

16. http://agents.www.media.mit.edu/groups/agents/projects/.

media society, now concerned as much with accessing and reusing existing media objects as with creating new ones.[17]

4. Variability

A new media object is not something fixed once and for all, but something that can exist in different, potentially infinite versions. This is another consequence of the numerical coding of media (principle 1) and the modular structure of a media object (principle 2).

Old media involved a human creator who manually assembled textual, visual, and/or audio elements into a particular composition or sequence. This sequence was stored in some material, its order determined once and for all. Numerous copies could be run off from the master, and, in perfect correspondence with the logic of an industrial society, they were all identical. New media, in contrast, is characterized by variability. (Other terms that are often used in relation to new media and that might serve as appropriate synonyms of *variable* are *mutable* and *liquid*.) Instead of identical copies, a new media object typically gives rise to many different versions. And rather than being created completely by a human author, these versions are often in part automatically assembled by a computer. (The example of Web pages automatically generated from databases using templates created by Web designers can be invoked here as well.) Thus the principle of variability is closely connected to automation.

Variability would also not be possible without modularity. Stored digitally, rather than in a fixed medium, media elements maintain their separate identities and can be assembled into numerous sequences under program control. In addition, because the elements themselves are broken into discrete samples (for instance, an image is represented as an array of pixels), they can be created and customized on the fly.

The logic of new media thus corresponds to the postindustrial logic of "production on demand" and "just in time" delivery logics that were themselves made possible by the use of computers and computer networks at all stages of manufacturing and distribution. Here, the "culture industry"

---

17. See my "Avant-Garde as Software," in *Ostranenie,* ed. Stephen Kovats (Frankfurt and New York: Campus Verlag, 1999) (http://visarts.ucsd.edu/~manovich).

(a term coined by Theodor Adorno in the 1930s) is actually ahead of most other industries. The idea that a customer might determine the exact features of her desired car at the showroom, transmit the specs to the factory, and hours later receive the car, remains a dream, but in the case of computer media, such immediacy is reality. Because the same machine is used as both showroom and factory, that is, the same computer generates and displays media—and because the media exists not as a material object but as data that can be sent through wires at the speed of light, the customized version created in response to the user's input is delivered almost immediately. Thus, to continue with the same example, when you access a Web site, the server immediately assembles a customized Web page.

Here are some particular cases of the variability principle (most of them will be discussed in more detail in later chapters):

1. Media elements are stored in a *media database;* a variety of end-user objects, which vary in resolution and in form and content, can be generated, either beforehand or on demand, from this database. At first, we might think that this is simply a particular technological implementation of the variability principle, but, as I will show in the "Database" section, in a computer age the database comes to function as a cultural form in its own right. It offers a particular model of the world and of the human experience. It also affects how the user conceives the data it contains.

2. It becomes possible to separate the levels of "content" (data) and interface. *A number of different interfaces can be created from the same data.* A new media object can be defined as one or more interfaces to a multimedia database.[18]

3. *Information about the user can be used by a computer program to customize automatically the media composition as well as to create elements themselves.* Examples: Web sites use information about the type of hardware and browser or user's network address to customize automatically the site the user will see; interactive computer installations use information about the user's body movements to generate sounds, shapes, and images, or to control the behavior of artificial creatures.

---

18. For an experiment in creating different multimedia interfaces to the same text, see my *Freud-Lissitzky Navigator* (http://visarts.ucsd.edu/~manovich/FLN).

4. A particular case of this customization is *branching-type interactivity* (sometimes also called "*menu-based* interactivity"). The term refers to programs in which all the possible objects the user can visit form a branching tree structure. When the user reaches a particular object, the program presents her with choices and allows her to choose among them. Depending on the value chosen, the user advances along a particular branch of the tree. In this case the information used by a program is the output of the user's cognitive process, rather than the network address or body position.

5. *Hypermedia* is another popular new media structure, which is conceptually close to branching-type interactivity (because quite often the elements are connected using a branch tree structure). In hypermedia, the multimedia elements making a document are connected through hyperlinks. Thus the elements and the structure are independent of each other—rather than hard-wired together, as in traditional media. The World Wide Web is a particular implementation of hypermedia in which the elements are distributed throughout the network. Hypertext is a particular case of hypermedia that uses only one media type—text. How does the principle of variability work in this case? We can think of all possible paths through a hypermedia document as being different versions of it. By following the links, the user retrieves a particular version of a document.

6. Another way in which different versions of the same media objects are commonly generated in computer culture is through *periodic updates.* For instance, modern software applications can periodically check for updates on the Internet and then download and install these updates, sometimes without any action on the part of the user. Most Web sites are also periodically updated either manually or automatically, when the data in the databases that drive the sites changes. A particularly interesting case of this "updateability" feature is those sites that continuously update information such as stock prices or weather.

7. One of the most basic cases of the variability principle is *scalability,* in which different versions of the same media object can be generated at various sizes or levels of detail. The metaphor of a map is useful in thinking about the scalability principle. If we equate a new media object with a physical territory, different versions of this object are like maps of this territory generated at different scales. Depending on the scale chosen, a map provides more or less detail about the territory. Indeed, different versions of a new media object may vary strictly quantitatively, that is, in the amount of de-

tail present: For instance, a full-size image and its icon, automatically generated by Photoshop; a full text and its shorter version, generated by the "Autosummarize" command in Microsoft Word; or the different versions that can be created using the "Outline" command in Word. Beginning with version 3 (1997), Apple's QuickTime format made it possible to embed a number of different versions that differ in size within a single QuickTime movie; when a Web user accesses the movie, a version is automatically selected depending on connection speed. A conceptually similar technique called "distancing" or "level of detail" is used in interactive virtual worlds such as VRML scenes. A designer creates a number of models of the same object, each with progressively less detail. When the virtual camera is close to the object, a highly detailed model is used; if the object is far away, a less detailed version is automatically substituted by a program to save unnecessary computation of detail that cannot be seen anyway.

New media also allow us to create versions of the same object that differ from each other in more substantial ways. Here the comparison with maps of different scales no longer works. Examples of commands in commonly used software packages that allow the creation of such qualitatively different versions are "Variations" and "Adjustment layers" in Photoshop 5 and the "writing style" option in Word's "Spelling and Grammar" command. More examples can be found on the Internet where, beginning in the mid-1990s, it become common to create a few different versions of a Web site. The user with a fast connection can choose a rich multimedia version, whereas the user with a slow connection can choose a more bare-bones version that loads faster.

Among new media artworks, David Blair's *Wax Web,* a Web site that is an "adaptation" of an hour-long video narrative, offers a more radical implementation of the scalability principle. While interacting with the narrative, the user can change the scale of representation at any point, going from an image-based outline of the movie to a complete script or a particular shot, or a VRML scene based on this shot, and so on.[19] Another example of how use of the scalability principle can create a dramatically new experience of an old

---

19. http://jefferson.village.virginia.edu/wax/.

media object is Stephen Mamber's database-driven representation of Hitchcock's *The Birds.* Mamber's software generates a still for every shot of the film; it then automatically combines all the stills into a rectangular matrix one shot per cell. As a result, time is spatialized, similar to the process in Edison's early Kinetoscope cylinders. Spatializing the film allows us to study its different temporal structures, which would be hard to observe otherwise. As in *WaxWeb,* the user can at any point change the scale of representation, going from a complete film to a particular shot.

As can be seen, the principle of variability is useful in allowing us to connect many important characteristics of new media that on first sight may appear unrelated. In particular, such popular new media structures as branching (or menu) interactivity and hypermedia can be seen as particular instances of the variability principle. In the case of branching interactivity, the user plays an active role in determining the order in which already generated elements are accessed. This is the simplest kind of interactivity; more complex kinds are also possible in which both the elements and the structure of the whole object are either modified or generated on the fly in response to the user's interaction with a program. We can refer to such implementations as *open interactivity* to distinguish them from the *closed interactivity* that uses fixed elements arranged in a fixed branching structure. Open interactivity can be implemented using a variety of approaches, including procedural and object-oriented computer programming, AI, AL, and neural networks.

As long as there exists some kernel, some structure, some prototype that remains unchanged throughout the interaction, open interactivity can be thought of as a subset of the variability principle. Here a useful analogy can be made with Wittgenstein's theory of family resemblance, later developed into the theory of prototypes by cognitive psychologists. In a family, a number of relatives will share some features, although no single family member may possess all of the features. Similarly, according to the theory of prototypes, the meanings of many words in a natural language derive not through logical definition but through proximity to a certain prototype.

Hypermedia, the other popular structure of new media, can also be seen as a particular case of the more general principle of variability. According to the definition by Halasz and Schwartz, hypermedia systems "provide their users with the ability to create, manipulate and/or examine a network of information-containing nodes interconnected by relational links."[20] Because in new media individual media elements (images, pages of text, etc.) always retain their individual identity (the principle of modularity), they can be "wired" together into more than one object. Hyperlinking is a particular way of achieving this wiring. A hyperlink creates a connection between two elements, for example, between two words in two different pages or a sentence on one page and an image in another, or two different places within the same page. Elements connected through hyperlinks can exist on the same computer or on different computers connected on a network, as in the case of the World Wide Web.

If in old media elements are "hardwired" into a unique structure and no longer maintain their separate identity, in hypermedia elements and structure are separate from each other. The structure of hyperlinks—typically a branching tree—can be specified independently from the contents of a document. To make an analogy with the grammar of a natural language as described in Noam Chomsky's early linguistic theory,[21] we can compare a hypermedia structure that specifies connections between nodes with the deep structure of a sentence; a particular hypermedia text can then be compared with a particular sentence in a natural language. Another useful analogy is computer programming. In programming, there is clear separation between algorithms and data. An algorithm specifies the sequence of steps to be performed on any data, just as a hypermedia structure specifies a set of navigation paths (i.e., connections between nodes) that potentially can be applied to any set of media objects.

The principle of variability exemplifies how, historically, changes in media technologies are correlated with social change. If the logic of old media corresponded to the logic of industrial mass society, the logic of new media fits the logic of the postindustrial society, which values individuality over conformity. In industrial mass society everyone was supposed to enjoy the same goods—and to share the same beliefs. This was also the logic of media technology. A media object was assembled in a media factory (such as a Hollywood studio). Millions of identical copies were produced from a

---

20. Frank Halasz and Mayer Schwartz, "The Dexter Hypertext Reference Model," *Communication of the ACM* (New York: ACM, 1994), 30.

21. Noam Chomsky, *Syntactic Structures* (The Hague and Paris: Mouton, 1957).

master and distributed to all the citizens. Broadcasting, cinema, and print media all followed this logic.

In a postindustrial society, every citizen can construct her own custom lifestyle and "select" her ideology from a large (but not infinite) number of choices. Rather than pushing the same objects/information to a mass audience, marketing now tries to target each individual separately. The logic of new media technology reflects this new social logic. Every visitor to a Web site automatically gets her own custom version of the site created on the fly from a database. The language of the text, the contents, the ads displayed— all these can be customized. According to a report in *USA Today* (9 November 1999), "Unlike ads in magazines or other real-world publications, 'banner' ads on Web pages change with every page view. And most of the companies that place the ads on the Web site track your movements across the Net, 'remembering' which ads you've seen, exactly when you saw them, whether you clicked on them, where you were at the time, and the site you have visited just before."[22]

Every hypertext reader gets her own version of the complete text by selecting a particular path through it. Similarly, every user of an interactive installation gets her own version of the work. And so on. In this way new media technology acts as the most perfect realization of the utopia of an ideal society composed of unique individuals. New media objects assure users that their choices—and therefore, their underlying thoughts and desires— are unique, rather than preprogrammed and shared with others. As though trying to compensate for their earlier role in making us all the same, descendants of the Jacquard loom, the Hollerith tabulator, and Zuse's cinema-computer are now working to convince us that we are all unique.

The principle of variability as presented here has some parallels to the concept of "variable media," developed by the artist and curator Jon Ippolito.[23] I believe that we differ in two key respects. First, Ippolito uses variability to describe a characteristic shared by recent conceptual and some digital art, whereas I see variability as a basic condition of all new media, not

---

22. "How Marketers 'Profile' Users," *USA Today* 9 November 1999, 2A.

23. See http://www.three.org. Our conversations helped me to clarify my ideas, and I am very grateful to Jon for the ongoing exchange.

only art. Second, Ippolito follows the tradition of conceptual art in which an artist can vary any dimension of the artwork, even its content; my use of the term aims to reflect the logic of mainstream culture in that versions of the object share some well-defined "data." This "data," which can be a well-known narrative (*Psycho*), an icon (Coca-Cola sign), a character (Mickey Mouse), or a famous star (Madonna), is referred to in the media industry as "property." Thus all cultural projects produced by Madonna will be automatically united by her name. Using the theory of prototypes, we can say that the property acts as a prototype, and different versions are derived from this prototype. Moreover, when a number of versions are being commercially released based on some "property," usually one of these versions is treated as the source of the "data," with others positioned as being derived from this source. Typically, the version that is in the same media as the original "property" is treated as the source. For instance, when a movie studio releases a new film, along with a computer game based on it, product tie-ins, music written for the movie, etc., the film is usually presented as the "base" object from which other objects are derived. So when George Lucas releases a new *Star Wars* movie, the original property—the original *Star Wars* trilogy—is referenced. The new movie becomes the "base" object, and all other media objects released along with it refer to this object. Conversely, when computer games such as *Tomb Raider* are remade into movies, the original computer game is presented as the "base" object.

Although I deduce the principle of variability from more basic principles of new media—numerical representation and modularity of information—the principle can also be seen as a consequence of the computer's way of representing data—and modeling the world itself—as variables rather than constants. As new media theorist and architect Marcos Novak notes, a computer—and computer culture in its wake—substitutes every constant with a variable.[24] In designing all functions and data structures, a computer programmer tries always to use variables rather than constants. On the level of the human-computer interface, this principle means that the user is given many options to modify the performance of a program or a media object, be it a

---

24. Marcos Novak, lecture at the "Interactive Frictions" conference, University of Southern California, Los Angeles, 6 June 1999.

computer game, Web site, Web browser, or the operating system itself. The user can change the profile of a game character, modify how folders appear on the desktop, how files are displayed, what icons are used, and so forth. If we apply this principle to culture at large, it would mean that every choice responsible for giving a cultural object a unique identity can potentially remain always open. Size, degree of detail, format, color, shape, interactive trajectory, trajectory through space, duration, rhythm, point of view, the presence or absence of particular characters, the development of plot—to name just a few dimensions of cultural objects in different media—can all be defined as variables, to be freely modified by a user.

Do we want, or need, such freedom? As the pioneer of interactive film-making Grahame Weinbren argues, in relation to interactive media, making a choice involves a moral responsibility.[25] By passing on these choices to the user, the author also passes on the responsibility to represent the world and the human condition in it. (A parallel is the use of phone or Web-based automated menu systems by big companies to handle their customers; while companies have turned to such systems in the name of "choice" and "freedom," one of the effects of this type of automation is that labor is passed from the company's employees to the customer. If before a customer would get the information or buy the product by interacting with a company employee, now she has to spend her own time and energy navigating through numerous menus to accomplish the same result.) The moral anxiety that accompanies the shift from constants to variables, from traditions to choices in all areas of life in a contemporary society, and the corresponding anxiety of a writer who has to portray it, is well rendered in the closing passage of a short story by the contemporary American writer Rick Moody (the story is about the death of his sister):[26]

I should fictionalize it more, I should conceal myself. I should consider the responsibilities of characterization, I should conflate her two children into one, or reverse

---

25. Grahame Weinbren, "In the Ocean of Streams of Story," *Millennium Film Journal* 28 (Spring 1995), http://www.sva.edu/MFJ/journalpages/MFJ28/GWOCEAN.HTML.

26. Rick Moody, *Demonology,* first published in *Conjunctions,* reprinted in *The KGB Bar Reader,* quoted in Vince Passaro, "Unlikely Stories," *Harper's Magazine* vol. 299, no. 1791 (August 1999), 88–89.

their genders, or otherwise alter them, I should make her boyfriend a husband, I should explicate all the tributaries of my extended family (its remarriages, its internecine politics), I should novelize the whole thing, I should make it multigenerational, I should work in my forefathers (stonemasons and newspapermen), I should let artifice create an elegant surface, I should make the events orderly, I should wait and write about it later, I should wait until I'm not angry, I shouldn't clutter a narrative with fragments, with mere recollections of good times, or with regrets, I should make Meredith's death shapely and persuasive, not blunt and disjunctive, I shouldn't have to think the unthinkable, I shouldn't have to suffer, I should address her here directly (these are the ways I miss you), I should write only of affection, I should make our travels in this earthly landscape safe and secure, I should have a better ending, I shouldn't say her life was short and often sad, I shouldn't say she had demons, as I do too.

5. Transcoding

Beginning with the basic, "material" principles of new media—numeric coding and modular organization—we moved to more "deep" and far-reaching ones—automation and variability. The fifth and last principle of cultural transcoding aims to describe what in my view is the most substantial consequence of the computerization of media. As I have suggested, computerization turns media into computer data. While from one point of view, computerized media still displays structural organization that makes sense to its human users—images feature recognizable objects; text files consist of grammatical sentences; virtual spaces are defined along the familiar Cartesian coordinate system; and so on—from another point of view, its structure now follows the established conventions of the computer's organization of data. Examples of these conventions are different data structures such as lists, records, and arrays; the already-mentioned substitution of all constants by variables; the separation between algorithms and data structures; and modularity.

The structure of a computer image is a case in point. On the level of representation, it belongs on the side of human culture, automatically entering in dialog with other images, other cultural "semes" and "mythemes." But on another level, it is a computer file that consists of a machine-readable header, followed by numbers representing color values of its pixels. On this level it enters into a dialog with other computer files. The dimensions of this dialog are not the image's content, meanings, or formal qualities, but rather file size, file type, type of compression used, file format, and so on. In short, these dimensions belong to the computer's own cosmogony rather than to human culture.

Similarly, new media in general can be thought of as consisting of two distinct layers—the "cultural layer" and the "computer layer." Examples of categories belonging to the cultural layer are the encyclopedia and the short story; story and plot; composition and point of view; mimesis and catharsis, comedy and tragedy. Examples of categories in the computer layer are process and packet (as in data packets transmitted through the network); sorting and matching; function and variable; computer language and data structure.

Because new media is created on computers, distributed via computers, and stored and archived on computers, the logic of a computer can be expected to significantly influence the traditional cultural logic of media; that is, we may expect that the computer layer will affect the cultural layer. The ways in which the computer models the world, represents data, and allows us to operate on it; the key operations behind all computer programs (such as search, match, sort, and filter); the conventions of HCI—in short, what can be called the computer's ontology, epistemology, and pragmatics—influence the cultural layer of new media, its organization, its emerging genres, its contents.

Of course, what I call "the computer layer" is not itself fixed but rather changes over time. As hardware and software keep evolving and as the computer is used for new tasks and in new ways, this layer undergoes continuous transformation. The new use of the computer as a media machine is a case in point. This use is having an effect on the computer's hardware and software, especially on the level of the human-computer interface, which increasingly resembles the interfaces of older media machines and cultural technologies—VCR, tape player, photo camera.

In summary, the computer layer and the culture layer influence each other. To use another concept from new media, we can say that they are being composited together. The result of this composite is a new computer culture—a blend of human and computer meanings, of traditional ways in which human culture modeled the world and the computer's own means of representing it.

Throughout the book, we will encounter many examples of the principle of transcoding at work. For instance, in "The Language of Cultural Interfaces," we will look at how conventions of the printed page, cinema, and traditional HCI interact in the interfaces of Web sites, CD-ROMs, virtual spaces, and computer games. The "Database" section will discuss how a database, originally a computer technology to organize and access data, is becoming a new cultural form in its own right. But we can also reinterpret some of the principles of new media already discussed as consequences of the transcoding principle. For instance, hypermedia can be understood as one cultural effect of the separation between an algorithm and a data structure, essential to computer programming. Just as in programming, where algorithms and data structures exist independently of each other, in hypermedia data is separated from the navigation structure. Similarly, the modular structure of new media can be seen as an effect of the modularity in structural computer programming. Just as a structural computer program consists of smaller modules that in turn consist of even smaller modules, a new media object has a modular structure.

In new media lingo, to "transcode" something is to translate it into another format. The computerization of culture gradually accomplishes similar transcoding in relation to all cultural categories and concepts. That is, cultural categories and concepts are substituted, on the level of meaning and/or language, by new ones that derive from the computer's ontology, epistemology, and pragmatics. New media thus acts as a forerunner of this more general process of cultural reconceptualization.

Given the process of "conceptual transfer" from the computer world to culture at large, and given the new status of media as computer data, what theoretical framework can we use to understand it? On one level new media is old media that has been digitized, so it seems appropriate to look at new media using the perspective of media studies. We may compare new media and old media such as print, photography, or television. We may also ask about the conditions of distribution and reception and patterns of use. We may also ask about similarities and differences in the material properties of each medium and how these affect their aesthetic possibilities.

This perspective is important and I am using it frequently in this book, but it is not sufficient. It cannot address the most fundamental quality of new media that has no historical precedent—programmability. Comparing new media to print, photography, or television will never tell us the whole story. For although from one point of view new media is indeed another type of media, from another it is simply a particular type of computer data, something stored in files and databases, retrieved and sorted, run through algorithms and written to the output device. That the data represent pixels and that this device happens to be an output screen is beside the point. The computer may perform perfectly the role of the Jacquard loom, but underneath it is fundamentally Babbage's Analytical Engine—after all, this was its identity for 150 years. New media may look like media, but this is only the surface.

New media calls for a new stage in media theory whose beginnings can be traced back to the revolutionary works of Harold Innis in the 1950s and Marshall McLuhan in the 1960s. To understand the logic of new media, we need to turn to computer science. It is there that we may expect to find the new terms, categories, and operations that characterize media that became programmable. *From media studies, we move to something that can be called "software studies"—from media theory to software theory.* The principle of transcoding is one way to start thinking about software theory. Another way, which this book experiments with, is to use concepts from computer science as categories of new media theory. Examples here are "interface" and "database." And last but not least, along with analyzing "material" and logical principles of computer hardware and software, we can also look at the human-computer interface and the interfaces of software applications used to author and access new media objects. The two chapters that follow are devoted to these topics.

What New Media Is Not

Having proposed a list of the key differences between new and old media, I now would like to address other potential candidates. Following are some of the popularly held notions about the difference between new and old media that I will subject to scrutiny:

1. New media is analog media converted to a digital representation. In contrast to analog media, which is continuous, digitally encoded media is discrete.

2. All digital media (texts, still images, visual or audio time data, shapes, 3-D spaces) share the same digital code. This allows different media types to be displayed using one machine—a computer—which acts as a multimedia display device.

3. New media allows for random access. In contrast to film or videotape, which store data sequentially, computer storage devices make it possible to access any data element equally fast.

4. Digitization inevitably involves loss of information. In contrast to an analog representation, a digitally encoded representation contains a fixed amount of information.

5. In contrast to analog media where each successive copy loses quality, digitally encoded media can be copied endlessly without degradation.

6. New media is interactive. In contrast to old media where the order of presentation is fixed, the user can now interact with a media object. In the process of interaction the user can choose which elements to display or which paths to follow, thus generating a unique work. In this way the user becomes the co-author of the work.

Cinema as New Media

If we place new media within a longer historical perspective, we will see that many of the principles above are not unique to new media, but can be found in older media technologies as well. I will illustrate this fact by using the example of the technology of cinema.

(1) New media is analog media converted to a digital representation. In contrast to analog media, which is continuous, digitally encoded media is discrete.

Indeed, any digital representation consists of a limited number of samples. For example, a digital still image is a matrix of pixels—a 2-D sampling of space. However, cinema was from its beginnings based on sampling—the sampling of time. Cinema sampled time twenty-four times a second. So we can say that cinema prepared us for new media. All that remained was to take this already discrete representation and to quantify it. But this is simply a mechanical step; what cinema accomplished was a much more difficult conceptual break—from the continuous to the discrete.

Cinema is not the only media technology emerging toward the end of the nineteenth century that employed a discrete representation. If cinema sampled time, fax transmission of images, starting in 1907, sampled a 2-D space; even earlier, the first television experiments (Carey 1875; Nipkow 1884) already involved sampling of both time and space.[27] However, reaching mass popularity much earlier than these other technologies, cinema was the first to make the principle of discrete representation of the visual public knowledge.

(2) All digital media (texts, still images, visual or audio time data, shapes, 3-D spaces) share the same digital code. This allows different media types to be displayed using one machine—a computer—which acts as a multimedia display device.

Although computer multimedia became commonplace only around 1990, filmmakers had been combining moving images, sound, and text

---

27. Albert Abramson, *Electronic Motion Pictures: A History of the Television Camera* (Berkeley: University of California Press, 1955), 15–24.

(whether the intertitles of the silent era or the title sequences of the later period) for a whole century. Cinema was thus the original modern "multimedia." We can also point to much earlier examples of multiple-media displays, such as medieval illuminated manuscripts that combine text, graphics, and representational images.

(3) New media allow for random access. In contrast to film or videotape, which store data sequentially, computer storage devices make it possible to access any data element equally fast.

For example, once a film is digitized and loaded in the computer's memory, any frame can be accessed with equal ease. Therefore, if cinema sampled time but still preserved its linear ordering (subsequent moments of time become subsequent frames), new media abandons this "human-centered" representation altogether—to put represented time fully under human control. Time is mapped onto two-dimensional space, where it can be managed, analyzed, and manipulated more easily.

Such mapping was already widely used in the nineteenth-century cinema machines. The Phenakisticope, the Zootrope, the Zoopraxiscope, the Tachyscope, and Marey's photographic gun were all based on the same principle—placing a number of slightly different images around the perimeter of a circle. Even more striking is the case of Thomas Edison's first cinema apparatus. In 1887 Edison and his assistant, William Dickson, began experiments to adopt the already proven technology of a phonograph record for recording and displaying motion pictures. Using a special picture-recording camera, tiny pinpoint-size photographs were placed in spirals on a cylindrical cell similar in size to the phonography cylinder. A cylinder was to hold 42,000 images, each so small ($\frac{1}{32}$ inch wide) that a viewer would have to look at them through a microscope.[28] The storage capacity of this medium was twenty-eight minutes—twenty-eight minutes of continuous time taken apart, flattened on a surface, and mapped onto a two-dimensional grid. (In short, time was prepared for manipulation and reordering, something soon to be accomplished by film editors.)

---

28. Charles Musser, *The Emergence of Cinema: The American Screen to 1907* (Berkeley: University of California Press, 1994), 65.

The Myth of the Digital

Discrete representation, random access, multimedia—cinema already contained these principles. So they cannot help us to separate new media from old media. Let us continue interrogating the remaining principles. If many principles of new media turn out to be not so new, what about the idea of digital representation? Surely, this is the one idea that radically redefines media? The answer is not so straightforward, however, because this idea acts as an umbrella for three unrelated concepts—analog-to-digital conversion (digitization), a common representational code, and numerical representation. Whenever we claim that some quality of new media is due to its digital status, we need to specify which of these three concepts is at work. For example, the fact that different media can be combined into a single digital file is due to the use of a common representational code, whereas the ability to copy media without introducing degradation is an effect of numerical representation.

Because of this ambiguity, I try to avoid using the word *digital* in this book. In "Principles of New Media" I showed that numerical representation is the one really crucial concept of the three. Numerical representation turns media into computer data, thus making it programmable. And this indeed radically changes the nature of media.

In contrast, as I will show below, the alleged principles of new media that are often deduced from the concept of digitization—that analog-to-digital conversion inevitably results in a loss of information and that digital copies are identical to the original—do not hold up under closer examination; that is, although these principles are indeed logical consequences of digitization, they do not apply to concrete computer technologies in the way in which they are currently used.

(4)   Digitization inevitably involves loss of information. In contrast to an analog representation, a digitally encoded representation contains a fixed amount of information.

In his important study of digital photography *The Reconfigured Eye,* William Mitchell explains this principle as follows: "There is an indefinite amount of information in a continuous-tone photograph, so enlargement usually reveals more detail but yields a fuzzier and grainier picture. . . . A digital image, on the other hand, has precisely limited spatial and tonal resolution and contains a fixed amount of information."[29] From a logical point of view, this principle is a correct deduction from the idea of digital representation. A digital image consists of a finite number of pixels, each having a distinct color or tonal value, and this number determines the amount of detail an image can represent. Yet in reality this difference does not matter. By the end of the 1990s, even cheap consumer scanners were capable of scanning images at resolutions of 1,200 or 2,400 pixels per inch. So while a digitally stored image is still comprised of a finite number of pixels, at such resolution it can contain much finer detail than was ever possible with traditional photography. This nullifies the whole distinction between an "indefinite amount of information in a continuous-tone photograph" and a fixed amount of detail in a digital image. The more relevant question is how much information in an image can be useful to the viewer. By the end of new media's first decade, technology had already reached the point where a digital image could easily contain much more information than anyone would ever want.

But even the pixel-based representation, which appears to be the very essence of digital imaging, cannot be taken for granted. Some computer graphics software has bypassed the main limitation of the traditional pixel grid—fixed resolution. *Live Picture,* an image-editing program, converts a pixel-based image into a set of mathematical equations. This allows the user to work with an image of virtually unlimited resolution. Another paint program, *Matador,* makes possible painting on a tiny image, which may consist of just a few pixels, as though it were a high-resolution image. (It achieves this by breaking each pixel into a number of smaller sub-pixels.) In both programs, the pixel is no longer a "final frontier"; as far as the user is concerned, it simply does not exist. Texture-mapping algorithms make the notion of a fixed resolution meaningless in a different way. They often store the same image at a number of different resolutions. During rendering, the texture map of arbitrary resolution is produced by interpolating two images that are closest to this resolution. (A similar technique is used by VR software, which stores the number of versions of a singular object at different degrees of detail.) Finally, certain compression techniques eliminate pixel-based

---

29. William J. Mitchell, *The Reconfigured Eye* (Cambridge, Mass: MIT Press, 1982), 6.

representation altogether, instead representing an image via different mathematical constructs (such as transforms).

(5)   In contrast to analog media where each successive copy loses quality, digitally encoded media can be copied endlessly without degradation.

Mitchell summarizes this as follows: "The continuous spatial and tonal variation of analog pictures is not exactly replicable, so such images cannot be transmitted or copied without degradation. . . . But discrete states can be replicated precisely, so a digital image that is a thousand generations away from the original is indistinguishable in quality from any one of its progenitors."[30] Therefore in digital culture, "an image file can be copied endlessly, and the copy is distinguishable from the original by its date since there is no loss of quality."[31] This is all true—in principle. In reality, however, there is actually much more degradation and loss of information between copies of digital images than between copies of traditional photographs. A single digital image consists of millions of pixels. All of this data requires considerable storage space in a computer; it also takes a long time (in contrast to a text file) to transmit over a network. Because of this, the software and hardware used to acquire, store, manipulate, and transmit digital images rely uniformly on *lossy compression*—the technique of making image files smaller by deleting some information. Examples of the technique include the JPEG format, which is used to store still images, and MPEG, which is used to store digital video on DVD. The technique involves a compromise between image quality and file size—the smaller the size of a compressed file, the more visible the visual artifacts introduced in deleting information become. Depending on the level of compression, these artifacts range from barely noticeable to quite pronounced.

One may argue that this situation is temporary, that once cheaper computer storage and faster networks become commonplace, lossy compression will disappear. Presently, however, the trend is quite the opposite, with lossy

---

30. Ibid., 6.
31. Ibid., 49.

compression becoming more and more the norm for representing visual information. If a single digital image already contains a lot of data, this amount increases dramatically if we want to produce and distribute moving images in a digital form. (One second of video, for instance, consists of thirty still images.) Digital television with its hundreds of channels and video on-demand services, the distribution of full-length films on DVD or over the Internet, fully digital post-production of feature films—all of these developments are made possible by lossy compression. It will be a number of years before advances in storage media and communication bandwidth will eliminate the need to compress audio-visual data. So rather than being an aberration, a flaw in the otherwise pure and perfect world of the digital, where not even a single bit of information is ever lost, lossy compression is the very foundation of computer culture, at least for now. Therefore, while in theory, computer technology entails the flawless replication of data, its actual use in contemporary society is characterized by loss of data, degradation, and noise.

The Myth of Interactivity

We have only one principle still remaining from the original list: interactivity.

> (6) New media is interactive. In contrast to old media where the order of presentation is fixed, the user can now interact with a media object. In the process of interaction the user can choose which elements to display or which paths to follow, thus generating a unique work. In this way the user becomes the co-author of the work.

As with *digital* I avoid using the word *interactive* in this book without qualifying it, for the same reason—I find the concept to be too broad to be truly useful.

In relation to computer-based media, the concept of interactivity is a tautology. Modern HCI is by definition interactive. In contrast to earlier interfaces such as batch processing, modern HCI allows the user to control the computer in real-time by manipulating information displayed on the screen. Once an object is represented in a computer, it automatically becomes interactive. Therefore, to call computer media "interactive" is meaningless—it simply means stating the most basic fact about computers.

Rather than evoking this concept by itself, I use a number of other concepts, such as menu-based interactivity, scalability, simulation, image-interface, and image-instrument, to describe different kinds of interactive structures and operations. The distinction between "closed" and "open" interactivity is just one example of this approach.

Although it is relatively easy to specify different interactive structures used in new media objects, it is much more difficult to deal theoretically with users' experiences of these structures. This aspect of interactivity remains one of the most difficult theoretical questions raised by new media. Without pretending to have a complete answer, I would like to address some aspects of the question here.

All classical, and even moreso modern, art is "interactive" in a number of ways. Ellipses in literary narration, missing details of objects in visual art, and other representational "shortcuts" require the user to fill in missing information.[32] Theater and painting also rely on techniques of staging and composition to orchestrate the viewer's attention over time, requiring her to focus on different parts of the display. With sculpture and architecture, the viewer has to move her whole body to experience the spatial structure.

Modern media and art pushed each of these techniques further, placing new cognitive and physical demands on the viewer. Beginning in the 1920s, new narrative techniques such as film montage forced audiences to bridge quickly the mental gaps between unrelated images. Film cinematography actively guided the viewer to switch from one part of a frame to another. The new representational style of semi-abstraction, which along with photography became the "international style" of modern visual culture, required the viewer to reconstruct represented objects from a bare minimum—a contour, a few patches of color, shadows cast by the objects not represented directly. Finally, in the 1960s, continuing where Futurism and Dada left off, new forms of art such as happenings, performance, and installation turned art explicitly participational—a transformation that, according to some new me-

---

32. Ernst Gombrich analyzes "the beholder's share" in decoding the missing information in visual images in his classic *Art and Illusion: A Study in the Psychology of Pictorial Representation* (Princeton, N.J.: Princeton University Press, 1960).

dia theorists, prepared the ground for the interactive computer installations that appeared in the 1980s.[33]

When we use the concept of "interactive media" exclusively in relation to computer-based media, there is the danger that we will interpret "interaction" literally, equating it with physical interaction between a user and a media object (pressing a button, choosing a link, moving the body), at the expense of psychological interaction. The psychological processes of filling-in, hypothesis formation, recall, and identification, which are required for us to comprehend any text or image at all, are mistakenly identified with an objectively existing structure of interactive links.[34]

This mistake is not new; on the contrary, it is a structural feature of the history of modern media. The literal interpretation of interactivity is just the latest example of a larger modern trend to externalize mental life, a process in which media technologies—photography, film, VR—have played a key role.[35] Beginning in the nineteenth century, we witness recurrent claims by the users and theorists of new media technologies, from Francis Galton (the inventor of composite photography in the 1870s) to Hugo Munsterberg, Sergei Eisenstein and, recently, Jaron Lanier, that these technologies externalize and objectify the mind. Galton not only claimed that "the ideal faces obtained by the method of composite portraiture appear to have a great deal

---

33. The notion that computer interactive art has its origins in new art forms of the 1960s is explored in Söke Dinkla, "The History of the Interface in Interactive Art," ISEA (International Symposium on Electronic Art) 1994 Proceedings (http://www.uiah.fi/bookshop/isea_proc/nextgen/08.html; "From Participation to Interaction: Toward the Origins of Interactive Art," in Lynn Hershman Leeson, ed., *Clicking In: Hot Links to a Digital Culture* (Seattle: Bay Press, 1996), 279–290. See also Simon Penny, "Consumer Culture and the Technological Imperative: The Artist in Dataspace," in Simon Penny, ed., *Critical Issues in Electronic Media* (Albany: State University of New York Press, 1993), 47–74.

34. This argument relies on a cognitivist perspective that stresses the active mental processes involved in comprehension of any cultural text. For examples of a cognitivist approach in film studies, see Bordwell and Thompson, *Film Art,* and David Bordwell, *Narration in the Fiction Film* (Madison: University of Wisconsin Press, 1989).

35. For a more detailed analysis of this trend, see my article "From the Externalization of the Psyche to the Implantation of Technology," in *Mind Revolution: Interface Brain/Computer,* ed. Florian Rötzer (Münich: Akademie Zum Dritten Jahrtausend, 1995), 90–100.

in common with . . . so-called abstract ideas" but in fact he proposed to re-name abstract ideas "cumulative ideas."[36] According to Münsterberg, who was a Professor of Psychology at Harvard University and an author of one of the earliest theoretical treatments of cinema entitled *The Film: A Psychologi-cal Study* (1916), the essence of film lies in its ability to reproduce or "objec-tify" various mental functions on the screen: "The photoplay obeys the laws of the mind rather than those of the outer world."[37] In the 1920s Eisenstein speculated that film could be used to externalize—and control—thinking. As an experiment in this direction, he boldly conceived a screen adaptation of Marx's *Capital*. "The content of CAPITAL (its aim) is now formulated: to teach the worker to think dialectically," Eisenstein writes enthusiastically in April of 1928.[38] In accordance with the principles of "Marxist dialectics" as canonized by the official Soviet philosophy, Eisenstein planned to present the viewer with the visual equivalents of thesis and anti-thesis so that the viewer could then proceed to arrive at synthesis, that is, the correct conclusion, as pre-programmed by Eisenstein.

In the 1980s, VR pioneer Jaron Lanier similarly saw VR technology as capable of completely objectifying—better yet, transparently merging with—mental processes. His descriptions of its capabilities did not dis-tinguish between internal mental functions, events, and processes and ex-ternally presented images. This is how, according to Lanier, VR can take over human memory: "You can play back your memory through time and classify your memories in various ways. You'd be able to run back through the experiential places you've been in order to be able to find people, tools."[39] Lanier also claimed that VR will lead to the age of "post-symbolic communication," communication without language or any other symbols. Indeed, why should there be any need for linguistic symbols if everyone

---

36. Quoted in Allan Sekula, "The Body and the Archive," *October* 39 (1987): 51.

37. Hugo Münsterberg, *The Photoplay: A Psychological Study* (New York: D. Appleton and Company, 1916), 41.

38. Sergei Eisenstein, "Notes for a Film of 'Capital,'" trans. Maciej Sliwowski, Jay Leuda, and Annette Michelson, *October* 2 (1976): 10.

39. Timothy Druckrey, "Revenge of the Nerds: An Interview with Jaron Lanier," *Afterimage* (May 1991), 9.

rather than being locked into a "prison-house of language" (Fredric Jameson),[40] will happily live in the ultimate nightmare of democracy—the single mental space that is shared by everyone, and where every communicative act is always ideal (Jürgen Habermas).[41] This is Lanier's example of how post-symbolic communication will function: "You can make a cup that someone else can pick when there wasn't a cup before, without having to use a picture of the word 'cup.'"[42] Here, as with the earlier technology of film, the fantasy of objectifying and augmenting consciousness, extending the powers of reason, goes hand in hand with the desire to see in technology a return to the primitive happy age of pre-language, pre-misunderstanding. Locked in virtual reality caves, with language taken away, we will communicate through gestures, body movements, and grimaces, like our primitive ancestors . . .

The recurrent claims that new media technologies externalize and objectify reasoning, and that they can be used to augment or control it, are based on the assumption of the isomorphism of mental representations and operations with external visual effects such as dissolves, composite images, and edited sequences. This assumption is shared not only by modern media inventors, artists, and critics but also by modern psychologists. Modern psychological theories of the mind, from Freud to cognitive psychology, repeatedly equate mental processes with external, technologically generated visual forms. Thus Freud in *The Interpretation of Dreams* (1900) compared the process of condensation with one of Francis Galton's procedures that became especially famous: making family portraits by overlaying a different negative image for each member of the family and then making a single print.[43] Writing in the same decade, the American psychologist Edward Titchener

---

40. Fredric Jameson, *The Prison-house of Language: A Critical Account of Structuralism and Russian Formalism* (Princeton, N.J.: Princeton University Press, 1972).

41. Jürgen Habermas, *The Theory of Communicative Action: Reason and Rationalization of Society* (The Theory of Communicative Action, Vol. 1), trans. Thomas McCarthy (Boston: Beacon Press, 1985).

42. Druckrey, "Revenge of the Nerds," 6.

43. Sigmund Freud, *Standard Edition of the Complete Psychological Works* (London: Hogarth Press, 1953), 4: 293.

opened the discussion of the nature of abstract ideas in his textbook of psychology by noting that "the suggestion has been made that an abstract idea is a sort of composite photograph, a mental picture which results from the superimposition of many particular perceptions or ideas, and which therefore shows the common elements distinct and the individual elements blurred."[44] He then proceeds to consider the pros and cons of this view. We should not wonder why Titchener, Freud, and other psychologists take the comparison for granted rather than presenting it as a simple metaphor—contemporary cognitive psychologists also do not question why their models of the mind are so similar to the computer workstations on which they are constructed. The linguist George Lakoff asserted that "natural reasoning makes use of at least some unconscious and automatic image-based processes such as superimposing images, scanning them, focusing on part of them,"[45] and the psychologist Philip Johnson-Laird proposed that logical reasoning is a matter of scanning visual models.[46] Such notions would have been impossible before the emergence of television and computer graphics. These visual technologies made operations on images such as scanning, focusing, and superimposition seem natural.

What to make of this modern desire to externalize the mind? It can be related to the demand of modern mass society for standardization. The subjects have to be standardized, and the means by which they are standardized need to be standardized as well. Hence the objectification of internal, private mental processes, and their equation with external visual forms that can easily be manipulated, mass produced, and standardized on their own. The private and individual are translated into the public and become regulated.

What before had been a mental process, a uniquely individual state, now became part of the public sphere. Unobservable and interior processes and representations were taken out of individual heads and placed outside—as drawings, photographs, and other visual forms. Now they could be discussed in public, employed in teaching and propaganda, standardized, and mass-

---

44. Edward Bradford Titchener, *A Beginner's Psychology* (New York: Macmillan, 1915), 114.

45. George Lakoff, "Cognitive Linguistics," *Versus* 44/45 (1986): 149.

46. Philip Johnson-Laird, *Mental Models: Towards a Cognitive Science of Language, Inference, and Consciousness* (Cambridge: Cambridge University Press, 1983).

distributed. What was private became public. What was unique became mass-produced. What was hidden in an individual's mind became shared.

Interactive computer media perfectly fits this trend to externalize and objectify the mind's operations. The very principle of hyperlinking, which forms the basis of interactive media, objectifies the process of association, often taken to be central to human thinking. Mental processes of reflection, problem solving, recall, and association are externalized, equated with following a link, moving to a new page, choosing a new image, or a new scene. Before we would look at an image and mentally follow our own private associations to other images. Now interactive computer media asks us instead to click on an image in order to go to another image. Before, we would read a sentence of a story or a line of a poem and think of other lines, images, memories. Now interactive media asks us to click on a highlighted sentence to go to another sentence. In short, we are asked to follow pre-programmed, objectively existing associations. Put differently, in what can be read as an updated version of French philosopher Louis Althusser's concept of "interpellation," we are asked to mistake the structure of somebody's else mind for our own.[47]

This is a new kind of identification appropriate for the information age of cognitive labor. The cultural technologies of an industrial society—cinema and fashion—asked us to identify with someone else's bodily image. Interactive media ask us to identify with someone else's mental structure. If the cinema viewer, male and female, lusted after and tried to emulate the body of the movie star, the computer user is asked to follow the mental trajectory of the new media designer.

47. Louis Althusser introduced his influential notion of ideological interpellation in "Ideology and Ideological State Apparatuses (Notes towards an Investigation)," in *Lenin and Philosophy,* trans. Ben Brewster (New York: Monthly Review Press, 1971).

The Interface

In 1984 the director of *Blade Runner,* Ridley Scott, was hired to create a commercial to introduce Apple Computer's new Macintosh. In retrospect, this event is full of historical significance. As Peter Lunenfeld has pointed out, *Blade Runner* (1982) and the Macintosh computer (1984)—released within two years of each other—defined the two aesthetics that, twenty years later, still rule contemporary culture, miring us in what he calls the "permanent present." One was a futuristic dystopia which combined futurism and decay, computer technology and fetishism, retro-styling and urbanism, Los Angeles and Tokyo. Since *Blade Runner*'s release, its techno-noir has been replayed in countless films, computer games, novels, and other cultural objects. And although a number of strong aesthetic systems have been articulated in the following decades, both by individual artists (Matthew Barney, Mariko Mori) and by commercial culture at large (the 1980s "postmodern" pastiche, the 1990s techno-minimalism), none of them has been able to challenge the hold of *Blade Runner* on our vision of the future.

In contrast to the dark, decayed, "postmodern" vision of *Blade Runner,* the Graphical User Interface (GUI), popularized by Macintosh, remained true to the modernist values of clarity and functionality. The user's screen was ruled by straight lines and rectangular windows that contained smaller rectangles of individual files arranged in a grid. The computer communicated with the user via rectangular boxes containing clean black type rendered against a white background. Subsequent versions of GUI added colors and made it possible for users to customize the appearance of many interface elements, thus somewhat diluting the sterility and boldness of the original monochrome 1984 version. Yet its original aesthetic survives in the displays of hand-held communicators such as Palm Pilot, cellular telephones, car navigation systems, and other consumer electronic products that use small LCD displays comparable in quality to the 1984 Macintosh screen.

Like *Blade Runner,* Macintosh's GUI articulated a vision of the future, although a very different one. In this vision, the lines between the human and its technological creations (computers, androids) are clearly drawn, and decay is not tolerated. In a computer, once a file is created, it never disappears except when explicitly deleted by the user. And even then deleted items can usually be recovered. Thus, if in "meatspace" we have to work to remember, in cyberspace we have to work to forget. (Of course while they run, OS and applications constantly create, write to, and erase various temporary files, as well as swap data between RAM and virtual memory files on a hard drive, but most of this activity remains invisible to the user.)

Also like *Blade Runner,* GUI vision came to influence many other areas of culture. This influence ranges from the purely graphical (for instance, the use of GUI elements by print and TV designers) to the more conceptual. In the 1990s, as the Internet progressively grew in popularity, the role of the digital computer shifted from being a particular technology (a calculator, symbol processor, image manipulator, etc.) to a filter for all culture, a form through which all kinds of cultural and artistic production were mediated. As the window of a Web browser replaced cinema and television screen, the art gallery wall, library and book, all at once, the new situation manifested itself: All culture, past and present, came to be filtered through a computer, with its particular human-computer interface.[1]

In semiotic terms, the computer interface acts as a code that carries cultural messages in a variety of media. When you use the Internet, everything you access—texts, music, video, navigable spaces—passes through the interface of the browser and then, in turn, the interface of the OS. In cultural communication, a code is rarely simply a neutral transport mechanism; usually it affects the messages transmitted with its help. For instance, it may make some messages easy to conceive and render others unthinkable. A code may also provide its own model of the world, its own logical system, or ideology; subsequent cultural messages or whole languages created with this code will be limited by its accompanying model, system, or ideology. Most modern cultural theories rely on these notions, which together I will refer to as the "non-transparency of the code" idea. For instance, according to the Whorf-Sapir hypothesis, which enjoyed popularity in the middle of the twentieth century, human thinking is determined by the code of natural language; the speakers of different natural languages perceive and think about the world differently.[2] The Whorf-Sapir hypothesis is an extreme expression of the "non-transparency of the code" idea; usually it is formulated in less extreme forms. But when we think about the case of the human-computer interface, applying a "strong" version of this idea makes sense. The interface

---

1. Stephen Johnson's *Interface Culture* makes a claim for the cultural significance of computer interface.

2. Other examples of cultural theories that rely on the "non-transparency of the code" idea are Yuri Lotman's theory of secondary modeling systems, George Lakoff's cognitive linguistics, Jacques Derrida's critique of logocentrism, and Marshall McLuhan's media theory.

shapes how the computer user conceives of the computer itself. It also determines how users think of any media object accessed via a computer. Stripping different media of their original distinctions, the interface imposes its own logic on them. Finally, by organizing computer data in particular ways, the interface provides distinct models of the world. For instance, a hierarchical file system assumes that the world can be organized in a logical multilevel hierarchy. In contrast, a hypertext model of the World Wide Web arranges the world as a nonhierarchical system ruled by metonymy. In short, far from being a transparent window into the data inside a computer, the interface brings with it strong messages of its own.

As an example of how the interface imposes its own logic on media, consider "cut and paste" operations, standard in all software running under the modern GUI. This operation renders insignificant the traditional distinction between spatial and temporal media, since the user can cut and paste parts of images, regions of space, and parts of a temporal composition in exactly the same way. It is also "blind" to traditional distinctions in scale: the user can cut and paste a single pixel, an image, or a whole digital movie in the same way. And last, this operation also renders insignificant the traditional distinctions between media: "cut and paste" can be applied to texts, still and moving images, sounds, and 3-D objects in the same way.

The interface comes to play a crucial role in the information society in yet another way. In this society, work and leisure activities not only increasingly involve computer use, but they also converge around the same interfaces. Both "work" applications (word processors, spreadsheet programs, database programs) and "leisure" applications (computer games, informational DVD) use the same tools and metaphors of GUI. The best example of this convergence is a Web browser employed both in the office and at home, both for work and for play. In this respect information society is quite different from industrial society, with its clear separation between the field of work and the field of leisure. In the nineteenth century Karl Marx imagined that a future communist state would overcome this work-leisure divide as well as the highly specialized and piecemeal character of modern work itself. Marx's ideal citizen would be cutting wood in the morning, gardening in the afternoon, and composing music in the evening. Today, the subject of the information society is engaged in even more activities during a typical day: inputting and analyzing data, running simulations, searching the Internet, playing computer games, watching streaming video, listening to music online, trading stocks, and so on. Yet in performing all these different activities, the user in essence is always using the same few tools and commands: a computer screen and a mouse; a Web browser; a search engine; cut, paste, copy, delete, and find commands.

If the human-computer interface has become a key semiotic code of the information society as well as its metatool, how does this affect the functioning of cultural objects in general and art objects in particular? As I have already noted, in computer culture it becomes common to construct a number of different interfaces to the same "content." For instance, the same data can be represented as a 2-D graph or as an interactive navigable space. Or, a Web site may guide the user to different versions of the site depending on the bandwidth of her Internet connection. Given these examples, we may be tempted to think of a new media artwork as also possessing two separate levels: content and interface. Thus, the old dichotomies *content—form* and *content—medium* can be rewritten as *content—interface.* But postulating such an opposition assumes that that artwork's content is independent of its medium (in an art historical sense) or its code (in a semiotic sense). Situated in some idealized medium-free realm, content is assumed to exist before its material expression. These assumptions are correct in the case of the visualization of quantified data; they also apply to classical art with its well-defined iconographic motives and representational conventions. But just as modern thinkers, from Whorf to Derrida, insisted on the "nontransparency of the code" idea, modern artists assumed that content and form cannot be separated. In fact, from the "abstraction" of the 1910s to the "process" of the 1960s, artists have continued to invent concepts and procedures to assure the impossibility of painting some preexistent content.

This leaves us with an interesting paradox. Many new media artworks have what can be called an "informational dimension," the condition that they share with all new media objects. The experience includes retrieving, looking at and thinking about quantified data. Therefore, when we refer to such artworks, we are justified in separating the levels of content and interface. At the same time, new media artworks have more traditional "experiential" or aesthetic dimensions, which justify their status as art rather than information design. These dimensions include a particular configuration of space, time, and surface articulated in the work; a particular sequence of the user's activities over time in interacting with the work; a particular formal, material, and phenomenological user experience. And it is the work's interface that creates its unique materiality and a unique user experience. To change the interface even slightly is to change the work dramatically. From this perspective, to think of an interface as a separate level, as something that can be arbitrarily varied, is to eliminate the status of a new media artwork as art.

There is another way to think about the difference between new media design and new media art in relation to the content—interface dichotomy. In contrast to design, in art the connection between content and form (or, in the case of new media, content and interface) is motivated; that is, the choice of a particular interface is motivated by a work's content to such degree that it can no longer be thought of as a separate level. Content and interface merge into one entity, and no longer can be taken apart.

Finally, the idea of content preexisting interface is challenged in yet another way by new media artworks that dynamically generate their data in real time. While in a menu-based interactive multimedia application or a static Web site, all data already exists before the user accesses it, in dynamic new media artworks, the data is created on the fly, or, to use the new media lingo, at run time. This can be accomplished in a variety of ways: procedural computer graphics, formal language systems, AI and AL programming. All these methods share the same principle: a programmer sets up some initial conditions, rules, or procedures that control the computer program generating the data. For the purposes of the present discussion, the most interesting of these approaches are AL and the evolution paradigm. In the AL approach, the interaction between a number of simple objects at run time leads to the emergence of complex global behaviors. These behaviors can only be obtained in the course of running the computer program; they cannot be predicted beforehand. The evolution paradigm applies the metaphor of evolution theory to the generation of images, shapes, animations, and other media data. The initial data supplied by the programmer acts as a genotype that is expanded into a full phenotype by the computer. In either case, the content of an artwork is the result of a collaboration between the artist/programmer and the computer program, or, if the work is interactive, between the artist, the computer program, and the user. New media artists who have most systematically explored the AL approach are the team of Christa Sommerer and Laurent Mignonneau. In their installation "Life Spacies," virtual organisms appear and evolve in response to the position, movement, and interactions of visitors. Artist/programmer Karl Sims also made key contributions to applying the evolution paradigm to media generation. In his installation "Galapagos" computer programs generate twelve different virtual organisms at every iteration; visitors select an organism that will continue to live, copulate, mutate, and reproduce.[3] Commercial products that use AL and evolution approaches include computer games such as the *Creatures* series (Mindscape Entertainment) and "virtual pet" toys such as Tamagochi.

In organizing this book, I wanted to highlight the importance of the interface category by placing its discussion right in the beginning. The two sections of this chapter present examples of different issues raised by this category—but they in no way exhaust it. In "The Language of Cultural Interface," I introduce the term "cultural interfaces" to describe interfaces used by stand-alone hypermedia (CD-ROM and DVD titles), Web sites, computer games, and other cultural objects distributed via computers. I analyze how the three cultural forms of the cinema, the printed word, and a general-purpose human-computer interface contributed to shaping the appearance and functionality of cultural interfaces during the 1990s.

The second section, "The Screen and the User," discusses the key element of the modern interface—the computer screen. As in the first section, I am interested in analyzing continuities between the computer interface and older cultural forms, languages, and conventions. This section positions the computer screen within a larger historical tradition and traces different stages in the development of this tradition—the static illusionistic image of Renaissance painting; the moving image of the film screen; the real-time image of radar and television; and the real-time interactive image of the computer screen.

---

3. http://www.ntticc.or.jp/permanent/index_e.html.

The Language of Cultural Interfaces

Cultural Interfaces

The term *human-computer interface* describes the ways in which the user interacts with a computer. HCI includes physical input and output devices such as a monitor, keyboard, and mouse. It also consists of metaphors used to conceptualize the organization of computer data. For instance, the Macintosh interface introduced by Apple in 1984 uses the metaphor of files and folders arranged on a desktop. Finally, HCI also includes ways of manipulating data, that is, a grammar of meaningful actions that the user can perform on it. Examples of actions provided by modern HCI are copy, rename, and delete a file; list the contents of a directory; start and stop a program; set the computer's date and time.

The term HCI was coined when the computer was used primarily as a tool for work. However, during the 1990s, the identity of the computer changed. In the beginning of the decade, the computer was still largely thought of as a simulation of a typewriter, paintbrush or drafting ruler—in other words, as a tool used to produce cultural content that, once created, would be stored and distributed in the appropriate media—printed page, film, photographic print, electronic recording. By the end of the decade, as Internet use became commonplace, the computer's public image was no longer solely that of a tool but also a universal media machine, which could be used not only to author, but also to store, distribute, and access all media.

As distribution of all forms of culture becomes computer-based, we are increasingly "interfacing" to predominantly cultural data—texts, photographs, films, music, virtual environments. In short, we are no longer interfacing to a computer but to culture encoded in digital form. I will use the term *cultural interface* to describe a human-computer-culture interface— the ways in which computers present and allow us to interact with cultural data. Cultural interfaces include the interfaces used by the designers of Web sites, CD-ROM and DVD titles, multimedia encyclopedias, on-line museums and magazines, computer games, and other new media cultural objects.

If you need to remind yourself what a typical cultural interface looked like in the second part of the 1990s, say 1997, go back in time and click to a random Web page. You are likely to see something that graphically resembles a magazine layout from the same decade. The page is dominated by text—headlines, hyperlinks, blocks of copy. Within this text are a few media elements—graphics, photographs, perhaps a QuickTime movie, and a VRML scene. The page also includes radio buttons and a pull-down menu that allows you to choose an item from the list. Finally, there is a search engine: Type a word or a phrase, hit the search button, and the computer will scan through a file or database trying to match your entry.

For another example of a prototypical cultural interface of the 1990s, you might load (assuming it would still run on your computer) the most well-known CD-ROM of the 1990s—*Myst* (Broderbund, 1993). Its opening clearly recalls a movie: credits slowly scroll across the screen, accompanied by a movie-like soundtrack to set the mood. Next, the computer screen shows an open book, awaiting the click of a mouse. Next, a familiar element of a Macintosh interface makes an appearance, reminding you that besides being a new movie/book hybrid, *Myst* is also a computer application: you can adjust the sound volume and graphics quality by selecting from a standard Macintosh-style menu at the upper top of the screen. Finally, you are taken inside the game, where the interplay between the printed word and cinema continues. A virtual camera frames images of an island that dissolve between each other. At the same time, you keep encountering books and letters, which take over the screen, providing with you with clues on how to progress in the game.

Given that computer media is simply a set of characters and numbers stored in a computer, there are numerous ways in which it could be presented to a user. Yet, as is the case with all cultural languages, only a few of these possibilities actually appear viable at any given historical moment. Just as early fifteenth-century Italian painters could only conceive of painting in a very particular way—quite different from, say, sixteenth-century Dutch painters—today's digital designers and artists use only a small set of action grammars and metaphors out of a much larger set of all possibilities.

Why do cultural interfaces—Web pages, CD-ROM titles, computer games—look the way they do? Why do designers organize computer data in certain ways and not in others? Why do they employ some interface metaphors and not others?

In my view, the language of cultural interfaces is largely made up from elements of other, already familiar cultural forms. In the following I will explore the contributions of three such forms to this language during its first decades—the 1990s. The three forms on which I will focus make their appearance in the opening sequence of the already discussed prototypical new media object of the 1990s—*Myst*. Its opening activates them before our eyes, one by one. The first form is cinema. The second is the printed word. The third is a general-purpose human-computer interface.

As should become clear, I use "cinema" and "printed word" as shortcuts. They stand not for particular objects, such as a film or a novel, but rather for larger cultural traditions (we can also use such terms as "cultural forms," "mechanisms," "languages," or "media"). "Cinema" thus includes the mobile camera, representations of space, editing techniques, narrative conventions, spectator activity—in short, different elements of cinematic perception, language, and reception. Their presence is not limited to the twentieth-century institution of fiction films; they can be found already in panoramas, magic lantern slides, theater, and other nineteenth-century cultural forms; similarly, since the middle of the twentieth century, they have been present not only in films but also in television and video programs. In the case of the "printed word," I am also referring to a set of conventions that have developed over many centuries (some even before the invention of print) and that today are shared by numerous forms of printed matter, from magazines to instruction manuals—a rectangular page containing one or more columns of text, illustrations or other graphics framed by the text, pages that follow each other sequentially, a table of contents, and index.

The modern human-computer interface has a much shorter history than the printed word or cinema—but it is still a history. Principles such as direct manipulation of objects on the screen, overlapping windows, iconic representation, and dynamic menus were gradually developed over a few decades, from the early 1950s to the early 1980s, when they finally appeared in commercial systems such as Xerox Star (1981), the Apple Lisa (1982), and most importantly the Apple Macintosh (1984).[4] Since then, they have become accepted conventions for operating a computer, and a cultural language in its own right.

Cinema, the printed word, the human-computer interface: Each of these traditions has developed its own unique way of organizing information, presenting it to the user, correlating space and time, and structuring human experience in the process of accessing information. Pages of text and a table of contents; 3-D spaces framed by a rectangular frame that can be navigated using a mobile point of view; hierarchical menus, variables, parameters, copy/paste and search/replace operations—these and other elements of the three traditions are shaping cultural interfaces today. Cinema, the printed word, and HCI are the three main reservoirs of metaphors and strategies for organizing information which feed cultural interfaces.

Treating them as if they occupied the same conceptual plane has an advantage—a theoretical bonus. It is only natural to think of them as belonging to two different kinds of cultural species, so to speak. If HCI is a general purpose tool which can be used to manipulate any kind of data, both the printed word and cinema are less general, and offer their own ways to organize particular types of data: text in the case of print, audio-visual narrative taking place in a 3-D space in the case of cinema. HCI is a system of controls to operate a machine; the printed word and cinema are cultural traditions, distinct ways of recording human memory and human experience, mechanisms for the cultural and social exchange of information. Bringing HCI, the printed word, and cinema together allows us to see that the three have more in common than we might have anticipated. On the one hand, being part of our culture now for half a century, HCI already represents a powerful cultural tradition, a cultural language offering its own ways of representing human memory and human experience. This language speaks in the form of discrete objects organized in hierarchies (hierarchical file system), or as catalogs (databases), or as objects linked together through hyperlinks (hypermedia). On the other hand, we begin to see that the printed word and cinema

---

4. Brad A. Myers, "A Brief History of Human Computer Interaction Technology," technical report CMU-CS-96-163 and Human Computer Interaction Institute Technical Report CMU-HCII-96-103 (Pittsburgh, Pa.: Carnegie Mellon University, Human-Computer Interaction Institute, 1996).

also can be thought of as interfaces, even though historically they have been tied to particular kinds of data. Each has its own grammar of actions, each comes with its own metaphors, each offers a particular physical interface. A book or a magazine is a solid object consisting of separate pages; actions include going from page to page linearly, marking individual pages, and using the table of contents. In the case of cinema, its physical interface is the particular architectural arrangement of the movie theater; its metaphor, a window opening up into a virtual 3-D space.

Today, as media is being "liberated" from traditional physical storage media—paper, film, stone, glass, magnetic tape—elements of the printed word interface and the cinema interface that previously were hardwired to content become "liberated" as well. A digital designer can freely mix pages and virtual cameras, tables of content and screens, bookmarks and points of view. No longer embedded within particular texts and films, these organizational strategies are now free floating in our culture, available for use in new contexts. In this respect, the printed word and cinema have indeed become interfaces—rich sets of metaphors, ways of navigating through content, ways of accessing and storing data. For a computer user, both conceptually and psychologically, their elements exist on the same plane as radio buttons, pull-down menus, command line calls, and other elements of the standard human-computer interface.

Let us now discuss some of the elements of these three cultural traditions—cinema, the printed word, and HCI—to see how they have shaped the language of cultural interfaces.

Printed Word

In the 1980s, as PCs and word processing software became commonplace, text became the first cultural medium to be subjected to digitization in a massive way. Already in the 1960s, two and a half decades before the concept of digital media was born, researchers were thinking about making the sum total of human written production—books, encyclopedias, technical articles, works of fiction, and so on—available online (Ted Nelson's *Xanadu* project[5]).

---

5. http://www.xanadu.net.

Text is unique among media types. It plays a privileged role in computer culture. On the one hand, it is one media type among others. But, on the other hand, it is a metalanguage of computer media, a code in which all other media are represented: coordinates of 3-D objects, pixel values of digital images, the formatting of a page in HTML. It is also the primary means of communication between a computer and a user: One types single line commands or runs computer programs written in a subset of English; the other responds by displaying error codes or text messages.[6]

If computers use text as their metalanguage, cultural interfaces in their turn inherit the principles of text organization developed by human civilization throughout its existence. One of these principles is a page—a rectangular surface containing a limited amount of information, designed to be accessed in some order, and having a particular relationship to other pages. In its modern form, the page was born in the first centuries of the Christian era when the clay tablet and papyrus roll were replaced by the codex—a collection of written pages stitched together on one side.

Cultural interfaces rely on our familiarity with the "page interface" while also trying to stretch its definition to include new concepts made possible by the computer. In 1984, Apple introduced a graphical user interface that presented information in overlapping windows stacked behind one another—essentially, a set of book pages. The user was given the ability to go back and forth between pages, as well as to scroll through individual pages. In this way, a traditional page was redefined as a virtual page, a surface that can be much larger than the limited surface of a computer screen. In 1987, Apple introduced the popular *Hypercard* program, which extended the page concept in new ways. Now, users were able to include multimedia elements within pages, as well as to establish links between pages regardless of their ordering. A few years later, designers of HTML stretched the concept of a page even further by enabling the creation of distributed documents; that is, different parts of a document are located on different computers connected through the network. With this development, a long process of gradual "vir-

---

6. XML, which is promoted as the replacement for HTML, enables any user to create her own customized markup language. The next stage in computer culture may involve authoring not simply new Web documents but new languages. For more information on XML, see http://www.ucc.ie/xml.

tualization" of the page reached a new stage. Messages written on clay tablets, which were almost indestructible, were replaced by ink on paper. Ink, in its turn, was replaced by bits of computer memory, making characters on an electronic screen. Now, with HTML, which allows parts of a single page to be located on different computers, the page becomes even more fluid and unstable.

The conceptual development of the page in computer media can also be read in a different way—not as a further development of a codex form, but as a return to earlier forms such as the papyrus roll of ancient Egypt, Greece, and Rome. Scrolling through the contents of a computer window or a World Wide Web page has more in common with unrolling than it does with turning the pages of a modern book. In the case of the Web of the 1990s, the similarity with a roll is even stronger because information is not available all at once, but rather arrives sequentially, top to bottom.

A good example of how cultural interfaces stretch the definition of a page while mixing together its different historical forms is the Web page created in 1997 by the British design collective antirom for HotWired's RGB Gallery.[7] The designers created a large surface containing rectangular blocks of text in different font sizes, arranged without any apparent order. The user is invited to skip from one block to another moving in any direction. Here, the different directions of reading used in different cultures are combined together on a single page.

By the mid-1990s, Web pages included a variety of media types—but they were still essentially traditional pages. Different media elements—graphics, photographs, digital video, sound, and 3-D worlds—were embedded within rectangular surfaces containing text. To this extent, a typical Web page was conceptually similar to a newspaper page, which is also dominated by text, with photographs, drawings, tables, and graphs embedded in between, along with links to other pages of the newspaper. VRML evangelists wanted to overturn this hierarchy by imaging in a future in which the World Wide Web is rendered as a giant 3-D space, with all the other media types, including text, existing within it.[8] Given that the history of a page

---

7. http://www.hotwired.com/rgb/antirom/index2.html.

8. See, for instance, Mark Pesce, "Ontos, Eros, Noos, Logos," the keynote address for the International Symposium on Electronic Arts (ISEA), 1995, http://www.xs4all.nl/~mpesce/iseakey.html.

stretches back for thousands of years, I think it is unlikely that it will disappear so quickly.

As the Web page became a new cultural convention, its dominance was challenged by two Web browsers created by artists—Web Stalker (1997) by the I/O/D collective[9] and Netomat (1999) by Maciej Wisniewski.[10] Web Stalker emphasizes the hypertextual nature of the Web. Instead of rendering standard Web pages, it renders the networks of hyperlinks these pages embody. When a user enters a URL for a particular page, Web Stalker displays all pages linked to that page as a line graph. Netomat similarly refuses the page convention of the Web. The user enters a word or a phrase that is passed to search engines. Netomat then extracts page titles, images, audio, or any other media type, as specified by the user, from the found pages and floats them across the computer screen. As can be seen, both browsers refuse the page metaphor, instead substituting their own metaphors—a graph showing the structure of links in the case of Web Stalker, a flow of media elements in the case of Netomat.

While the 1990s' Web browsers and other commercial cultural interfaces have retained the modern page format, they also have come to rely on a new way of organizing and accessing texts that has little precedent within the book tradition—hyperlinking. We may be tempted to trace hyperlinking to earlier forms and practices of non-sequential text organization, such as the Torah's interpretations and footnotes, but it is actually fundamentally different from them. Both the Torah's interpretations and footnotes imply a master-slave relationship between one text and another. But in the case of hyperlinking as implemented by HTML and earlier by Hypercard, no such relationship of hierarchy is assumed. The two sources connected through a hyperlink have equal weight; neither one dominates the other. Thus the acceptance of hyperlinking in the 1980s can be correlated with contemporary culture's suspicion of all hierarchies, and preference for the aesthetics of collage in which radically different sources are brought together within a singular cultural object.

Traditionally, texts encoded human knowledge and memory, instructed, inspired, convinced, and seduced their readers to adopt new

---

9. http://www.backspace.org/iod.

10. http://www.netomat.net.

ideas, new ways of interpreting the world, new ideologies. In short, the printed word was linked to the art of rhetoric. While it is probably possible to invent a new rhetoric of hypermedia that will use hyperlinking not to distract the reader from the argument (as is often the case today), but rather to further convince her of an argument's validity, the sheer existence and popularity of hyperlinking exemplifies the continuing decline of the field of rhetoric in the modern era. Ancient and medieval scholars classified hundreds of different rhetorical figures. In the middle of the twentieth century, linguist Roman Jakobson, under the influence of the computer's binary logic, information theory, and cybernetics to which he was exposed at MIT where he was teaching, radically reduced rhetoric to just two figures—metaphor and metonymy.[11] Finally, in the 1990s, World Wide Web hyperlinking has privileged the single figure of metonymy at the expense of all others.[12] The hypertext of the World Wide Web leads the reader from one text to another, ad infinitum. Contrary to popular images of computer media as collapsing all human culture into a single giant library (which implies the existence of some ordering system), or a single giant book (which implies a narrative progression), it is perhaps more accurate to think of the new media culture as an infinite flat surface where individual texts are placed in no particular order, like the Web page designed by antirom for HotWired. Expanding this comparison further, we can note that Random Access Memory, the concept behind the group's name, also implies a lack of hierarchy: Any RAM location can be accessed as quickly as any other. In contrast to the older storage media of book, film, and magnetic tape, where data is organized sequentially and linearly, thus suggesting the presence of a narrative or a rhetorical trajectory, RAM "flattens" the data. Rather than seducing the user through a careful arrangement of arguments and examples, points and counterpoints, changing rhythms of presentation (i.e., the rate of data streaming, to use contemporary language), simulated false paths, and dramatically presented conceptual

---

11. Roman Jakobson, "Deux aspects du langage et deux types d'aphasie," in *Temps Modernes*, no. 188 (January 1962).

12. XLM diversifies types of links available by including bidirectional links, multiway links, and links to a span of text rather than a simple point.

breakthroughs, cultural interfaces, like RAM itself, bombard the user with all the data at once.[13]

In the 1980s many critics described one of the key effects of "postmodernism" as that of spatialization—privileging space over time, flattening historical time, refusing grand narratives. Computer media, which evolved during the same decade, accomplished this spatialization quite literally. It replaced sequential storage with random-access storage; hierarchical organization of information with a flattened hypertext; psychological movement of narrative in novels and cinema with physical movement through space, as witnessed by endless computer animated fly-throughs or computer games such as *Myst, Doom,* and countless others. In short, time became a flat image or a landscape, something to look at or navigate through. If there is a new rhetoric or aesthetic possible here, it may have less to do with the ordering of time by a writer or an orator, and more with spatial wandering. The hypertext reader is like Robinson Crusoe, walking across the sand, picking up a navigation journal, a rotten fruit, an instrument whose purpose he does not know; leaving imprints that, like computer hyperlinks, follow from one found object to another.

Cinema

The printed word tradition that initially dominated the language of cultural interfaces is becoming less important, while the part played by cinematic elements is becoming progressively stronger. This is consistent with a general trend in modern society toward presenting more and more information in the form of time-based audiovisual moving image sequences, rather than as text. As new generations of both computer users and computer designers grow up in a media-rich environment dominated by television rather than by printed texts, it is not surprising that they favor cinematic language over the language of print.

A hundred years after cinema's birth, cinematic ways of seeing the world, of structuring time, of narrating a story, of linking one experience to the

---

13. This may imply that new digital rhetoric may have less to do with arranging information in a particular order and more to do simply with selecting what is included and what is not included in the total corpus presented.

next, have become the basic means by which computer users access and interact with all cultural data. In this respect, the computer fulfills the promise of cinema as a visual Esperanto—a goal that preoccupied many film artists and critics in the 1920s, from Griffith to Vertov. Indeed, today millions of computer users communicate with each other through the same computer interface. And in contrast to cinema where most "users" are able to understand cinematic language but not speak it (i.e., make films), all computer users can speak the language of the interface. They are active users of the interface, employing it to perform many tasks: send e-mail, organize files, run various applications, and so on.

The original Esperanto never became truly popular. Cultural interfaces, in contrast, are widely used and easily learned. We have what is an unprecedented situation in the history of cultural languages—a language designed by a rather small group of people that is immediately adopted by millions of computer users. How is it possible that people around the world adopt today something that a twenty-something programmer in Northern California hacked together just the night before? Shall we conclude that we are somehow biologically "wired" to the interface language, in the same way as we are "wired" to different natural languages according to the original hypothesis of Noam Chomsky?

The answer is of course no. Users are able to acquire new cultural languages, whether cinema a hundred years ago, or cultural interfaces today, because these languages are based on previous and already familiar cultural forms. In the case of cinema, the cultural forms that went into its making include theater, magic lantern shows, and other nineteenth-century forms of public entertainment. Cultural interfaces in turn draw on older cultural forms such as cinema and the printed word. I have already discussed some ways in which the printed word tradition structures interface language; now it is cinema's turn.

I will begin with probably the most important case of cinema's influence on cultural interfaces—the mobile camera. Originally developed as part of 3-D computer graphics technology for such applications as computer-aided design, flight simulators, and computer movie making, during the 1980s and 1990s the camera model became as much of an interface convention as scrollable windows or cut-and-paste operations. It became an accepted way of interacting with any data represented in three dimensions—which in computer culture means literally anything and everything—the results of a physical simulation, an architectural site, the design of a new molecule, statistical data, the structure of a computer network, and so on. As computer culture gradually spatializes all representations and experiences, they are subjected to the camera's particular grammar of data access. Zoom, tilt, pan, and track—we now use these operations to interact with data spaces, models, objects, and bodies.

Abstracted from its historical temporary "imprisonment" within the physical body of a movie camera directed at physical reality, a virtualized camera also becomes an interface to all types of media and information beside 3-D space. As an example, consider the GUI of the leading computer animation software—PowerAnimator from Alias/Wavefront.[14] In this interface, each window, regardless of whether it displays a 3-D model, a graph, or even plain text, contains Dolly, Track, and Zoom buttons. It is particularly important that the user is expected to dolly and pan over text as if it were a 3-D scene. In this interface, cinematic vision triumphs over the print tradition, with the camera subsuming the page. The Gutenberg galaxy turns out to be just a subset of the Lumières' universe.

Another feature of cinematic perception that persists in cultural interfaces is a rectangular framing of represented reality.[15] Cinema itself inherited this framing from Western painting. Since the Renaissance, the frame has acted as a window onto a larger space that is assumed to extend beyond the frame. This space is cut by the frame's rectangle into two parts: "onscreen space," the part that is inside the frame, and the part that is outside. In the

---

14. See http://www.aw.sgi.com/pages/home/pages/products/pages/poweranimator_film_sgi/.
15. In *The Address of the Eye,* Vivian Sobchack discusses the three metaphors of frame, window, and mirror that underlie modern film theory. The metaphor of the frame comes from modern painting and is central to formalist theory, which is concerned with signification. The metaphor of the window underlies realist film theory (Bazin), which stresses the act of perception. Realist theory follows Alberti in conceptualizing the cinema screen as a transparent window onto the world. Finally, the metaphor of the mirror is central to psychoanalytic film theory. In terms of these distinctions, my discussion here is concerned with the window metaphor. The distinctions themselves, however, open up a very productive space for thinking further about the relationships between cinema and computer media, in particular, the cinema screen and the computer window. See Vivian Sobchack, *The Address of the Eye: A Phenomenology of Film Experience* (Princeton, N.J.: Princeton University Press, 1992).

famous formulation of Leon Battista Alberti, the frame acts as a window onto the world. Or, in the more recent formulation of French film theorist Jacques Aumont and his co-authors, "The onscreen space is habitually perceived as included within a more vast scenographic space. Even though the onscreen space is the only visible part, this larger scenographic part is nonetheless considered to exist around it."[16]

Just as a rectangular frame in painting and photography presents a part of a larger space outside it, a window in HCI presents a partial view of a larger document. But if in painting (and later in photography), the framing chosen by an artist is final, computer interface benefits from a new invention introduced by cinema—the mobility of the frame. Just as a kino-eye can move around a space revealing its different regions, a computer user can scroll through a window's contents.

It is not surprising to see that screen-based interactive 3-D environments, such as VRML words, also use cinema's rectangular framing, since they rely on other elements of cinematic vision, specifically, a mobile virtual camera. It may be surprising, however, to realize that the Virtual Reality interface, often promoted as the most "natural" interface of all, utilizes the same framing.[17] As in cinema, the world presented to a VR user is cut by a rectangular frame. As in cinema, this frame presents a partial view of a larger space.[18] As in cinema, the virtual camera moves around to reveal different parts of this space.

Of course, the camera is now controlled by the user and in fact is identified with her own sight. Yet it is crucial that in VR one sees the virtual world through a rectangular frame, and that this frame always presents only part of

16. Jacques Aumont et al., *Aesthetics of Film* (Austin: University of Texas Press, 1992), 13.

17. By VR interface, I mean the common forms of a head-mounted or head-coupled directed display employed in VR systems. For a popular review of such displays written when the popularity of VR was at its peak, see Steve Aukstakalnis and David Blatner, *Silicon Mirage: The Art and Science of Virtual Reality* (Berkeley, CA: Peachpit Press, 1992), pp. 80–98. For a more technical treatment, see Dean Kocian and Lee Task, "Visually Coupled Systems Hardware and the Human Interface," in *Virtual Environments and Advanced Interface Design,* ed. Woodrow Barfield and Thomas Furness III (New York and Oxford: Oxford University Press, 1995), 175–257.

18. See Kocian and Task for details on the field of view of various VR displays. Although it varies widely between different systems, the typical size of the field of view in commercial head-mounted displays (HMD) available in the first part of the 1990s was thirty to fifty degrees.

a larger whole. This frame creates a distinct subjective experience that is much closer to cinematic perception than it is to unmediated sight.

Interactive virtual worlds, whether accessed through a screen-based or VR interface, are often discussed as the logical successor to cinema and potentially the key cultural form of the twenty-first century just as cinema was the key cultural form of the twentieth century. These discussions usually focus on issues of interaction and narrative; thus, the typical scenario for twenty-first century cinema involves a user represented as an avatar existing literally "inside" the narrative space, rendered with photorealistic 3-D computer graphics, interacting with virtual characters and perhaps other users, and affecting the course of narrative events.

It is an open question whether this and similar scenarios indeed represent an extension of cinema, or if they rather should be thought of as a continuation of theatrical traditions such as improvisational or avant-garde theater. But what undoubtedly can be observed is how virtual technology's dependence on cinema's mode of seeing and language is becoming progressively stronger. This coincides with the move from proprietary and expensive VR systems to more widely available and standardized technologies, such as VRML. (The following examples refer to a particular VRML browser— WebSpace Navigator 1.1 from SGI.[19] Other VRML browsers have similar features.)

The creator of a VRML world can define a number of viewpoints that are loaded with the world.[20] These viewpoints automatically appear in a special menu in a VRML browser that allows the user to step through them, one by one. Just as in cinema, ontology is coupled with epistemology: the world is designed to be viewed from particular points of view. The designer of a virtual world is thus a cinematographer as well as an architect. The user can wander around the world, or she can save time by assuming the familiar position of a cinema viewer for whom the cinematographer has already chosen the best viewpoints.

Equally interesting is another option that controls how a VRML browser moves from one viewpoint to the next. By default, the virtual camera trav-

---

19. http://webspace.sgi.com/WebSpace/Help/1.1/.

20. See John Hartman and Josie Wernecke, *The VRML 2.0 Handbook: Building Moving Worlds on the Web* (Reading, Mass.: Addison-Wesley, 1996), 363.

els smoothly through space from the current viewpoint to the next as though on a dolly, its movement automatically calculated by the software. Selecting the "jump cuts" option makes it cut from one view to the next. Both modes are obviously derived from cinema. Both are more efficient than trying to explore the world on its own.

With a VRML interface, nature is firmly subsumed under culture. The eye is subordinated to the kino-eye. The body is subordinated to the virtual body of the virtual camera. While the user can investigate the world on her own, freely selecting trajectories and viewpoints, the interface privileges cinematic perception—cuts, precomputed, dolly-like motions, preselected viewpoints.

The area of computer culture where the cinematic interface is being transformed into a cultural interface most aggressively is computer games. By the 1990s, game designers had moved from two to three dimensions and had begun to incorporate cinematic language in an increasingly systematic fashion. Games began to feature lavish opening cinematic sequences (called "cinematics" in the game business) that set the mood, established the setting, and introduced the narrative. Frequently, the whole game would be structured as an oscillation between interactive fragments requiring the user's input and noninteractive cinematic sequences, that is, "cinematics." As the decade progressed, game designers created increasingly complex—and increasingly cinematic—interactive virtual worlds. Regardless of a game's genre, it came to rely on cinematography techniques borrowed from traditional cinema, including the expressive use of camera angles and depth of field, and dramatic lighting of 3-D computer-generated sets to create mood and atmosphere. In the beginning of the decade, many games such as *The 7th Guest* (Trilobyte, 1993) or *Voyeur* (Philips Interactive Media, 1994) used digital video of actors superimposed over 2-D or 3-D backgrounds; by its end, they had switched to fully synthetic characters rendered in real time.[21] This switch allowed game designers to go beyond the branching-type structure of earlier games based on digital video in which all possible scenes had to be taped beforehand. In contrast, 3-D characters animated in real time move

---

21. Examples of the earlier trend are *Return to Zork* (Activision, 1993) and *The 7th Guest* (Trilobyte/Virgin Games, 1993). Examples of the later trend are *Soulblade* (Namco, 1997) and *Tomb Raider* (Eidos, 1996).

arbitrarily around the space, and the space itself can change during the game. (For instance, when a player returns to an already visited area, she will find any objects that she left there earlier.) This switch also made virtual words more cinematic, as characters could be better visually integrated with their environments.[22]

A particularly important example of how computer games use—and extend—cinematic language is their implementation of a dynamic point of view. In driving and flying simulators and in combat games such as *Tekken 2* (Namco, 1994–), events like car crashes and knockdowns are automatically replayed from a different point of view. Other games such as the *Doom* series (Id Software, 1993–) and *Dungeon Keeper* (Bullfrog Productions, 1997) allow the user to switch between the point of view of the hero and a top-down bird's-eye view. Designers of online virtual worlds such as Active Worlds provide their users with similar capabilities. Nintendo goes even further by dedicating four buttons on its N64 joypad to controlling the view of the action. While playing Nintendo games such as *Super Mario 64* (Nintendo, 1996) the user can continuously adjust the position of the camera. Some Sony Playstation games such as *Tomb Raider* (Eidos, 1996) also use the buttons on the Playstation joypad for changing point of view. Some games such as *Myth: The Fallen Lords* (Bungie, 1997) use an AI engine (computer code that controls simulated "life" in the game, such as human characters that the player encounters) to automatically control the camera.

The incorporation of virtual/camera controls into the very hardware of game consoles is truly a historic event. Directing the virtual camera becomes as important as controlling the hero's actions. This fact is admitted by the game industry itself. Of the four key features of *Dungeon Keeper* advertized on its package, for instance, the first two concern control of the camera: "switch your perspective," "rotate your view," "take on your friend," "unveil hidden

---

22. Critical literature on computer games, and in particular, their visual language, remains slim. Useful facts on the history of computer games, descriptions of different genres, and interviews with designers can be found in Chris McGowan and Jim McCullaugh, *Entertainment in the Cyber Zone* (New York: Random House, 1995). Another useful source is J. C. Herz, *Joystick Nation: How Videogames Ate Our Quarters, Won Our Hearts, and Rewired Our Minds* (Boston: Little, Brown, 1997).

levels." In games such as this one, cinematic perception functions as the sub-ject in its own right,[23] suggesting the return of "The New Vision" movement of the 1920s (Moholy-Nagy, Rodchenko, Vertov, and others), which fore-grounded the new mobility of the photo and film camera, and made uncon-ventional points of view a key part of its poetics.

The fact that computer games and virtual worlds continue to encode, step by step, the grammar of a kino-eye in software and in hardware is not an ac-cident, but rather is consistent with the overall trajectory of the computeri-zation of culture since the 1940s—the automation of all cultural operations. This automation gradually moves from basic to more complex operations: from image processing and spell checking to software-generated characters, 3-D worlds, and Web sites. A side effect of this automation is that once par-ticular cultural codes are implemented in low-level software and hardware, they are no longer seen as choices but as unquestionable defaults. To take the automation of imaging as an example, in the early 1960s the newly emerg-ing field of computer graphics incorporated a linear one-point perspective into 3-D software, and later directly into the hardware.[24] As a result, linear perspective became the default mode of vision in computer culture, whether we are speaking of computer animation, computer games, visualization, or VRML worlds. Now we are witnessing the next stage of this process—the translation of a cinematic grammar of points of view into software and hard-ware. As Hollywood cinematography is translated into algorithms and com-puter chips, its conventions become the default method of interacting with any data subjected to spatialization. (At SIGGRAPH '97 in Los Angeles, one of the presenters called for the incorporation of Hollywood-style editing in multi-user virtual worlds software. In such implementation, user interaction with other avatar(s) will be automatically rendered using classical Holly-wood conventions for filming dialog.[25]) To use the terms of "The Virtual

---

23. *Dungeon Keeper* (Bullfrog Productions, 1997).

24. For a more detailed discussion of the history of computer imaging as gradual automation, see my articles "Mapping Space: Perspective, Radar, and Computer Graphics," and "Automa-tion of Sight from Photography to Computer Vision."

25. Moses Ma's presentation on the panel "Putting a Human Face on Cyberspace: Designing Avatars and the Virtual Worlds They Live In," SIGGRAPH '97, 7 August 1997.

Cinematographer: A Paradigm for Automatic Real-Time Camera Control and Directing," a 1996 paper authored by Microsoft researchers, the goal of research is to encode "cinematographic expertise," translating "heuristics of filmmaking" into computer software and hardware.[26] Element by element, cinema is being poured into a computer: first, one-point linear perspective; next, the mobile camera and rectangular window; next, cinematography and editing conventions; and, of course, digital personas based on acting conventions borrowed from cinema, to be followed by make-up, set design, and the narrative structures themselves. Rather than being merely one cultural language among others, cinema is now becoming *the* cultural interface, a toolbox for all cultural communication, overtaking the printed word.

Cinema, the major cultural form of the twentieth century, has found a new life as the toolbox of the computer user. Cinematic means of perception, of connecting space and time, of representing human memory, thinking, and emotion have become a way of work and a way of life for millions in the computer age. Cinema's aesthetic strategies have become basic organizational principles of computer software. The window into a fictional world of a cinematic narrative has become a window into a datascape. In short, what was cinema is now the human-computer interface.

I will conclude this section by discussing a few artistic projects that, in different ways, offer alternatives to this trajectory—a trajectory that, again, involves the gradual translation of elements and techniques of cinematic perception and language into a de-contextualized set of tools to be used as an interface to any data. In the process of this translation, cinematic perception is divorced from its original material embodiment (camera, film stock), as well as from the historical context of its formation. If in cinema the camera functions as a material object, coexisting spatially and temporally with the world it is showing us, it has now becomes a set of abstract operations. The art projects that I discuss below refuse this separation of cinematic vision from the material world. They reunite perception and material reality by making the camera and what it records a part of the ontology of a virtual world. They

---

26. Li-wei He, Michael Cohen, and David Salesin, "The Virtual Cinematographer: A Paradigm for Automatic Real-Time Camera Control and Directing," SIGGRAPH '96 (http://research.microsoft.com/SIGGRAPH96/96/VirtualCinema.htm).

also refuse the universalization of cinematic vision by computer culture, which (just as postmodern visual culture in general) treats cinema as a toolbox, a set of "filters" that can be used to process any input. In contrast, each of these projects employs a unique cinematic strategy that has a specific relation to the particular virtual world it reveals to the user.

In *The Invisible Shape of Things Past,* Joachim Sauter and Dirk Lüsenbrink of the Berlin-based ART+COM collective created a truly innovative cultural interface for accessing historical data about Berlin's history.[27] The interface de-virtualizes cinema, so to speak, by putting the records of cinematic vision back into their historical and material context. As the user navigates through a 3-D model of Berlin, she comes across elongated shapes lying on city streets. These shapes, which the authors call "filmobjects," correspond to documentary footage recorded at corresponding points in the city. To create each shape, the original footage is digitized and the frames are stacked one after another in depth, with the original camera parameters determining the exact shape. The user can view the footage by clicking on the first frame. As the frames are displayed one after another, the shape becomes correspondingly thinner.

In following the general trend of computer culture toward spatialization of every cultural experience, this cultural interface spatializes time, representing it as a shape in a 3-D space. This shape can be thought of as a book, with individual frames stacked one after another like book pages. The trajectory through time and space followed by a camera becomes a book to be read, page by page. The records of the camera's vision become material objects, sharing space with the material reality that gave rise to this vision. Cinema is solidified. This project, then, can be also understood as a virtual monument to cinema. The (virtual) shapes situated around the (virtual) city remind us of the era when cinema was the defining form of cultural expression—as opposed to a toolbox for data retrieval and use.

Hungarian-born artist Tamás Waliczky openly refuses the default mode of vision imposed by computer software—one-point linear perspective. Each of his computer-animated films *The Garden* (1992), *The Forest* (1993) and *The Way* (1994) utilizes a particular perspectival system: a water-drop

---

27. See http://www.artcom.de/projects/invisible_shape/welcome.en.

perspective in *The Garden,* a cylindrical perspective in *The Forest,* and a reverse perspective in *The Way.* Working with computer programmers, the artist created custom-made 3-D software to implement these perspectival systems. Each of the systems has an inherent relationship to the subject of the film in which it is used. In *The Garden,* the subject is the perception of a small child, for whom the world does not yet have an objective existence. In *The Forest,* the mental trauma of emigration is translated into the endless roaming of a camera through the forest, which is actually just a set of transparent cylinders. Finally, in *The Way,* the self-sufficiency and isolation of a Western subject are conveyed by the use of a reverse perspective.

In Waliczky's films the camera and the world are made into a single whole, whereas in *The Invisible Shape of Things Past* the records of the camera are placed back into the world. Rather than simply subjecting his virtual worlds to different types of perspectival projection, Waliczky modified the spatial structure of the worlds themselves. In *The Garden,* a child playing in a garden becomes the center of the world; as she moves around, the actual geometry of all the objects around her is transformed, with objects becoming bigger as she gets closer to them. To create *The Forest,* a number of cylinders were placed inside each other, each cylinder mapped with a picture of a tree, repeated a number of times. In the film, we see a camera moving through this endless static forest in a complex spatial trajectory—but this is an illusion. In reality, the camera does move, but the architecture of the world is constantly changing as well, because each cylinder is rotating at its own speed. As a result, the world and our perception of it are fused together.

HCI: Representation versus Control

The development of the human-computer interface, until recently, has had little to do with the distribution of cultural objects. Following some of the main applications from the 1940s until the early 1980s, when the current generation of the GUI was developed and reached the mass market together with the rise of the PC, we can list the most significant: real-time control of weapons and weapon systems; scientific simulation; computer-aided design; and finally, office work with the secretary functioning as prototypical computer user—filing documents in folders, emptying the trash can, creating and editing documents ("word processing"). Today, as the computer is beginning to host very different applications for access and manipulation of cultural data and cultural experiences, their interfaces still rely on old metaphors and action grammars. Cultural interfaces predictably use elements of a general-purpose HCI such as scrollable windows containing text and other data types, hierarchical menus, dialogue boxes, and command-line input. For instance, a typical "art collection" CD-ROM tries to recreate "the museum experience" by presenting a navigable 3-D rendering of a museum space, while still resorting to hierarchical menus that allow the user to switch between different museum collections. Even in the case of *The Invisible Shape of Things Past,* which uses a unique interface solution of "filmobjects" not directly traceable to either old cultural forms or general-purpose HCI, the designers still rely on HCI convention in the use of a pull-down menu to switch between different maps of Berlin.

In their important study of new media, *Remediation,* Jay David Bolter and Richard Grusin define *medium* as "that which remediates."[28] In contrast to a modernist view that aims to define the essential properties of every medium, Bolter and Grusin propose that all media work by "remediating," that is, translating, refashioning, and reforming other media, both on the level of content and form. If we think of the human-computer interface as another medium, its history and present development definitely fit this thesis. The history of the human-computer interface is that of borrowing and reformulating, or, to use new media lingo, reformatting other media, both past and present—the printed page, film, television. But along with borrowing the conventions of most other media and eclectically combining them together, HCI designers also heavily borrow "conventions" of the human-made physical environment, beginning with Macintosh's use of the desktop metaphor. And, more than any medium before it, HCI is like a chameleon that keeps changing its appearance, responding to how computers are used in any given period. For instance, if in the 1970s the designers at Xerox PARC modeled the first GUI on the office desk because they imagined that the computer they were designing would be used in the office, in the 1990s the primary use of computers as media-access machines led to the borrowing of interfaces of already familiar media devices such as the VCR or audio CD player controls.

---

28. Jay David Bolter and Richard Grusin, *Remediation: Understanding New Media* (Cambridge, Mass: MIT Press, 1999), 19.

In general, cultural interfaces of the 1990s try to walk an uneasy path between the richness of control provided in general-purpose HCI and the "immersive" experience of traditional cultural objects such as books and movies. Modern general-purpose HCI, be it the MAC OS, Windows, or UNIX, allow their users to perform complex and detailed actions on computer data: acquire information about an object, copy it, move it to another location, change the way data is displayed, etc. In contrast, a conventional book or a film positions the user inside an imaginary universe whose structure is fixed by the author. Cultural interfaces attempt to mediate between these two fundamentally different and ultimately incompatible approaches.

As an example, consider how cultural interfaces conceptualize the computer screen. If a general-purpose HCI clearly identifies to the user that certain objects can be acted on while others cannot (icons representing files but not the desktop itself), cultural interfaces typically hide the hyperlinks within a continuous representational field. (This technique was already so widely accepted by the 1990s that the designers of HTML offered it early on to users by implementing the "imagemap" feature.) The field can be a two-dimensional collage of different images, a mixture of representational elements and abstract textures, or a single image of a space such as a city street or a landscape. By trial and error, clicking all over the field, the user discovers that some parts of this field are hyperlinks. This concept of a screen combines two distinct pictorial conventions—the older Western tradition of pictorial illusionism in which a screen functions as a window into a virtual space, something for the viewer to look into but not act upon; and the more recent convention of graphical human-computer interfaces that divides the computer screen into a set of controls with clearly delineated functions, thereby essentially treating it as a virtual instrument panel. As a result, the computer screen becomes a battlefield for a number of incompatible definitions—depth and surface, opaqueness and transparency, image as illusionary space and image as instrument for action.

The computer screen also functions both as a window into an illusionary space and as a flat surface carrying text labels and graphical icons. We can relate this to a similar understanding of a pictorial surface in the Dutch art of the seventeenth century. In her classic study *The Art of Describing,* art historian Svetlana Alpers discusses how Dutch painting of the period functioned as both map and picture, combining different kinds of information and knowledge of the world.[29]

Here is another example of how cultural interfaces try to find a middle ground between the conventions of general-purpose HCI and the conventions of traditional cultural forms. Again we encounter tension and struggle—in this case, between standardization and originality. One of the main principles of modern HCI is the consistency principle. It dictates that menus, icons, dialogue boxes, and other interface elements should be the same in different applications. The user knows that every application will contain a "file" menu, or that if she encounters an icon that looks like a magnifying glass, it can be used to zoom on documents. In contrast, modern culture (including its "postmodern" stage) stresses originality: Every cultural object is supposed to be different from the rest, and if it is quoting other objects, these quotes have to be defined as such. Cultural interfaces try to accommodate both the demand for consistency and the demand for originality. Most of them contain the same set of interface elements with standard semantics, such as "home," "forward," and "backward" icons. But because every Web site and CD-ROM strives to have its own distinct design, these elements are always designed differently from one product to the next. For instance, many games such as *War Craft II* (Blizzard Entertainment, 1996) and *Dungeon Keeper* give their icons a "historical" look consistent with the mood of the imaginary universe portrayed in the game.

The language of cultural interfaces is a hybrid. It is a strange, often awkward mix between the conventions of traditional cultural forms and the conventions of HCI—between an immersive environment and a set of controls, between standardization and originality. Cultural interfaces try to balance the concept of a surface in painting, photography, cinema, and the printed page as something to be looked at, glanced at, read, but always from some distance, without interfering with it, with the concept of the surface in a computer interface as a virtual control panel, similar to the control panel on

---

29. See Svetlana Alpers, *The Art of Describing: Dutch Art in the Seventeenth Century* (Chicago: University of Chicago Press, 1983). See particularly the chapter "Mapping Impulse."

a car, plane, or any other complex machine.[30] Finally, on yet another level, the traditions of the printed word and of cinema also compete between themselves. One wants the computer screen to be a dense and flat information surface, whereas the other insists that it become a window into a virtual space.

To see that this hybrid language of the cultural interfaces of the 1990s represents only one historical possibility, consider a very different scenario. Potentially, cultural interfaces could completely rely on already existing metaphors and action grammars of a standard HCI, or, at least, rely on them much more than they actually do. They do not have to "dress up" HCI with custom icons and buttons, or hide links within images, or organize the information as a series of pages or a 3-D environment. For instance, texts can be presented simply as files inside a directory rather than as a set of pages connected by custom-designed icons. This strategy of using standard HCI to present cultural objects is encountered quite rarely. In fact, I am aware of only one project that seems to use it completely consciously, as though by choice rather than by necessity—a CD-ROM by Gerald Van Der Kaap entitled *BlindRom V.0.9.* (Netherlands, 1993). The CD-ROM includes a standard-looking folder named "Blind Letter." Inside the folder there are a large number of text files. You do not have to learn yet another cultural interface, search for hyperlinks hidden in images, or navigate through a 3-D environment. Reading these files requires simply opening them in standard Macintosh SimpleText, one by one. This simple technique works very well. Rather than distracting the user from experiencing the work, the computer interface becomes part and parcel of the work. Opening these files, I felt that I was in the presence of a new literary form for a new medium, perhaps the real medium of a computer—its interface.

As the examples here illustrate, cultural interfaces try to create their own language rather than simply using the general-purpose HCI. In doing so, these

---

30. This historical connection is illustrated by popular flight simulator games in which the computer screen is used to simulate the control panel of a plane, that is, the very type of object from which computer interfaces have developed. The conceptual origin of the modern GUI in a traditional instrument panel can be seen even more clearly in the first graphical computer interfaces of the late 1960s and early 1970s, which used tiled windows. The first tiled window interface was demonstrated by Douglas Engelbart in 1968.

interfaces try to negotiate between metaphors and ways of controlling a computer developed in HCI, and the conventions of more traditional cultural forms. Indeed, neither extreme is ultimately satisfactory by itself. It is one thing to use a computer to control weapons or analyze statistical data, it is another to use it to represent cultural memories, values, and experiences. Interfaces developed for the computer in the role of calculator, control mechanism, or communication device are not necessarily suitable for a computer playing the role of cultural machine. Conversely, if we simply mimic the existing conventions of older cultural forms such as the printed word and cinema, we will not take advantage of all the new capacities offered by the computer: its flexibility in displaying and manipulating data, interactive control by the user, ability to run simulations, etc.

Today the language of cultural interfaces is in its early stage, as was the language of cinema a hundred years ago. We do not know what the final result will be, or even if it will ever completely stabilize. Both the printed word and cinema eventually achieved stable forms that underwent little change for long periods of time, in part because of the material investments in their means of production and distribution. Given that computer language is implemented in software, potentially it could keep changing forever. But there is one thing we can be sure of. We are witnessing the emergence of a new cultural metalanguage, something that will be at least as significant as the printed word and cinema before it.

The Screen and the User

Contemporary human-computer interfaces offer radical new possibilities for art and communication. Virtual reality allows us to travel through nonexistent three-dimensional spaces. A computer monitor connected to a network becomes a window through which we can enter places thousands of miles away. Finally, with the help of a mouse or a video camera, a computer can be transformed into an intelligent being capable of engaging us in dialogue.

VR, telepresence, and interactivity are made possible by the recent technology of the digital computer. However, they are made real by a much older technology—the screen. It is by looking at a screen—a flat, rectangular surface positioned at some distance from the eyes—that the user experiences the illusion of navigating through virtual spaces, of being physically present somewhere else or of being hailed by the computer itself. If computers have become a common presence in our culture only in the last decade, the screen, on the other hand, has been used to present visual information for centuries—from Renaissance painting to twentieth-century cinema.

Today, coupled with the computer, the screen is rapidly becoming the main means of accessing any kind of information, be it still images, moving images, or text. We are already using it to read the daily newspaper; to watch movies; to communicate with co-workers, relatives, and friends; and, most important, to work. We may debate whether our society is a society of spectacle or of simulation, but, undoubtedly, it is a society of the screen. What are the different stages of the screen's history? What are the relationships between the physical space where the viewer is located, her body, and the screen space? What are the ways in which computer displays both continue and challenge the tradition of the screen?[31]

A Screen's Genealogy

Let us start with the definition of a screen. The visual culture of the modern period, from painting to cinema, is characterized by an intriguing phenomenon—the existence of *another* virtual space, another three-dimensional world enclosed by a frame and situated inside our normal space. The frame separates two absolutely different spaces that somehow coexist. This phenomenon is what defines the screen in the most general sense, or, as I will call it, the "classical screen."

What are the properties of a classical screen? It is a flat, rectangular surface. It is intended for frontal viewing—as opposed to a panorama for instance. It exists in our normal space, the space of our body, and acts as a window into another space. This other space, the space of representation, typically has a scale different from the scale of our normal space. Defined in this way, a screen describes equally well a Renaissance painting (recall Alberti's formulation referred to above) and a modern computer display. Even proportions have not changed in five centuries; they are similar for a typical fifteenth-century painting, a film screen, and a computer screen. In this respect it is not accidental that the very names of the two main formats of

---

31. My analysis here focuses on the continuities between the computer screen and preceding representational conventions and technologies. For alternative readings that take up the differences between the two, see the excellent articles by Vivian Sobchack, "Nostalgia for a Digital Object: Regrets on the Quickening of QuickTime," in *Millennium Film Journal* 4–23, No. 34 (Fall 1999) and Norman Bryson, "Summer 1999 at TATE," available from Tate Gallery, 413 West 14th Street, New York City. Bryson writes: "Though the [computer] screen is able to present a scenographic depth, it is obviously unlike the Albertian or Renaissance window; its surface never vanishes before the imaginary depths behind it, it never truly opens into depth. But the PC screen does not behave like the modernist image, either. It cannot foreground the materiality of the surface (of pigments on canvas) since it has no materiality to speak of, other than the play of shifting light." Both Sobchack and Bryson stress the difference between the traditional image frame and the multiple windows of a computer screen. "Basically," writes Bryson, "the whole order of the frame is abolished, replaced by the order of superimposition or tiling."

computer displays point to two genres of painting: A horizontal format is referred to as "landscape mode," whereas the vertical format is referred to as "portrait mode."

A hundred years ago a new type of screen, which I will call the "dynamic screen," became popular. This new type retains all the properties of a classical screen while adding something new: It can display an image changing over time. This is the screen of cinema, television, video. The dynamic screen also brings with it a certain relationship between the image and the spectator—a certain *viewing regime,* so to speak. This relationship is already implicit in the classical screen, but now it fully surfaces. A screen's image strives for complete illusion and visual plenitude, while the viewer is asked to suspend disbelief and to identify with the image. Although the screen in reality is only a window of limited dimensions positioned inside the physical space of the viewer, the viewer is expected to concentrate completely on what she sees in this window, focusing her attention on the representation and disregarding the physical space outside. This viewing regime is made possible by the fact that the singular image, whether a painting, movie screen, or television screen, completely fills the screen. This is why we are so annoyed in a movie theater when the projected image does not precisely coincide with the screen's boundaries: It disrupts the illusion, making us conscious of what exists outside the representation.[32]

Rather than being a neutral medium of presenting information, the screen is aggressive. It functions to filter, to *screen out,* to take over, rendering nonexistent whatever is outside its frame. Of course, the degree of this filtering varies between cinema viewing and television viewing. In cinema viewing, the viewer is asked to merge completely with the screen's space. In television viewing (as it was practiced in the twentieth century), the screen is smaller, lights are on, conversation between viewers is allowed, and the act of viewing is often integrated with other daily activities. Still, overall this viewing regime has remained stable—until recently.

---

32. The degree to which a frame that acts as a boundary between the two spaces is emphasized seems to be proportional to the degree of identification expected from the viewer. Thus in cinema, where the identification is most intense, the frame as a separate object does not exist at all—the screen simply ends at its boundaries—whereas both in painting and television the framing is much more pronounced.

This stability has been challenged by the arrival of the computer screen. On the one hand, rather than showing a single image, a computer screen typically displays a number of coexisting windows. Indeed, the coexistence of a number of overlapping windows is a fundamental principle of the modern GUI. No single window completely dominates the viewer's attention. In this sense, the possibility of simultaneously observing a few images that coexist within one screen can be compared with the phenomenon of zapping— the quick switching of television channels that allows the viewer to follow more than program.[33] In both instances, the viewer no longer concentrates on a single image. (Some television sets enable a second channel to be watched within a smaller window positioned in a corner of the main screen. Perhaps future TV sets will adopt the window metaphor of a computer.) A window interface has more to do with modern graphic design, which treats a page as a collection of different but equally important blocks of data such as text, images, and graphic elements, than with the cinematic screen.

On the other hand, with VR, the screen disappears altogether. VR typically uses a head-mounted display whose images completely fill the viewer's visual field. No longer is the viewer looking at a rectangular, flat surface from a certain distance, a window into another space. Now she is fully situated within this other space. Or, more precisely, we can say that the two spaces— the real, physical space and the virtual, simulated space—coincide. The virtual space, previously confined to a painting or a movie screen, now completely encompasses the real space. Frontality, rectangular surface, difference in scale are all gone. The screen has vanished.

Both situations—window interface and VR—disrupt the viewing regime that characterizes the historical period of the dynamic screen. This regime, based on an identification of viewer and screen image, reached its culmination in the cinema, which goes to an extreme to enable this identification (the bigness of the screen, the darkness of the surrounding space).

Thus, the era of the dynamic screen that began with cinema is now ending. And it is this disappearance of the screen—its splitting into many windows in window interface, its complete takeover of the visual field in

---

33. Here I agree with the parallel suggested by Anatoly Prokhorov between window interface and montage in cinema.

VR—that allows us today to recognize it as a cultural category and begin to trace its history.

The origins of the cinema's screen are well known. We can trace its emergence to the popular spectacles and entertainments of the eighteenth and nineteenth centuries: magic lantern shows, phantasmagoria, eidophusikon, panorama, diorama, zoopraxiscope shows, and so on. The public was ready for cinema, and when it finally appeared, it was a huge public event. Not by accident, the "invention" of cinema was claimed by at least a dozen individuals from a half-dozen countries.[34]

The origin of the computer screen is a different story. It appears in the middle of this century, but it does not become a public presence until much later; and its history has not yet been written. Both of these facts are related to the context in which it emerged: As with all the other elements of modern human-computer interface, the computer screen was developed for military use. Its history has to do not with public entertainment but with military surveillance.

The history of modern surveillance technologies begins with photography. With the advent of photography came an interest in using it for aerial surveillance. Félix Tournachon Nadar, one of the most eminent photographers of the nineteenth century, succeeded in exposing a photographic plate at 262 feet over Bièvre, France in 1858. He was soon approached by the French Army to attempt photo reconnaissance but rejected the offer. In 1882, unmanned photo balloons were already in the air; a little later, they were joined by photo rockets both in France and in Germany. The only innovation of World War I was to combine aerial cameras with a superior flying platform—the airplane.[35]

Radar became the next major surveillance technology. Massively employed in World War II, it provided important advantages over photography. Previously, military commanders had to wait until pilots returned from surveillance missions and film was developed. The inevitable delay between time of surveillance and delivery of the finished image limited photography's usefulness because by the time a photograph was produced, enemy positions

---

34. For these origins see, for instance, C. W. Ceram, *Archeology of the Cinema* (New York: Harcourt Brace and World, 1965).

35. Beaumont Newhall, *Airborne Camera* (New York: Hastings House, 1969).

could have changed. However, with radar, imaging became instantaneous, and this delay was eliminated. The effectiveness of radar had to do with a new means of displaying an image—a new type of screen.

Consider the imaging technologies of photography and film. The photographic image is a permanent imprint corresponding to a single referent—whatever is in front of the lens when the photograph is taken. It also corresponds to a limited time of observation—the time of exposure. Film is based on the same principles. A film sequence, composed of a number of still images, represents the sum of referents and the sum of exposure times of these individual images. In either case, the image is fixed once and for all. Therefore the screen can only show past events.

With radar, we see for the first time the mass employment (television is founded on the same principle but its mass employment comes later) of a fundamentally new type of screen, a screen that gradually comes to dominate modern visual culture—video monitor, computer screen, instrument display. What is new about such a screen is that its image can change in real time, reflecting changes in the referent, whether the position of an object in space (radar), any alteration in visible reality (live video) or changing data in the computer's memory (computer screen). The image can be continually updated *in real time.* This is the third type of screen after classic and dynamic—the screen of real time.

The radar screen changes, tracking the referent. But while it appears that the element of time delay, always present in the technologies of military surveillance, is eliminated, in fact, time enters the real-time screen in a new way. In older, photographic technologies, all parts of an image are exposed simultaneously, whereas now the image is produced through sequential scanning—circular in the case of radar, horizontal in the case of television. Therefore, the different parts of the image correspond to different moments in time. In this respect, a radar image is more similar to an audio record, since consecutive moments in time become circular tracks on a surface.[36]

---

36. This is more than a conceptual similarity. In the late 1920s, John H. Baird invented "phonovision," the first method for the recording and playback of a television signal. The signal was recorded on Edison's phonograph record by a process very similar to that of making an audio recording. Baird named his recording machine the "phonoscope." Albert Abramson, *Electronic Motion Pictures* (University of California Press, 1955), 41–42.

What this means is that the image, in a traditional sense, no longer exists! And it is only by habit that we still refer to what we see on the real-time screen as "images." It is only because the scanning is fast enough and because, sometimes, the referent remains static, that we see what looks like a static image. Yet, such an image is no longer the norm, but the exception of a more general, new kind of representation for which we do not yet have a term.

The principles and technology of radar were worked out independently by scientists in the United States, England, France, and Germany during the 1930s. After the beginning of the War, however, only the U.S. had the resources necessary to continue radar development. In 1940, at MIT, a team of scientists was assembled to work in the Radiation Laboratory, or the "Rad Lab," as it came to be called. The purpose of the lab was radar research and production. By 1943, the "Rad Lab" occupied 115 acres of floor space; it had the largest telephone switchboard in Cambridge and employed four thousand people.[37]

Next to photography, radar provided a superior way to gather information about enemy locations. In fact, it provided too much information, more information than one person could deal with. Historical footage from the early days of the war shows a central command room with a large, table-size map of Britain.[38] Small pieces of cardboard in the form of planes are positioned on the map to show the locations of actual German bombers. A few senior officers scrutinize the map. Meanwhile, women in army uniforms constantly change the location of the cardboard pieces by moving them with long sticks as information is transmitted from dozens of radar stations.[39]

Was there a more effective way to process and display information gathered by radar? The computer screen, as well as most other key principles and technologies of the modern human-computer interface—interactive control, algorithms for 3-D wireframe graphics, bit-mapped graphics—was developed as a way of solving this problem.

The research again took place at MIT. The Radiation Laboratory was dismantled after the end of the war, but soon the Air Force created another

---

37. *Echoes of War* (Boston: WGBH Boston, 1989), videotape.

38. Ibid.

39. Ibid.

secret laboratory in its place—Lincoln Laboratory. The purpose of Lincoln Laboratory was to work on human factors and new display technologies for SAGE—"Semi-Automatic Ground Environment," a command center to control the U.S. air defenses established in the mid-1950s.[40] Historian of computer technology Paul Edwards writes that SAGE's job "was to link together radar installations around the USA's perimeter, analyze and interpret their signals, and direct manned interceptor jets toward the incoming bee. It was to be a total system, one whose 'human components' were fully integrated into the mechanized circuit of detection, decision and response."[41]

The creation of SAGE and the development of an interactive human-computer interface were largely the result of a particular military doctrine. In the 1950s, the American military thought that a Soviet attack on the U.S. would entail sending a large number of bombers simultaneously. Therefore, it seemed necessary to create a center that could receive information from all U.S. radar stations, track the large number of enemy bombers, and coordinate a counterattack. The computer screen and other components of the modern human-computer interface owe their existence to this particular military idea. (As someone who was born in the Soviet Union and now works on the history of new media in the United States, I find this bit of history truly fascinating.)

An early version of the center was called "the Cape Cod network," since it received information from radars situated along the coast of New England. The center operated right out of the Barta Building on the MIT campus. Each of eighty-two Air Force officers monitored his own computer display, which showed the outline of the New England Coast and the location of key radars. Whenever an officer noticed a dot indicating a moving plane, he

---

40. On SAGE, see the excellent social history of early computing by Paul Edwards, *The Closed World: Computers and the Politics of Discourse in Cold War America* (Cambridge, Mass.: MIT Press, 1996). For a shorter summary of his argument, see Paul Edwards, "The Closed World: Systems Discourse, Military Policy and Post–World War II U.S. Historical Consciousness," in *Cyborg Worlds: The Military Information Society,* eds. Les Levidow and Kevin Robins (London: Free Association Books, 1989). See also Howard Rheingold, *Virtual Reality* (New York: Simon and Schuster, 1991), 68–93.

41. Edwards, "The Closed World" (1989), 142.

would tell the computer to follow the plane. To do this, the officer simply had to touch the dot with a special "light pen."[42]

Thus, the SAGE system contained all the main elements of the modern human-computer interface. The light pen, designed in 1949, can be considered a precursor of the contemporary mouse. More importantly, at SAGE, the screen came to be used not only to display information in real time, as in radar and television, but also to give commands to the computer. Rather than acting solely as a means of displaying an image of reality, the screen became a vehicle for directly affecting reality.

Using the technology developed for SAGE, Lincoln researchers created a number of computer graphics programs that relied on the screen as a means of inputting and outputting information from a computer. These included programs for displaying brain waves (1957), simulating planet and gravitational activity (1960), and creating 2-D drawings (1958).[43] The most well-known of these programs was "Sketchpad." Designed in 1962 by Ivan Sutherland, a graduate student supervised by Claude Shannon, it widely publicized the idea of interactive computer graphics. With Sketchpad, a human operator could create graphics directly on a computer screen by touching the screen with a light pen. Sketchpad exemplified a new paradigm of interacting with computers: By changing something on the screen, the operator changed something in the computer's memory. The real-time screen became interactive.

This, in short, is the history of the birth of the computer screen. But even before the computer screen became widely used, a new paradigm emerged— the simulation of an interactive three-dimensional environment without a screen. In 1966, Ivan Sutherland and his colleagues began research on the prototype of VR. The work was cosponsored by the Advanced Research Projects Agency (ARPA) and the Office of Naval Research.[44]

"The fundamental idea behind the three-dimensional display is to present the user with a perspective image which changes as he moves," wrote

42. "Retrospectives II: The Early Years in Computer Graphics at MIT, Lincoln Lab, and Harvard," in *SIGGRAPH '89 Panel Proceedings* (New York: The Association for Computing Machinery, 1989), 22–24.

43. Ibid., 42–54.

44. Rheingold, *Virtual Reality,* 105.

Sutherland in 1968.[45] The computer tracked the position of the viewer's head and adjusted the perspective of the computer graphic image accordingly. The display itself consisted of two six-inch-long monitors mounted next to the temples. They projected an image that appeared superimposed over the viewer's field of vision.

The screen disappeared. It had completely taken over the visual field.

The Screen and the Body

I have presented one possible genealogy of the modern computer screen. In my genealogy, the computer screen represents an interactive type, a subtype of the real-time type, which is a subtype of the dynamic type, which is a subtype of the classical type. My discussion of these types relied on two ideas. First, the idea of temporality—the classical screen displays a static, permanent image; the dynamic screen displays a moving image of the past; and finally, the real-time screen shows the present. Second, the relationship between the space of the viewer and the space of representation (I defined the screen as a window into the space of representation that itself exists in our normal space).

Let us now look at the screen's history from another angle—the relationship between the screen and the body of the viewer. This is how Roland Barthes describes the screen in "Diderot, Brecht, Eisenstein," written in 1973:

Representation is not defined directly by imitation: even if one gets rid of notions of the "real," of the "vraisemblable," of the "copy," there will still be representation for as long as a subject (author, reader, spectator or voyeur) casts his *gaze* towards a horizon on which he cuts out a base of a triangle, his eye (or his mind) forming the apex. The "Organon of Representation" (which is today becoming possible to write because there are intimations of *something else*) will have as its dual foundation the sovereignty of the act of cutting out [*découpage*] and the unity of the subject of action. . . . The scene, the picture, the shot, the cut-out rectangle, here we have the very *condition* that allows us to conceive theater, painting, cinema, literature, all those arts, that is, other than music and which could be called *dioptric arts*.[46]

---

45. Quoted in ibid., 104.

46. Roland Barthes, "Diderot, Brecht, Eisenstein," in *Image/Music/Text,* trans. Stephen Heath (New York: Farrar, Straus, and Giroux, 1977), 69–70.

For Barthes, the screen becomes an all-encompassing concept that covers the functioning of even non-visual representation (literature), although he does make an appeal to a particular visual model of linear perspective. At any rate, his concept encompasses all the types of representational apparatuses I have discussed: painting, film, television, radar, and computer display. In each of these, reality is cut by the rectangle of a screen: "a pure cut-out segment with clearly defined edges, irreversible and incorruptible; everything that surrounds it is banished into nothingness, remains unnamed, while everything that it admits within its field is promoted into essence, into light, into view."[47] This act of cutting reality into a sign and nothingness simultaneously doubles the viewing subject, who now exists in two spaces: the familiar physical space of her real body and the virtual space of an image within the screen. This split comes to the surface with VR, but it already exists in painting and other *dioptric arts.*

What is the price the subject pays for the mastery of the world, focused and unified by the screen?

The Draughtsman's Contract, a 1982 film by Peter Greenaway, concerns an architectural draftsman hired to produce a set of drawings of a country house. The draughtsman employs a simple drawing tool consisting of a square grid. Throughout the film, we repeatedly see the draughtsman's face through the grid, which looks like prison bars. It is as if the subject who attempts to catch the world, immobilizing and fixing it within the representational apparatus (here, perspectival drawing), is trapped by the apparatus himself. The subject is imprisoned.

I take this image as a metaphor for what appears to be a general tendency of the Western screen-based representational apparatus. In this tradition, the body must be fixed in space if the viewer is to see the image at all. From Renaissance monocular perspective to modern cinema, from Kepler's camera obscura to nineteenth-century camera lucida, the body has to remain still.[48]

---

47. Ibid.

48. Although in the following I discuss the immobility of the subject of a screen in the context of the history of representation, we can also relate this condition to the history of communication. In ancient Greece, communication was understood as an oral dialogue between people. It was also assumed that physical movement stimulated dialogue and the process of thinking. Aristotle and his pupils walked around while discussing philosophical problems. In

The imprisonment of the body takes place on both the conceptual and literal levels; both kinds of imprisonment already appear with the first screen apparatus, Alberti's perspectival window, which, according to many interpreters of linear perspective, presents the world as seen by a singular eye—static, unblinking, and fixated. As described by Norman Bryson, perspective "followed the logic of the Gaze rather than the Glance, thus producing a visual take that was eternalized, reduced to one 'point of view' and disembodied."[49] Bryson argues that "the gaze of the painter arrests the flux of phenomena, contemplates the visual field from a vantage point outside the mobility of duration, in an eternal moment of disclosed presence."[50] Correspondingly, the world, as seen by this immobile, static, and atemporal Gaze, which belongs more to a statue than a living body, becomes equally immobile, reified, fixated, cold and dead. Referring to Dürer's famous print of a draftsman drawing a nude through a screen of perspectival threads, Martin Jay notes that "a reifying male look" turns "its targets into stone"; consequently, "the marmoreal nude is drained of its capacity to arouse desire."[51] Similarly, John Berger compares Alberti's window to "a safe let into a wall, a safe into which the visible has been deposited."[52] And in *The Draughtsman's Contract,* the draughtsman, time and again, tries to eliminate all motion, any sign of life, from the scenes he is rendering.

With perspectival machines, the imprisonment of the subject also happens in a literal sense. From the onset of the adaptation of perspective, artists and draftsmen attempted to aid the laborious manual process of creating perspectival images, and between the sixteenth and nineteenth centuries various "perspectival machines" were constructed.[53] By the first decades of the

---

the Middle Ages, a shift occured from dialogue between subjects to communication between a subject and an information storage device, that is, a book. A medieval book chained to a table can be considered a precursor to the screen that "fixes" its subject in space.

49. As summarized by Martin Jay, "Scopic Regimes of Modernity," in *Vision and Visuality,* ed. Hal Foster (Seattle: Bay Press, 1988), 7.

50. Quoted in ibid., 7.

51. Ibid., 8.

52. Quoted in ibid., 9.

53. For a survey of perspectival instruments, see Martin Kemp, *The Science of Art* (New Haven: Yale University Press, 1990), 167–220.

sixteenth century, Dürer had described a number of such machines.[54] Many varieties were invented, but regardless of the type, the artist had to remain immobile throughout the process of drawing.

Along with perspectival machines, a whole range of optical apparatuses was in use, particularly for depicting landscapes and conducting topographical surveys. The most popular optical apparatus was the camera obscura.[55] *Camera obscura* literally means "dark chamber," and was founded on the premise that if rays of light from an object or a scene pass through a small aperture, they will cross and reemerge on the other side to form an image on a screen. In order for the image to become visible, however, "it is necessary that the screen be placed in a chamber in which light levels are considerably lower than those around the object."[56] Thus, in one of the earliest depictions of the camera obscura, in Kircher's *Ars magna Lucis et umbrae* (Rome, 1649), we see the subject enjoying the image inside a tiny room, oblivious to the fact that he has had to imprison himself inside this "dark chamber" in order to see the image on the screen.

Later, a smaller tent-type camera obscura—a movable prison, so to speak—became popular. It consisted of a small tent mounted on a tripod, with a revolving reflector and lens at its apex. Having positioned himself inside the tent, which provided the necessary darkness, the draftsman would then spend hours meticulously tracing the image projected by the lens.

Early photography continued the trend toward the imprisonment of the subject and the object of representation. During photography's first decades, exposure times were quite long. The daguerreotype process, for instance, required exposures of four to seven minutes in the sun and from twelve to sixty minutes in diffused light. So, similar to the drawings produced with the help of the camera obscura, which depicted reality as static and immobile, early photographs represented the world as stable, eternal, unshakable. And when photography ventured to represent living things, they had to be immobilized. Thus, portrait studios universally employed various clamps to assure the steadiness of the sitter throughout the lengthy time of exposure. Reminiscent of torture instruments, the iron clamps firmly held the subject in

---

54. Ibid., 171–172.
55. Ibid., 200.
56. Ibid.

place—a subject who voluntarily became the prisoner of the machine in order to see her own image.[57]

Toward the end of the nineteenth century, the petrified world of the photographic image was shattered by the dynamic screen of the cinema. In "The Work of Art in the Age of Mechanical Reproduction," Walter Benjamin expressed his fascination with the new mobility of the visible: "Our taverns and our metropolitan streets, our offices and furnished rooms, our railroad stations and our factories appeared to have us locked up hopelessly. When came the film and burst this prison-world asunder by the dynamite of the tenth of a second, so that now, in the midst of its far-flung ruins and debris, we calmly and adventurously go traveling."[58]

The cinema screen enabled audiences to take a journey through different spaces without leaving their seats; in the words of film historian Anne Friedberg, it created "a mobilized virtual gaze."[59] However, the cost of this virtual mobility was a new, institutionalized immobility of the spectator. All around the world large prisons were constructed that could hold hundreds of prisoners—movie houses. The prisoners could neither talk to one another nor move from seat to seat. While they were taken on virtual journeys, their bodies remained still in the darkness of collective cameras obscura.

The formation of this viewing regime took place in parallel with the shift from what film theorists call "primitive" to "classical" film language.[60] An important part of this shift, which took place in the 1910s, was the new functioning of the virtual space represented on the screen. During the "primitive" period, the space of the film theater and the screen space were clearly separated, much like in theater or vaudeville. Viewers were free to interact, come and go, and maintain a psychological distance from the virtual world of the cinematic narrative. In contrast, classical film addressed each viewer as a separate individual and positioned him inside its virtual world

---

57. Anesthesiology emerges approximately at the same time.

58. Walter Benjamin, "The Work of Art in the Age of Mechanical Reproduction," in *Illuminations,* ed. Hannah Arendt (New York: Schocken Books, 1969), 238.

59. Anne Friedberg, *Window Shopping: Cinema and the Postmodern* (Berkeley: University of California Press, 1993), 2.

60. See, for instance, David Bordwell, Janet Steiger, and Kristin Thompson, *The Classical Hollywood Cinema* (New York: Columbia University Press, 1985).

narrative. As noted by a contemporary in 1913, "[spectators] should be put in the position of being a 'knot hole in the fence' at every stage in the play."[61] If "primitive cinema keeps the spectator looking across a void in a separate space,"[62] classical cinema positions the spectator in terms of the best viewpoint of each shot, inside the virtual space.

This situation is usually conceptualized in terms of the spectator's identification with the camera eye. The body of the spectator remains in her seat while her eye is coupled with a mobile camera. However, it is also possible to conceptualize this differently. We can imagine that the camera does not, in fact, move at all, but rather remains stationary, coinciding with the spectator's eyes. Instead, it is the virtual space as a whole that changes its position with each shot. Using the contemporary vocabulary of computer graphics, we can say that this virtual space is rotated, scaled, and zoomed always to give the spectator the best viewpoint. As in a striptease, the space slowly disrobes itself, turning, presenting itself from different sides, teasing, stepping forward and retracting, always leaving something covered so that the spectator must wait for the next shot . . . a seductive dance that begins all over with the next scene. All the spectator has to do is remain immobile.

Film theorists have taken this immobility to be the essential feature of the institution of cinema. Anne Friedberg writes: "As everyone from Baudry (who compares cinematic spectation to the prisoners in Plato's cave) to Musser points out, the cinema relies on the immobility of the spectator, seated in an auditorium."[63] Film theoretician Jean-Louis Baudry, probably more than anyone else, emphasizes immobility as the foundation of cinematic illusion, quoting Plato: "In this underground chamber they have been from childhood, chained by the leg and also by the neck, so that they cannot move and can only see what is in front of them, because the chains will not

---

61. Quoted in ibid., 215.

62. Ibid., 214.

63. Friedberg, *Window Shopping,* 134. She refers to Jean-Louis Baudry, "The Apparatus: Metapsychological Approaches to the Impression of Reality in the Cinema," in *Narrative, Apparatus, Ideology,* ed. Philip Rosen (New York: Columbia University Press, 1986) and Charles Musser, *The Emergence of Cinema: The American Screen to 1907* (New York: Charles Scribner and Sons, 1990).

let them turn their heads."[64] This immobility and confinement, according to Baudry, enables the prisoners/spectators to mistake representations for their perceptions thereby regressing to childhood when the two were indistinguishable. Rather than a historical accident, the immobility of the spectator, according to Baudry's psychoanalytic explanation, is the essential condition of cinematic pleasure.

Alberti's window, Dürer's perspectival machines, the camera obscura, photography, cinema—in all of these screen-based apparatuses, the subject has to remain immobile. In fact, as Friedberg perceptively points out, the progressive mobilization of the image in modernity was accompanied by the progressive imprisonment of the viewer: "as the 'mobility' of the gaze became more 'virtual'—as techniques were developed to paint (and then to photograph) realistic images, as mobility was implied by changes in lighting (and then cinematography)—the observer became more immobile, passive, ready to receive the constructions of a virtual reality placed in front of his or her unmoving body."[65]

What happens to this tradition with the arrival of a screen-less representational apparatus—VR? On the one hand, VR constitutes a fundamental break with this tradition. It establishes a radically new type of relationship between the body of the viewer and the image. In contrast to cinema, where the mobile camera moves independently of the immobile spectator, now the spectator actually has to move in physical space in order to experience movement in virtual space. It is as though the camera were mounted on the user's head. Thus, to look up in virtual space, one has to look up in physical space; to step forward "virtually" one has to step forward in actuality, and so on.[66] The spectator is no longer chained, immobilized, anesthetized by the apparatus that serves her ready-made images; now she has to work, to speak, in order to see.

At the same time, VR imprisons the body to an unprecedented extent. This can clearly be seen in the earliest VR system designed by Sutherland

---

64. Quoted in Baudry, "The Apparatus," 303.

65. Friedberg, *Window Shopping,* 28.

66. A typical VR system adds other ways of moving around, for instance, the ability to move forward in a single direction by simply pressing a button on a joystick. To change the direction, however, the user still has to change the position of his/her body.

and his colleagues in the 1960s. According to Howard Rheingold's history of VR, "Sutherland was the first to propose mounting small computer screens in binocular glasses—far from an easy hardware task in the early 1960s—and thus immerse the user's point of view inside the computer graphic world."[67] Rheingold further wrote:

In order to change the appearance of the computer-generated graphics when the user moves, some kind of gaze-tracking tool is needed. Because the direction of the user's gaze was most economically and accurately measured at that time by means of a mechanical apparatus, and because the HMD [head-mounted display] itself was so heavy, the users of Sutherland's early HMD systems found their head locked into machinery suspended from the ceiling. The user put his or her head into a metal contraption that was known as the "Sword of Damocles" display.[68]

A pair of tubes connected the display to tracks in the ceiling, "thus making the user a captive of the machine in a physical sense."[69] The user was able to turn around and rotate her head in any direction, but could not move away from the machine more than a few steps. Like today's computer mouse, the body was tied to the computer. In fact, the body was reduced to nothing less—and nothing more—than a giant mouse, or more precisely, a giant joystick. Instead of moving a mouse, the user had to turn her own body. Another comparison that comes to mind is the apparatus built in the late nineteenth century by Etienne-Jules Marey to measure the frequency of the wing movements of a bird. The bird was connected to the measuring equipment by wires that were long enough to enable it to flap its wings in midair but not fly anywhere.[70]

The paradox of VR, that it requires the viewer to move in order to see an image and at the same time physically ties her to a machine, is interestingly dramatized in a "cybersex" scene in the movie *Lawnmower Man* (Brett Leonard, 1992). In the scene, the heroes, a man and a woman, are situated in

---

67. Rheingold, *Virtual Reality,* 104.

68. Ibid., 105.

69. Ibid., 109.

70. Marta Braun, *Picturing Time: The Work of Etienne-Jules Marey (1830–1904)* (Chicago: University of Chicago Press, 1992), 34–35.

the same room, each fastened to a separate circular frame that allows the body to rotate 360 degrees in all directions. During "cybersex" the camera cuts back and forth between virtual space (i.e., what the heroes see and experience) and physical space. In the virtual world represented by psychedelic computer graphics, their bodies melt and morph together, disregarding all the laws of physics, while in the real world each of them simply rotates within his or her own frame.

The paradox reaches its extreme in one of the most long-standing VR projects—the Super Cockpit developed by the U.S. Air Force in the 1980s.[71] Instead of using his eyes to follow the terrain outside the plane and the dozens of instrument panels inside the cockpit, the pilot wears a head-mounted display that presents both kinds of information in a more efficient way. What follows is a description of the system from *Air & Space* magazine:

When he climbed into his F16C, the young fighter jock of 1998 simply plugged in his helmet and flipped down his visor to activate his Super Cockpit system. The virtual world he saw exactly mimicked the world outside. Salient terrain features were outlined and rendered in three dimensions by the two tiny cathode ray tubes focused at his personal viewing distance. . . . His compass heading was displayed as a large band of numbers on the horizon line, his projected flight path a shimmering highway leading out toward infinity.[72]

If in most screen-based representations (painting, cinema, video) as well as typical VR applications, the physical and virtual worlds have nothing to do with each other, here the virtual world is synchronized precisely with the physical one. The pilot positions himself in the virtual world in order to move through the physical one at a supersonic speed with his representational apparatus securely fastened to his body, more securely than ever before in the history of the screen.

Representation versus Simulation
In summary, VR continues the screen's tradition of viewer immobility by fastening the body to a machine, while at the same time it creates an

---

71. Rheingold, *Virtual Reality,* 201–209.

72. Quoted in ibid., 201.

unprecedented new condition by requiring the viewer to move. We may ask whether this new condition is without historical precedent, or whether it fits within an alternative representational tradition that encourages the movement of the viewer.

I began my discussion of the screen by emphasizing that a screen's frame separates two spaces that have *different* scales—the physical and the virtual. Although this condition does not necessarily lead to the immobilization of the spectator, it does discourage any movement on her part: Why move when she can't enter the represented virtual space anyway? This is well dramatized in *Alice in Wonderland* when Alice struggles to become just the right size in order to enter the other world.

The alternative tradition of which VR is a part can be found whenever the scale of a representation is the same as the scale of our human world so that the two spaces are continuous. This is the tradition of simulation rather than that of representation bound to a screen. The simulation tradition aims to blend virtual and physical spaces rather than to separate them. Therefore, the two spaces have the same scale; their boundary is de-emphasized (rather than being marked by a rectangular frame, as in the representation tradition); the spectator is free to move around the physical space.

To analyze further the different logic of the two traditions, we may compare their typical representatives—frescoes and mosaics, on the one hand, and Renaissance painting, on the other. The former create an illusionary space that starts behind the surface of an image. Importantly, frescoes and mosaics (as well as wall paintings) are inseparable from architecture. In other words, they cannot not be moved anywhere. In contrast, the modern painting, which first makes its appearance during the Renaissance, is essentially mobile. Separate from a wall, it can be transported anywhere. (It is tempting to connect this new mobility of representation with the tendency of capitalism to make all signs as mobile as possible.)

But, at the same time, an interesting reversal takes place. Interaction with a fresco or a mosaic, which itself cannot be moved, does not assume immobility on the part of the spectator, while the mobile Renaissance painting does presuppose such immobility. It is as though the imprisonment of the spectator is the price for the new mobility of the image. This reversal is consistent with the different logic of the representation and simulation traditions. The fact that the fresco and mosaic are "hardwired" to their architectural setting allows the artist to create a continuity between virtual and physical space. In contrast, a painting can be put in an arbitrary setting, and therefore, such continuity can no longer be guaranteed. Responding to this new condition, a painting presents a virtual space that is clearly distinct from the physical space where the painting and spectator are located. At the same time, its imprisons the spectator through a perspective model or other techniques so that she and the painting form one system. Therefore, if in the simulation tradition, the spectator exists in a single coherent space—the physical space and the virtual space that continues it—in the representational tradition, the spectator has a double identity. She simultaneously exists in physical space and in the space of representation. This split of the subject is the tradeoff for the new mobility of the image as well as for the newly available possibility to represent any arbitrary space, rather than having to simulate the physical space where an image is located.

While the representational tradition came to dominate post-Renaissance culture, the simulation tradition did not disappear. In fact, the nineteenth century, with its obsession with naturalism, pushed simulation to the extreme with the wax museum and the dioramas of natural history museums. Another example of the simulation tradition is sculpture on a human scale, for instance, Auguste Rodin's "The Burghers of Calais." We think of such sculptures as part of a post-Renaissance humanism that puts the human at the center of the universe, when in fact they are aliens, black holes uniting our world with another universe, a petrified universe of marble or stone that exists in parallel to our own.

VR continues the tradition of simulation. However, it introduces one important difference. Previously, the simulation depicted a fake space continuous with and extended from the normal space. For instance, a wall painting created a pseudo landscape that appeared to begin at the wall. In VR, either there is no connection between the two spaces (e.g., I am in a physical room while the virtual space is an underwater landscape) or, conversely, the two completely coincide (e.g., the Super Cockpit project). In either case, the actual physical reality is disregarded, dismissed, abandoned.

In this respect, the nineteenth-century panorama can be thought of as a transitional form between classical simulations (wall paintings, human-size sculpture, diorama) and VR. Like VR, the panorama creates a 360-degree space. Viewers are situated in the center of this space, and they are encouraged to move around the central viewing area in order to see different parts of the panorama.[73] But in contrast to wall paintings and mosaics that, after all, act as decorations of a real space, the physical space of action, now this physical space is subordinate to the virtual space. In other words, the central viewing area is conceived as a continuation of fake space, rather than vice versa, as before—and this is why it is usually empty. It is empty so that we can pretend that it continues the battlefield, or the view of Paris, or whatever else the panorama represents.[74] From here we are one step away from VR, where physical space is totally disregarded, and all "real" actions take place in virtual space. The screen disappeared because what was behind it simply took over.

And what about the immobilization of the body in VR that connects it to the screen tradition? Dramatic as it is, this immobilization probably represents the last act in the long history of the body's imprisonment. All around us are the signs of increasing mobility and the miniaturization of communication devices—mobile telephones and electronic organizers, pagers and laptops, phones and watches that offer Web surfing, Gameboys, and similar handheld game units. Eventually, the VR apparatus may be reduced to a chip implanted in the retina and connected by wireless transmission to the Net. From that moment on, we will carry our prisons with us—not in order to blissfully confuse representations and perceptions (as in cinema), but rather always to "be in touch," always connected, always "plugged-in." The retina and the screen will merge.

This futuristic scenario may never become a reality. For now, we clearly live in the society of the screen. Screens are everywhere—the screens of airline agents, data-entry clerks, secretaries, engineers, doctors, and pilots; the screens of ATM machines, supermarket checkouts, automobile dashboards,

---

73. Here I disagree with Friedberg, who writes, "Phantasmagorias, panoramas, dioramas— devices that concealed their machinery—were dependent on the relative immobility of their spectators" (23).

74. In some nineteenth-century panoramas, the central area was occupied by the simulation of a vehicle consistent with the subject of the panorama, such as a part of a ship. We can say that in this case the virtual space of the simulation completely takes over the physical space; that is, physical space has no identity of its own—not even such minimal negative identity as emptiness. It completely serves the simulation.

and, of course, the screens of computers. Rather than disappearing, the screen threatens to take over our offices and homes. Both computer and television monitors are getting bigger and flatter; eventually, they will become wall-sized. Architects such as Rem Koolhaas design *Blade Runner*-like buildings whose façades have been transformed into giant screens.[75]

Dynamic, real-time, and interactive, a screen is still a screen. Interactivity, simulation, and telepresence: As was the case centuries ago, we are still looking at a flat, rectangular surface, existing in the space of our body and acting as a window into another space. We still have not left the era of the screen.

---

75. I am referring here to Rem Koolhaas's unrealized project for a new building for ZKM in Karlsruhe, Germany. See Rem Koolhaas and Bruce Mau, *S, M, L, XL* (New York: Monacelli Press, 1995).

3

The Operations

Just as there is no "innocent eye," there is no "pure computer." A traditional artist perceives the world through the filters of already existing cultural codes, languages, and representational schemes. Similarly, a new media designer or user approaches the computer through a number of cultural filters, some of which I discussed in the preceding chapter. The human-computer interface models the world in distinct ways; it also imposes its own logic on digital data. Existing cultural forms such as the printed word and cinema bring their own powerful conventions of organizing information. These forms further interact with the conventions of the human-computer interface to create what I called "cultural interfaces"—new sets of conventions for organizing cultural data. Finally, constructs such as the screen contribute an additional layer of conventions.

The metaphor of a series of filters assumes that at each stage, from barebones digital data to particular media objects, creative possibilities are being increasingly restricted. It is important, therefore, to note that each of these stages can also be seen as progressively more enabling; that is, although the programmer who would directly deal with binary values stored in memory would be as "close to the machine" as possible, it would also take forever to get the computer to do anything. Indeed, the history of software is one of increasing abstraction. By increasingly removing the programmer and the user from the machine, software allows them to accomplish more faster. From machine language, programmers moved to Assembler, and from there to high-level languages such as COBOL, FORTRAN, and C, as well as very high-level languages designed for programming in a particular area, such as Macromedia Director's LINGO and HTML. The use of computers to author media developed along similar lines. If the few artists working with computers in the 1960s and 1970s had to write their own programs in high-level computer languages, beginning with the Macintosh, most artists, designers and occasional users came to use menu-based software applications—image editors, paint and layout programs, Web editors, and so on. This evolution of software toward higher levels of abstraction is fully compatible with the general trajectory governing the computer's development and use: automation.

In this chapter, I will take the next step in describing the language of new media. I started by analyzing the properties of computer data (chapter 1), and then looked at the human-computer interface (chapter 2). Continuing this bottom-up movement, this chapter takes up the layer of technology that runs on top of the interface—application software. Software programs enable new media designers and artists to create new media objects—and at the same time, they act as yet another filter which shapes their imagination of what is possible to do with a computer. Similarly, software employed by end users to access these objects, such as Web browsers, image viewers, or media players, shape their understanding of what new media are. For example, digital media players such as Windows 98 Media Player or RealPlayer emulate the interfaces of linear-media machines such as VCRs. They provide such commands as play, stop, eject, rewind, and fast forward. In this way, they make new media simulate old media, all the while hiding new properties such as random access.

Rather than analyzing particular software programs, I will address more general techniques, or commands, common to many of them. Regardless of whether a new media designer is working with quantitative data, text, images, video, 3-D space, or combinations of them, she employs the same techniques—copy, cut, paste, search, composite, transform, filter. The existence of such techniques, which are not media-specific, is another consequence of media's status as computer data. I will call these typical techniques of working with computer media *operations.* This chapter will discuss three examples of operations—selection, compositing, and teleaction.

While operations are embedded in software, they are not tied to it. They are employed not only within the computer but also in the social world outside it. They are not only ways of working with computer data but also general ways of working, ways of thinking, and ways of existing in a computer age.

The communication between the larger social world and software use and design is a two-way process. As we work with software and use the operations embedded in it, these operations become part of how we understand ourselves, others, and the world. Strategies of working with computer data become our general cognitive strategies. At the same time, the design of software and the human-computer interface reflects a larger social logic, ideology, and imaginary of the contemporary society. So if we find particular operations dominating software programs, we may also expect to find them at work in the culture at large. In discussing the three operations of *selecting, compositing,* and *teleaction* in this chapter, I will illustrate this general thesis with particular examples. Other examples of operations embedded in software and hardware and found at work in contemporary culture at large are *sampling* and *morphing.*[1]

---

1. Sampling across media is the subject of the Ph.D. dissertation (in progress) by Tarleton Gillespie (Department of Communication, University of California, San Diego); morphing is

As I have already noted, one difference between an industrial society and an information society is that in the latter, both work and leisure often involve the use of the same computer interfaces. This new, closer relationship between work and leisure is complemented by a closer relationship between authors and readers (or, more generally, between producers of cultural objects and their users). This does not mean that new media completely collapse the difference between producers and users, or that every new media text exemplifies Roland Barthes' concept of the "readerly text." Rather, as we shift from an industrial society to an information society, from old media to new media, the overlap between producers and users becomes significantly larger. This holds true for the software the two groups use, their respective skills and expertise, the structure of typical media objects, and the operations they perform on computer data.

While some software products are aimed at either professional producers or end users, other software is used by both groups: Web browsers and search engines, word processors, media-editing applications such as Photoshop (the latter routinely employed in postproduction of Hollywood feature films) or Dreamweaver. Further, differences in functionality and pricing between professional and amateur software are quite small (a few hundred dollars or less), compared to the real gap between equipment and formats used by professionals and amateurs before new media. For instance, differences between 35mm and 8mm film equipment and cost of production, or between professional video (formats such as D-1 and Beta SP; editing decks, switchers, Digital Video Effects (DVE), and other editing hardware) and amateur video (VHS) are in the hundreds of thousands of dollars. Similarly, the gap in skills between professionals and amateurs has also become smaller. For instance, although employing Java or DHTML for Web design in the late 1990s was the domain of professionals, many Web users were also able to create basic Web pages using such programs as FrontPage, HomePage, or Word.

At the same time, new media do not change the nature of the professional-amateur relationship. The gap becomes much smaller but it still exists. And it will always exist, because it is systematically maintained by

the subject of Vivian Sobchack, ed., *Meta-Morphing: Visual Transformation and the Culture of Quick-Change* (Minneapolis: University of Minnesota Press, 1999).

professional producers themselves in order to survive. With old media, such as photography, film, and video, this gap involved three key areas—technology, skills, and aesthetics.[2] With new media, a new area has emerged. As "professional" technology becomes accessible to amateurs, new media professionals create new standards, formats, and design expectations to maintain their status. The continuous introduction of new Web design "features" along with the techniques to create them that followed the public debut of HTML around 1993—rollover buttons and pull-down menus, DHTML and XML, Javascript scripts and Java applets—can in part be explained as a strategy employed by professionals to keep themselves ahead of ordinary users.

On the level of new media products, the overlap between producers and users can be illustrated by computer games. Game companies often release so-called "level editors," special software that allows players to create their own game environments for the game they purchased. Additional software that allows users to modify games is released by third parties or written by game fans themselves. This phenomenon is referred to as "game patching." As described by Anne-Marie Schleiner, "game patches (or game add-ons, mods, levels, maps, or wads) refer to the alterations of preexisting game source code in terms of graphics, game characters, architecture, sound and game play. Game patching in the 1990s has evolved into a kind of popular hacker art form with numerous shareware editors available on the Internet for modifying most games."[3]

Every commercial game is also expected to feature an extensive "options" area allowing the player to customize various aspects of the game. Thus, the player becomes somewhat of a game designer, although her creativity involves selecting combinations of different options rather than making something from scratch. I will discuss the concept of creativity as selection in more detail in the "Menus, Filters, Plug-ins" section.

Although some operations are the domain of new media professionals, and others, the domain of end users, the two groups also employ some of the same operations, including copy, cut and paste, sort, search, filter, transcode,

---

2. See my article "'Real' Wars: Esthetics and Professionalism in Computer Animation," *Design Issues* 6, no. 1 (Fall 1991): 18–25.

3. *Switch 5,* no. 2 (http://switch.sjsu.edu/CrackingtheMaze).

and rip. This chapter will discuss three examples of operations. "Selection" is an operation employed both by professional designers and end users. "Compositing" is used exclusively by designers. The third operation, "tele-action," is an example of an operation typically used by users.

Although this chapter focuses on software operations, the concept of an operation can be also employed to think about other technologically-based cultural practices. We can connect it to other more familiar terms such as "procedure," "practice," and "method." At the same time, it would be a mistake to reduce the concept of an operation to a "tool" or "medium." In fact, one of the assumptions underlying this book is that these traditional concepts do not work very well in relation to new media, and thus we need new concepts like "interface" and "operation." On the one hand, operations are usually in part automated in a way in which traditional tools are not. On the other hand, like computer algorithms, they can be inscribed as a series of steps; that is, they exist as concepts before being materialized in hardware and software. In fact, most new media operations, from morphing to texture mapping, from searching and matching to hyperlinking, begin as algorithms published in computer science papers; eventually, these algorithms become commands in standard software applications. Thus, for instance, when the user applies a particular Photoshop filter to an image, the main Photoshop programs invoke a separate program that corresponds to this filter. The program reads in the pixel values, performs some actions on them, and writes modified values to the screen.

Thus operations should be seen as another case of a more general principle of new media—transcoding. Encoded in algorithms and implemented as software commands, operations exist independently of the media data to which they can be applied. The separation of algorithms and data in programming becomes the separation of operations and media data.

As an example of the operation in other areas of culture, consider the architectural practice of Peter Eisenman. His projects use different operations provided by CAD programs as the basis of the design of a building's exterior and/or interior form. Eisenman systematically utilizes the full range of computer operations available—extrusion, twisting, extension, displacement, morphing, warping, shifting, scaling, rotation, and so on.[4]

---

4. Peter Eisenman, *Diagram Diaries* (New York: Universe Publishing, 1999), 238–239.

Another example is provided by clothing design by Issey Miyake. Each of his designs is the result of a particular conceptual procedure translated into a technological process.[5] For instance, *Just Before* (Spring/Summer 1998 collection) is a gigantic roll of identical dresses with suggested lines of demarcation already incorporated into the fabric. An individual dress can be cut out from the roll in a variety of possible ways. *Dunes* (Spring/Summer 1998 collection) is based on the operation of shrinking. A model is cut two times larger than its final size; next, patches and pieces of tape are fitted in key places; finally, it is shrunk down to size by dipping it into a special solution. This sequence of operations creates a particular wrinkled texture except in those places protected by patches and tapes.

Dunes exemplifies an important feature of operations: They can be combined together in a sequence. The designer can manipulate the resulting script, removing and adding new operations. This script exists separately from the data to which it can be applied. Thus, the script of *Dunes* consists of cutting the model, applying patches and tapes to key areas, and shrinking. It can be applied to different designs and fabrics. New media software designers and users have even more flexibility. New filters can be "plugged into" the program, extending the range of operations available. The script can be edited using special scripting languages. It can also be saved and later applied to a different object. Designers and users can automatically apply the script to a number of objects and even instruct the computer automatically to invoke the script at a particular time or if a particular condition occurs. An example of the former is backup or disk defragmenter programs often designated to start at a particular time at night. An example of the later is filtering e-mail messages in e-mail programs such as Eudora or Microsoft Outlook. While retrieving new e-mail messages from the server, the program can move e-mail messages into a particular folder (or delete them, or raise their priority, etc.) if the message header or address contains a particular string.

---

5. "Issey Miyake Making Things," an exhibition at Fondation Cartier, Paris, October 13, 1998–January 17, 1999.

The Logic of Selection

Viewpoint Datalabs International is selling thousands of 3-D geometric models widely used by computer animators and designers. Its catalog describes the models as follows: "VP4370: Man, Extra Low Resolution. VP4369: Man, Low Resolution. VP4752: Man, Muscular in Shorts and Tennis Shoe. VP5200. Man, w/Beard, Boxer Shorts . . ."[6] Adobe Photoshop 5.0 comes with more than one hundred filters that allow the user to modify an image in numerous ways; After Effects 4.0, the standard for compositing moving images, is shipped with eighty effects plug-ins; thousands more are available from third parties.[7] Macromedia Director 7 comes with an extensive library of "behaviors"—ready-to-use pieces of computer code.[8] Softimage|3D (v3.8), the leading 3-D modeling and animation software, is shipped with over four hundred textures that can be applied to 3-D objects.[9] QuickTime 4 from Apple, a format for digital video, comes with fifteen built-in filters and thirteen built-in video transitions.[10] The Geocities Web site, which pioneered the concept of hosting users' Web sites for free in exchange for placing ad banners on users' pages, gives users access to a

---

6. http://www.viewpoint.com.

7. http://www.adobe.com.

8. http://www.macromedia.com.

9. http://www.aw.sgi.com.

10. http://www.apple.com/quicktime/authoring/tutorials.html.

collection of over forty thousand clip art images for customizing their sites.[11] Index Stock Imagery offers 375,000 stock photos available for use in Web banner ads.[12] Microsoft Word 97 Web Page Wizard allows the user to create a simple Web by selecting from eight predetermined styles described by such terms as "Elegant," "Festive," and "Professional." Microsoft Chat 2.1 asks the user to specify her avatar (a character or graphic icon representing a user in a virtual world) by choosing among twelve built-in cartoon characters. During the online session, the user can further customize the selected character by interpolating between eight values that represent eight fundamental emotions as defined by Microsoft programmers.

These examples illustrate a new logic of computer culture. New media objects are rarely created completely from scratch; usually they are assembled from ready-made parts. Put differently, in computer culture, authentic creation has been replaced by selection from a menu. In the process of creating a new media object, the designer selects from libraries of 3-D models and texture maps, sounds and behaviors, background images and buttons, filters, and transitions. Every authoring and editing software comes with such libraries. In addition, both software manufacturers and third parties sell separate collections that work as "plug-ins"; that is, they appear as additional commands and ready-to-use media elements under the software's menus. The Web provides a further source of plug-ins and media elements, with numerous collections available for free.

New media users are similarly asked to select from predefined menus of choices when using software to create documents or access various Internet services. Here are a few examples: selecting a predefined style when creating a Web page in Microsoft Word or similar program, selecting one of the "Auto-Layouts" when creating a slide in PowerPoint, selecting a predetermined avatar upon entering a multi-user virtual world such as Palace, selecting a predetermined viewpoint when navigating a VRML world.

All in all, selecting from a library or menu of predefined elements or choices is a key operation for both professional producers of new media and end users. This operation makes the production process more efficient for

---

11. http://geocities.yahoo.com.

12. http://www.turneupheat.com.

professionals, and it makes end users feel that they are not just consumers but "authors" creating a new media object or experience. What are the historical origins of this new cultural logic? How can we describe theoretically the particular dynamics of standardization and invention that comes with it? Is the model of authorship put forward specific to new media or can we already find it at work in old media?

Ernst Gombrich and Roland Barthes, among others, have critiqued the romantic ideal of the artist creating totally from scratch, pulling images directly from his imagination, or inventing new ways to see the world all on his own.[13] According to Gombrich, the realist artist can only represent nature by relying on already established "representational schemes"; the history of illusion in art involves slow and subtle modifications of these schemes over many generations of artists. In his famous essay "The Death of the Author," Barthes offers an even more radical criticism of the idea of the author as solitary inventor alone responsible for the work's content. As Barthes puts it, "The Text is a tissue of quotations drawn from the innumerable centers of culture."[14] Even though a modern artist may only be reproducing, or, at best, combining preexisting texts, idioms, and schemas in new ways, the actual material process of art making, nevertheless, supports the romantic ideal. An artist operates like God creating the Universe—she starts with an empty canvas or a blank page. Gradually filling in the details, she brings a new world into existence.

Such a process, manual and painstakingly slow, was appropriate for the age of pre-industrial artisan culture. In the twentieth century, as the rest of the culture moved to mass production and automation, literally becoming a "culture industry" (Theodor Adorno), the fine arts, however, continued to insist on its artisan model. Only in the 1910s when some artists began to assemble collages and montages from already existing cultural "parts" did the industrial method of production enter the realm of art. Photomontage became the most "pure" expression of this new method. By the early 1920s, photomontage practitioners had already created (or rather, constructed)

---

13. E. H. Gombrich, *Art and Illusion;* Roland Barthes, "The Death of the Author," in *Image/Music/Text.*

14. Barthes, "The Death of the Author," 142.

some of the most remarkable images of modern art such as *Cut with the Cake-Knife* (Hannah Höch, 1919), *Metropolis* (Paul Citroën, 1923), *The Electrification of the Whole Country* (Gustav Klutsis, 1920), and *Tatlin at Home* (Raoul Hausmann, 1920), to mention just a few examples. Although photomontage became an established practice of Dadaists, Surrealists, and Constructivists in the 1920s, and Pop artists in the 1960s, the creation from scratch, as exemplified by painting and drawing, nevertheless remained the main operation of modern art.

In contrast, electronic art from its very beginning was based on a new principle: *modification of an already existing signal.* The first electronic instrument designed in 1920 by the Russian scientist and musician Lev Theremin contained a generator producing a sine wave; the performer simply modified its frequency and amplitude.[15] In the 1960s, video artists began to build video synthesizers based on the same principle. The artist was no longer a romantic genius generating a new world purely out of his imagination; he became a technician turning a knob here, pressing a switch there—an accessory to the machine.

Substitute a simple sine wave with a more complex signal (sounds, rhythms, melodies), add a whole bank of signal generators, and you have arrived at the modern music synthesizer, the first instrument that embodies the logic of all new media—selection from a menu of choices.

The first music synthesizers appeared in the 1950s, followed by video synthesizers in the 1960s, DVE in the late 1970s—the bank of effects used by video editors—and computer software in the eighties such as the 1984 MacDraw, which came with a repertoire of basic shapes. The process of art making has finally caught up with modern times. It has become synchronized with the rest of modern society, where everything from objects to people's identities is assembled from ready-made parts. Whether assembling an outfit, decorating an apartment, choosing dishes from a restaurant menu, or choosing which interest group to join, the modern subject proceeds through life by selecting from numerous menus and catalogs of items. With electronic and digital media, art making similarly entails choosing from

---

15. Bulat Galeyev, *Soviet Faust: Lev Theremin—Pioneer of Electronic Art* (in Russian) (Kazan, 1995), 19.

ready-made elements—textures and icons supplied by a paint programs, 3-D models that come with a 3-D modeling program, melodies and rhythms built into a music synthesis program.

While previously the great text of culture from which the artist created her own unique "tissue of quotations" was bubbling and shimmering somewhere below consciousness, now it has become externalized (and greatly reduced in the process)—2-D objects, 3-D models, textures, transitions, effects available as soon as the artist turns on the computer. The World Wide Web takes this process to the next level: it encourages the creation of texts that consist entirely of pointers to other texts that are already on the Web. One does not have to add any original writing; it is enough to select from what already exists. Put differently, now anybody can become a creator by simply providing a new menu, that is, by making a new selection from the total corpus available.

The same logic applies to branching-type interactive new media objects. In a branching-type interactive program, the user, upon reaching a particular object, selects which branch to follow next by clicking a button, clicking on part of an image, or choosing from a menu. The visual result of making a choice is that either a whole screen or its part(s) change. A typical interactive program of the 1980s and early 1990s was self-contained, that is, it ran on a computer that was not networked. Designers of self-contained programs could, therefore, expect undivided attention from a user, and, accordingly, it was safe to change the whole screen after a user had made a selection. The effect was similar to turning pages in a book. The book metaphor was promoted by the first popular hypermedia authoring software—Apple's HyperCard (1987); a good example of its use can be found in *Myst* (Broderbund, 1993). *Myst* presents the player with still images that completely fill the screen. When the player clicks on the right or left parts of an image, it is replaced by another image. In the second half of the 1990s, as most interactive documents migrated to the Web where it is much easier to move from one site to another, it became important to give all pages of the site a common identity and also visually to display the page's position in relation to the site's branching-tree structure. Consequently, with the help of technologies such as HTML frames, Dynamic HTML, and Flash, interactive designers established a different convention. Now, parts of the screen, which typically contain the company logo, top-level menus, and the page's path, remain constant while other parts change dynamically. (Microsoft and Macromedia sites provide good examples of this new convention.)[16] Regardless of whether making a selection leads the user to a whole new screen or only changes part of it, the user still navigates through a branching structure consisting of pre-defined objects. Although more complex types of interactivity can be created by a computer program that controls and modifies the media object at run-time, the majority of interactive media uses fixed branching-tree structures.

It is often claimed that the user of a branching interactive program be-comes its coauthor: By choosing a unique path through the elements of a work, she supposedly creates a new work. But it is also possible to see this process in a different way. If a complete work is the sum of all possible paths through its elements, then the user following a particular path accesses only a part of this whole. In other words, the user is activating only a part of the total work that already exists. Just as with the example of Web pages that consist of nothing but links to other pages, here the user does not add new objects to a corpus, but only selects a subset. This is a new type of authorship that corresponds neither to the premodern (before Romanticism) idea of mi-nor modification to the tradition nor to the modern (nineteenth century and first half of the twentieth century) idea of a creator-genius revolting against it. It does, however, fit perfectly with the logic of advanced industrial and post-industrial societies, where almost every practical act involves choosing from some menu, catalog, or database. In fact, as I have already noted, new media is the best available expression of the logic of identity in these soci-eties—choosing values from a number of predefined menus.

How can a modern subject escape from this logic? In a society saturated with brands and labels, people respond by adopting a minimalist aesthetic and a hard-to-identify clothing style. Writing about an empty loft as an ex-pression of a minimalist ideal, architecture critic Herbert Muschamp points out that people "reject exposing the subjectivity when one piece of stuff is preferred to another." The opposition between an individualized inner world and an objective, shared, neutral world outside becomes reversed:

The private living space has taken on the guise of objectivity: neutral, value-free, as if this were a found space, not an impeccably designed one. The world outside,

---

16. http://www.microsoft.com; http://www.macromedia.com.

meanwhile, has become subjectified, rendered into a changing collage of personal whims and fancies. This is to be expected in a culture dominated by the distribution system. That system, exists, after all, not to make things but to sell them, to appeal to individual impulses, tastes, desires. As a result, the public realm has become a collective repository of dreams and designs from which the self requires refuge.[17]

How can one accomplish a similar escape in new media? It can only be accomplished by refusing all options and customization, and, ultimately, by refusing all forms of interactivity. Paradoxically, by following an interactive path, one does not construct a unique self but instead adopts already preestablished identities. Similarly, choosing values from a menu or customizing one's desktop or an application automatically makes one participate in the "changing collage of personal whims and fancies" mapped out and coded into software by the companies. Thus, short of using the command-line interface of UNIX, which can be thought of as an equivalent of the minimalist loft in the realm of computing, I would prefer using Microsoft Windows exactly the way it was installed at the factory instead of customizing it in the hope of expressing my "unique identity."

"Postmodernism" and Photoshop

As I noted in this chapter's introduction, computer operations encode existing cultural norms in their design. "The logic of selection" is a good example of this. What was a set of social and economic practices and conventions is now encoded in the software itself. The result is a new form of control, soft but powerful. Although software does not directly prevent its users from creating from scratch, its design on every level makes it "natural" to follow a different logic—that of selection.

Although computer software "naturalizes" the model of authorship as selection from libraries of predefined objects, we can already find this model at work in old media, such as magic lantern slides shows.[18] As film historian Charles Musser points out, in contrast to modern cinema where authorship

---

17. Herbert Muschamp, "Blueprint: The Shock of the Familiar," *New York Times Magazine* 13 December 1998, 66.

18. Musser, *The Emergence of Cinema.*

extends from preproduction to postproduction but does not cover exhibition (i.e., the theatrical presentation of a film is completely standardized and does not involve making creative decisions), in magic lantern slide shows the exhibition was a highly creative act. The magic lantern exhibitioner was, in fact, an artist who skillfully arranged a presentation of slides bought from distributors. This is a perfect example of authorship as selection: An author puts together an object from elements that she herself did not create. The creative energy of the author goes into the selection and sequencing of elements rather than into original design.

Although not all modern media arts follow this authorship model, the technological logic of analog media strongly supports it. Stored on industrially manufactured materials such as film stock or magnetic tape, media elements can be more easily isolated, copied, and assembled in new combinations. In addition, various media manipulation machines, such as the tape recorder and film slicer, make the operations of selection and combination easier to perform. In parallel, we witness the development of archives of various media that enable the author to draw on already existing media elements rather than always having to record new elements themselves. For instance, in the 1930s German photojournalist Dr. Otto Bettmann started what later became known as "the Bettmann Archive"; at the time of its acquisition by Bill Gates's Corbis Corporation in 1995, it contained sixteen million photographs, including some of the most frequently used images of the twentieth century. Similar archives have been created for film and audio media. Using "stock" photographs, movie clips, and audio recordings became the standard practice of modern media production.

To summarize: The practice of putting together a media object from already existing commercially distributed media elements existed with old media, but new media technology further standardized it and made it much easier to perform. What before involved scissors and glue now involves simply clicking on "cut" and "paste." And, by encoding the operations of selection and combination into the very interfaces of authoring and editing software, new media "legitimizes" them. Pulling elements from databases and libraries becomes the default; creating them from scratch becomes the exception. The Web acts as a perfect materialization of this logic. It is one gigantic library of graphics, photographs, video, audio, design layouts, software code, and texts; and every element is free because it can be saved to the user's computer with a single mouse click.

It is not accidental that the development of GUI, which legitimized a "cut and paste" logic, as well as media manipulation software such as Photoshop, which popularized a plug-in architecture, took place during the 1980s—the same decade when contemporary culture became "postmodern." In evoking this term, I follow Fredric Jameson's usage of postmodernism as "a periodizing concept whose function is to correlate the emergence of new formal features in culture with the emergence of a new type of social life and a new economic order."[19] As became apparent by the early 1980s, culture, for critics such as Jameson, no longer tried to "make it new." Rather, endless recycling and quoting of past media content, artistic styles, and forms became the new "international style" and the new cultural logic of modern society. Rather than assembling more media recordings of reality, culture is now busy reworking, recombining, and analyzing already accumulated media material. Invoking the metaphor of Plato's cave, Jameson writes that postmodern cultural production "can no longer look directly out of its eyes at the real word but must, as in Plato's cave, trace its mental images of the world on its confining walls."[20] In my view, this new cultural condition found its perfect reflection in the emerging computer software of the 1980s that privileged selection from ready-made media elements over creating them from scratch. And to a large extent it is this software that in fact made postmodernism possible. The shift of all cultural production first to electronic tools such as switchers and DVEs (1980s) and then to computer-based tools (1990s) greatly eased the practice of relying on old media content to create new productions. It also made the media universe much more self-referential because when all media objects are designed, stored, and distributed using a single machine—the computer—it becomes much easier to borrow elements from existing objects. Here again, the Web is the perfect expression of this logic, since new Web pages are routinely created by copying and modifying existing Web pages. This applies both to home users creating their own home pages and to professional Web, hypermedia, and game development companies.

---

19. Fredric Jameson, "Postmodernism and Consumer Society," in *Postmodernism and its Discontents,* ed. E. Ann Kaplan (London and New York: Verso, 1988): 15.

20. Jameson, "Postmodernism and Consumer Society," 20.

From Object to Signal

Selecting ready-made elements to become part of the content of a new media object is only one aspect of the "logic of selection." While working on the object, the designer also typically selects and applies various filters and "effects." All these filters, whether manipulating image appearance, creating a transition between moving images, or applying a filter to a piece of music, involve the same principle: the algorithmic modification of an existing media object or its parts. Since computer media consist of samples that are represented in a computer as numbers, a computer program can access every sample in turn and modify its value according to some algorithm. Most image filters work in this way. For instance, to add noise to an image, a program such as Photoshop reads in the image file pixel by pixel, adds a randomly generated number to the value of each pixel, and writes out a new image file. Programs can also work on more than one media object at once. For instance, to blend two images together, a program reads in values of corresponding pixels from the two images; it then calculates a new pixel value based on the percentages of existing pixel values; this process is repeated for all the pixels.

Although we can find their precursors in old media (for instance, hand colorization of silent film), filter operations really come into their own with electronic media technologies. All electronic media technologies of the nineteenth and twentieth centuries are based on modifying a signal by passing it through various filters. These include technologies for real-time communication such as the telephone, broadcasting technologies used for mass distribution of media products such as radio and television, and technologies to synthesize media such as video and audio synthesizers that originate with the instrument designed by Theremin in 1920.

In retrospect, the shift from a material object to a signal accomplished by electronic technologies represents a fundamental conceptual step towards computer media. In contrast to a permanent imprint in some material, a signal can be modified in real time by passing it through a filter or filters. Moreover, in contrast to manual modifications of a material object, an electronic filter can modify the signal all at once. Finally, and most important, all machines for electronic media synthesis, recording, transmission, and reception include controls for signal modification. As a result, an electronic signal does not have a singular identity—a particular state qualitatively different from all other possible states. Consider, for example, the loudness control of a radio receiver or the brightness control of an analog television set. They do not have any privileged values. In contrast to a material object, the electronic signal is essentially mutable.

This mutability of electronic media is just one step away from the "variability" of new media. As already discussed, a new media object can exist in numerous versions. For instance, in the case of a digital image, we can change its contrast and color, blur or sharpen it, turn it into a 3-D shape, use its values to control sound, and so on. But, to a significant extent, an electronic signal is already characterized by similar variability because it can exist in numerous states. For example, in the case of a sine wave, we can modify its amplitude or frequency; each modification produces a new version of the original signal without affecting its structure. Therefore, in essence, television and radio signals are already new media. Put differently, in the progression from material object to electronic signal to computer media, the first shift is more radical than the second. All that happens when we move from analog electronics to digital computers is that the range of variations is greatly expanded. This happens because, first, modern digital computers separate hardware and software, and, second, because an object is now represented as numbers, that is, it has become computer data that can be modified by software. In short, a media object becomes "soft"—with all the implications contained in this metaphor.

The experimental filmmaker Hollis Frampton, whose reputation rests on his remarkable structural films and who, toward the end of his life, came to be interested in computer media, seemed already to understand this fundamental importance of the shift from material object to electronic signal.[21] He wrote in one of his essays:

Since the New Stone Age, all the arts have tended, through accident or design, toward a certain fixity in their object. If Romanticism deferred stabilizing the artifact, it nonetheless placed its trust, finally, in a specialized dream of *statis:* the 'assembly line' of the Industrial Revolution was at first understood as responsive to copious imagination.

---

21. Peter Lunenfeld discusses the relevance of Frampton to new media in his *Snap to Grid* (Cambridge, Mass.: MIT Press, 2000).

If the television assembly line has by now run riot (half a billion people can watch a wedding as consequential as mine or yours) it has also confuted itself in its own malleability.

We're all familiar with the parameters of expression: Hue, Saturation, Brightness, Contrast. For the adventurous, there remain the twin deities Vertical Hold and Horizontal Hold . . . and, for those aspiring to the pinnacles, Fine Tuning.[22]

With new media, "malleability" becomes "variability"; that is, while the analog television set allowed the viewer to modify the signal in just a few dimensions such as brightness and hue, new media technologies give the user much more control. A new media object can be modified in numerous dimensions, and these modifications can be expressed numerically. For instance, the user of a Web browser can instruct the browser to skip all multimedia elements; tell it to enlarge font size while displaying a page, or completely substitute the original font with a different one. The user can also reshape the browser window to any size and proportion as well as change the spatial and color resolution of the display itself. Further, a designer can specify that different versions of the same Web site will be displayed depending upon the bandwidth of the user's connection and the resolution of her display. For instance, a user accessing the site via a high-speed connection and a high resolution screen will get a rich multimedia version, while the user accessing the same site via the small LCD display of a handheld electronic device will receive just a few lines of text. More radically, a number of completely different interfaces can be constructed from the same data, from a database to a virtual environment. In short, the new media object is something that can exist in numerous versions and numerous incarnations.

To conclude this discussion of the operation of selection, I would like to invoke a particular cultural figure, a new kind of author for whom this operation is key—the DJ who creates music in real-time by mixing existing music tracks and who is dependent on various electronic hardware devices. In the 1990s, the DJ acquired new cultural prestige, becoming a required presence at art openings and book release parties, in hip restaurants and hotels,

---

22. Hollis Frampton, "The Withering Away of the State of the Art," in *Circles of Confusion* (Rochester: Visual Studies Workshop), 169.

in the pages of *Art Forum* and *Wired.* The rise of this figure can be directly correlated to the rise of computer culture. The DJ best demonstrates its new logic: selection and combination of preexistent elements. The DJ also demonstrates the true potential of this logic to create new artistic forms. Finally, the example of the DJ also makes it clear that selection is not an end in and of itself. The essence of the DJ's art is the ability to mix selected elements in rich and sophisticated ways. In contrast to the "cut and paste" metaphor of modern GUI that suggests that selected elements can be simply, almost mechanically, combined, the practice of live electronic music demonstrates that true art lies in the "mix."

Compositing

From Image Streams to Modular Media

The movie *Wag the Dog* (Barry Levinson, 1997) contains a scene in which a Washington spin doctor and a Hollywood producer are editing fake news footage designed to win public support for a nonexistent war. The footage shows a girl, a cat in her arms, running through a destroyed village. If a few decades earlier creating such a shot would have required staging and then filming the whole thing on location, computer tools make it possible today to create it in real time. Now the only live element is the girl, played by a professional actress. The actress is videotaped against a blue screen. The other two elements in the shot, the destroyed village and the cat, come from a database of stock footage. Scanning through the database, the producers try different versions of these elements; a computer updates the composite scene in real time.

The logic of this shot is typical of the new media production process, regardless of whether the object under construction is a video or film shot, as in *Wag the Dog;* a 2-D still image; a sound track; a 3-D virtual environment; a computer game scene; or a sound track. In the course of production, some elements are created specifically for the project; others are selected from databases of stock material. Once all the elements are ready, they are composited together into a single object; that is, they are fitted together and adjusted in such a way that their separate identities become invisible. The fact that they come from diverse sources and were created by different people at different times is hidden. The result is a single seamless image, sound, space, or scene.

As used in the field of new media, the term "digital compositing" has a particular and well-defined meaning. It refers to the process of combining a number of moving image sequences, and possibly stills, into a single sequence with the help of special compositing software such as After Effects (Adobe), Compositor (Alias|Wavefront), or Cineon (Kodak). Compositing was formally defined in a paper published in 1984 by two scientists working for Lucasfilm, who make a significant analogy between compositing and computer programming:

Experience has taught us to break down large bodies of source code into separate modules in order to save compilation time. An error in one routine forces only the recompilation of its module and the relatively quick reloading of the entire program. Similarly, small errors in coloration or design in one object should not force "recompilation" of the entire image.

Separating the image into elements that can be independently rendered saves enormous time. Each element has an associated matte, coverage information that designates the shape of the element. The compositing of those elements makes use of the mattes to accumulate the final image.[23]

Most often, the composited sequence simulates a traditional film shot; that is, it looks like something that took place in real physical space and was filmed by a real film camera. To achieve this effect, all elements comprising the finished composite—for example, footage shot on location, referred to in the industry as a "live plate"; footage of actors shot in front of a blue screen; and 3-D computer-generated elements—are aligned in perspective, and modified so that they have the same contrast and color saturation. To simulate depth of field, some elements are blurred while others are sharpened. Once all elements are assembled, a virtual-camera move through the simulated space may be added to increase its "reality effect." Finally, artifacts such as film grain or video noise can be added. In summary, digital compositing can be broken down into three conceptual steps:

1. Construction of a seamless 3-D virtual space from different elements.
2. Simulation of a camera move through this space (optional).
3. Simulation of the artifacts of a particular media (optional).

---

23. Thomas Porter and Tom Duff, "Compositing Digital Images," *Computer Graphics* 18, no. 3 (July 1984): 253–259.

If 3-D computer animation is used to create a virtual space from scratch, compositing typically relies on existing film or video footage. Therefore I need to explain why I claim the result of a composite is a virtual space. Let us consider two different examples of compositing. A compositor may use a number of moving and still images to create a totally new 3-D space and then generate a camera move through it. For example, in *Cliffhanger* (Renny Harlin, 1993), a shot of the main hero, played by Sylvester Stallone, which was filmed in the studio against a blue screen, was composited with the shot of a mountain landscape. The resulting shot shows Stallone high in the mountains hanging over an abyss. In other cases, new elements will be added (or removed from) a live action sequence without changing either its perspective or the camera move. For example, a 3-D computer-generated creature can be added to a live action shot of an outdoor location, as in the many dinosaur shots in *Jurassic Park* (Steven Spielberg, special effects by Industrial Light and Magic, 1993). In the first example, it is immediately clear that the composited shot represents something that never took place in reality. In other words, the result of the composite is a virtual space. In the second example, it may appear at first that the existing physical space is preserved. However, here as well, the final result is a virtual world that does not really exist. Put differently, what exists is simply a field of grass, *without* dinosaurs.

Digital compositing is routinely used to put together TV commercials and music videos, computer game scenes, shots in feature films, and most other moving images in computer culture. Throughout the 1990s, Hollywood directors increasingly came to rely on compositing to assemble larger and larger parts of a film. In 1999 George Lucas released *Star Wars: Episode 1* (1999); according to Lucas, 95 percent of the film was assembled on a computer. As I will discuss below, digital compositing as a technique to create moving images goes back to video keying and optical printing in cinema; but what before was a rather special operation now becomes the norm for creating moving imagery. Digital compositing also greatly expanded the range of this technique, allowing control of the transparency of individual layers and the combination of a potentially unlimited number of layers. For instance, a typical special effects shot from a Hollywood film may consist of a few hundred, or even thousands, of layers. Although in some situations, a few layers can be combined in real time automatically (virtual sets technology), compositing, in general, is a time-consuming and difficult operation. This is one aspect of the before-mentioned scene from *Wag the Dog* that is misrepresented; to create the composite shown in this scene would require many hours.

Digital compositing exemplifies a more general operation of computer culture—assembling together a number of elements to create a single seamless object. Thus we can distinguish between compositing in the wider sense (the general operation) and compositing in a narrow sense (assembling movie image elements to create a photorealistic shot). The latter meaning corresponds to the accepted usage of the term "compositing." For me, compositing in a narrow sense is a particular case of a more general operation—a typical operation in assembling any new media object.

As a general operation, compositing is a counterpart of selection. Since a typical new media object is put together from elements that come from different sources, these elements need to be coordinated and adjusted to fit together. Although the logic of these two operations—selection and compositing—may suggest that they always follow one another (first selection, then compositing), in practice their relationship is more interactive. Once an object is partially assembled, new elements may need to be added; existing elements may need to be reworked. This interactivity is made possible by the modular organization of a new media object on different scales. Throughout the production process, elements retain their separate identities and, therefore, can be easily modified, substituted, or deleted. When the object is complete, it can be "output" as a single "stream" in which separate elements are no longer accessible. An example of an operation which "collapses" elements into a single stream is the "flatten image" command in Adobe Photoshop 5.0. Another example is recording a digitally composited moving image sequence on film, which was a typical procedure in Hollywood film production in the 1980s and 1990s.

Alternatively, the completed object may retain the modular structure when it is distributed. For instance, in many computer games the player can interactively control characters, moving them in space. In some games, the user moves 2-D images of characters, called "sprites," over the background image; in others, everything is represented as a 3-D object, including characters. In either case, the elements are adjusted during production to form a single whole, stylistically, spatially, and semantically; while playing the game the user can move the elements within the programmed limits.

In general, *a 3-D computer graphics representation is more "progressive" than a 2-D image because it allows true independence of elements; as such, it may gradually replace image streams such as photographs, 2-D drawings, films, video.* In other words, a 3-D computer graphics representation is more modular than a 2-D still image or a 2-D moving image stream. This modularity makes it easier for a designer to modify the scene at any time. It also gives the scene additional functionality. For instance, the user may "control" the character, moving him or her around the 3-D space. Scene elements can be also reused in later productions. Finally, modularity also allows for the more efficient storage and transmission of a media object. To transmit a video clip over a network, for example, all pixels that make up this clip have to be sent over, whereas to transmit a 3-D scene requires only sending the coordinates of the objects in it. This is how on-line virtual worlds, on-line computer games, and networked military simulators work: First, copies of all objects making up a world are downloaded to a user's computer; after this, the server has only to keep sending their new 3-D coordinates.

If the general trajectory of computer culture is from 2-D images towards 3-D computer graphics representations, digital compositing represents an intermediary historical step between the two. A composited space consisting of a number of moving-image layers is more modular than a single shot of a physical space. The layers can be repositioned against each other and adjusted separately. Such a representation, however, is not as modular as a true 3-D virtual space because each of the layers retains its own perspective. When and where moving image "streams" will be replaced completely by 3-D computer-generated scenes will depend not only on cultural acceptance of the computer scene's look but also on economics. A 3-D scene is much more functional than a film or video shot of the same scene, but, if it is to contain a similar level of detail, it may be much more expensive to generate.

The general evolution of all media types toward increased modularity, and the particular evolution of the moving image in the same direction, can be traced through the history of popular-media file formats. QuickTime developers early on specified that a single QuickTime movie may consist of a number of separate tracks, just as a still Photoshop image consists of a number of layers. QuickTime 4 format (1999) included eleven different track types, including video track, sound track, text track, and sprite track (graphic objects which can be moved independently of video).[24] By placing

---

24. http://www.apple.com/quicktime/resources/qt4/us/help/QuickTime%20Help.htm.

different media on different tracks that can be edited and exported independently, QuickTime encourages designers to think in modular terms. In addition, a movie may contain a number of video tracks that can act as layers in a digital composite. By using alpha channels (masks saved with video tracks) and different modes of track interaction (such as partial transparency), the QuickTime user can create complex compositing effects within a single QuickTime movie, without having to resort to any special compositing software. In effect, QuickTime architects embedded the practice of digital compositing in the media format itself. What previously required special software can now be done simply by using the features of the Quick-Time format itself.

Another example of a media format evolving towards more and more data modularity is MPEG.[25] The early version of the format, MPEG-1 (1992), was defined as "the standard for storage and retrieval of moving pictures and audio on storage media." The format specified a compression scheme for video and/or audio data conceptualized in a traditional way. In contrast, MPEG-7 (to be approved in 2001) is defined as "the content representation standard for multimedia information search, filtering, management and processing." It is based on a different concept of media composition that consists of a number of media objects of various types, from video and audio to 3-D models and facial expressions, and information on how these objects are combined. MPEG-7 provides an abstract language to describe such a scene. The evolution of MPEG, thus, allows us to trace the conceptual evolution in how we understand new media—from a traditional "stream" to a modular composition, more similar in its logic to a structural computer program than a traditional image or film.

The Resistance to Montage
The connection between the aesthetics of postmodernism and the operation of selection also applies to compositing. Together, these two operations simultaneously reflect and enable the postmodern practice of pastiche and quotation. They work in tandem: One operation is used to select elements and styles from the "database of culture"; another is used to assemble them

---

25. http://drogo.cset.it/mpeg.

into new objects. Thus, along with selection, compositing is the key operation of postmodern, or computer-based, authorship.

At the same time, we should think of the aesthetic and the technological as aligned but ultimately separate layers, to use the metaphor of digital technology itself. The logic of the postmodern aesthetics of the 1980s and the logic of the computer-based compositing of the 1990s are not the same. In the postmodern aesthetics of the eighties, historical references and media quotes are maintained as distinct elements; boundaries between elements are well defined (the examples are David Salle's paintings, Barbara Kruger's montages, and various music videos). Interestingly, this aesthetic corresponds to the electronic and early digital tools of the period, such as video switchers, keyers, DVE, and computer graphics cards with limited color resolution. These tools enabled hard-edge "copy and paste" operations but not smooth, multilayer composites. (A lot can be made of the fact that one of the key postmodern artists of the 1980s, Richard Prince, who became well known for his "appropriation" photographs, was operating one of the earliest computer-based photo editing systems in the late 1970s as part of his commercial job before he started making "appropriation" photographs.) Compositing in the 1990s supports a different aesthetic characterized by smoothness and continuity. Elements are now blended together, and boundaries erased rather than emphasized. This aesthetic of continuity can best be observed in television spots and special effects sequences of feature films that were actually put together through digital compositing (i.e., compositing in the narrow, technical sense). For instance, the computer-generated dinosaurs in *Jurassic Park* are made to blend perfectly with the landscape, just as the live actors, 3-D virtual actors, and computer-rendered ship are made to blend together in *Titanic* (James Cameron, special effects by Digital Domain, 1997). But the aesthetics of continuity can also be found in other areas of new media. Computer-generated morphs allow for a continuous transition between two images—an effect which before would be accomplished through a dissolve or cut.[26] Many computer games also obey the aesthetics of continuity in that, in cinematic terms, they are single-takes. They

---

26. For an excellent theoretical analysis of morphing, see Vivian Sobchack, "'At the Still Point of the Turning World': Meta-Morphing and Meta-Stasis," in Sobchack, ed., *Meta-Morphing*.

have no cuts. From beginning to end, they present a single continuous trajectory through a 3-D space. This is particularly true of first-person shooters such as *Quake.* The lack of montage in these games fits in with the first-person point of view they employ. These games simulate the continuity of a human experience, guaranteed by the laws of physics. While modern telecommunication, from the telegraph, telephone, and television to telepresence and the World Wide Web allowed us to suspend these laws, moving almost instantly from one virtual location to another with the toggle of a switch or press of a button, in real life we still obey physics: In order to move from one point to another, we have to pass through every point in between.

All these examples—smooth composites, morphing, uninterrupted navigation in games—have one thing in common: where old media relied on montage, new media substitutes the aesthetics of continuity. A film cut is replaced by a digital morph or digital composite. Similarly, the instant changes in time and space characteristic of modern narrative, both in literature and cinema, are replaced by the continuous noninterrupted first-person narrative of games and VR. Computer multimedia also does not use any montage. The desire to correlate different senses, or, to use new media lingo, different media tracks, which preoccupied many artists throughout the twentieth century including Kandinsky, Skriabin, Eisenstein, and Godard, to mention just a few, is foreign to multimedia. Instead, it follows the principle of simple addition. Elements in different media are placed next to each other without any attempt to establish contrast, complementarity, or dissonance between them. This is best illustrated by Web sites of the 1990s that typically contain JPEG images, QuickTime clips, audio files, and other media elements, side by side.

We can also find strong anti-montage tendencies in the modern GUI. In the middle of the 1980s Apple published guidelines for interface design for all Macintosh application software. According to these guidelines, an interface should communicate the same messages through more than one sense. For instance, an alert box appearing on the screen should be accompanied by a sound. This alignment of different senses can be compared to the naturalistic use of different media in traditional film language—a practice attacked by Eisenstein and other montage filmmakers. Another example of the anti-montage tendency in GUI is the peaceful coexistence of multiple information objects on the computer screen, exemplified by a number of simultaneously opened windows. Just as with media elements in a Web, the user can add more and more windows without establishing any conceptual tension between them.

The aesthetics of continuity cannot be fully deduced from compositing technology, although in many cases it would not be possible without it. Similarly, the montage aesthetics that dominates much of modern art and media should not be thought of simply as the result of available tools; since these tools, with their possibilities and limitations, have also contributed to its development. For instance, a film camera enables one to shoot film footage of a certain limited length; to create a longer film, the separate pieces have to be put together. This is typical in editing where the pieces are trimmed and then glued together. Not surprisingly, modern film language is built on discontinuities: short shots replace one another; point of view changes from shot to shot. The Russian montage school pushes such discontinuities to the extreme, but, with very few exceptions, such as Andy Warhol's early films and *Wavelength* by Michael Snow, all film schools are based on them.

In computer culture, montage is no longer the dominant aesthetic, as it was throughout the twentieth century, from the avant-garde of the 1920s up until the postmodernism of the 1980s. Digital compositing, in which different spaces are combined into a single seamless virtual space, is a good example of the alternative aesthetics of continuity; moreover, compositing in general can be understood as a counterpart to montage aesthetics. Montage aims to create visual, stylistic, semantic, and emotional dissonance between different elements. In contrast, compositing aims to blend them into a seamless whole, a single gestalt. Since I have already evoked the DJ as someone who exemplifies "authoring by selection," I will use this figure once again as an example of how the anti-montage aesthetics of continuity cuts across culture and is not limited to the creation of computer-generated still and moving images and spaces. The DJ's art is measured by his ability to go from one track to another seamlessly. A great DJ is thus a compositor and anti-montage artist par excellence. He is able to create a perfect temporal transition from very different musical layers; and he can do this in real time, in front of a dancing crowd.

In discussing selection from a menu, I pointed out that this operation is typical of both new media and culture at large. Similarly, the operation of compositing is not limited to new media. Consider, for instance, the frequent use of one or more layers of semi-transparent materials in contemporary packaging and architecture. The result is a visual composite, since a viewer can see both what is in front and what is behind the layer. It is interesting that one architectural project that explicitly refers to computer culture—The Digital House (Hariri and Hariri, project, 1988)—systematically employs such semitransparent layers throughout.[27] If in the famous glass house of Mies van der Rohe, the inhabitant looks out at nature through glass walls, the more complex plan of "The Digital House" creates the possibility of seeing through a number of interior spaces at once. Thus the inhabitant of the house is constantly faced with complex visual composites.

Having discussed compositing as a general operation of new media and as a counterpart of selection, I will now focus on a more particular case—compositing in the narrow sense, that is, the creation of a single moving image sequence from a number of separate sequences, and (optionally) stills, using special compositing software. Today, digital compositing is responsible for an increasing number of moving images—all special effects in cinema, computer games, virtual worlds, most television visuals, and even television news. Most often, the moving image constructed through compositing presents a fake 3-D world. I say "fake" because, regardless of whether a compositor creates a totally new 3-D space from different elements (*Cliffhanger,* for example), or only adds elements to live action footage (*Jurassic Park,* for example), the resulting moving image shows something that does not exist in reality. Digital compositing thus belongs together with other simulation techniques. These are the techniques used to create fake realities and thus, ultimately, to deceive the viewer—fashion and makeup, realist painting, dioramas, military decoys, and VR. Why has digital compositing acquired such prominence? If we are to create an archeology that will connect digital compositing with previous techniques of visual simulation, where should we locate the essential historical breaks? Or, to ask the question differently: What is the historical logic driving the evolution of these techniques? Shall we expect computer culture gradually to abandon pure lens-based imaging (still photography, film, video), replacing it instead with composited images and ultimately with 3-D computer-generated simulations?

Archeology of Compositing: Cinema

I will start my archeology of compositing with Potemkin's villages. According to the historical myth, at the end of the eighteenth century, Russian ruler

---

27. Terence Riley, *The Un-private House* (New York: Museum of Modern Art, 1999).

Catherine the Great decided to travel around Russia to observe firsthand how the peasants lived. The first minister and Catherine's lover, Potemkin, ordered the construction of special fake villages along her projected route. Each village consisted of a row of pretty facades. The facades faced the road; at the same time, to conceal their artifice, they were positioned at a considerable distance. Since Catherine never left her carriage, she returned from her journey convinced that all peasants lived in happiness and prosperity.

This extraordinary arrangement can be seen as a metaphor for life in the Soviet Union where I grew up in the 1970s. There, the experience of all citizens was split between the ugly reality of their lives and the official shining facades of ideological pretense. However, the split took place not only on a metaphorical but also on a literal level, particularly in Moscow—the showcase Communist city. When prestigious foreign guests visited Moscow, they, like Catherine the Great, were taken around in limousines that always followed a few special routes. Along these routes, every building was freshly painted, shop windows displayed consumer goods, and drunks were absent, having been picked up by the militia early in the morning. The monochrome, rusty, half-broken, amorphous Soviet reality was carefully hidden from the view of the passengers.

In turning selected streets into facades, Soviet rulers adopted the eighteenth-century technique of creating a fake reality. But, the twentieth century brought with it a much more effective technology for creating fake realities—cinema. By replacing the window of a carriage or car with a screen showing projected images, cinema opened up new possibilities for simulation.

Fictional cinema, as we know it, is based upon lying to the viewer. A perfect example is the construction of a cinematic space. Traditional fiction film transports us into a space—a room, a house, a city. Usually, none of these exists in reality. What exists are a few fragments carefully constructed in a studio. Out of these disjointed fragments, a film synthesizes the illusion of a coherent space.

The development of techniques to accomplish this synthesis coincides with the shift in American cinema between approximately 1907 and 1917 from a so-called primitive to classical film style. Before the classical period, the space of film theater and the screen space were clearly separated, much like in theater or vaudeville. Viewers were free to interact, come and go, and maintain a psychological distance from the cinematic narrative. Correspondingly, the early cinema's system of representation was *presentational:* Actors played to the audience, and the style was strictly frontal.[28] The composition of shots also emphasized frontality.

In contrast, as I discussed earlier, classical Hollywood film positions each viewer inside the fictional space of the narrative. The viewer is asked to identify with the characters and to experience the story from their points of view. Accordingly, the space no longer acts as a theatrical backdrop. Instead, through new compositional principles, staging, set design, deep focus cinematography, lighting, and camera movement, the viewer is situated at the optimum viewpoint of each shot. The viewer is "present" inside a space that does not really exist.

In general, Hollywood cinema has always been careful to hide the artificial nature of its space, but there is one exception: the rear-screen projection shots introduced in the 1930s. A typical shot shows actors sitting inside a stationary vehicle; a film of a moving landscape is projected on the screen behind the car's windows. The artificiality of rear-screen projection shots stands in striking contrast to the smooth fabric of Hollywood cinematic style in general.

The synthesis of a coherent space out of distinct fragments is only one example of how fictional cinema fakes reality. A film in general is comprised of separate image sequences. These sequences can come from different physical locations. Two consecutive shots of what looks like one room may correspond to two locations inside one studio. They can also correspond to locations in Moscow and Berlin, or Berlin and New York. The viewer will never know.

This is the key advantage of cinema over older fake-reality technologies, be they eighteenth-century Potemkin villages or nineteenth-century panoramas and dioramas. Before cinema, simulation was limited to the construction of a fake space inside a real space visible to the viewer. Examples include theater decorations and military decoys. In the nineteenth century, panorama offered a small improvement: By enclosing a viewer within a 360-degree view, the area of fake space was expanded. Louis-Jacques Daguerre introduced another innovation by having viewers move from one set to another in his London diorama. As described by the historian Paul Johnson, its

---

28. On the presentational system of early cinema, see Musser, *The Emergence of Cinema,* 3.

"amphitheater, seating 200, pivoted through a 73-degree arc, from one 'picture' to another. Each picture was seen through a 2,800-square-foot-window."[29] But already in the eighteenth century, Potemkin had pushed this technique to its limit: He created a giant facade—a diorama stretching for hundreds of miles—along which the viewer (Catherine the Great) passed. In contrast, in cinema a viewer remains stationary: what moves is the film itself.

Therefore if the older simulation technologies were limited by the materiality of a viewer's body, existing in a particular point in space and time, film overcomes this spatial and temporal limitation. It achieves this by substituting recorded images for unmediated human sight and by editing these images together. Through editing, images that could have been shot in different geographic locations or at different times create the illusion of a contiguous space and time.

Editing, or montage, is the key twentieth-century technology for creating fake realities. Theoreticians of cinema have distinguished between many kinds of montage, but for the purpose of sketching an archeology of the technologies of simulation that led to digital compositing I will distinguish between two basic techniques. The first technique is temporal montage: Separate realities form consecutive moments in time. The second technique is montage within a shot. It is the opposite of the first: separate realities form contingent parts of a single image. The first technique of temporal montage is much more common; this is what we usually mean by "montage" in film. It defines the cinematic language as we know it. In contrast, montage within a shot is used more rarely throughout film history. An example of this technique is the dream sequence in *The Life of an American Fireman* by Edward Porter in 1903, in which an image of a dream appears over a man's sleeping head. Other examples include split screens that, beginning in 1908, show the different interlocutors of a telephone conversation; the superimposition of images and multiple screens by avant-garde filmmakers in the 1920s (for instance, the superimposed images in Vertov's *Man with a Movie Camera* and the three-part screen in Gance Abel's 1927 *Napoléon*); rear-screen projection shots; and deep focus and special compositional strategies used to juxtapose

---

29. Paul Johnson, *The Birth of the Modern: World Society, 1815–1830* (London: Orion House, 1992), 156.

close and faraway scenes (for instance, a character looking through a window, as in *Citizen Kane, Ivan the Terrible,* and *Rear Window.*)[30]

In a fiction film, temporal montage serves a number of functions. As I have already pointed out, it creates a sense of presence in a virtual space. It is also utilized to change the meaning of individual shots (recall Kuleshov's effect) or, more precisely, to construct a meaning from separate pieces of profilmic reality. However, the use of temporal montage extends beyond the construction of an artistic fiction. Montage also becomes a key technology for ideological manipulation, through its employment in propaganda films, documentaries, news, commercials, and so on. The pioneer of the ideological montage is, once again, Vertov. In 1923 Vertov analyzed how he put together episodes of his news program *Kino-Pravda* ("Cinema-Truth") from shots filmed in different locations and at different times. Here is one example of his montage: "the bodies of the people's heroes are being lowered into the graves (filmed in Astrakhan in 1918); the graves are being covered with earth (Kronshtad, 1921); gun salute (Petrograd, 1920); eternal memory, people take off their hats (Moscow, 1922)." Here is another example: "montage of the greetings by the crowd and montage of the greetings by the machines to the comrade Lenin, filmed at different times."[31] As theorized by Vertov, film can overcome its indexical nature through montage, by presenting a viewer with objects that never existed in reality.

Archeology of Compositing: Video

Outside cinema, montage within a shot becomes a standard technique of modern photography and design (the photomontages of Alexander Rodchenko, El Lissitzky, Hannah Höch, John Heartfield, and countless other lesser-known twentieth-century designers). However, in the realm of the moving image, temporal montage dominates. Temporal montage is cinema's main operation for creating fake realities.

After World War II, a gradual shift takes place from film-based to electronic image recording and editing. This shift brings with it a new

---

30. The examples of *Citizen Kane* and *Ivan the Terrible* are taken from Aumont et al., *Aesthetics of Film,* 41.

31. Dziga Vertov, "Kinoki: Perevorot" (Kinoki: A revolution), *LEF* 3 (1923): 140.

technique—keying. One of the most basic techniques used today in any video and television production, keying refers to combining two different image sources. Any area of uniform color in one video image can be cut out and substituted with another source. Significantly, this new source can be a live video camera positioned somewhere, a prerecorded tape, or computer-generated graphics. The possibilities for creating fake realities are multiplied once again.

When electronic keying became part of standard television practice in the 1970s, the construction not only of still but also moving images finally began routinely to rely on montage within a shot. In fact, rear projection and other special effects shots, which had occupied a marginal place in classical film, became the norm: the weatherman in front of weather map, announcer in front of news footage, singer in front of animation in a music video.

An image created through keying presents a hybrid reality, composed of two different spaces. Television normally relates these spaces semantically but not visually. To take a typical example, we may be shown an image of an announcer sitting in a studio; behind her, in a cutout, we see news footage of a city street. The two spaces are connected through their meanings (the announcer discusses events shown in the cutout), but visually they are disjointed, as they share neither the same scale nor the same perspective. If classical cinematic montage creates the illusion of a coherent space and hides its work, electronic montage openly presents the viewer with an apparent visual clash of different spaces.

What will happen if the two spaces seamlessly merge? This operation forms the basis of the remarkable video *Steps* directed by Polish-born filmmaker Zbigniew Rybczynski in 1987. *Steps* is shot on videotape and uses keying; it also utilizes film footage and makes inadvertent reference to virtual reality. In this way, Rybczynski connects three generations of fake-reality technologies: analog, electronic, and digital. He also reminds us that it was the 1920s Soviet filmmakers who first fully realized the possibilities of montage, possibilities that continue to be expanded by electronic and digital media.

In the video, a group of American tourists is invited into a sophisticated video studio to participate in a kind of virtual reality/time machine experiment. The group is positioned in front of a blue screen. Next, the tourists find themselves literally inside the famous Odessa steps sequence from Sergei Eisenstein's *Potemkin* (1925). Rybczynski skillfully keys the shots of the people in the studio into the shots from *Potemkin,* creating a single co-herent space. At the same time, he emphasizes the artificiality of this space by contrasting the color video images of the tourists with Eisenstein's origi-nal grainy black-and-white footage. The tourists walk up and down the steps, snap pictures of the attacking soldiers, play with a baby in a crib. Gradually, the two realities begin to interact and mix: Some Americans fall down the steps after being shot by soldiers from Eisenstein's sequence; a tourist drops an apple that is picked up by a soldier.

The Odessa steps sequence, already a famous example of cinematic mon-tage, becomes just one element in a new ironic remix by Rybczynski. The original shots, already edited by Eisenstein, are now edited again with video images of the tourists, using both temporal montage and montage within a shot, the latter done through video keying. A "film look" is juxtaposed with a "video look," color is juxtaposed with black and white, the "presentness" of video is juxtaposed with the "always already" of film.

In *Steps,* Eisenstein's sequence becomes a generator for numerous kinds of juxtapositions, superimpositions, mixes and remixes. But Rybczynski treats this sequence not only as a single element of his own montage but also as a singular, physically existing space. In other words, the Odessa steps se-quence is read as a single shot corresponding to a real space, a space that could be visited like any other tourist attraction.

Along with Rybczynski, another filmmaker who systematically experi-mented with the possibilities of electronic montage within a shot is Jean-Luc Godard. While in the 1960s, Godard was actively exploring new possibili-ties of temporal montage such as jump cut, in later video works such as *Scé-nario du film "Passion"* (1982) and *Histoire(s) du cinéma* (1989–) he developed a unique aesthetics of continuity that relies on electronically mixing a num-ber of images together within a single shot. If Rybczynski's aesthetics is based on the operation of video keying, Godard's aesthetics similarly relies on a single operation available to any video editor—mixing. Godard uses the electronic mixer to create very slow cross-dissolves between images, cross-dissolves that seem never to resolve in a singular image, ultimately becom-ing the film itself. In *Histoire(s) du cinéma,* Godard mixes together two, three, or more images; images gradually fade in and out, but never disappear completely, staying on the screen for a few minutes at a time. This tech-nique can be interpreted as the representation of ideas or mental images floating around in our minds, coming in and out of mental focus. Another variation of the same technique used by Godard is to move from one image to another by oscillating between the two. The images flicker back and forth over and over, until the second image finally replaces the first. This technique can be also interpreted as an attempt to represent the mind's movement from one concept, mental image, or memory to another—the attempt, in other words, to represent what, according to Locke and other associationist philosophers, is the basis of our mental life—forming associations.

Godard wrote: "There are no more simple images. . . . The whole world is too much for an image. You need several of them, a chain of images . . ."[32] Accordingly, Godard always uses multiple images, images cross-dissolved together, coming together and separating. The electronic mixing that replaces both temporal montage and montage within the shot becomes for Godard an appropriate technique to visualize this "vague and complicated system that the whole world is continually entering and watching."[33]

Digital Compositing

The next generation in simulation technologies is digital compositing. On first glance, computers do not bring any conceptually new techniques for creating fake realities. They simply expand the possibilities of joining together different images within one shot. Rather than *keying* together images from two video sources, we can now *composite* an unlimited number of image layers. A shot may consist of dozens, hundreds, or thousands of image layers. These image may all have different origins—film shot on location ("live plates"), computer-generated sets or virtual actors, digital matte paintings, archival footage, and so on. Following the success of *Terminator 2* and *Jurassic Park,* most Hollywood films began to utilize digital compositing to create a least some of their shots.

Thus historically, a digitally composed image, like an electronically keyed image, can be seen as a continuation of montage within a shot. But while electronic keying creates disjointed spaces that remind us of the avantgarde collages of Rodchenko or Moholy-Nagy from the 1920s, digital com-

---

32. Jean-Luc Godard, *Son + Image,* ed. Raymond Bellour (New York: Museum of Modern Art, 1992), 171.
33. Ibid.

posing brings back the nineteenth-century techniques of creating smooth "combination prints" like those of Henry Peach Robinson and Oscar G. Reijlander.

But this historical continuity is deceptive. Digital compositing does represent a qualitatively new step in the history of visual simulation because it allows the creation of *moving* images of nonexistent worlds. Computer-generated characters can move within real landscapes; conversely, real actors can move and act within synthetic environments. In contrast to nineteenth-century "combination prints," which emulated academic painting, digital composites simulate the established language of cinema and television. Regardless of the particular combination of live-action elements and computer-generated elements that make up the composited shot, the camera can pan, zoom, and dolly through it. Interactions between the elements of a virtual world over time (for instance, the dinosaur attacking the car), along with the ability to look at this world from different viewpoints, become the guarantee of its authenticity.

The new ability to create a virtual world that moves—and that can be moved through—comes at a price. Although compositing fake news-footage takes place in real time in *Wag the Dog,* aligning numerous elements to create a convincing composite is, in reality, a time-consuming task. For instance, the forty-second sequence in *Titanic* in which the camera flies over the computer-generated ship, populated by computer-generated characters, took many months to produce and its total cost was $1.1 million.[34] In contrast, although images of such complexity are out of reach for video keying, it is possible to combine three image sources in real-time. (This trade-off between image-construction time and its complexity is similar to another trade-off I have already noted—that between image-construction time and its functionality; that is, images created with 3-D computer graphics are more functional than image streams recorded by film or video cameras, but in most cases, they are much more time-consuming to generate.)

If a compositor restricts the composite to just a few images, as was done with electronic keying, compositing can also be created in real time. The

---

34. See Paula Parisi, "Lunch on the Deck of the Titanic," *Wired* 6.02 (February 1998) (http://www.wired.com/wired/archive/6.02/cameron.html).

resulting illusion of a seamless space is stronger than what was possible with electronic keying. An example of real-time compositing is Virtual Sets technology, which was first introduced in the early 1990s and since then has been making its way into television studios around the world. This technology allows compositing video-image and computer-generated 3-D elements on the fly. (Actually, because the generation of computer elements is computation-intensive, the final image transmitted to the audience may be seconds behind the original image picked up by television camera.) A typical application of Virtual Sets involves composing an image of an actor over a computer-generated set. The computer reads the position of the video camera and uses this information to render the image of the set in proper perspective. The illusion is made more convincing by generating shadows and/or reflections of the actor and integrating them into the composite. Because of the relatively low resolution of analog television, the resulting effect is quite convincing. A particularly interesting application of Virtual Sets is the replacement and insertion of arena-tied advertising messages during live TV broadcasts of sports and entertainment events. Computer-synthesized advertising messages can be inserted into the playing field or other empty areas of the arena in the proper perspective, as though they were actually present in physical reality.[35]

Digital compositing represents a fundamental break with previous techniques for visual deception in another way. Throughout the history of representation, artists and designers have focused on the problem of creating a convincing illusion within a single image, whether a painting, film frame, or a view seen by Catherine the Great through the window of her carriage. Set making, one-point perspective, chiaroscuro, trick photography, and other cinematography techniques were all developed to solve this problem. Film montage introduced a new paradigm—creating an effect of presence in a virtual world by joining different images over time. Temporal montage became the dominant paradigm for the visual simulation of nonexistent spaces.

As the examples of digital composing for film and Virtual Sets applications for television demonstrate, the computer era introduces a different par-

---

35. *IMadGibe: Virtual Advertising for Live Sport Events,* a promotional flyer by ORAD, P.O. Box 2177, Kfar Saba 44425, Israel, 1998.

adigm. This paradigm is concerned not with time but with space. It can be seen as the next step in the development of techniques for creating a single convincing image of nonexistent spaces—painting, photography, cinematography. Having mastered this task, the culture came to focus on how to join seamlessly a number of such images into one coherent whole (electronic keying, digital compositing). Whether composing a live video of a newscaster with a 3-D computer-generated set or composing thousands of elements to create the images of *Titanic, the problem is no longer how to generate convincing individual images but how to blend them together.* Consequently, what is important now is what happens on the edges where different images are joined. The borders where different realities come together is the new arena where the Potemkins of our era try to outdo one another.

Compositing and New Types of Montage

In the beginning of this section, I pointed out that the use of digital compositing to create continuous spaces out of different elements can be seen as an example of the larger anti-montage aesthetics of computer culture. Indeed, if at the beginning of the twentieth century, cinema discovered that it could simulate a single space through temporal montage—a time-based mosaic of different shots—by the end of the century, it had arrived at a technique to accomplish a similar result without montage. In digital compositing, the elements are not juxtaposed but blended, their boundaries erased rather than foregrounded.

At the same time, by relating digital compositing to the theory and practice of film montage, we can better understand how this new key technique of assembling moving images redefines our concept of a moving image. While traditional film montage privileges temporal montage over montage within a shot—technically the latter was much more difficult to achieve—compositing makes them equal. More precisely, it erases the strict conceptual and technical separation between the two. Consider, for instance, the interface layout typical of many programs for computer-based editing and digital compositing, such as Adobe Premiere 4.2, a popular editing program, and Alias|Wavefront Composer 4.0, a professional compositing program. In this interface, the horizontal dimension represents time, while the vertical dimension represents the spatial order of the different image layers making up each image. A moving image sequence appears as a number of blocks staggered vertically, with each block standing for a particular image layer. Thus if Pudovkin, one of the theorists and practitioners of the Russian montage movement the 1920s, conceived of montage as a one-dimensional line of bricks, now it becomes a 2-D brick wall. This interface makes montage in time and montage within a shot equal in importance.

If the Premiere interface conceptualizes editing as an operation in 2-D dimensions, the interface of one of the most popular compositing programs, After Effects 4.0, adds a third dimension. Following the conventions of traditional film and video editing, Premiere assumes that all image sequences are the same size and proportion; in fact, it makes working with images that do not conform to the standard three-by-four frame ratio rather difficult. In contrast, the user of After Effects places image sequences of arbitrary sizes and proportions within the larger frame. Breaking with the conventions of old moving image media, the interface of After Effects assumes that the individual elements making up a moving image can freely move, rotate, and change proportions over time.

Sergei Eisenstein already used the metaphor of many-dimensional space in his writings on montage, naming one of his articles *Kino cheturekh izmereneii* (The Filmic Fourth Dimension).[36] However, his theories of montage ultimately focused on one dimension—time. Eisenstein formulated a number of principles, such as counterpoint, that can be used to coordinate changes in different visual dimensions over time. The examples of visual dimensions he considered are graphic directions, volumes, masses, space, and contrast.[37] When the sound film became a possibility, Eisenstein extended these principles to handle what, in computer language, can be called "synchronization" of visual and audio tracks; and later he added the dimension of color.[38] Eisenstein also developed a different set of principles ("methods of montage") according to which different shots can be edited together to form a longer sequence. The examples of "methods of montage" include metric montage, which uses absolute lengths of shots to establish a "beat," and

36. Sergei Eisenstein, "The Filmic Fourth Dimension," in *Film Form,* trans. Jay Leyda (New York: Harcourt Brace and Company, 1949).

37. Eisenstein, "A Dialectical Approach to Film Form," in *Film Form.*

38. Eisenstein, "Statement" and "Synchronization of Senses," in *Film Sense,* trans. Jay Leyda (New York: Harcourt Brace and Company, 1942).

rhythmic montage, which is based on pattern of movement within the shots. These methods can be used by themselves to structure a sequence of shots, but they also can be combined within a single sequence.

The new logic of a digital moving image contained in the operation of compositing runs against Eisenstein's aesthetics with its focus on time. Digital compositing makes the dimensions of space (3-D fake space being created by a composite and 2½-D space of all the layers being composited) and frame (separate images moving in 2-D within the frame) as important as time. In addition, the possibility of embedding hyperlinks within a moving sequence introduced in QuickTime 3 and other digital formats adds yet another spatial dimension.[39] The typical use of hyperlinking in digital movies is to link elements of a movie with information displayed outside of it. For instance, when a particular frame is displayed, a specific Web page can be loaded in another window. This practice "spatializes" a moving image: No longer completely filling the screen, it is now just one window among many.

In summary, if film technology, film practice, and film theory privilege the temporal development of a moving image, computer technology privileges spatial dimensions. The new spatial dimensions can be defined as follows:

1. spatial order of layers in a composite (2½-D space),
2. virtual space constructed through compositing (3-D space),
3. 2-D movement of layers in relation to the image frame (2-D space),
4. relationship between the moving image and linked information in the adjustment windows (2-D space).

These dimensions should be added to the list of visual and sound dimensions of the moving image elaborated by Eisenstein and other filmmakers. Their use opens new possibilities for cinema as well as poses a new challenge for film theory. *No longer just a subset of audio-visual culture, the digital moving image becomes a part of audio-visual-spatial culture.*

---

39. For an excellent theoretical analysis of QuickTime and digital moving images in general, see Vivian Sobchack's "Nostalgia for a Digital Object."

Of course, simple use of these dimensions in and of itself does not result in montage. Most images and spaces of contemporary culture are juxtapositions of different elements; calling any such juxtaposition "montage" renders the term meaningless. Media critic and historian Erkki Hutamo suggests that we should reserve the use of the term "montage" for "strong" cases, and I will follow his suggestion here.[40] Thus to qualify as an example of montage, a new media object should fulfill two conditions: Juxtapositions of elements should follow a particular system, and these juxtapositions should play a key role in how the work establishes its meaning, and its emotional and aesthetic effects. These conditions would also apply to the particular case of new spatial dimensions of digital moving images. By establishing a logic that controls the changes and the correlation of values on these dimensions, digital filmmakers can create what I will call *spatial montage.*

Although digital compositing is usually used to create a seamless virtual space, this does not have to be its only goal. Borders between different worlds do not have to be erased; different spaces do not have to be matched in perspective, scale, and lighting; individual layers can retain their separate identities rather than being merged into a single space; different worlds can clash semantically rather than form a single universe. I will conclude this section by invoking a few more works, which, together with videos by Rybczynski and Godard, point to the new aesthetic possibilities of digital compositing if it is not used in the service of traditional realism. Although all these works were created before digital compositing became available, they explore its aesthetic logic—for compositing is, first and foremost, a conceptual, not only a technological operation. I will use these works to introduce two other montage methods based on compositing: *ontological montage* and *stylistic montage.*

Rybczynski's film *Tango* (1982), made when he was still living in Poland, uses layering as a metaphor for the particular overcrowdedness characteristic of socialist countries in the second half of the twentieth century, and for human cohabitation in general. A number of people perform various actions moving in loops through the same small room, apparently unaware of each other. Rybczynski offsets the loops in such a way that even though his characters keep moving through the same points in space, they never run into one an-

---

40. Private communication, Helsinki, 4 October 1999.

other. Compositing, achieved in *Tango* through optical printing, allows the filmmaker to superimpose a number of elements, or whole words, within a single space. (In this film, each person moving through the room can be said to form a separate world.) As in *Steps,* these worlds are matched in perspective and scale—and yet the viewer knows that the scene being shown could not occur in normal human experience at all given the laws of physics, or is highly unlikely to occur given the conventions of human life. In the case of *Tango,* the depicted scene could have occurred physically, but the probability of such an occurrence is close to zero. Works such as *Tango* and *Steps* develop what I will call an *ontological montage:* the coexistence of ontologically incompatible elements within the same time and space.

The films of Czech filmmaker Konrad Zeman exemplify another montage method based on compositing, which I will call *stylistic montage.* In a career spanning from the 1940s to the 1980s, Zeman used a variety of special effect techniques to create juxtapositions of stylistically diverse images in different media. He juxtaposes different media in time, cutting from a live-action shot to a shot of a model or documentary footage, as well as within the same shot. For example, a shot may combine filmed human figures, an old engraving used for background, and a model. Of course, such artists as Picasso, Braque, Picabia, and Max Ernst were creating similar juxtaposition of elements in different media in still images already before the World War II. However, in the realm of the moving image, stylistic montage only came to the surface in the 1990s when the computer became the meeting ground for different generations of media formats used in the twentieth century—35mm and 8mm film, amateur and professional video, and early digital film formats. While previously, filmmakers usually worked with a single format throughout the whole film, the accelerated replacement of different analog and digital formats since the 1970s made the coexistence of stylistically diverse elements a norm rather than the exception for new media objects. Compositing can be used to hide this diversity—or it can be used to foreground it, creating it artificially if necessary. For instance, the film *Forrest Gump* emphasizes stylistic differences between various shots; this simulation of different film and video artifacts is an important aspect of its narrative system.

In Zeman's films such as *Baron Prásil* (Baron Munchhausen, 1961) and *Na komete* (On the Comet, 1970), live-action footage, etchings, miniatures, and other elements are layered together in a self-conscious and ironic way. Like

Rybczynski, Zeman keeps a coherent perspectival space in his films while making us aware that it is constructed. One of his devices is to superimpose filmed actors over an old etching used as a background. In Zeman's aesthetics, neither graphic nor cinematographic elements dominate; the two are blended together in equal proportion, creating a unique visual style. At the same time, Zeman subordinates the logic of feature filmmaking to the logic of animation; that is, the shots in his films that combine live-action footage with graphic elements position all elements on parallel planes; the elements move parallel to the screen. This is the logic of an animation stand where the stack of images is arranged parallel to each other, rather than live-action cinema where the camera typically moves through 3-D space. As we will see in the "Digital Cinema" section, this subordination of live action to animation is the logic of digital cinema in general.

St. Petersburg artist Olga Tobreluts, who uses digital compositing, also respects the illusion of a coherent perspectival space, while continuously playing tricks with it. In *Gore ot Uma* (1994; directed by Olga Komarova), a video work based on a famous play written by the nineteenth-century Russian writer Aleksandr Griboedov, Tobreluts overlays images representing radically different realities (a close-up of plants; animals in the zoo) on the windows and walls of various interior spaces. In one shot, two characters converse in front of a window behind which we see a flock of soaring birds taken from Alfred Hitchcock's *The Birds;* in another, a delicate computer-rendered design keeps morphing on the wall behind a dancing couple. In these and similar shots, Tobreluts aligns the two realities in perspective but not in scale. The result is an ontological montage—and also a new kind of montage within a shot. Which is to say, if the avant-garde of the 1920s, and MTV in its wake, juxtaposed radically different realities within a single image, and if Hollywood digital artists use computer compositing to glue different images into a seamless illusionistic space, Zeman, Rybczynski, and Tobreluts explore the creative space between these two extremes. The space between modernist collage and Hollywood cinematic realism is new terrain for cinema ready for exploration with the help of digital compositing.

Teleaction

Representation versus Communication

Teleaction, the third operation that I will discuss in this chapter, may appear to be qualitatively different from the first two, selecting and compositing. It is not employed to create new media, only to access it. Therefore, we may at first think that teleaction does not have a direct effect on the language of new media.

Of course, this operation is made possible by designers of computer hardware and software. For instance, numerous Web cameras allow users to observe remote locations; most Web sites also include hyperlinks that allow the user to "teleport" from one remote server to another. At the same time, in the case of many commercial sites, designers try to prevent users from leaving the site. To use industry lingo (circa 1999), a designer wants to make each user "hardcore" (i.e., make her stay on the site); the goal of commercial Web design is to create "stickiness" (a measure of how long an individual user stays on a particular Web site), and increase "eyeball hang time" (Web-site loyalty). So although it is the end user who employs the operation of teleaction, it is the designer who makes it (im)possible. Still, no new media objects are being generated when the user follows a hyperlink to another Web site, or uses telepresence to observe or act in a remote location, or communicates in real time with other users using Internet chat, or just makes a plain old-fashioned telephone call. In short, once we begin dealing with verbs and nouns which begin with *tele-,* we are no longer dealing with the traditional cultural domain of representation. Instead, we enter a new conceptual space, which this book has not explored so far—telecommunication. How can we start navigating it?

When we think of the end of the nineteenth century, we think of the birth of cinema. In the preceding decades, and the one immediately following the 1890s, most other modern media technologies were developed, enabling the recording of still images of visible reality (photography) and sound (the phonograph), as well as real-time transmission of images, sounds, and text (telegraph, television, the fax, telephone, and radio). Yet, more than any of these other inventions, it was the introduction of cinema that impressed itself most strongly on public memory. The year we remember and celebrate is 1895, not 1875 (the first television experiments of Carey) or 1907 (the introduction of the fax). Clearly, we are more impressed (or at least, we were until the arrival of the Internet) with modern media's ability to record aspects of reality and then use these recordings to simulate it for our senses than with its real-time communication aspect. If we were given the choice to be among the Lumiere's first audience or to be among the first users of the telephone, we would choose the former. Why? The reason is that the new recording technologies led to the development of new arts in a way that real-time communication did not. The fact that aspects of sensible reality can be recorded and that these recordings can be later combined, reshaped, and manipulated—in short, edited—made possible the new media-based arts that were soon to dominate the twentieth century: fiction films, radio concerts, music programs, television serials, and news programs. Despite persistent experiments of avant-garde artists with the modern technologies of real-time communication—radio in the 1920s, video in the 1970s, the Internet in the 1990s—the ability to communicate over a physical distance in real time did not seem by itself to inspire fundamentally new aesthetic principles the way film or tape recording did.

Since their beginning in the nineteenth century, modern media technologies have developed along two distinct trajectories. The first is representational technologies—film, audio and video magnetic tape, various digital storage formats. The second is real-time communication technologies, that is, everything that begins with *tele*—telegraph, telephone, telex, television, telepresence. Such new twentieth-century cultural forms as radio and, later, television emerge at the intersections of these two trajectories. In this meeting, the technologies of real-time communication became subordinated to the technologies of representation. Telecommunication was used for distribution, as with broadcasting, which enabled a twentieth century radio listener or television viewer to receive a transmission in real time. But a typical broadcast, whether film, play, or musical performance, was a traditional aesthetic object, that is, a construction utilizing elements of familiar reality and created by professionals previous to transmission. For instance, although television retained some live programs such as news and talk shows following the adoption of video tape recorders, the majority of programming came to be prerecorded.

Attempts by some artists from the 1960s onward to substitute a traditionally defined aesthetic object with other concepts such as "process," "practice," and "concept" only highlight the stronghold of the traditional concept on our cultural imagination. The concept of an aesthetic object as an *object,* that is, a self-contained structure limited in space and/or time, is fundamental to all modern thinking about aesthetics. For instance, in his *Languages of Art* (1976), which outlines one of the most influential aesthetic theories of the last decades, philosopher Nelson Goodman names the following four symptoms of the aesthetic—syntactic density, semantic density, syntactic repleteness, and the ability to exemplify.[41] These characteristics assume a finite object in space and/or time—a literary text, a musical or dance performance, a painting, a work of architecture. For another example of how modern aesthetic theory relies on the concept of a fixed object, we can look at the influential article "From Work to Text" by Roland Barthes. In this article, Barthes establishes an opposition between the traditional notion of a "work" and a new notion of "text," about which he advances seven "propositions."[42] As can be seen from these propositions, Barthes's notion of a "text" is an attempt to go beyond the traditional aesthetic object understood as something clearly delineated from other objects semantically and physically—yet ultimately Barthes retains the traditional concept. His notion of a "text" still assumes a reader "reading," in the most general sense, something previously "written." In short, while a "text" is interactive, hypertextual, distributed, and dynamic (to translate Barthes's propositions into new media terms), it is still a finite object.

By foregrounding telecommunication, both real-time and asynchronous, as a fundamental cultural activity, the Internet asks us to reconsider the very

---

41. Nelson Goodman, *Languages of Art,* 2d ed. (Indianapolis: Hackett, 1976), 252–253.

42. Barthes, "From Work to Text," in *Image/Music/Text.*

paradigm of an aesthetic object. Is it necessary for the concept of the aesthetic to assume representation? Does art necessary involve a finite object? Can telecommunication between users by itself be the subject of an aesthetic? Similarly, can the user's search for information be understood aesthetically? In short, if a user accessing information and a user telecommunicating with other(s) are as common in computer culture as a user interacting with a representation, can we expand our aesthetic theories to include these two new situations?

I find these to be hard questions; but as a way to begin approaching them, I will offer an analysis of different kinds of "tele" operations summed up by my term "teleaction."

Telepresence: Illusion versus Action

In the opening sequence of the movie *Titanic* (James Cameron, 1997), we see an operator sitting at the controls. The operator is wearing a head-mounted display that shows an image transmitted from a remote location. This display allows him to remotely control a small vehicle, and with its help, explore the insides of the "Titanic" lying on the bottom of the ocean. In short, the operator is "telepresent."

With the rise of the Web, telepresence, which until recently was restricted to a few specialized industrial and military applications, has become a more familiar experience. A search on Yahoo! for "interesting devices connected to the Net" returns links to a variety of Net-based telepresence applications: coffee machines, robots, an interactive model railroad, audio devices and, of course, the ever-popular web cams.[43] Some of these devices, such as most web cams, do not allow for true telepresence—you get images from a remote location but you cannot act on them. Others, however, are true telepresence links that allow the user to perform actions remotely.

Remote video cameras and remotely navigated devices such as the one featured in *Titanic* exemplify the notion of being "present" in a physically remote location. At the same time, the experience of daily navigating the Web also involves telepresence on a more basic level. By following hyperlinks, the user "teleports" from one server to another, from one physical location to the

---

43. http://www.yahoo.com.

next. If we are still fetishizing video-based telepresence as portrayed in *Titanic,* this is only because we are slow to accept the primacy of information space over physical space in computer culture. But in fact, the ability to "teleport" instantly from one server to another, to be able to explore a multitude of documents located on computers around the world, all from one location, is much more important that being able to perform physical actions in one remote location.

I will discuss telepresence in this section in its accepted, more narrow meaning: the ability to see and act at a distance. And just as I constructed one possible archeology of digital compositing, here I would like to construct one possible historical trajectory leading to computer-based telepresence. If digital compositing can be placed along with other technologies for creating fake reality such as fashion and makeup, realist paintings, dioramas, military decoys, and VR, telepresence can be thought of as one example of *representational technologies used to enable action, that is, to allow the viewer to manipulate reality through representations.* Other examples of these action-enabling technologies are maps, architectural drawings, and x-rays. All of them allow their users to act at a distance. Given this, what are the new possibilities for action offered by telepresence in contrast to these older technologies? This question will guide my discussion of telepresence here.

If we look at the word itself, *telepresence* means presence at a distance. But presence where? Interactive media designer and theorist Brenda Laurel defines *telepresence* as "a medium that allows you to take your body with you into some other environment . . . you get to take some subset of your senses with you into another environment. And that environment may be a computer-generated environment, it may be a camera-originated environment, or it may be a combination of the two."[44] According to this definition, telepresence encompasses two different situations—being "present" in a synthetic computer-generated environment (what is commonly referred to as "virtual reality") and being "present" in a real remote physical location via a live video image. Scott Fisher, one of the developers of the NASA Ames Virtual

---

44. Brenda Laurel, quoted in Rebecca Coyle, "The Genesis of Virtual Reality," in *Future Visions: New Technologies of the Screen,* ed. Philip Hayward and Tana Wollen (London: British Film Institute, 1993), 162.

Environment Workstation—the first modern VR system—similarly does not distinguish between being "present" in a computer-generated environment or a real remote physical location. Describing the Ames system, he writes: "Virtual environments at the Ames system are synthesized with 3-D computer-generated imagery, or are remotely sensed by user-controlled, stereoscopic video camera configurations."[45] Fisher uses "virtual environments" as an all-encompassing term, reserving "telepresence" for the second situation: "presence" in a remote physical location.[46] I will follow his usage here.

Popular media has downplayed the concept of telepresence in favor of virtual reality. Photographs of the Ames system, for instance, have often been featured to illustrate the idea of an escape from any physical space into a computer-generated world. The fact that a head-mounted display can also show a televised image of a remote physical location is hardly ever mentioned.

Yet, from the point of view of the history of the technologies of action, telepresence is a much more radical technology than virtual reality, or computer simulations in general. Let us consider the difference between the two.

Like the fake reality technologies that preceded it, virtual reality provides the subject with the illusion of being present in a simulated world. Virtual reality adds a new capability: It allows the subject to actively change this world. In other words, the subject is given control over a fake reality. For instance, an architect can modify an architectural model, a chemist can try different molecule configurations, a tank driver can shoot at a model of a tank, and so on. But, what is modified in each case is nothing but data stored in a computer's memory! The user of any computer simulation has power over a virtual world, which only exists inside a computer.

Telepresence allows the subject to control not just the simulation but reality itself. Telepresence provides the ability to manipulate remotely physical reality in real time through its image. The body of the teleoperator is transmitted, in real time, to another location where it can act on the subject's

---

45. Fisher, 430 (emphasis mine).

46. Fisher defines telepresence as "a technology which would allow remotely situated operators to receive enough sensory feedback to feel like they are really at a remote location and are able to do different kinds of tasks." Scott Fisher, "Visual Interface Environments," in *The Art of Human-Computer Interface Design,* ed. Brenda Laurel (Reading, Mass.: Addison-Wesley, 1990), 427.

behalf—repairing a space station, doing underwater excavation, or bombing a military base in Iraq or Yugoslavia.

Thus, the essence of telepresence is that it is anti-presence. I do not have to be physically present in a location to affect reality at this location. A better term would be *teleaction.* Acting over distance. In real time.

Catherine the Great was fooled into mistaking painted facades for real villages. Today, from thousands of miles away—as was demonstrated during the Gulf War—we can send a missile equipped with a television camera close enough to tell the difference between a target and a decoy. We can direct the flight of the missile using the image transmitted back by its camera, we can carefully fly towards the target, and using the same image, we can blow the target away. All that is needed is to position the computer cursor over the right place in the image and press a button.

Image-Instruments[47]

How new is this use of images? Does it originate with telepresence? Since we are accustomed to consider the history of visual representations in the West in terms of illusion, it may seem that to use images to enable action is a completely new phenomenon. However, French philosopher and sociologist Bruno Latour proposes that certain kinds of images have always functioned as instruments of control and power, power being defined as the ability to mobilize and manipulate resources across space and time.

One example of such image-instruments analyzed by Latour are perspectival images. Perspective establishes the precise and reciprocal relationship between objects and their signs. We can go from objects to signs (two-dimensional representations), but we can also go from such signs to three-dimensional objects. This reciprocal relationship allows us not only to represent reality but also to control it.[48] For instance, we cannot measure the sun in space directly, but we only need a small ruler to measure it on a photograph (the perspectival image par excellence).[49] And even if we could fly

---

47. I am grateful to Thomas Elsaesser for suggesting the term "image-instrument" and also for making a number of other suggestions regarding the "Teleaction" section as a whole.
48. Bruno Latour, "Visualization and Cognition: Thinking with Eyes and Hands," *Knowledge and Society: Studies in the Sociology of Culture Past and Present,* 6 (1986): 1–40.
49. Ibid., 22.

around the sun, we would still be better off studying the sun through its representations, which we can bring back from the trip—because now we have unlimited time to measure, analyze, and catalog them. We can move objects from one place to another by simply moving their representations: "You can see a church in Rome, and carry it with you in London in such a way as to reconstruct it in London, or you can go back to Rome and amend the picture." Finally, we can also represent absent things and plan our movement through space by working on representations: "One cannot smell or hear or touch Sakhalin Island, but you can look at the map and determine at which bearing you will see the land when you send the next fleet."[50] All in all, perspective is more than just a sign system that reflects reality—it makes possible the manipulation of reality through the manipulation of its signs.

Perspective is only one example of image-instruments. Any representation that systematically captures some features of reality can be used as an instrument. In fact, most types of representations that do not fit into the history of illusionism—diagrams and charts, maps and x-rays, infrared and radar images—belong to the second history, that of representations as instruments for action.

Telecommunication

Given that images have always been used to affect reality, does telepresence bring anything new? A map, for instance, already allows for a kind of tele-action: It can be used to predict the future and therefore change it. To quote Latour again, "One cannot smell or hear or touch Sakhalin Island, but you can look at the map and determine at which bearing you will see the land when you send the next fleet."

In my view, there are two fundamental differences between old image-instruments and telepresence. Because telepresence involves electronic transmission of video images, the construction of representations takes place instantaneously. Making a perspectival drawing or a chart, taking a photograph or shooting film, takes time. Now I can use a remote video camera that capture images in real-time, sending these images back to me without any delay. This allows me to monitor any visible changes in a remote location

---

50. Ibid., 8.

(weather conditions, movements of troops, and so on), adjusting my actions accordingly. Depending upon what information I need, radar can be used instead of a video camera. In either case, an image-instrument displayed by a real-time screen is formed in real time.

The second difference is directly related to the first. The ability to receive visual information about a remote place in real time allows us to manipulate physical reality in this place, also in real-time. If power, according to Latour, includes the ability to manipulate resources at a distance, then teleaction provides a new and unique kind of power—real-time remote control. I can drive a toy vehicle, repair a space station, do an underwater excavation, operate on a patient, or kill—all from a distance.

What technology is responsible for this new power? Since a teleoperator typically acts with the help of a live video image (for instance, when remotely operating a moving vehicle such as in the opening sequence of *Titanic*), we may think at first that it is the technology of video, or, more precisely, of television. The original, nineteenth-century meaning of television was "vision at a distance." Only after the 1920s, when television was equated with broadcasting, did this meaning fade away. However, during the preceding half century (television research began in the 1870s), television engineers were mostly concerned with the problem of how to transmit consecutive images of a remote location to enable "remote seeing."

If images are transmitted at regular intervals, if these intervals are short enough, and if the images have sufficient detail, the viewer will have enough reliable information about the remote location for teleaction. The early television systems used slow mechanical scanning and resolution as low as thirty lines. In the case of modern television systems, the visible reality is being scanned at the resolution of a few hundred lines sixty times a second. This provides enough information for most telepresence tasks.

Now, consider the *Telegarden* project by Ken Goldberg and his associates.[51] In this Web telerobotics project, the Web users operate a robotic arm to plant seeds in a garden. Instead of continuously refreshed video, the project uses user-driven still images. The image shows the garden from the viewpoint of the video camera attached to the robotic arm. When the arm is

---

51. http://telegarden.aec.at.

moved to a new location, a new still image is transmitted. These still images provide enough information for the particular teleaction in this project—planting the seeds.

As this example indicates, it is possible to teleact without video. More generally, we can say that different kinds of teleaction require different temporal and spatial resolutions. If the operator needs immediate feedback on her actions (the example of remote operation of a vehicle is again appropriate here), a frequent update of images is essential. But in the case of planting a garden using a remote robot arm, user-triggered still images are sufficient.

Now consider another example of telepresence. Radar images are obtained by scanning the surrounding area once every few seconds. The visible reality is reduced to a single point. A radar image does not contain any indications about shapes, textures, or colors present in a video image—it only records the position of an object. Yet this information is quite sufficient for the most basic teleaction—the destruction of an object.

In this extreme case of teleaction, the image is so minimal that it hardly can be called an image at all. However, it is still sufficient for real-time remote action. What is crucial is that the information is transmitted in real time.

If we put the examples of video-based and radar-based telepresence together, the common denominator turns out to be not video but electronic transmission of signals. In other words, the technology that makes teleaction in real time possible is electronic telecommunication, itself made possible by two discoveries of the nineteenth century—electricity and electromagnetism. Coupled with a computer used for real-time control, electronic telecommunication leads to a new and unprecedented relationship between objects and their signs. It makes instantaneous not only the process by which objects are turned into signs but also the reverse process—the manipulation of objects through these signs.

Umberto Eco once defined a sign as something that can be used to tell a lie. This definition correctly describes one function of visual representations—to deceive. But in the age of electronic telecommunication we need a new definition: A sign is something which can be used to teleact.

Distance and Aura

Having analyzed the operation of telepresence in its more narrow and conventional meaning as a physical presence in a remote environment, I now want to come back to a more general sense of telepresence—real-time communication with a physically remote location. This meaning fits all "tele" technologies, from television, radio, fax, and telephone to Internet hyperlinking and chat. Again, I want to ask the same question as before: What is different about more recent telecommunication technologies as opposed to older ones?

To address this question, I will juxtapose the arguments by two key theoreticians of old and new media—Walter Benjamin and Paul Virilio. These arguments come from two essays written half a century apart—Benjamin's celebrated "The Work of Art in the Age of Mechanical Reproduction" (1936)[52] and Virilio's "Big Optics" (1992).[53] Benjamin's and Virilio's essays focus on the same theme—the disruption caused by a cultural artifact, specifically, a new communication technology (film in the case of Benjamin, telecommunication in the case of Virilio), in the familiar patterns of human perception; in short, the intervention of technology into human nature. But what is human nature, and what is technology? How does one draw the boundary between the two in the twentieth century? Both Benjamin and Virilio solve this problem in the same way. They equate nature with spatial distance between the observer and the observed, and they see technologies as destroying this distance. As we will see, these two assumptions lead them to interpret the prominent new technologies of their times in a very similar way.

Benjamin starts with his now famous concept of aura—the unique presence of a work of art, a historical or natural object. We may think that an object has to be close by if we are to experience its aura but, paradoxically, Benjamin defines aura "as the unique phenomenon of a distance" (224). "If, while resting on a summer afternoon, you follow with your eyes a mountain range on the horizon or a branch which casts its shadow over you, you

---

52. Benjamin, "The Work of Art in the Age of Mechanical Reproduction."

53. Paul Virilio, "Big Optics," in *On Justifying the Hypothetical Nature of Art and the Non-Identicality within the Object World,* ed. Peter Weibel (Cologne, 1992). Virilio's argument can also be found in his other texts, for instance, "Speed and Information: Cyberspace Alarm!" in *CTHEORY* (www.ctheory.com/a30-cyberspace_alarm.html) and *Open Sky,* trans. Julie Rose (London: Verso, 1997).

experience the aura of those mountains, of that branch" (225). Similarly, writes Benjamin, a painter "maintains in his work a natural distance from reality" (235). This respect for distance common to both natural perception and painting is overturned by the new technologies of mass reproduction, particularly photography and film. The cameraman, whom Benjamin compares to a surgeon, "penetrates deeply into its [reality's] web" (237); his camera zooms in order to "pry an object from its shell" (225). Due to its new mobility, glorified in such films as *Man with a Movie Camera,* the camera can be anywhere, and with its superhuman vision it can obtain a close-up of any object. These close-ups, writes Benjamin, satisfy the desire of the masses "to bring things 'closer' spatially and humanly," "to get hold of an object at very close range" (225). When photographs are brought together within a single magazine or newreel, both the scale and unique locations of the objects are discarded—thus answering the demand of mass society for a "universal equality of things."

Writing about telecommunication and telepresence, Virilio also uses the concept of distance to understand their effect. In Virilio's reading, these technologies collapse physical distances, uprooting familiar patterns of perception that ground our culture and politics. Virilio introduces the terms "Small Optics" and "Big Optics" to underline the dramatic nature of this change. Small Optics are based on geometric perspective shared by human vision, painting, and film. It involves distinctions between near and far, between an object and a horizon against which the object stands out. Big Optics is real-time electronic transmission of information, "the active optics of time passing at the speed of light."

As Small Optics are replaced by Big Optics, the distinctions characteristic of Small Optics era are erased. If information from any point can be transmitted with the same speed, the concepts of near and far, horizon, distance, and space itself no longer have any meaning. So, if for Benjamin the industrial age displaced every object from its original setting, for Virilio the post-industrial age eliminates the dimension of space altogether. At least in principle, every point on earth is now instantly accessible from any other point on earth. As a consequence, Big Optics locks us in a claustrophobic world without any depth or horizon; the earth becomes our prison.

Virilio asks us to notice "the progressive derealization of the terrestrial horizon, . . . resulting in an impending primacy of real time perspective of undulatory optics over real space of the linear geometrical optics of the Quattrocento."[54] He mourns the destruction of distance, geographic grandeur, the vastness of natural space, the vastness that guaranteed time delay between events and our reactions, giving us time for critical reflection necessary to arrive at a correct decision. The regime of Big Optics inevitably leads to real-time politics, a politics that requires instant reactions to events transmitted with the speed of light, and that, ultimately, can only be efficiently handled by computers responding to each other.

Given the surprising similarity of Benjamin's and Virilio's accounts of new technologies, it is telling how differently they draw the boundaries between the natural and the cultural, between what is already assimilated within human nature and what is still new and threatening. Writing in 1936, Benjamin uses the real landscape and a painting as examples of what is natural for human perception. This natural state is invaded by film, which collapses distances, bringing everything equally close, and destroys aura. Virilio, writing half a century later, draws the lines quite differently. If for Benjamin film still represents an alien presence, for Virilio it has already become part of our human nature, the continuation of our natural sight. Virilio considers human vision, the Renaissance perspective, painting, and film as all belonging to the Small Optics of geometric perspective, in contrast to the Big Optics of instant electronic transmission.

Virilio postulates a historical break between film and telecommunication, between Small Optics and Big Optics. It is also possible to read the movement from the first to the second in terms of continuity—if we are to use the concept of modernization. Modernization is accompanied by a disruption of physical space and matter, a process that privileges interchangeable and mobile signs over original objects and relations. In the words of art historian Jonathan Crary (who draws on Deleuze and Guattari's *Anti-Oedipus* and on Marx's *Grandrisse*), "Modernization is the process by which capitalism uproots and makes mobile that which is grounded, clears away or obliterates that which impedes circulation, and makes exchangeable what is singular."[55] The concept of modernization fits equally well with Benjamin's account of

---

54. Virilio, "Big Optics," 90.

55. Jonathan Crary, *Techniques of the Observer: On Vision and Modernity in the Nineteenth Century* (Cambridge, Mass.: MIT Press, 1990), 10.

film and Virilio's account of telecommunication, the latter but a more advanced stage in the continual process of turning objects into mobile signs. Before, different physical locations met within a single magazine spread or film newsreel; now, they meet within a single electronic screen. Of course, the signs themselves now exist as digital data, which makes their transmission and manipulation even easier. Also, in contrast to photographs, which remain fixed once they are printed, computer representation makes every image inherently mutable—creating signs that are no longer just mobile but also forever modifiable.[56] Yet, significant as they are, these are ultimately quantitative rather than qualitative differences—with one exception.

As can be seen from my discussion above, in contrast to photography and film, electronic telecommunication can function as two-way communication. Not only can the user immediately obtain images of various locations, bringing them together within a single electronic screen, but, via telepresence, she can also be "present" in these locations. In other words, she can affect change on material reality over physical distance in real time.

Film, telecommunication, telepresence. Benjamin's and Virilio's analyses make it possible for us to understand the historical effect of these technologies in terms of progressive diminishing and, finally, the complete elimination of something that both writers see as a fundamental condition of human perception—spatial distance, the distance between the subject who is seeing and the object being seen. This reading of the distance involved in vision as something positive, as a necessary ingredient of human culture, provides an important alternative for a much more dominant tendency in modern thought to read distance negatively. This negative reading is then used to attack the visual sense as a whole. Distance becomes responsible for creating the gap between spectator and spectacle, for separating subject and object, for putting the first in the position of transcendental mastery and rendering the second inert. Distance allows the subject to treat the Other as object; in short, it makes objectification possible. Or, as a French fisherman summarized these arguments to a young Lacan who was looking at a sardine can floating on the surface of the sea, years before

---

56. This point is argued in Mitchell, *The Reconfigured Eye.*

he became a famous psychoanalyst: "You see the can? Do you see it? Well, it doesn't see you!"[57]

In Western thought, vision has always been understood and discussed in opposition to touch, so, inevitably, the denigration of vision (to use Martin Jay's term)[58] leads to the elevation of touch. Thus criticism of vision predictably leads to a new theoretical interest in the idea of the haptic. We may be tempted, for instance, to read the lack of distance characteristic of the act of touching as allowing for a different relationship between subject and object. Benjamin and Virilio block this seemingly logical line of argument, since they both stress the aggression potentially present in touching. Rather than understanding touch as a respectful and careful contact or as a caress, they present it as an unceremonious and aggressive disruption of matter.

Thus the standard connotations of vision and touch become reversed. For Benjamin and Virilio, distance guaranteed by vision preserves the aura of an object, its position in the world, while the desire "to brings things 'closer'" destroys objects' relations to each other, ultimately obliterating the material order altogether and rendering the notions of distance and space meaningless. So even if we are to disagree with their arguments about new technologies and to question their equation of natural order and distance, the critique of the vision—touch opposition is something we should retain. Indeed, in contrast to older action-enabling representational technologies, real-time image instruments literally allow us to touch objects over distance, thus making possible their easy destruction as well. The potential aggressiveness of looking turns out to be rather more innocent than the actual aggression of electronically enabled touch.

---

57. Jacques Lacan, *The Four Fundamental Concepts of Psycho-Analysis,* ed. Jacques-Alain Miller (New York: W. W. Norton, 1978), 95.

58. Martin Jay, *Downcast Eyes: The Denigration of Vision in Twentieth-Century French Thought* (Berkeley: University of California Press, 1993).

The Illusions

Zeuxis was a legendary Greek painter who lived in the fifth century B.C. The story of his competition with Parrhasius exemplifies the concern with illusionism that was to occupy Western art throughout much of its history. According to the story, Zeuxis painted grapes with such skill that birds began to fly down to eat from the painted vine.[1]

RealityEngine is a high-performance graphics computer that was manufactured by Silicon Graphics Inc. in the last decade of the twentieth century A.D. Optimized to generate real-time, interactive, photorealistic 3-D graphics, it is used to create computer games and special effects for feature films and TV, and to run scientific visualization models and computer-aided design software. Last but not least, RealityEngine is routinely employed to run high-end VR environments—the latest achievement in the West's struggle to outdo Zeuxis.

In terms of the images it can generate, RealityEngine may not be superior to Zeuxis. Yet it can do other tricks unavailable to the Greek painter. For instance, it allows the viewer to move around virtual grapes, touch them, lift them in the palm of one's hand. And this ability of the viewer to interact with a representation may be as important in contributing to the overall reality effect as the images themselves. Which makes RealityEngine a formidable contender to Zeuxis.

In the twentieth century, art has largely rejected the goal of illusionism, the goal that was so important to it before; as a consequence, it has lost much of its popular support. The production of illusionistic representations has become the domain of mass culture and of media technologies—photography, film, and video. The creation of illusions has been delegated to optical and electronic machines.

Today, everywhere, these machines are being replaced by new, digital illusion generators—computers. The production of all illusionistic images is becoming the sole province of PCs and Macs, Onyxes and RealityEngines.[2]

This massive replacement is one of the key economic factors that keeps the new media industries expanding. As a consequence, these industries are

---

1. For a detailed analysis of this story, see Stephen Bann, *The True Vine: On Western Representation and the Western Tradition* (Cambridge: Cambridge University Press, 1989).

2. Onyx is a faster version of RealityEngine, which was also manufactured by Silicon Graphics. See www.sgi.com.

obsessed with visual illusionism. This obsession is particularly strong in the field of computer imaging and animation. The annual SIGGRAPH convention is a competition between Zeuxis and Parrhasius on an industrial scale: about forty thousand people gather on a trade floor around thousands of new hardware and software displays, all competing with each other to deliver the best illusionistic images. The industry frames each new technological advance in image acquisition and display in terms of the ability of computer technologies to catch up and surpass the visual fidelity of analog media technologies. On their side, animators and software engineers are perfecting the techniques for synthesizing photorealistic images of sets and human actors. The quest for a perfect simulation of reality drives the whole field of VR. In a different sense, the designers of human-computer interfaces are also concerned with illusion. Many of them believe that their main goal is to make the computer invisible, that is, to construct an interface which is completely "natural." (In reality, what they usually mean by "natural" is simply older, already assimilated technologies, such as office stationery and furniture, cars, VCR controls, and telephones.)

Continuing our bottom-up trajectory in examining new media, we have now arrived at the level of appearance. Although the industry's obsession with illusionism is not the sole factor responsible for making new media look they way they do, it is definitely one of the key factors. Focusing on the issue of illusionism, I will address different questions raised by it in this chapter. How is the "reality effect" of a synthetic image different from that of optical media? Has computer technology redefined our standards of illusionism as determined by our earlier experience with photography, film, and video? "Synthetic Realism as Bricolage" and "The synthetic Image and its Subject" provide two possible answers to these questions. In these sections, I investigate the new "internal" logic of the computer-generated illusionistic image by comparing lens-based and computer-imaging technologies. In the third section, "Illusion, Narrative, and Interactivity," I ask how visual illusionism and interactivity work together (as well as against each other), in virtual worlds, computer games, military simulators, and other interactive new media objects and interfaces.

The discussions in these sections do not by any means exhaust the topic of illusionism in new media. As examples of other interesting questions that the topic of illusionism in new media may generate, I will list three below.

1. A parallel can be established between the gradual turn of computer imaging toward representational and photorealistic (the industry term for synthetic images that look as through they were created using traditional photography or cinematography) images from the end of the 1970s through the early 1980s and the similar turn toward representational painting and photography in the art world during the same period.[3] In the art world, we witness photorealism, neo-expressionism, and postmodern "simulation" photography. In the computer world, during the same period, we may note the rapid development of the key algorithms for photorealistic 3-D image synthesis such as Phong shading, texture mapping, bump mapping, reflection mapping, and cast shadows, as well as the development of the first paint programs in the mid-1970s that allowed the manual creation of representational images, and eventually, toward the end of the 1980s, software such as Photoshop. In contrast, from the 1960s until late 1970s, computer imaging was mostly abstract because it was algorithm-driven and the technologies for inputting photographs into a computer were not easily accessible.[4] Similarly, the art world was dominated by non-representational movements, such as conceptual art, minimalism, and performance, or at least approached representation with a strong sense of irony and distance, as in the case of pop art. (It is possible to argue that the "simulation" artists of the 1980s also used "appropriated" images ironically, but in their case, the distance between the media and the artists' images visually became very small or even non-existent.)

2. In the twentieth century, a particular kind of image created by still photography and cinematography came to dominate modern visual culture. Some of its qualities are linear perspective, depth of field effect (so only a part of 3-D space is in focus), particular tonal and color range, and motion blur (rapidly moving objects appear smudged). Considerable research had to be accomplished before it became possible to simulate all these visual artifacts with computers. And even armed with special software, the designer still has to spend significant time manually recreating the look of photogra-

---

3. I am grateful to Peter Lunenfeld for pointing out this connection to me.

4. For an overview of the early history of computer art, which includes the discussion of the "turn to illusionism," see Frank Dietrich, "Visual Intelligence: The First Decade of Computer Art," in *IEEE Computer Graphics and Applications* 5, no. 7 (July 1985): 32–45.

phy or film. In other words, computer software does not produce such images by default. The paradox of digital visual culture is that although all imaging is becoming computer-based, the dominance of photographic and cinematic imagery is becoming even stronger. But rather than being a direct, "natural" result of photo and film technology, these images are constructed on computers. 3-D virtual worlds are subjected to depth of field and motion blur algorithms; digital video is run through special filters that simulate film grain; and so on.

Visually, these computer-generated or manipulated images are indistinguishable from traditional photo and film images, whereas on the level of "material" they are quite different, as they are made from pixels or represented by mathematical equations and algorithms. In terms of the kinds of operations that can be performed on them, they are also quite different from the images of photography and film. These operations, such as "copy and paste," "add," "multiply," "compress," and "filter" reflect, first of all, the logic of computer algorithms and the human-computer interface; only secondarily do they refer to dimensions inherently meaningful to human perception. (In fact, we can think of these operations as well as HCI in general as balancing between the two poles of computer logic and human logic, by which I mean the everyday ways of perception, cognition, causality, and motivation—in short, human everyday existence.)

Other aspects of the new logic of computer images can be derived from the general principles of new media: Many operations involved in their synthesis and editing are automated, they typically exist in many versions, they include hyperlinks, they act as interactive interfaces (thus, an image is something we expect to enter rather than stay on its surface), and so on. To summarize, *the visual culture of a computer age is cinematographic in its appearance, digital on the level of its material, and computational (i.e., software driven) in its logic.* What are the interactions between these three levels? Can we expect that cinematographic images (I use the phrase here to include the images of both traditional analog and computer-simulated cinematography and photography) will at some point be replaced by very different images whose appearance will be more in tune with their underlying computer-based logic?

My own feeling is that the answer to this question is no. Cinematographic images are very efficient for cultural communication. Because they share many qualities with natural perception, they are easily processed by the brain. Their similarity to "the real thing" allows designers to provoke emotions in viewers, as well as effectively visualize nonexistent objects and scenes. And because computer representation turns these images into numerically coded data that is discrete (pixels) and modular (layers), they become subject to all the economically beneficial effects of computerization—algorithmic manipulation, automation, variability, and so on. A digitally coded cinematographic image thus has two identities, so to speak: One satisfies the demands of human communication; another makes it suitable for computer-based practices of production and distribution.

3. Available theories and histories of illusion in art and media, from Gombrich's *Art and Illusion* and André Bazin's "The Myth of Total Cinema" to Stephen Bann's *The True Vine,* only deal with visual dimensions.[5] In my view, most of these theories have three arguments in common. These arguments concern three different relationships—image and physical reality, image and natural perception, present and past images:

1.   Illusionistic images share some features with the represented physical reality (for instance, the number of an object's angles).
2.   Illusionistic images share some features with human vision (for instance, linear perspective).
3.   Each period offers some new "features" that are perceived by audiences as an "improvement" over the previous period (for instance, the evolution of cinema from silent to sound to color).[6]

Until the arrival of computer media, these theories were sufficient because the human desire to simulate reality indeed focused on its visual appearance (although not exclusively—think, for instance, of the tradition of automata). Today, while still useful, the traditional analysis of visual illusionism needs to be supplemented by new theories. The reason is that the reality effect in many areas of new media only partially depends on an image's

---

5. André Bazin, *What is Cinema?* vol. 1 (Berkeley: University of California Press, 1967–71); Bann, *The True Vine.*

6. On the history of illusionism in cinema, see the influential theoretical analysis by Jean-Louis Comolli, "Machines of the Visible," *The Cinematic Apparatus,* ed. Teresa De Lauretis and Steven Heath (New York: St. Martin's Press), 1980. I discuss Comolli's argument in more detail in the "Synthetic Realism and Its Discontents" section.

appearance. Such areas of new media as computer games, motion simulators, virtual worlds, and VR, in particular, exemplify how computer-based illusionism functions differently. Rather than utilizing the single dimension of visual fidelity, they construct the reality effect on a number of dimensions, of which visual fidelity is but one. These new dimensions include active bodily engagement with a virtual world (for instance, the user of VR moves the whole body); the involvement of other senses beside vision (spatialized audio in virtual worlds and games, use of touch in VR, joysticks with force feedback, special vibrating and moving chairs for computer games and motion rides); and the accuracy of the simulation of physical objects, natural phenomena, anthropomorphic characters, and humans.

This last dimension, in particular, calls for an extensive analysis because of the variety of methods and subjects of simulation. If the history of illusionism in art and media largely revolves around the simulation of how things look, for computer simulation this is but one goal among many. Besides visual appearance, simulation in new media aims to model realistically how objects and humans act, react, move, grow, evolve, think, and feel. Physically-based modeling is used to simulate the behavior of inanimate objects and their interactions, such as a ball bouncing of the floor or a glass shattering. Computer games regularly use physical modeling to simulate collisions between objects and vehicle behavior—for instance, a car being bounced against the walls of the racing tracks, or the behavior of a plane in a flight simulation. Other methods such as AL, formal grammars, fractal geometry, and various applications of the complexity theory (popularly referred to as "chaos theory") are used to simulate natural phenomena such as waterfalls and ocean waves, and animal behavior (flocking birds, schools of fish). Yet another important area of simulation that also relies on many different methods is virtual characters and avatars, extensively used in movies, games, virtual worlds, and human-computer interfaces. Examples include enemies and monsters in *Quake;* army units in *WarCraft* and similar games; human-like creatures in *Creatures* and other AL games and toys; and anthropomorphic interfaces such as Microsoft Office Assistant in Windows 98—an animated character that periodically pops out in a small window offering help and tips. The goal of human simulation in itself can be further broken down into a set of various subgoals—simulation of human psychological states, human behavior, motivations, and emotions. (Thus, ultimately, the fully "realistic" simulation of a human being requires not only completely fulfilling the vision of the original AI paradigm but also going beyond it—since original AI was aimed solely at simulating human perception and thinking processes but not emotions and motivations.) Yet another kind of simulation involves modeling the dynamic behavior of whole systems composed from organic and/or nonorganic elements over time (for instance, the popular series of Sim games such as *SimCity* or *SimAnts,* which simulate a city and an ant colony, respectively).

And even in the visual dimension—the one dimension that new media "reality engines" share with traditional illusionistic techniques—things work very differently. New media change our concept of what an image is—because they turn a viewer into an active user. As a result, an illusionistic image is no longer something a subject simply looks at, comparing it with memories of represented reality to judge its reality effect. The new media image is something the user actively *goes into,* zooming in or clicking on individual parts with the assumption that they contain hyperlinks (for instance, imagemaps in Web sites). Moreover, *new media turn most images into image-interfaces and image-instruments.* The image becomes interactive, that is, it now functions as an interface between a user and a computer or other devices. The user employs an *image-interface* to control a computer, asking it to zoom into the image or display another one, start a software application, connect to the Internet, and so on. The user employs *image-instruments* to directly affect reality—move a robotic arm in a remote location, fire a missile, change the speed of a car and set the temperature, and so on. To evoke a term often used in film theory, new media move us from identification to action. What kinds of actions can be performed via an image, how easily they can be accomplished, their range—all these play a part in the user's assessment of the reality effect of the image.

Synthetic Realism and Its Discontents

"Realism" is the concept that inevitably accompanies the development and assimilation of 3-D computer graphics. In media, trade publications, and research papers, the history of technological innovation and research is presented as a progression toward realism—the ability to simulate any object in such a way that its computer image is indistinguishable from a photograph. At the same time, it is constantly pointed out that this realism is qualitatively different from the realism of optically based image technologies (photography, film), for the simulated reality is not indexically related to the existing world.

Despite this difference, the ability to generate three-dimensional stills does not represent a radical break in the history of the visual representation of the multitude comparable to the achievements of Giotto. A Renaissance painting and a computer image employ the same technique (a set of consistent depth cues) to create an illusion of space—existent or imaginary. The real break is the introduction of a moving synthetic image—interactive 3-D computer graphics and computer animation. With these technologies, a viewer has the experience of moving around a simulated 3-D space—something one cannot do with an illusionistic painting.

To better understand the nature of the "realism" of the synthetic moving image, it is relevant to consider a contiguous practice of the moving image—the cinema. I will approach the problem of "realism" in 3-D computer animation starting from the arguments advanced in film theory in regard to cinematic realism.

This section considers finished 3-D computer animations created beforehand and then incorporated in a film, television program, Web site, or computer game. In the case of animations generated by a computer in real-time, and thus dependent not only on available software but also on hardware capabilities, a somewhat different logic applies. An example of a new media object from the 1990s that uses both types of animation is a typical computer game. The interactive parts of the game are animated in real time. Periodically, the game switches to a "full motion video" mode. "Full motion video" is either a digital video sequence or a 3-D animation that has been prerendered and therefore has a higher level of detail—and thus "realism"—than the animations done in real time. The last section of this chapter, "Image, Narrative, and Illusion," considers how such temporal shifts, which are not limited to games but are typical of interactive new media objects in general, affect their "realism."

Technology and Style in Cinema

The idea of cinematic realism is associated first and foremost with André Bazin, for whom cinematic technology and style move toward a "total and complete representation of reality."[7] In "The Myth of Total Cinema," Bazin claims that the idea of cinema existed long before the medium actually appeared and that the development of cinema technology "little by little made a reality out of original 'myth'."[8] In this account, the modern technology of cinema is a realization of the ancient myth of mimesis, just as the development of aviation is a realization of the myth of Icarus. In another influential essay, "The Evolution of the Language of Cinema," Bazin reads the history of film style in similar teleological terms: The introduction of depth of field at the end of the 1930s and the subsequent innovations of Italian neorealists in the 1940s gradually allow the spectator to have a more intimate relation with the image than is possible in reality. The essays differ not only in that the first interprets film technology whereas the second concentrates on film style, but also in their distinct approaches to the problem of realism. In the first essay realism stands for the approximation of phenomenological qualities of reality, "the reconstruction of a perfect illusion of the outside world in sound, color and relief."[9] In the second essay, Bazin emphasizes that a realistic

---

7. Bazin, *What Is Cinema?* 20.

8. Ibid., 21.

9. Ibid., 20.

representation should also approximate the perceptual and cognitive dynamics of natural vision. For Bazin, this dynamic involves active exploration of visual reality. Consequently, he interprets the introduction of depth of field as a step toward realism because now the viewer can freely explore the space of film image.[10]

Against Bazin's "idealist" and evolutionary account, Jean-Louis Comolli proposes a "materialist" and fundamentally nonlinear reading of the history of cinematic technology and style. The cinema, Comolli tells us, "is born immediately as a social machine . . . from the anticipation and confirmation of its social profitability; economic, ideological and symbolic."[11] Comolli thus proposes to read the history of cinema techniques as an intersection of technical, aesthetic, social, and ideological determinations; however, his analyses clearly privilege the ideological function of the cinema. For Comolli, this function is "'objective' duplication of the 'real' itself conceived as specular reflection" (133). Along with other representational cultural practices, cinema works endlessly to reduplicate the visible, thus sustaining the illusion that it is the phenomenal forms that constitute the social "real"—rather than the "invisible" relations of productions. To fulfill its function, cinema must maintain and constantly update its "realism." Comolli sketches this process using two alternative figures—addition and substitution.

In terms of technological developments, the history of realism in the cinema is one of addition. First, additions are necessary to maintain the process of disavowal that for Comolli defines the nature of cinematic spectatorship (132). Each new technological development (sound, panchromatic stock, color) points out to viewers just how "unrealistic" the previous image was and also reminds them that the present image, even though more realistic, will also be superseded in the future—thus constantly sustaining the state of disavowal. Second, because cinema functions in a structure with other visual media, it has to keep up with their changing level of realism. For instance, by the 1920s the spread of photographic images that offered richer gradations of tones made the cinematic image seem harsh by comparison, and the film industry was forced to change to panchromatic stock to keep up

---

10. Ibid., 36–37.
11. Comolli, "Machines of the Visible," 122.

with the standard of photographic realism (131). This example is a good illustration of Comolli's reliance on Althusserian structuralist Marxism. Unprofitable economically for the film industry, this change is "profitable" in more abstract terms for the social structure as a whole, helping to sustain the ideology of the real/visible.

In terms of cinematic style, the history of realism in cinema is one of substitution of cinematic techniques. For instance, while the change to panchromatic stock adds to image quality, it leads to other losses. If earlier cinematic realism was maintained through the effects of depth, now "depth (perspective) loses its importance in the production of 'reality effects' in favor of shade, range, color" (131). So theorized, realistic effect in the cinema appears as a constant sum in an equation with a few variables that change historically and have equal weight: If more shading or color is "put in," perspective can be "taken out." Comolli follows the same logic of substitution/substraction in sketching the development of cinematic style in its first two decades: The early cinematographic image announces its realism through an abundance of moving figures and the use of deep focus; later, these devices fade away and others, such as fictional logic, psychological characters, coherent space-time of narration, take over (130).

While for Bazin realism functions as an Idea (in a Hegelian sense), for Comolli it plays an ideological role (in a Marxist sense); for David Bordwell and Janet Staiger, realism in film is connected first and foremost with the industrial organization of cinema. Put differently, Bazin draws the idea of realism from mythological, utopian thinking. For him, realism is found in the space between reality and a transcendental spectator. Comolli sees realism as an effect produced between the image and the historical viewer and continuously sustained through the ideologically determined additions and substitutions of cinematic technologies and techniques. Bordwell and Staiger locate realism within the institutional discourses of film industries, implying that it is a rational and pragmatic tool in industrial competition.[12] Emphasizing that cinema is an industry like any other, Bordwell and Staiger attribute the changes in cinematic technology to factors shared by all modern industries—efficiency, product differentiation, maintenance of a standard of qual-

---

12. Bordwell and Staiger, "Technology, Style, and Mode of Production," 243–261.

ity (247). One of the advantages of adopting an industrial model is that it allows the authors to look at specific agents—manufacturing and supplying
firms and professional associations (250). The latter are particularly important, since it is in their discourses (conferences, trade meetings, and publications) that the standards and goals of stylistic and technical innovations are
articulated.

Bordwell and Staiger agree with Comolli that the development of cinematic technology is not linear; however, they claim that it is not random either, as the professional discourses articulate goals of the research and set the
limits for permissible innovations (260). According to Bordwell and Staiger,
realism is one of these goals. They believe that such a definition of a realism
is specific to Hollywood:

"Showmanship," realism, invisibility: such cannons guided the SMPE [Society of
Motion Picture Engineers] members toward understanding the acceptable and un-
acceptable choices in technical innovations, and these too became teleological. In another industry, the engineer's goal might be an unbreakable glass or a lighter alloy.
In the film industry, the goals were not only increased efficiency, economy, and flexibility but also spectacle, concealment of artifice, and what Goldsmith [1934 president of SMPE] called "the production of an acceptance semblance of reality." (258)

Bordwell and Staiger are satisfied with Goldsmith's definition of realism
as "the production of an acceptance semblance of reality." However, such a
general and transhistorical definition does not seem to have any specificity
for Hollywood and thus cannot really account for the direction of technological innovation. Moreover, although they claim to have successfully reduced realism to a rational and functional notion, in fact they have not
managed to eliminate Bazin's idealism. It reappears in the comparison between the goals of innovation in film and other industries. If the aviation industry expends effort developing "lighter alloy," does this not remind us of
the myth of Icarus; and is there not something mythical and fairytale-like
about "unbreakable glass"?

Technology and Style in Computer Animation
How can these three influential accounts of cinematic realism be used to approach the problem of realism in 3-D computer animation? Bazin, Comolli,
and Bordwell and Staiger offer us three different strategies, three different

starting points. Bazin builds his argument by comparing the changing quality of the cinematic image with the phenomenological impression of visual reality. Comolli's analysis suggests a different strategy—to think of the history of computer graphics technologies and changing stylistic conventions as a chain of substitutions that function to sustain the reality effect for audiences. Finally, to follow Bordwell and Staiger's approach is to analyze the relationship between the character of realism in computer animation and the particular industrial organization of the computer graphics industry. (For instance, we can ask how this character is affected by the cost difference between hardware and software development.) Further, we should pay attention to professional organizations in the field and their discourses that articulate the goals of research including "admonitions about the range and nature of permissible innovations" (Bordwell and Staiger, 260). I will try the three strategies in turn.

If we follow Bazin's approach and compare images drawn from the history of 3-D computer graphics with the visual perception of natural reality, his evolutionary narrative appears to be confirmed. During the 1970s and the 1980s, computer images progressed towards a fuller and fuller illusion of reality—from wireframe displays to smooth shadows, detailed textures, and aerial perspective; from geometric shapes to moving animal and human figures; from Cimabue to Giotto to Leonardo and beyond. Bazin's idea that deep focus cinematography allowed the spectator a more active position in relation to the film image, thus bringing cinematic perception closer to real life perception, also finds a recent equivalent in interactive computer graphics, where the user can freely explore the virtual space of the display from different points of view. And with such extensions of computer graphics technology as virtual reality, the promise of Bazin's "total realism" appears to be closer than ever, literally within arm's reach of the VR user.

The history of the style and technology of computer animation can also be seen in a different way. Comolli reads the history of realistic media as a constant trade-off of codes, a chain of substitutions producing the reality effect for audiences, rather than as an asymptotic movement toward the axis labeled "reality." His interpretation of the history of film style is first of all supported by the shift he observes between the cinematic style of the 1900s and the 1920s, the example I have already mentioned. Early film announces its realism by excessive representations of deep space achieved through every possible means: deep focus, moving figures, frame compositions which emphasize the effect of linear perspective. In the 1920s, with the adaptation of panchromatic film stock, "depth (perspective) loses its importance in the production of 'reality effects' in favor of shade, range, color" (Comolli, 131). A similar trade-off of codes can be observed during the short history of commercial 3-D computer animation, which begins around 1980. Initially, the animations were schematic and cartoon-like because the objects could only be rendered in wireframe or facet-shaded form. Illusionism was limited to the indication of an object's volume. To compensate for this limited illusionism in the representation of objects, computer animations of the early 1980s ubiquitously showed deep space. This was done by emphasizing linear perspective (mostly, through the excessive use of grids) and by building animations around rapid movement in depth in the direction perpendicular to the screen. These strategies are exemplified by the computer sequences of the Disney movie *Tron,* released in 1982. Toward the end of the 1980s, with commercial availability of such techniques as smooth shading, texture mapping, and cast shadows, the representation of objects in animations approached more closely the ideal of photorealism. At this time, the codes by which early animation signaled deep space started to disappear. In place of rapid in-depth movements and grids, animations began to feature lateral movements in shallow space.

The observed substitution of realistic codes in the history of 3-D computer animation seems to confirm Comolli's argument. The introduction of new illusionistic techniques dislodges old ones. Comolli explains this process of sustaining the reality effect from the point of view of audiences. Following Bordwell and Staiger's approach, we can consider the same phenomenon from the producer's point of view. For the production companies, the constant substitution of codes is necessary to stay competitive. As in every industry, the producers of computer animation stay competitive by differentiating their products. To attract clients, a company has to be able to offer some novel effects and techniques. But why do the old techniques disappear? The specificity of the industrial organization of the computer animation field is that it is driven by software innovation. (In this respect, the field is closer to the computer industry as a whole than it is to the film industry or to graphic design.) New algorithms to produce new effects are constantly developed. To stay competitive, a company has to incorporate quickly the new software into their offerings. Animations are designed to show off the latest algorithm. Correspondingly, the effects possible with older algorithms are featured less often—available to everybody else in the field, they no longer signal "state of the art." Thus, the trade-off of codes in the history of computer animation can be related to the competitive pressure to utilize quickly the latest achievements of software research.

While commercial companies employ programmers capable of adopting published algorithms for the production environment, the theoretical work of developing these algorithms mainly takes place in academic computer science departments and in the research groups of top computer companies such as Microsoft and SGI. To pursue further the question of realism, we need to ask about the direction of this work. Do computer graphics researchers share a common goal?

In analyzing the same question for the film industry, Bordwell and Staiger claim that realism "was rationally adopted as an engineering aim" (258). They attempt to discover the specificity of Hollywood's conception of realism in the discourses of professional organizations such as the SMPE. For the computer graphics industry, the major professional organization is SIGGRAPH. Its annual conventions combine a trade show, a festival of computer animation, and a scientific conference where the best new research work is presented. The conferences also serve as the meeting place for researchers, engineers, and commercial designers. If the research has a common direction, we can expect to find its articulations in SIGGRAPH proceedings.

Indeed, a typical research paper includes a reference to realism as the goal of investigations in the computer graphics field. For example, a 1987 paper presented by three highly recognized scientists offers this definition of realism:

Reys is an image rendering system developed at Lucasfilm Ltd. and currently in use at Pixar. In designing Reys, our goal was an architecture optimized for fast high-quality rendering of complex animated scenes. By fast we mean being able to compute a feature-length film in about a year; *high quality means virtually indistinguishable from live action motion picture photography; and complex means as visually rich as real scenes.*[13]

According to this definition, achieving synthetic realism means attaining two goals—the simulation of the codes of traditional cinematography and the

---

13. R. Cook, L. Carpenter, and E. Catull, "The Reys Image Rendering Architecture," *Computer Graphics* 21.4 (1987): 95 (emphasis mine).

simulation of the perceptual properties of real life objects and environments. The first goal, the simulation of cinematographic codes, was in principle solved early on, as these codes are well-defined and few in number. Every current professional computer animation system incorporates a virtual camera with variable length lens, depth of field effects, motion blur, and controllable lights that simulate the lights available to a traditional cinematographer.

The second goal, the simulation of "real scenes," turned out to be more complex. Creating a computer time-based representation of an object involves solving three separate problems—the representation of an object's shape, the effects of light on its surface, and the pattern of movement. To have a general solution for each problem requires an exact simulation of underlying physical properties and processes—a task whose extreme mathematical complexity renders it impossible to execute. For instance, to simulate fully the shape of a tree would involve mathematically "growing" every leaf, every branch, every piece of bark; and to simulate fully the color of a tree's surface, a programmer would have to consider every other object in the scene, from grass to clouds to other trees. In practice, computer graphics researchers have resorted to solving particular local cases, developing a number of *unrelated* techniques for simulation of *some* kinds of shapes, materials, lighting effects, and movements.

The result is a realism that is highly uneven. Of course, one may suggest that this is not an entirely new development and that it can already be observed in the history of twentieth-century optical and electronic representational technologies, which allow for a more precise rendering of certain features of visual reality at the expense of others. For instance, both color film and color television were designed to assure acceptable rendering of human flesh tones at the expense of other colors. However, the limitations of synthetic realism are qualitatively different.

In the case of optically based representation, the camera records already existing reality. Everything that exists can be photographed. Camera artifacts, such as depth of field, film grain, and limited tonal range, affects the image as a whole.

In the case of 3-D computer graphics, the situation is quite different. Now reality itself has to be constructed from scratch before it can be photographed by a virtual camera. Therefore, the photorealistic simulation of "real scenes" is practically impossible, as techniques available to commercial animators only cover the particular phenomena of visual reality. An animator using a particular software package can, for instance, easily create the shape of a human face, but not hair; materials such as plastic or metal but not cloth or leather; the flight of a bird but not the jumps of a frog. The realism of computer animation is highly uneven, reflecting the range of problems addressed and solved.

What determined which particular problems received priority in research? To a large extent, this was determined by the needs of the early sponsors of this research—the Pentagon and Hollywood. I am not concerned here to trace fully the history of these sponsorships. What is important for my argument is that the requirements of military and entertainment applications led researchers to concentrate on the simulation of the particular phenomena of visual reality, such as landscapes and moving figures.

One of the original motivations behind the development of photorealistic computer graphics was its application for flight simulators and other training technology.[14] And since simulators require synthetic landscapes, a lot of research went into techniques to render clouds, rugged terrain, trees, and aerial perspective. Thus the work that led to the development of the famous technique to represent natural shapes, such as mountains, using fractal mathematics was done at Boeing.[15] Other well-known algorithms to simulate natural scenes and clouds were developed by the Grumman Aerospace Corporation.[16] The latter technology was used for flight simulators and also was applied to pattern recognition research in target tracking by a missile.[17]

Another major sponsor was the entertainment industry, which was lured by the promise of lowering the costs of film and television production. In 1979 Lucasfilm, Ltd., George Lucas's company, organized a computer animation research division. It hired the best computer scientists in the field to produce animations for special effects. Research for the effects in such films as *Star Trek II: The Wrath of Khan* (Nicholas Meyer, Paramount Pictures,

---

14. Cynthia Goodman, *Digital Visions* (New York: Harry N. Abrams, 1987), 22, 102.

15. L. Carpenter, A. Fournier, and D. Fussell, "Fractal Surfaces," *Communications of the ACM,* 1981.

16. Geoffrey Y. Gardner, "Simulation of Natural Scenes Using Textured Quadric Surfaces," *Computer Graphics* 18.3 (1984): 21–30.

Geoffrey Y. Gardner, "Visual Simulation of Clouds," *Computer Graphics* 19.3 (1985): 297–304.

17. Gardner, "Simulation of Natural Scenes," 19.

special effects by Industrial Light and Magic, 1982) and *Return of the Jedi* (Richard Marquand, Lucasfilm Ltd., special effects by Industrial Light and Magic, 1983) led to the development of important algorithms that became widely used.[18]

Along with creating particular effects for films such as star fields and explosions, a lot of research activity has been dedicated to the development of moving humanoid figures and synthetic actors. This is not surprising since commercial film and video productions center around human characters. Significantly, the first time computer animation was used in a feature film (*Looker*, Michael Crichton, Warner Brothers, 1981) was to create a three-dimensional model of an actress. One of the early attempt to simulate human facial expressions featured synthetic replicas of Marilyn Monroe and Humphrey Bogart.[19] In another acclaimed 3-D animation, produced by Kleiser-Wolczak Construction Company in 1988, a synthetic human figure was humorously cast as Nestor Sextone, a candidate for the presidency of the Synthetic Actors Guild.

The task of creating fully synthetic human actors has turned out to be more complex than was originally anticipated. Researchers continue to work on this problem. For instance, the 1992 SIGGRAPH conference presented a session on "Humans and Clothing" that featured such papers as "Dressing Animated Synthetic Actors with Complex Deformable Clothes"[20] and "A Simple Method for Extracting the Natural Beauty of Hair."[21] Meanwhile, Hollywood has created a new genre of films (*Terminator 2, Jurassic Park, Casper, Flubber,* etc.) structured around "the state of the art" in digital actor simulation. In computer graphics it is still easier to create the fantastic and extraordinary than to simulate ordinary human beings. Consequently, each of these films is centered around an unusual character who, in fact, consists

---

18. William T. Reeves, "Particle Systems—A Technique for Modeling a Class of Fuzzy Objects," *ACM Transactions on Graphics* 2.3 (1983): 91–108.

19. Nadia Magnenat-Thalmann, and Daniel Thalmann, "The Direction of Synthetic Actors in the Film *Rendezvous in Montreal*," *IEEE Computer Graphics and Applications,* December 1987.

20. M. Carignan, "Dressing Animated Synthetic Actors with Complex Deformable Clothes," *Computer Graphics* 26.2 (1992): 99–104.

21. K. Anjyo, Y. Usami, and T. Kurihara, "A Simple Method for Extracting the Natural Beauty of Hair," *Computer Graphics* 26.2 (1992): 111–120.

of a series of special effects—morphing into different shapes, exploding into particles, and so on.

The preceding analysis applies to the period during which the techniques of 3-D animation were undergoing continuous development—from the middle 1970s to the middle 1990s. By the end of this period, the software tools became relatively stable; at the same time, the dramatically decreased cost of hardware led to a significant reduction of the time it takes to render complex animations. Put differently, the animators were now able to use more complex geometric and rendering models, thus achieving a stronger reality effect. *Titanic* (1997) featured hundreds of computer-animated "extras," and ninety-five percent of *Star Wars: Episode 1* (1999) was constructed on a computer. However, the dynamics that characterized the early period of prerendered computer animation returned in new areas of new media—computer games and virtual worlds (such as VRML and Active Worlds scenes), which all use 3-D computer graphics generated in realtime. Here the Bazinian evolution towards fuller and fuller realism that characterized the development of computer animation in the 1970s and the 1980s was replayed once again at accelerated speed. As the speed of CPUs and graphics cards kept increasing, computer games moved from the flat shading of the original *Doom* (1993) to the more detailed world of *Unreal* (Epic Games, 1997), which featured shadows, reflections, and transparency. In the area of virtual worlds designed to run on typical computers without specialized graphics accelerators, the same evolution proceeded at a much slower pace.

The Icons of Mimesis

Although the privileging of certain areas in research can be attributed to the needs of sponsors, other areas receive consistent attention for a different reason. To support the idea of progress of computer graphics toward realism, researchers privilege particular subjects that culturally connote the mastery of illusionistic representation.

Historically, the idea of illusionism has been connected with the success in representation of certain subjects. The original episode in the history of Western painting, which I have already invoked, is the story of the competition of Zeuxis and Parrhasius. The grapes painted by Zeuxis symbolize his skill in creating living nature out of the inanimate matter of paint. Further examples in the history of art include the celebration of the mimetic skill of those painters who were able to simulate another symbol of living nature—

human flesh. Not surprisingly, throughout the history of computer animation, the simulation of the human figure has served as a yardstick for measuring the progress of the whole field.

The painting tradition has its own iconography of subjects connoting mimesis; moving image media rely on a different set of subjects. Steven Neale describes how early film demonstrated its authenticity by representing moving nature: "What was lacking [in photographs] was the wind, the very index of real, natural movement. Hence the obsessive contemporary fascination, not just with movement, not just with scale, but also with waves and sea spray, with smoke and spray."[22] Computer graphics researchers resort to similar subjects to signify the realism of animation. "Moving nature" presented at SIGGRAPH conferences have included animations of smoke, fire, sea waves, and moving grass.[23] These privileged signs of realism overcompensate for the inability of computer graphics researchers to simulate fully "real scenes."

In summary, the differences between cinematic and synthetic realism begin on the level of ontology. New realism is partial and uneven, rather than analog and uniform. The artificial reality that can be simulated with 3-D computer graphics is fundamentally incomplete, full of gaps and white spots.

Who determines what will be filled and what will remain a gap in the simulated world? As I have noted, the available computer graphics techniques reflect the particular needs of the military and industrial groups which paid for their development. The ability of certain subjects to connote the mastery of illusionism also makes researchers pay more attention to some areas of the map, so to speak, and ignore others. In addition, as computer graphics techniques migrate from specialized markets toward mass consumers, they become biased in yet another way.

---

22. Steve Neale, *Cinema and Technology* (Bloomington: Indiana University Press, 1985), 52.

23. The following are just a few well-known classics in the field devoted to this research: Nelson Max, "Vectorized Procedure Models for Natural Terrain: Waves and Islands in the Sunset," *Computer Graphics* 15.3 (1981); Ken Perlin, "An Image Synthesizer," *Computer Graphics* 19.3 (1985): 287–296; William T. Reeves, "Particle Systems—A Technique for Modeling a Class of Fuzzy Objects"; William T. Reeves and Ricki Blau, "Approximate and Probabilistic Algorithms for Shading and Rendering Structured Particle Systems," *Computer Graphics* 19.3 (1985): 313–322.

The amount of labor involved in constructing reality from scratch on a computer makes it hard to resist the temptation to utilize preassembled, standardized objects, characters, and behaviors readily provided by software manufacturers—fractal landscapes, checkerboard floors, complete characters, and so on. As discussed in the "Selection" section, every program comes with libraries of ready-to-use models, effects, or even complete animations. For instance, a user of the Dynamation program (a part of the popular Alias|Wavefront 3-D software) can access complete preassembled animations of moving hair, rain, a comet's tail, or smoke, with a single mouse click. If even professional designers rely on ready-made objects and animations, the end users of virtual worlds on the Internet, who usually do not have graphic or programming skills, have no other choice. Not surprisingly, VRML software companies and Web virtual world providers encourage users to choose from the libraries of 3-D objects and avatars that they supply. Worlds Inc., the provider of Worlds software used to create on-line virtual 3-D chat environments, offers its users a library of one hundred 3-D avatars.[24] The Active Worlds, which offers "3D community based environments on the Internet," allows its over one million users (April 1999 data) to choose from over one thousand different worlds, some of which are provided by a company and others built by users themselves.[25] As the complexity of these worlds increases, we can expect a whole market for detailed virtual sets, characters with programmable behaviors, and even complete environments (a bar with customers, a city square, a famous historical episode, etc.) from which a user can put together her or his own "unique" virtual world. And although companies such as Active Worlds provide end users with software that allows them to build and customize quickly their virtual dwellings, avatars, and whole virtual universes, each of these constructs has to adhere to standards established by the company. Thus, behind the freedom on the surface lies standardization on a deeper level. While a hundred years ago, the user of a Kodak camera was asked merely to push a button, she still had the freedom to point the camera at anything. Now, "You push the button, we do the rest" has become "You push the button, we create your world."

---

24. http://www.worlds.com.

25. http://www.activeworlds.com.

I hope that this section has demonstrated that the accounts of realism developed in film theory can be usefully employed to talk about realism in new media. But that does not mean that the question of computer realism is exhausted. In the twentieth century, new technologies of representation and simulation replace each other in rapid succession, thereby creating a perpetual lag between our experience of their effects and our understanding of this experience. The reality effect of a moving image is a case in point. As film scholars were producing increasingly detailed studies of cinematic realism, film itself was already being undermined by 3-D computer animation. Indeed, consider the following chronology.

Bazin's *Evolution of the Language of Cinema* is a compilation of three articles written between 1952 and 1955. In 1951 the viewers of the popular television show "See it Now" for the first time saw a computer graphics display, generated by the MIT computer Whirlwind, built in 1949. One animation was of a bouncing ball, another of a rocket's trajectory.[26]

Comolli's *Machines of the Visible* was given as a paper at the seminal conference on the cinematic apparatus in 1978. The same year saw the publication of a crucial paper for the history of computer graphics research. It presented a method to simulate bump textures, which is still one of the most powerful techniques of synthetic photorealism.[27]

Bordwell and Staiger's chapter, "Technology, Style, and Mode of Production," forms a part of the comprehensive *The Classical Hollywood Cinema: Film Style and Mode of Production to 1960,* published in 1985. By this year, most of the fundamental photorealistic techniques had been discovered and turnkey computer animation systems were already employed by media production companies.

As 3-D synthetic imagery is used more and more widely in contemporary visual culture, the problem of realism has to be studied afresh. And while many theoretical accounts developed in relation to cinema do hold when applied to synthetic imaging, we cannot assume that any concept or model can be taken for granted. Redefining the very concepts of representation, illusion, and simulation, new media challenge us to understand in new ways how visual realism functions.

---

26. Goodman, *Digital Visions,* 18–19.

27. J. F. Blinn, "Simulation of Wrinkled Surfaces," *Computer Graphics* 12, no. 3 (August 1978): 286–92.

The Synthetic Image and Its Subject

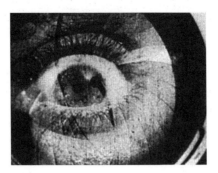

As we saw, the achievement of photorealism is the main goal of research in the field of computer graphics. The field defines photorealism as the ability to simulate any object in such a way that its computer image is indistinguishable from its photograph. Since this goal was first articulated at the end of the 1970s, significant progress has been made toward getting closer to this goal: Compare, for instance, the computer images of *Tron* (1982) with those of *Star Wars: Episode 1* (1999). Yet common opinion still holds that synthetic 3-D images generated by computer graphics are not yet (or perhaps will never be) as "realistic" in rendering visual reality as images obtained through a photographic lens. In this section, I will suggest that this common opinion is mistaken. Such synthetic photographs are already more "realistic" than traditional photographs. In fact, they are too real.

This seemingly paradoxical argument will become less strange once we place the current preoccupation with photorealism in a larger historical framework, considering not only the present and recent past (computer imaging and analog film, respectively) but also the more distant past and the future of visual illusionism. For although the computer graphics field tries desperately to replicate the particular kind of images created by twentieth-century film technology, these images represent only one episode in a longer history of visual culture. We should not assume that the history of illusion ends with 35mm frames projected on the screen across the movie hall—even if a film camera is replaced with computer software, a film projector is replaced with a digital projector, and the film reel itself is replaced with data transmitted over a computer network.

Georges Méliès, the Father of Computer Graphics

When a future historian writes about the computerization of cinema in the 1990s, she will highlight such movies as *Terminator 2* and *Jurassic Park*. Along with a few others, these films by James Cameron and Steven Spielberg were responsible for turning Hollywood around: from extreme skepticism about computer animation in the early 1990s to a full embrace by the middle of the decade. These two movies, along with the host of others that followed in their wake, dramatically demonstrated that total synthetic realism seemed to be in sight. Yet they also exemplified the triviality of what at first may appear to be an outstanding technical achievement—the ability to fake visual reality. For what is faked is, of course, not reality but photographic reality, reality as seen by the camera lens. In other words, what computer graphics have (almost) achieved is not realism, but rather only *photorealism*— the ability to fake not our perceptual and bodily experience of reality but only its photographic image.[28] This image exists outside our consciousness, on a screen—a window of limited size that presents a still imprint of a small part of outer reality, filtered through a lens with limited depth of field, and then filtered through the film's grain and limited tonal range. It is only this film-based image that computer graphics technology has learned to simulate. And the reason we may think that computer graphics has succeeded in faking reality is that, over the course of the last hundred and fifty years, we have come to accept the image of photography and film as reality.

What is faked is only a film-based image. Once we came to accept the photographic image as reality, the way to its future simulation was open. What remained were small details—the development of digital computers (1940s) followed by a perspective-generating algorithm (early 1960s), and then working out how to make a simulated object solid with shadow, reflection, and texture (1970s), and finally simulating artifacts of the lens such as motion blur and depth of field (1980s). So, while the distance from the first computer graphics images, circa 1960, to the synthetic dinosaurs of *Jurassic Park* in the 1990s is tremendous, we should not be too impressed. Conceptually, photorealistic computer graphics had already appeared with Félix Nadar's photographs in the

---

28. Research in VR aims to go beyond the screen image to simulate both the perceptual and bodily experience of reality.

1840s and certainly with the first films of Georges Méliès in the 1890s. Conceptually, they are the inventors of 3-D photorealistic computer graphics.

In saying this, I do not want to negate the human ingenuity and the tremendous amount of labor that today goes into creating computer-generated special effects. Indeed, if our civilization has any equivalent to medieval cathedrals, it is special effects Hollywood films. They are truly epic both in their scale and attention to detail. Assembled by thousands of highly skilled craftsmen over the course of years, each such movie is the ultimate display of collective craftsmanship that we have today. But if medieval masters left after themselves material wonders of stone and glass inspired by religious faith, today our craftsmen leave only pixel sets to be projected on movie theater screens or played on computer monitors. These are immaterial cathedrals made of light; and appropriately, they often still have religious referents, both in the stories (consider, for example, the Christian references in *Star Wars: Episode 1:* Skywalker was conceived without a father, etc.) and in the grandeur and transcendence of their virtual sets.

Jurassic Park and Socialist Realism

Consider one of these immaterial cathedrals: *Jurassic Park.* This triumph of computer simulation took more than two years of work by dozens of designers, animators, and programmers at Industrial Light and Magic (ILM), one of the premier companies specializing in the production of computer animation for feature films in the world today. Because a few seconds of computer animation often requires months and months of work, only the huge budget of a Hollywood blockbuster could pay for such extensive and highly detailed computer-generated scenes as those of *Jurassic Park.* Most of the 3-D computer animation produced today has a much lower degree of photorealism, and this photorealism, as I have shown in the previous section, is uneven, higher for some kinds of objects and lower for others. And even for ILM, the photorealistic simulation of human beings, the ultimate goal of computer animation, still remains impossible. (Some scenes in the 1997 *Titanic* feature hundreds of synthetic human figures, yet they appear for a few seconds and are quite small, being far away from the camera.)

Typical images produced with 3-D computer graphics still appear unnaturally clean, sharp, and geometric looking. Their limitations especially stand out when juxtaposed with a normal photograph. Thus one of the landmark achievements of *Jurassic Park* was the seamless integration of film footage of real scenes with computer-simulated objects. To achieve this integration, computer-generated images had to be degraded; their perfection had to be diluted to match the imperfection of film's graininess.

First, the animators needed to figure out the resolution at which to render computer graphics elements. If the resolution were too high, the computer image would have more detail than the film image, and its artificiality would become apparent. Just as medieval masters guarded their painting secrets, leading computer graphics companies used to carefully guard the resolution of images they simulate.

Once computer-generated images are combined with film images, additional tricks are used to diminish their perfection. With the help of special algorithms, the straight edges of computer-generated objects are softened. Barely visible noise is added to the overall image to blend computer and film elements. Sometimes, as in the final battle between the two protagonists in *Terminator 2,* the scene is staged in a particular location (in this example, a smoky factory), which justifies the addition of smoke or fog to blend further the film and synthetic elements.

So, although we normally think that synthetic photographs produced with computer graphics are inferior to real photographs, in fact, they are *too perfect.* But beyond that we can also say that, paradoxically, they are also *too real.*

The synthetic image is free of the limitations of both human and camera vision. It can have unlimited resolution and an unlimited level of detail. It is free of the depth-of-field effect, this inevitable consequence of the lens, so everything is in focus. It is also free of grain—the layer of noise created by film stock and by human perception. Its colors are more saturated, and its sharp lines follow the economy of geometry. From the point of view of human vision, it is hyperreal. And yet, it is completely realistic. The synthetic image is the result of a different, more perfect than human, vision.

Whose vision is it? It is the vision of a computer, a cyborg, an automatic missile. It is a realistic representation of human vision in the future when it will be augmented by computer graphics and cleansed of noise. It is the vision of a digital grid. *Synthetic computer-generated imagery is not an inferior representation of our reality, but a realistic representation of a different reality.*

By the same logic, we should not consider clean, skinless, too flexible, and at the same time too jerky, human figures in 3-D computer animation as unrealistic, as imperfect approximations to the real thing—our bodies. They are perfectly realistic representations of a cyborg body yet to come, of a world reduced to geometry, where efficient representation via a geometric model becomes the basis of reality. The synthetic image simply represents the future. In other words, *if a traditional photograph always points to a past event, a synthetic photograph points to a future event.*

Is this a totally new situation? Was there already an aesthetic that consistently pointed to the future? In order to help us locate this aesthetic historically, I will invoke a painting by the Russian-born conceptual artists Komar and Melamid. Called *Bolsheviks Returning Home after a Demonstration* (1981–82), it depicts two workers, one carrying a red flag, who come across a tiny dinosaur, smaller than a human hand, standing in the snow. Part of the 'Nostalgic Socialist Realism' series, this painting was created a few years after the painters had arrived in the United States, well before Hollywood embraced computer-generated visuals. Yet it seems to comment on such movies as *Jurassic Park* and on Hollywood as a whole, connecting its fictions with the fictions of Soviet history as depicted by Socialist Realism, the official style of Soviet art from the early 1930s until the late 1950s.

Taking the hint from this painting, we are now in a position to characterize the aesthetics of *Jurassic Park.* This aesthetic is one of Soviet Socialist Realism. Socialist realism wanted to show the future in the present by projecting the perfect world of future socialist society onto a visual reality familiar to the viewer—the streets, interiors, and faces of Russia in the middle of the twentieth century—tired and underfed, scared and exhausted from fear, unkempt and gray. Socialist realism had to retain enough of then-everyday reality while showing how that reality would look in the future when everyone's body would be healthy and muscular, every street modern, every face transformed by the spirituality of communist ideology. This is how socialist realism differs from pure science fiction, which does not have to carry any feature of today's reality into the future. In contrast, Socialist Realism had to superimpose the future on the present, projecting the Communist ideal onto the very different reality familiar to viewers. Importantly, Socialist realism never depicted this future directly: There is not a single Socialist Realist work of art set in the future. Science fiction as a genre did not exist in Russia from the early 1930s until Stalin's death. The idea was not to make the workers dream about the perfect future while closing their eyes to imperfect reality, but rather to make them see the signs of this future in the reality around them. This is one of the meanings behind Vertov's notion of the "communist decoding of the world." To decode the world in such a way means to recognize the future all around you.

The same superimposition of the future onto the present happens in *Jurassic Park*. It tries to show the future of sight itself—the perfect cyborg vision, free of noise and capable of grasping infinite details. This vision is exemplified by the original computer-graphics images before they were blended with film images. But just as Socialist Realist paintings blended the perfect future with the imperfect reality, *Jurassic Park* blends the future supervision of computer graphics with the familiar vision of the film image. In *Jurassic Park,* the computer image bends down before the film image; its perfection is undermined by every possible means and is also masked by the film's content. As already discussed, computer-generated images, originally clean and sharp, free of focus and grain, are degraded in a variety of ways: Resolution is reduced; edges are softened; depth of field and grain effect artificially added. Additionally, the very content of the film—prehistoric dinosaurs that come to life—can be interpreted as another way to mask the potentially disturbing reference to our cyborg future. The dinosaurs are present to tell us that computer images belong safely to a past long gone—even though we have every reason to believe that they are messengers from a future still to come.

In that respect *Jurassic Park* and *Terminator 2* are opposites. If in *Jurassic Park* the dinosaurs function to convince us that computer imagery belongs to the past, the Terminator in *Terminator 2* is more "honest." He himself is a messenger from the future—a cyborg who can take on human appearance. His true form is that of a futuristic alloy. In perfect correspondence with this logic, this form is represented with computer graphics. While his true body perfectly reflects its surrounding reality, the very nature of these reflections shows us the future of human and machine sight. The reflections are extrasharp and clean, without any blur. This is indeed the look produced by the reflection mapping algorithm, one of the standard techniques to achieve photorealism. Thus to represent the Terminator who comes from the future, designers used the standard computer graphics techniques without degrading them; in contrast, in *Jurassic Park* the dinosaurs that come from the past were created by systematically degrading computer images. What of course is the past in this movie is the film medium itself—its grain, its depth of focus, its motion blur, its low resolution.

This, then, is the paradox of 3-D photorealistic computer animation. Its images are not inferior to those of traditional photography. They are perfectly real—all too real.

Illusion, Narrative, and Interactivity

Having analyzed computer illusionism from the point of view of its production and the longer history of visual illusion, I now want to look at it from a different perspective. While existing theories of illusionism assume that the subject acts strictly as a viewer, new media, more often than not, turn the subject into a user. The subject is expected to interact with a representation—click on menus or the image itself, making selections and decisions. What effect does interactivity have on the reality effect of an image? What is more important for the realism of a representation: faithfully simulating physical laws and human motivations, or accurately simulating the visual aspects of reality? For instance, does a racing game that uses a precise collision model but poor visuals feel more real than a game that has richer images but a less precise model? Or do the simulation dimensions and the visual dimensions support each other, adding up to a total effect?

In this section, I will focus on a particular aspect of the more general question of the production of illusionism in interactive computer objects. The aspect that I will consider has to do with time. Web sites, virtual worlds, computer games and many other types of hypermedia applications are characterized by a peculiar temporal dynamic—constant, repetitive oscillation between an illusion and its suspense. These new media objects keep reminding us of their artificiality, incompleteness, and constructedness. They present us with a perfect illusion only next to reveal its underlying machinery.

Web surfing in the 1990s provides a perfect example. A typical user may be spending equal time looking at a page and waiting for the next page to download. During waiting periods, the act of communication itself—bits traveling through the network—becomes the message. The user keeps checking whether the connection is being made, glancing back and forth between the animated icon and the status bar. Using Roman Jakobson's model of communication functions, we can say that communication comes to be dominated by contact, or the phatic function—it is centered on the physical channel and the very act of connection between addresser and addressee.[29]

Jakobson writes about verbal communication between two people who, in order to check whether the channel works, address each other: "Do you hear me?" "Do you understand me?" But in Web communication there is no human addresser, only a machine. So as the user keeps checking whether the information is coming, she actually addresses the machine itself. Or rather, the machine addresses the user. The machine reveals itself; it reminds the user of its existence—not only because the user is forced to wait but also because she is forced to witness how the message is being constructed over time. A page fills in part by part, top to bottom; text comes before images; images arrive in low resolution and are gradually refined. Finally, everything comes together in a smooth sleek image—the image that will be destroyed with the next click.

Interaction with most 3-D virtual worlds is characterized by the same temporal dynamic. Consider the technique called "distancing" or "level of detail," which for years has been used in VR simulations and later was adapted to 3-D games and VRML scenes. The idea is to render the models more crudely when the user is moving through virtual space; when the user stops, details gradually fill in. Another variation of the same technique involves creating a number of models of the same object, each with progressively less detail. When the virtual camera is close to an object, a highly detailed model is used; if the object is far away, a lesser detailed version is substituted to save unnecessary computation.

A virtual world that incorporates these techniques has a fluid ontology that is affected by the actions of the user. As the user navigates through space, the objects switch back and forth between pale blueprints and fully fleshed out illusions. The immobility of a subject guarantees a complete illusion; the slightest movement destroys it.

---

29. See Roman Jakobson, "Closing Statement: Linguistics and Poetics," in *Style in Language,* ed. Thomas Sebeok (Cambridge, Mass.: MIT Press, 1960).

Navigating a QuickTime VR movie is characterized by a similar dynamic. In contrast to the nineteenth-century panorama that it closely emulates, QuickTime VR continuously deconstructs its own illusion. The moment you begin to pan through the scene, the image becomes jagged. And if you try to zoom into the image, all you get are oversized pixels. The representational machine keeps hiding and revealing itself.

Compare this dynamic to traditional cinema or realist theater, which aims at all cost to maintain the continuity of the illusion for the duration of the performance. In contrast to such totalizing realism, new media aesthetics has a surprising affinity to twentieth-century leftist avant-garde aesthetics. Playwright Bertold Brecht's strategy of revealing the conditions of an illusion's production, echoed by countless other leftist artists, has become embedded in hardware and software themselves. Similarly, Walter Benjamin's concept of "perception in the state of distraction"[30] has found a perfect realization. The periodic reappearance of the machinery, the continuous presence of the communication channel in the message, prevent the subject from falling into the dream world of illusion for very long, make her alternate between concentration and detachment.

While virtual machinery itself already acts as an avant-garde director, the designers of interactive media, such as games, DVD titles, interactive cinema, and interactive television programs, often consciously attempt to structure the subject's temporal experience as a series of periodic shifts. The subject is forced to oscillate between the roles of viewer and user, shifting between perceiving and acting, between following the story and actively participating in it. During one segment, the computer screen presents the viewer with an engaging cinematic narrative. Suddenly the image freezes, menus and icons appear, and the viewer is forced to act—make choices, click, push buttons. The purest example of such cyclical organization of the user's experience is the computer games that alternate between FMV (full motion video) segments and segments requiring the user's input, such as the *Wing Commander* series. Moscow media theorist Anatoly Prokhorov describes these shifts in terms of two different identities of the computer screen—transparent and opaque. The screen keeps shifting from transparent to

---

30. Benjamin, "The Work of Art in the Age of Mechanical Reproduction."

opaque—from a window to fictional 3-D universe to a solid surface, full of menus, controls, text, and icons.[31] Three-dimensional space becomes surface; a photograph becomes a diagram; a character becomes an icon. To use the opposition introduced in the "Cultural Interfaces" section, we can say that the screen keeps alternating between the dimensions of representation and control. What at one moment was a fictional universe becomes a set of buttons that demand action.

The effect of these shifts on the subject is hardly one of liberation and enlightenment. While modernist avant-garde theater and film directors deliberately highlighted the machinery and conventions involved in producing and keeping the illusion in their works—for instance, having actors directly address the audience or pulling away the camera to show the crew and the set—the systematic "auto-deconstruction" performed by computer objects, applications, interfaces, and hardware does not seem to distract the user from giving in to the reality effect. The cyclical shifts between illusion and its destruction appear neither to distract from it nor support it. It is tempting to compare these temporal shifts to the shot/counter-shot structure in cinema and to understand them as a new kind of suturing mechanism. By having periodically to complete the interactive text through active participation, the subject is interpolated in it. Thus if we adopt the notion of suture, it would follow that the periodic shifts between illusion and its suspension are necessary to fully involve the subject in the illusion.[32]

Yet clearly we are dealing with something that goes beyond the old-style realism of the analog era. We can call this new realism *metarealism* since it incorporates its own critique inside itself. Its emergence can be related to a larger cultural change. The old realism corresponded to the functioning of ideology during modernity—totalization of a semiotic field, "false consciousness," complete illusion. But today ideology functions differently: It continuously and skillfully deconstructs itself, presenting the subject with countless "scandals" and "investigations." The leaders of the middle of the twentieth century were presented as invincible—as always in the right, and,

---

31. Private communication, September 1995, St. Petersburg.

32. On theories of suture in relation to cinema, see chapter 5 of Kaja Silverman, *The Subject of Semiotics* (New York: Oxford University Press, 1983).

in the case of Stalin and Hitler, as true saints incapable of any human sin. Today we expect to hear about scandals involving our leaders, yet these scandals do not really diminish their credibility. Similarly, contemporary television commercials often make fun of themselves and of advertising in general; this does not prevent them from selling whatever they are designed to sell. Auto-critique, scandal, and revelation of its machinery became new structural components of modern ideology: witness the 1998 episode when MTV created an illusion on its Web site that somebody hacked it. The ideology does not demand that the subject blindly believe it, as it did early in the twentieth century; rather, it puts the subject in the master position of someone who knows very well that she is being fooled, and generously lets herself be fooled. You know, for instance, that creating a unique identity through a commercial mass-produced style is meaningless—but you buy the expensively styled clothes anyway, choosing from a menu—"military," "bohemian," "flower child," "inner city," "clubbing," and so on. The periodic shifts between illusion and its suspension in interactive media, described here, can be seen as another example of the same general phenomenon. Like classical ideology, classical realism demands that the subject completely accept the illusion for as along as it lasts. In contrast, the new metarealism is based on oscillation between illusion and its destruction, between immersing a viewer in illusion and directly addressing her. In fact, the user is put in a much stronger position of mastery than ever before when she is "deconstructing" commercials, newspaper reports of scandals, and other traditional noninteractive media. The user invests in the illusion precisely because she is given control over it.

If this analysis is correct, the possible counterargument—that this oscillation between interactivity and illusion is simply an artifact of the current technology and that advances in hardware will eliminate it—would not work. The oscillation analyzed here is not an artifact of computer technology but a structural feature of modern society, present not just in interactive media but in numerous other social realms and on many different levels.

This may explain the popularity of this particular temporal dynamics in interactive media, but it does not address another question: Does it work aesthetically? Can Brecht and Hollywood be married? Is it possible to create a new temporal aesthetics, even a language, based on cyclical shifts between perception and action? In my view, the most successful example of such an aesthetics already in existence is a military simulator, the only mature form of interactive narrative. It perfectly blends perception and action, cinematic realism and computer menus. The screen presents the subject with an illusionistic virtual world while periodically demanding quick actions—shooting at the enemy, changing the direction of a vehicle, and so on. In this art form, the roles of viewer and actant are blended perfectly—but there is a price to pay. The narrative is organized around a single and clearly defined goal—staying alive.

Games modeled after simulators—first of all, first-person shooters such as *Doom, Quake,* and *Tomb Raider,* but also flight and racing simulators—have been quite successful. In contrast to interactive narratives, such as *Wing Commander, Myst, Riven,* or *Bad Day on the Midway,* that are based on temporal oscillation between two distinct states—noninteractive movie-like sequences and interactive game play—first-person shooters are based on the coexistence of the two states—which are also two states of the subject (perception and action) and two states of a screen (transparent and opaque). As you run through the corridors shooting at enemies or controlling the car on the racetrack, you also keep your eyes on the readouts, which tell you about the "health" of your character, the damage level of your vehicle, the availability of ammunition, and so on.

As a conclusion, I would like to offer a different interpretation of the temporal oscillation in new media that will relate it not to the social realm outside new media but rather to other similar effects specific to computer culture itself. The oscillation between illusionary segments and interactive segments forces the user to switch between different mental sets—different kinds of cognitive activity. These switches are typical of modern computer usage in general. At one moment, the user might be analyzing quantitative data; the next, using a search engine, then starting a new application, or navigating through space in a computer game; next perhaps, using a search engine again, and so on. In fact, the modern HCI that allows the user to run a number of programs at the same time and keep a number of windows open on the screen at once posits multitasking as the social and cognitive norm. This multitasking demands from the user "cognitive multitasking"—rapidly alternating between different kinds of attention, problem solving, and other cognitive skills. All in all, modern computing requires of the user intellectual problem solving, systematic experimentation, and the quick learning of new tasks.

Just as any particular software application is embedded, both metaphorically and literally, within the larger framework of the operating system, new media embeds cinema-style illusions within the larger framework of an interactive control surface. Illusion is subordinated to action, depth to surface, window to imaginary universe to control panel. From commanding a dark movie theater, the cinema image, this twentieth-century illusion and therapy machine par excellence, becomes just a small window on a computer screen, one stream among many others coming to us through the network, one file among numerous others on our hard drives.

5

The Forms

August 5, 1999. I am sitting in the lobby of Razorfish Studios, which was named by *Adweek* one of the top ten interactive agencies in the world for 1998.[1] The company's story is Silicon Alley legend. It was founded in 1995 by two partners in their East Village loft; by 1997 it had forty-five employees; by 1999 the number grew to six hundred (this includes a number of companies around the world that Razorfish acquired). Razorfish projects range from screen savers to a Charles Schwab online trading Web site. At the time of my visit, the studios were housed on two floors of a building on Grand Street in Soho, between Broadway and Mercer, a few blocks from Prada, Hugo Boss, and other designer shops. The large, open space houses loosely positioned workspaces occupied mostly by twenty-something employees (although I notice one busy programmer who cannot be older then eighteen). The design of the space functions (intentionally so) as a metaphor for computer culture's key themes—interactivity, lack of hierarchy, modularity. In contrast to traditional office architecture, where the reception area acts as a gateway between the visitor and the company, here the desk looks like just another workstation, set aside from the entrance. On entering the space you can go to the reception desk, or you can directly make your way to any workstation on the floor. Stylishly dressed young employees of both genders appear and disappear in the elevator at regular intervals. It is fairly quiet, except for the little noises made by numerous computers as they save and retrieve files. One of the cofounders, still in his early thirties, gives me a quick tour of the place. Although Razorfish is the established design leader in the virtual world of computer screens and networks, our tour is focused on the physical world. He proudly points out that the workers are scattered around the open space regardless of their job titles—a programmer next to an interface designer next to a Web designer. He notes that the reception area, composed of a desk and two semicircular sofas, mimics the Razorfish logo. He talks about Razorfish's plans to venture into product design: "Our goal is to provide a total user experience. Right now, a client thinks that if he needs a design for buttons on the screen, he hires Razorfish; but if he needs real buttons, he goes to another shop. We want to change this."

The original 1970s paradigm of the Graphical User Interface (GUI) emulated familiar physical interfaces—a file cabinet, a desk, a trash can, a control panel.

---

1. http://www.adweek.com.

After leaving Razorfish Studios, I stop at Venus by Patricia Field, a funky store on West Broadway where I buy an orange and blue wallet that has two plastic buttons on its cover, an emulation of the forward and reverse buttons of a Web browser. The buttons do not do anything (yet); they simply signify "computer." Over the course of twenty years, the culture has come full circle. If with GUI the physical environment migrated into the computer screen, now the conventions of GUI are migrating back into our physical reality. The same trajectory can be traced in relation to other conventions, or forms, of computer media. A collection of documents and a navigable space, already traditional methods of organizing both data and human experience of the world itself, became two of the forms that today can be found in most areas of new media. The first form is a database, used to store any kind of data—from financial records to digital movie clips; the second form is a virtual interactive 3-D space, employed in computer games, motion rides, VR, computer animation, and human-computer interfaces. In migrating to a computer environment, the collection and the navigable space were not left unchanged; on the contrary, they came to incorporate a computer's particular techniques for structuring and accessing data, such as modularity, as well as its fundamental logic—that of computer programming. So, for instance, a computer database is quite different from a traditional collection of documents: It allows one to quickly access, sort, and reorganize millions of records; it can contain different media types, and it assumes multiple indexing of data, since each record besides the data itself contains a number of fields with user-defined values.

Today, in accordance with the transcoding principle, these two computer-based forms migrate back into culture at large, both literally and conceptually. A library, a museum—in fact, any large collection of cultural data—is replaced by a computer database. At the same time, a computer database becomes a new metaphor that we use to conceptualize individual and collective cultural memory, a collection of documents or objects, and other phenomena and experiences. Similarly, computer culture uses 3-D navigable space to visualize any kind of data—molecules, historical records, files in a computer, the Internet as a whole, the semantics of human language. (For instance, the software from plumbdesign renders an English thesaurus as a structure in 3-D space.)[2] And, with many computer games, the human ex-

2. http://www.plumbdesign.com/thesaurus/.

perience of being in the world and the narrative itself are represented as continuous navigation through space (think, for example, of *Tomb Raider*). In short, the computer database and the 3-D computer-based virtual space have become true cultural forms—general ways used by the culture to represent human experience, the world, and human existence in this world.

Why does computer culture privilege these forms over other possibilities?[3] We may associate the first genre with work (the postindustrial labor of information processing) and the second with leisure and fun (computer games), yet this very distinction is no longer valid in computer culture. As I noted in the introduction to the "Interface" chapter, increasingly the same metaphors and interfaces are used at work and at home, for business and for entertainment. For instance, the user navigates through a virtual space both to work and to play, whether analyzing scientific data or killing enemies in *Quake*.

We may arrive at a better explanation if we look at how these two forms are used in new media design. From one perspective, all new media design can be reduced to these two approaches; that is, creating works in new media can be understood as either constructing the right interface to a multimedia database or as defining navigation methods through spatialized representations. The first approach is typically used in self-contained hypermedia and Web sites—in short, whenever the main goal is to provide an interface to data. The second approach is used in most computer games and virtual worlds. What is the logic here? Web sites and hypermedia programs usually aim to give the user efficient access to information, whereas games and virtual worlds aim to psychologically "immerse" the user in an imaginary universe. It is appropriate that the database has emerged as the perfect vehicle for the first goal while navigable space meets the demands of the second. It accomplishes the same effects that before were created by literary and cinematic narrative.

---

3. According to Janet Murray, digital environments have four essential properties: They are procedural, participatory, spatial, and encyclopedic. As can be seen, spatial and encyclopedic can be correlated with the two forms I describe here—navigable space and the database. Janet Murray, *Hamlet on the Holodeck—The Future of Narrative in Cyberspace* (Cambridge, Mass.: MIT Press, 1997), 73.

Sometimes, one alone of these two goals, information access and psychological engagement with an imaginary world, shapes the design of a new media object. An example of the former would be a search engine site; an example of the latter would be games such as *Riven* or *Unreal.* However, in general these two goals should be thought of as extreme cases of a single conceptual continuum. Such a supposedly "pure" example of an information-oriented object as a Yahoo, Hotbot, or other search site aims to "immerse" the user in its universe, prevent her from going to other sites. And such supposedly pure "psychological immersion" objects as *Riven* or *Unreal* have a strong "information processing" dimension. This dimension makes playing these games more like reading a detective story or playing chess than being engaged with traditional literary and film fictional narrative. Gathering clues and treasures; constantly updating a mental map of the universe of the game, including the positions of pathways, doors, places to avoid, and so on; keeping track of one's ammunition, health, and other levels—all this aligns playing a computer game with other "information processing" tasks typical of computer culture, like searching the Internet, scanning news groups, pulling records from a database, using a spreadsheet, or data mining large data stores.

Often, the two goals of information access and psychological engagement compete within the same new media object. *Along with surface versus depth, the opposition between information and "immersion" can be thought of as a particular expression of the more general opposition characteristic of new media—between action and representation.* And just as is the case with the surface and depth opposition, the results of this competition are often awkward and uneasy. For instance, an image that embeds within itself a number of hyperlinks offers neither a true psychological "immersion" nor easy navigation because the user has to search for hyperlinks. Appropriately, games such as *Johnny Mnemonic* (SONY, 1995) that aspired to become true interactive movies, chose to avoid hyperlinks and menus altogether, instead relying on a keyboard as the sole source of interactive control.

Narratology, the branch of modern literary theory devoted to the theory of narrative, distinguishes between narration and description. Narration is those parts of the narrative that move the plot forward; description is those parts that do not. Examples of description are passages that describe the landscape, or a city, or a character's apartment. In short, to use the language of the information age, description passages present the reader with descriptive information. As its name itself implies, narratology paid most attention to narration and hardly any to description. But in the information age, narration and description have changed roles. If traditional cultures provided people with well-defined narratives (myths, religion) and little "stand-alone" information, today we have too much information and too few narratives that can tie it all together. For better or worse, information access has become a key activity of the computer age. Therefore, *we need something that can be called "info-aesthetics"—a theoretical analysis of the aesthetics of information access as well as the creation of new media objects that "aestheticize" information processing.* In an age when all design has become "information design," and, to paraphrase the title of the famous book by the architectural historian Sigfried Giedion,[4] "the search engine takes command," information access is no longer just a key form of work but also a new key category of culture. Accordingly, it demands that we deal with it theoretically, aesthetically, and symbolically.

---

4. Sigfried Giedion, *Mechanization Takes Command, a Contribution to Anonymous History* (New York: Oxford University Press, 1948).

The Database

The Database Logic

After the novel, and subsequently cinema, privileged narrative as the key form of cultural expression of the modern age, the computer age introduces its correlate—the database. Many new media objects do not tell stories; they do not have a beginning or end; in fact, they do not have any development, thematically, formally, or otherwise that would organize their elements into a sequence. Instead, they are collections of individual items, with every item possessing the same significance as any other.

Why does new media favor the database form over others? Can we explain its popularity by analyzing the specificity of the digital medium and of computer programming? What is the relationship between the database and another form that has traditionally dominated human culture—narrative? These are the questions I will address in this section.

Before proceeding, I need to comment on my use of the word *database*. In computer science, *database* is defined as a structured collection of data. The data stored in a database is organized for fast search and retrieval by a computer and therefore, it is anything but a simple collection of items. Different types of databases—hierarchical, network, relational, and object-oriented—use different models to organize data. For instance, the records in hierarchical databases are organized in a treelike structure. Object-oriented databases store complex data structures, called "objects," which are organized into hierarchical classes that may inherit properties from classes higher in the chain.[5]

---

5. "Database," *Encyclopædia Britannica Online,* http://www.eb.com:180/cgi-bin/g?DocF=micro/160/23.html.

New media objects may or may not employ these highly structured database models; however, from the point of view of the user's experience, a large proportion of them are databases in a more basic sense. They appear as collections of items on which the user can perform various operations—view, navigate, search. The user's experience of such computerized collections is, therefore, quite distinct from reading a narrative or watching a film or navigating an architectural site. Similarly, a literary or cinematic narrative, an architectural plan, and a database each present a different model of what a world is like. It is this sense of database as a cultural form of its own that I want to address here. Following art historian Ervin Panofsky's analysis of linear perspective as a "symbolic form" of the modern age, we may even call database a new symbolic form of the computer age (or, as philosopher Jean-François Lyotard called it in his famous 1979 book *The Postmodern Condition,* "computerized society"),[6] a new way to structure our experience of ourselves and of the world. Indeed, if after the death of God (Nietzsche), the end of grand Narratives of Enlightenment (Lyotard), and the arrival of the Web (Tim Berners-Lee), the world appears to us as an endless and unstructured collection of images, texts, and other data records, it is only appropriate that we will be moved to model it as a database. But it is also appropriate that we would want to develop a poetics, aesthetics, and ethics of this database.

Let us begin by documenting the dominance of the database form in new media. The most obvious examples are popular multimedia encyclopedias, collections by definition, as well as other commercial CD-ROM (or DVD), that feature collections of recipes, quotations, photographs, and so on.[7] The identity of a CD-ROM as a storage media is projected onto another plane, thereby becoming a cultural form in its own right. Multimedia works that have "cultural" content appear to particularly favor the database form. Consider, for instance, the "virtual museums" genre—CD-ROMs that take the user on a tour through a museum collection. A museum becomes a database of images representing its holdings, which can be accessed in different

---

6. Jean-François Lyotard, *The Postmodern Condition: A Report on Knowledge,* trans. Geoff Bennington and Brian Massumi (Minneapolis: University of Minnesota Press, 1984), 3.

7. As early as 1985, Grolier, Inc. issued a text-only *Academic American Encyclopedia* on CD-ROM. The first multimedia encyclopedia was *Compton's MultiMedia Encyclopedia,* published in 1989.

ways—chronologically, by country, or by artist. Although such CD-ROMs often simulate the traditional museum experience of moving from room to room in a continuous trajectory, this narrative method of access does not have any special status in comparison to other access methods offered by CD-ROMs. Thus narrative becomes just one method of accessing data among many. Another example of a database form is a multimedia genre that does not have an equivalent in traditional media—CD-ROMs devoted to a single cultural figure such as a famous architect, film director, or writer. Instead of a narrative biography, we are presented with a database of images, sound recordings, video clips, and/or texts that can be navigated in a variety of ways.

CD-ROMs and other digital storage media proved to be particularly receptive to traditional genres that already had a database-like structure, such as the photo album; they also inspired new database genres, like the database biography. Where the database form really flourished, however, is the Internet. As defined by original HTML, a Web page is a sequential list of separate elements—text blocks, images, digital video clips, and links to other pages. It is always possible to add a new element to the list—all you have to do is to open a file and add a new line. As a result, most Web pages are collections of separate elements—texts, images, links to other pages, or sites. A home page is a collection of personal photographs. A site of a major search engine is a collection of numerous links to other sites (along with a search function, of course). A site of a Web-based TV or radio station offers a collection of video or audio programs along with the option to listen to the current broadcast, but this current program is just one choice among many other programs stored on the site. Thus the traditional broadcasting experience, which consists solely of a real-time transmission, becomes just one element in a collection of options. Similar to the CD-ROM medium, the Web offered fertile ground to already existing database genres (for instance, bibliography) and also inspired the creation of new ones such as sites devoted to a person or a phenomenon (Madonna, the Civil War, new media theory, etc.) that, even if they contain original material, inevitably center around a list of links to other Web pages on the same person or phenomenon.

The open nature of the Web as a medium (Web pages are computer files that can always be edited) means that Web sites never have to be complete; and they rarely are. They always grow. New links are continually added to what is already there. It is as easy to add new elements to the end of a list as it is to insert them anywhere in it. All this further contributes to the anti-narrative logic of the Web. If new elements are being added over time, the result is a collection, not a story. Indeed, how can one keep a coherent narrative or any other development trajectory through the material if it keeps changing?

Commercial producers have experimented with ways to explore the database form inherent to new media, with offerings ranging from multimedia encyclopedias to collections of software and collections of pornographic images. In contrast, many artists working with new media at first uncritically accepted the database form as a given. Thus they became blind victims of database logic. Numerous artists' Web sites are collections of multimedia elements documenting their works in other media. In the case of many early artists' CD-ROMs as well, the tendency was to fill all the available storage space with different material—the main work, documentation, related texts, previous works, and so on.

As the 1990s progressed, artists increasingly began to approach the database more critically.[8] A few examples of projects investigating database politics and possible aesthetics are Chris Marker's "IMMEMORY," Olga Lialina's "Anna Karenina Goes to Paradise,"[9] Stephen Mamber's "Digital Hitchcock," and Fabian Wagmister's ". . . two, three, many Guevaras." The artist who has explored the possibilities of a database most systematically is George Legrady. In a series of interactive multimedia works ("The Anecdoted Archive," 1994; "[the clearing]," 1994; "Slippey Traces," 1996; "Tracing," 1998) he used different types of databases to create "an information structure where stories/things are organized according to multiple thematic connections."[10]

Data and Algorithm

Of course, not all new media objects are explicitly databases. Computer games, for instance, are experienced by their players as narratives. In a game,

---

8. See *AI and Society* 13.3, a special issue on database aesthetics, ed. Victoria Vesna (http://arts. ucsb.edu/~vesna/AI_Society/); *SWITCH* 5, no. 3, "The Database Issue" (http://switch.sjsu. edu/).

9. http://www.teleportacia.org/anna.

10. George Legrady, personal communication, 16 September 1998.

the player is given a well-defined task—winning the match, being first in a race, reaching the last level, or attaining the highest score. It is this task that makes the player experience the game as a narrative. Everything that happens to her in a game, all the characters and objects she encounters, either take her closer to achieving the goal or further away from it. Thus, in contrast to a CD-ROM and Web database, which always appear arbitrary because the user knows additional material could have been added without modifying the logic, in a game, from the user's point of view, all the elements are motivated (i.e., their presence is justified).[11]

Often the narrative shell of a game ("You are the specially trained commando who has just landed on a lunar base; your task is to make your way to the headquarters occupied by the mutant base personnel . . .") masks a simple algorithm well-familiar to the player—kill all the enemies on the current level, while collecting all the treasures it contains; go to the next level and so on until you reach the last level. Other games have different algorithms. Here is the algorithm of the legendary *Tetris:* When a new block appears, rotate it in such a way so that it will complete the top layer of blocks on the bottom of the screen, thus making this layer disappear. The similarity between the actions expected of the player and computer algorithms is too uncanny to be dismissed. While computer games do not follow a database logic, they appear to be ruled by another logic—that of the algorithm. They demand that a player execute an algorithm in order to win.

An algorithm is the key to the game experience in a different sense as well. As the player proceeds through the game, she gradually discovers the rules that operate in the universe constructed by this game. She learns its hidden logic—in short, its algorithm. Therefore, in games in which the game play departs from following an algorithm, the player is still engaged with an algorithm albeit in another way: She is discovering the algorithm of

---

11. Bordwell and Thompson define motivation in cinema in the following way: "Because films are human constructs, we can expect that any one element in a film will have some justification for being there. This justification is the motivation for that element." Here are some examples of motivation: "When Tom jumps from the balloon to chase a cat, we motivate his action by appealing to notions of how dogs are likely to act when cats are around"; "The movement of a character across a room may motivate the moving of the camera to follow the action and keep the character within a frame." Bordwell and Thompson, *Film Art,* 5th ed., 80.

the game itself. I mean this both metaphorically and literally: For instance, in a first-person shooter such as *Quake* the player may eventually notice that, under such and such conditions, the enemies will appear from the left; that is, she will literally reconstruct a part of the algorithm responsible for the game play. Or, in a different formulation of the legendary author of Sim games, Will Wright, "playing the game is a continuous loop between the user (viewing the outcomes and inputting decisions) and the computer (calculating outcomes and displaying them back to the user). The user is trying to build a mental model of the computer model."[12]

This is another example of the general principle of transcoding discussed in the first chapter—the projection of the ontology of a computer onto culture itself. If in physics the world is made of atoms and in genetics it is made of genes, computer programming encapsulates the world according to its own logic. The world is reduced to two kinds of software objects that are complementary to each other—data structures and algorithms. Any process or task is reduced to an algorithm, a final sequence of simple operations that a computer can execute to accomplish a given task. And any object in the world—be it the population of a city, or the weather over the course of a century, or a chair, or a human brain—is modeled as a data structure, that is, data organized in a particular way for efficient search and retrieval.[13] Examples of data structures are arrays, linked lists, and graphs. Algorithms and data structures have a symbiotic relationship. The more complex the data structure of a computer program, the simpler the algorithm needs to be, and vice versa. Together, data structures and algorithms are two halves of the ontology of the world according to a computer.

The computerization of culture involves the projection of these two fundamental parts of computer software—and of the computer's unique ontology—onto the cultural sphere. If CD-ROMs and Web databases are cultural manifestations of one half of this ontology—data structures—then computer games are manifestations of the second half—algorithms. Games (sports, chess, cards, etc.) are one cultural form that require algorithm-like

---

12. McGowan and McCullaugh, *Entertainment in the Cyber Zone*, 71.

13. This is true for a procedural programming paradigm. In an object-oriented programming paradigm, represented by such computer languages as Java and C++, algorithms and data structures are modeled together as objects.

behavior from players; consequently, many traditional games were quickly simulated on computers. In parallel, new genres of computer games such as the first-person shooter came into existence. Thus, as was the case with database genres, computer games both mimic already existing games and create new game genres.

It may appear at first sight that data is passive and algorithms active—another example of the passive-active binary categories so loved by human cultures. A program reads in data, executes an algorithm, and writes out new data. We may recall that before "computer science" and "software engineering" became established names in the computer field, this was called "data processing"—a name which remained in use for the few decades during which computers were mainly associated with performing calculations over data. However, the passive/active distinction is not quite accurate because data does not just exist—it has to be generated. Data creators have to collect data and organize it, or create it from scratch. Texts need to written, photographs need to be taken, video and audio material need to be recorded. Or they need to be digitized from already existing media. In the 1990s, when the new role of the computer as a Universal Media Machine became apparent, already computerized societies went into a digitizing craze. All existing books and videotapes, photographs, and audio recordings started to be fed into computers at an ever-increasing rate. Steven Spielberg created the Shoah Foundation, which videotaped and then digitized numerous interviews with Holocaust survivors; it would take one person forty years to watch all the recorded material. The editors of the journal *Mediamatic,* who devoted a whole issue to the topic of "the storage mania" (Summer 1994) wrote: "A growing number of organizations are embarking on ambitious projects. Everything is being collected: culture, asteroids, DNA patterns, credit records, telephone conversations; it doesn't matter."[14] In 1996, the financial company T. Rowe Price stored eight hundred gigabytes of data; by the fall of 1999 this number rose to ten terabytes.[15]

Once digitized, the data has to be cleaned up, organized, and indexed. The computer age brought with it a new cultural algorithm: reality→

---

14. *Mediamatic* 8, no. 1 (Summer 1994), 1860.

15. Bob Laird, "Information Age Losing Memory," *USA Today,* 25 October 1999.

media→data→database. The rise of the Web, this gigantic and always changing data corpus, gave millions of people a new hobby or profession—data indexing. There is hardly a Web site that does not feature at least a dozen links to other sites; therefore, every site is a type of database. And, with the rise of Internet commerce, most large-scale commercial sites have become real databases, or rather front-ends to company databases. For instance, in the fall of 1998, Amazon.com, an online bookstore, had three million books in its database; and the maker of the leading commercial database *Oracle* has offered *Oracle 8i,* fully integrated with the Internet and featuring unlimited database size, natural-language queries, and support for all multimedia data types.[16] Jorge Luis Borges's story about a map equal in size to the territory it represents is rewritten as a story about indexes and the data they index. But now the map has become larger than the territory. Sometimes, much larger. Porno Web sites exposed the logic of the Web at its extreme by constantly reusing the same photographs from other porno Web sites. Only rare sites featured the original content. On any given date, the same few dozen images would appear on thousands of sites. Thus, the same data would give rise to more indexes than the number of data elements themselves.

Database and Narrative

As a cultural form, the database represents the world as a list of items, and it refuses to order this list. In contrast, a narrative creates a cause-and-effect trajectory of seemingly unordered items (events). Therefore, database and narrative are natural enemies. Competing for the same territory of human culture, each claims an exclusive right to make meaning out of the world.

In contrast to most games, most narratives do not require algorithm-like behavior from their readers. However, narratives and games are similar in that the user must uncover their underlying logic while proceeding through them—their algorithm. Just like the game player, the reader of a novel gradually reconstructs the algorithm (here I use the term metaphorically) that the writer used to create the settings, the characters, and the events. From this perspective, I can rewrite my earlier equations between the two parts of

---

16. http://www.amazon.com/exec/obidos/subst/misc/company-info.html/, http://www.oracle.com/database/oracle8i/.

the computer's ontology and its corresponding cultural forms. Data structures and algorithms drive different forms of computer culture. CD-ROMs, Web sites, and other new media objects organized as databases correspond to the data structure, whereas narratives, including computer games, correspond to algorithm.

In computer programming, data structures and algorithms need each other; they are equally important for a program to work. What happens in the cultural sphere? Do databases and narratives have the same status in computer culture?

Some media objects explicitly follow a database logic in their structure whereas others do not; but under the surface, practically all of them are databases. In general, creating a work in new media can be understood as the construction of an interface to a database. In the simplest case, the interface simply provides access to the underlying database. For instance, an image database can be represented as a page of miniature images; clicking on a miniature will retrieve the corresponding record. If a database is too large to display all of its records at once, a search engine can be provided to allow the user to search for particular records. But the interface can also translate the underlying database into a very different user experience. The user may be navigating a virtual three-dimensional city composed from letters, as in Jeffrey Shaw's interactive installation "Legible City."[17] Or she may be traversing a black-and-white image of a naked body, activating pieces of text, audio, and video embedded in its skin (Harwood's CD-ROM "Rehearsal of Memory.")[18] Or she may be playing with virtual animals that come closer or run away depending upon her movements (Scott Fisher et al., VR installation "Menagerie.")[19] Although each of these works engages the user in a set of behaviors and cognitive activities that are quite distinct from going through the records of a database, all of them are databases. "Legible City" is a database of three-dimensional letters that make up a city. "Rehearsal of Memory" is a database of texts and audio and video clips that are accessed through the interface of a body. And "Menagerie" is a database of virtual animals, including their shapes, movements, and behaviors.

---

17. http://artnetweb.com/guggenheim/mediascape/shaw.html.

18. Harwood, *Rehearsal of Memory,* CD-ROM (London: Artec and Bookworks, 1996.)

19. http://www.telepresence.com/MENAGERIE.

The database becomes the center of the creative process in the computer age. Historically, the artist made a unique work within a particular medium. Therefore the interface and the work were the same; in other words, the level of an interface did not exist. With new media, the content of the work and the interface are separated. It is therefore possible to create different interfaces to the same material. These interfaces may present different versions of the same work, as in David Blair's *WaxWeb*.[20] Or they may be radically different from each other, as in Olga Lialina's Last Real Net Art Museum.[21] This is one of the ways in which the principle of *variability* of new media manifests itself. But now we can give this principle a new formulation. *The new media object consists of one or more interfaces to a database of multimedia material.* If only one interface is constructed, the result will be similar to a traditional art object, but this is an exception rather than the norm.

This formulation places the opposition between database and narrative in a new light, thus redefining our concept of narrative. The "user" of a narrative is traversing a database, following links between its records as established by the database's creator. An interactive narrative (which can be also called a *hypernarrative* in an analogy with hypertext) can then be understood as the sum of multiple trajectories through a database. A traditional linear narrative is one among many other possible trajectories, that is, a particular choice made within a hypernarrative. Just as a traditional cultural object can now be seen as a particular case of a new media object (i.e., a new media object that has only one interface), traditional linear narrative can be seen as a particular case of hypernarrative.

This "technical," or "material," change in the definition of narrative does not mean that an arbitrary sequence of database records is a narrative. To qualify as a narrative, a cultural object has to satisfy a number of criteria, which literary theorist Mieke Bal defines as follows: It should contain both an actor and a narrator; it also should contain three distinct levels consisting of the text, the story, and the fabula; and its "contents" should be "a series of connected events caused or experienced by actors."[22] Obviously, not

20. http://jefferson.village.virginia.edu/wax/.

21. http://myboyfriendcamebackfromth.ewar.ru.

22. Mieke Bal, *Narratology: Introduction to the Theory of Narrative* (Toronto: University of Toronto Press, 1985), 8.

all cultural objects are narratives. However, in the world of new media, the word *narrative* is often used as an all-inclusive term, to cover up the fact that we have not yet developed a language to describe these new strange objects. It is usually paired with another overused word—*interactive.* Thus a number of database records linked together so that more than one trajectory is possible is assumed to constitute an "interactive narrative." But merely to create these trajectories is of course not sufficient; the author also has to control the semantics of the elements and the logic of their connection so that the resulting object will meet the criteria of narrative as outlined above. Another erroneous assumption frequently made is that, by creating her own path (i.e., choosing the records from a database in a particular order), the user constructs her own unique narrative. However, if the user simply accesses different elements, one after another, in a usually random order, there is no reason to assume that these elements will form a narrative at all. Indeed, why should an arbitrary sequence of database records, constructed by the user, result in "a series of connected events caused or experienced by actors"?

In summary, database and narrative do not have the same status in computer culture. In the database/narrative pair, database is the unmarked term.[23] Regardless of whether new media objects present themselves as linear narratives, interactive narratives, databases, or something else, underneath, on the level of material organization, they are all databases. In new media, the database supports a variety of cultural forms that range from direct translation (i.e., a database stays a database) to a form whose logic is the opposite of the logic of the material form itself—narrative. More precisely, a database can support narrative, but there is nothing in the logic of the medium itself that would foster its generation. It is not surprising, then, that databases occupy a significant, if not the largest, territory of the new media landscape. What is more surprising is why the other end of the spectrum—narratives—still exist in new media.

---

23. The theory of markedness was first developed by linguists of the Prague School in relation to phonology, but subsequently applied to all levels of linguistic analysis. For example, "rooster" is a marked term and "chicken" an unmarked term. Whereas "rooster" is used only in relation to males, "chicken" is applicable to both males and females.

Paradigm and Syntagm

The dynamics that exist between database and narrative are not unique in new media. The relation between the structure of a digital image and the languages of contemporary visual culture is characterized by the same dynamics. As defined by all computer software, a digital image consists of a number of separate layers, each layer containing particular visual elements. Throughout the production process, artists and designers manipulate each layer separately; they also delete layers and add new ones. Keeping each element as a separate layer allows the content and the composition of an image to be changed at any point—deleting a background, substituting one person for another, moving two people closer together, blurring an object, and so on. What would a typical image look like if the layers were merged together? The elements contained on different layers would become juxtaposed, resulting in a montage look. Montage is the default visual language of composite organization of an image. However, just as database supports both the database form and its opposite—narrative—a composite organization of an image on the material level (and compositing software on the level of operations) supports two opposing visual languages. One is modernist-MTV montage—two-dimensional juxtaposition of visual elements designed to shock due to its impossibility in reality. The other is the representation of familiar reality as seen by a film camera (or its computer simulation, in the case of 3-D graphics). During the 1980s and 1990s, all image-making technologies became computer-based, thus turning all images into composites. In parallel, a renaissance of montage took place in visual culture, in print, broadcast design, and new media. This is not unexpected—after all, this is the visual language dictated by the composite organization. What needs to be explained is why photorealist images continue to occupy such a significant space in our computer-based visual culture.

It would be surprising, of course, if photorealist images suddenly disappeared completely. The history of culture does not contain such sudden breaks. Similarly, we should not expect that new media would completely replace narrative with database. New media does not radically break with the past; rather, it distributes weight differently between the categories that hold culture together, foregrounding what was in the background, and vice versa. As Frederick Jameson writes in his analysis of another shift, that from modernism to postmodernism: "Radical breaks between periods do not generally involve complete changes but rather the restructuration of a certain number of elements already given: features that in an earlier period of system were subordinate become dominant, and features that had been dominant again become secondary."[24]

The database/narrative opposition is a case in point. To further understand how computer culture redistributes weight between the two terms of opposition in computer culture, I will bring in the semiological theory of syntagm and paradigm. According to this model, originally formulated by Ferdinand de Saussure to describe natural languages such as English and later expanded by Roland Barthes and others to apply to other sign systems (narrative, fashion, food, etc.), the elements of a system can be related in two dimensions—the syntagmatic and paradigmatic. As defined by Barthes, "The syntagm is a combination of signs, which has space as a support."[25] To use the example of natural language, the speaker produces an utterance by stringing together elements, one after another, in a linear sequence. This is the syntagmatic dimension. Now let us look at the paradigmatic dimension. To continue with the example of the language user, each new element is chosen from a set of other related elements. For instance, all nouns form a set; all synonyms of a particular word form another set. In the original formulation of Saussure, "The units which have something in common are associated in theory and thus form groups within which various relationships can be found."[26] This is the paradigmatic dimension.

Elements in the syntagmatic dimension are related *in praesentia,* while elements in the paradigmatic dimension are related *in absentia.* For instance, in the case of a written sentence, the words that comprise it materially exist on a piece of paper, while the paradigmatic sets to which these words belong only exist in the writer's and reader's minds. Similarly, in the case of a fashion outfit, the elements that compose it, such as skirt, blouse, and jacket, are present in reality, while pieces of clothing that could have been present instead—different skirt, different blouse, different jacket—exist only in the viewer's imagination. Thus, syntagm is explicit and paradigm is implicit; one is real and the other is imagined.

---

24. Fredric Jameson, "Postmodernism and Consumer Society," in *The Anti-Aesthetic: Essays on Postmodern Culture,* ed. Hal Foster (Seattle: Bay Press, 1983), 123.

25. Barthes, *Elements of Semiology,* 58.

26. Quoted in ibid., 58.

Literary and cinematic narratives work in the same way. Particular words, sentences, shots, and scenes that make up a narrative have a material existence; other elements that form the imaginary world of an author or a particular literary or cinematic style, and that could have appeared instead, exist only virtually. Put differently, the database of choices from which narrative is constructed (the paradigm) is implicit; while the actual narrative (the syntagm) is explicit.

New media reverse this relationship. Database (the paradigm) is given material existence, while narrative (the syntagm) is dematerialised. Paradigm is privileged, syntagm is downplayed. Paradigm is real; syntagm, virtual. To see this, consider the new media design process. The design of any new media object begins with assembling a database of possible elements to be used. (Macromedia Director calls this database "cast," Adobe Premiere calls it "project," ProTools calls it a "session," but the principle is the same.) This database is the center of the design process. It typically consists of a combination of original and stock material such as buttons, images, video and audio sequences, 3-D objects, behaviors, and so on. Throughout the design process, new elements are added to the database; existing elements are modified. The narrative is constructed by linking elements of this database in a particular order, that is by designing a trajectory leading from one element to another. On the material level, a narrative is just a set of links; the elements themselves remain stored in the database. Thus the narrative is virtual while the database exists materially.

The paradigm is privileged over syntagm in yet another way in interactive objects presenting the user with a number of choices at the same time— which is what typical interactive interfaces do. For instance, a screen may contain a few icons; clicking on each icon leads the user to a different screen. On the level of an individual screen, these choices form a paradigm of their own that is explicitly presented to the user. On the level of the whole object, the user is made aware that she is following one possible trajectory among many others. In other words, she is selecting one trajectory from the paradigm of all trajectories that are defined.

Other types of interactive interfaces make the paradigm even more explicit by presenting the user with an explicit menu of all available choices. In such interfaces, all of the categories are always available, just a mouse click away. The complete paradigm is present before the user, its elements neatly arranged in a menu. This is another example of how new media make explicit the psychological processes involved in cultural communication. Other examples include the (already discussed) shift from creation to selection, which externalizes and codifies the database of cultural elements existing in the creator's mind, as well as the very phenomena of interactive links. As I noted in chapter one, new media takes "interaction" literally, equating it with a strictly physical interaction between a user and a computer, at the expense of psychological interaction. The cognitive processes involved in understanding any cultural text are erroneously equated with an objectively existing structure of interactive links.

Interactive interfaces foreground the paradigmatic dimension and often make explicit paradigmatic sets. Yet they are still organized along the syntagmatic dimension. Although the user is making choices at each new screen, the end result is a linear sequence of screens that she follows. This is the classical syntagmatic experience. In fact, it can be compared to constructing a sentence in a natural language. Just as a language user constructs a sentence by choosing each successive word from a paradigm of other possible words, a new media user creates a sequence of screens by clicking on this or that icon at each screen. Obviously, there are many important differences between these two situations. For instance, in the case of a typical interactive interface, there is no grammar, and paradigms are much smaller. Yet the similarity of basic experience in both cases is quite interesting; in both cases, it unfolds along a syntagmatic dimension.

Why does new media insist on this language-like sequencing? My hypothesis is that they follow the dominant semiological order of the twentieth century—that of cinema. As I will discuss in more detail in the next chapter, cinema replaced all other modes of narration with a sequential narrative, an assembly line of shots that appear on the screen one at a time. For centuries, a spatialized narrative in which all images appear simultaneously dominated European visual culture; in the twentieth century it was relegated to "minor" cultural forms such as comics or technical illustrations. "Real" culture of the twentieth century came to speak in linear chains, aligning itself with the assembly line of the industrial society and the Turing machine of the postindustrial era. New media continue this mode, giving the user information one screen at a time. At least, this is the case when it tries to become "real" culture (interactive narratives, games); when it simply functions as an interface to information, it is not ashamed to present much more information on the screen at once, whether in the form of tables, normal or pull-down menus, or lists. In particular, the experience of a user filling in an online form can be compared to precinematic spatialized narrative: in both cases, the user follows a sequence of elements that are presented simultaneously.

A Database Complex

To what extent is the database form intrinsic to modern storage media? For instance, a typical music CD is a collection of individual tracks grouped together. The database impulse also drives much of photography throughout its history, from William Henry Fox Talbot's *Pencil of Nature* to August Sander's monumental typology of modern German society *Face of Our Time,* to Bernd and Hilla Becher's equally obsessive cataloging of water towers. Yet the connection between storage media and database forms is not universal. The prime exception is cinema. Here the storage media support the narrative imagination.[27] Why then, in the case of photography storage media, does technology sustain database, whereas in the case of cinema it gives rise to a modern narrative form par excellence? Does this have to do with the method of media access? Shall we conclude that random-access media, such as computer storage formats (hard drives, removable disks, CD-ROMs, DVD), favor database, whereas sequential-access media, such as film, favor narrative? This does not hold either. For instance, a book, the perfect random-access medium, supports database forms such as photoalbums as well as narrative forms such as novels.

Rather than trying to correlate database and narrative forms with modern media and information technologies, or deduce them from these technologies, I prefer to think of them as two competing imaginations, two basic creative impulses, two essential responses to the world. Both have existed long before modern media. The ancient Greeks produced long narratives, such as Homer's epic poems *The Iliad* and *The Odyssey;* they also produced encyclopedias. The first fragments of a Greek encyclopedia to have survived were the work of Speusippus, a nephew of Plato. Diderot wrote novels—and also was in charge of the monumental *Encyclopédie,* the largest publishing

27. Christian Metz, "The Fiction Film and Its Spectator: A Metapsychological Study," in *Apparatus,* ed. Theresa Hak Kyung Cha (New York: Tanam Press, 1980), p. 402.

project of the eighteenth century. Competing to make meaning out of the world, database and narrative produce endless hybrids. It is hard to find a pure encyclopedia without any traces of a narrative in it and vice versa. For instance, until alphabetical organization became popular a few centuries ago, most encyclopedias were organized thematically, with topics covered in a particular order (typically, corresponding to the seven liberal arts.) At the same time, many narratives, such as the novels by Cervantes and Swift, and even Homer's epic poems—the founding narratives of the Western tradition—traverse an imaginary encyclopedia.

Modern media is the new battlefield for the competition between database and narrative. It is tempting to read the history of this competition in dramatic terms. First, the medium of visual recording—photography— privileges catalogs, taxonomies, and lists. While the modern novel blossoms, and academicians continue to produce historical narrative paintings throughout the nineteenth century, in the realm of the new techno-image of photography, database rules. The next visual recording medium— film—privileges narrative. Almost all fictional films are narratives, with few exceptions. Magnetic tape used in video does not bring any substantial changes. Next, storage media—computer-controlled digital storage devices—privilege databases once again. Multimedia encyclopedias, virtual museums, pornography, artists' CD-ROMs, library databases, Web indexes, and, of course, the Web itself: The database is more popular than ever before.

The digital computer turns out to be the perfect medium for the database form. Like a virus, databases infect CD-ROMs and hard drives, servers and Web sites. Can we say that the database is the cultural form most characteristic of a computer? In her 1978 article "Video: The Aesthetics of Narcissism," probably the single most well-known article on video art, art historian Rosalind Krauss argued that video is not a physical medium but a psychological one. In her analysis, "Video's real medium is a psychological situation, the very terms of which are to withdraw attention from an external object— an Other—and invest it in the Self."[28] In short, video art is a support for the

---

28. Rosalind Krauss, "Video: The Aesthetics of Narcissism," in John Hanhardt, ed. *Video Culture* (Rochester: Visual Studies Workshop, 1987), 184.

psychological condition of narcissism.[29] Does new media similarly function to play out a particular psychological condition, something that might be called a "database complex"? In this respect, it is interesting that a database imagination has accompanied computer art from its very beginning. In the 1960s, artists working with computers wrote programs to systematically explore the combinations of different visual elements. In part, they were following art world trends such as minimalism. Minimalist artists executed works of art according to preexistent plans; they also created series of images or objects by systematically varying a single parameter. So when minimalist artist Sol LeWitt spoke of an artist's idea as "the machine which makes the work," it was only logical to substitute the human executing the idea with a computer.[30] At the same time, since the only way to make pictures with a computer was by writing a computer program, the logic of computer programming itself pushed computer artists in the same directions. Thus, for artist Frieder Nake, a computer was a "Universal Picture Generator," capable of producing every possible picture out of a combination of available picture elements and colors.[31] In 1967 he published a portfolio of twelve drawings

----

29. This analysis can also be applied to many interactive computer installations. The user of such an installation is presented with her own image; the user is given the possibility to play with this image and also to observe how her movements trigger various effects. In a different sense, most new media, regardless of whether it represents to the user her image or not, can be said to activate the narcissistic condition because they represent to the user her actions and their results. In other words, it functions as a new kind of mirror that reflects not only the human image but human activities. This is a different kind of narcissism—not passive contemplation but action. The user moves the cursor around the screen, clicks on icons, presses the keys on the keyboard, and so on. The computer screen acts as a mirror of these activities. Often this mirror does not simply reflect but greatly amplifies the user's actions—a second difference from traditional narcissism. For instance, clicking on a folder icon activates an animation accompanied by sound; pressing a button on a game pad sends a character off to climb a mountain; and so on. But even without this amplification, the modern GUI functions as a mirror, always representing the image of the user in the form of a cursor moving around the screen.

30. Quoted in Sam Hunter and John Jacobus, *Modern Art: Painting, Sculpture, and Architecture,* 3d ed. (New York: Abrams, 1992), 326.

31. Frank Dietrich, "Visual Intelligence: The First Decade of Computer Art (1965–1975)," *IEEE Computer Graphics and Applications* (July 1985), 39.

that were obtained by successfully multiplying a square matrix by itself. Another early computer artist Manfred Mohr produced numerous images that recorded various transformations of a basic cube.

Even more remarkable were films by John Whitney, the pioneer of computer filmmaking. His films such as *Permutations* (1967), *Arabesque* (1975) and others systematically explored the transformations of geometric forms obtained by manipulating elementary mathematical functions. Thus they substituted successive accumulation of visual effects for narrative, figuration, or even formal development. Instead they presented the viewer with databases of effects. This principle reaches its extreme in Whitney's early film *Catalog,* which was made with an analog computer. In his important book on new forms of cinema of the 1960s entitled *Expanded Cinema* (1970), critic Gene Youngblood writes about this remarkable film: "The elder Whitney actually never produced a complete, coherent movie on the analog computer because he was continually developing and refining the machine while using it for commercial work. . . . However, Whitney did assemble a visual catalogue of the effects he had perfected over the years. This film, simply titled *Catalog,* was completed in 1961 and proved to be of such overwhelming beauty that many persons still prefer Whitney's analogue work over his digital computer films."[32] One is tempted to read *Catalog* as one of the founding moments of new media. As discussed in the "Selection" section, all software for media creation today arrives with endless "plug-ins"—the banks of effects that with a press of a button generate interesting images from any input whatsoever. In parallel, much of the aesthetics of computerized visual culture is effects-driven, especially when a new techno-genre (computer animation, multimedia, Web sites) is first becoming established. For instance, countless music videos are variations of Whitney's *Catalog*—the only difference is that the effects are applied to the images of human performers. This is yet another example of how the logic of a computer—in this case, the ability of a computer to produce endless variations of elements and to act as a filter, transforming its input to yield a new output—becomes the logic of culture at large.

---

32. Gene Youngblood, *Expanded Cinema* (New York: E. P. Dutton and Co., 1970), 210.

Database Cinema: Greenaway and Vertov

Although the database form may be inherent to new media, countless attempts to create "interactive narratives" testify to our dissatisfaction with the computer in the sole role of encyclopedia or catalog of effects. We want new media narratives, and we want these narratives to be different from the narratives we have seen or read before. In fact, regardless of how often we repeat in public that the modernist notion of medium specificity ("every medium should develop its own unique language") is obsolete, we do expect computer narratives to showcase new aesthetic possibilities that did not exist before digital computers. In short, we want them to be new media specific. Given the dominance of the database in computer software and the key role it plays in the computer-based design process, perhaps we can arrive at new kinds of narrative by focusing our attention on how narrative and database can work together. How can a narrative take into account the fact that its elements are organized in a database? *How can our new abilities to store vast amounts of data, to automatically classify, index, link, search, and instantly retrieve it, lead to new kinds of narratives?*

Peter Greenaway, one of the few prominent film directors concerned with expanding cinema's language, once complained that "the linear pursuit—one story at a time told chronologically—is the standard format of cinema." Pointing out that cinema lags behind modern literature in experimenting with narrative, he asked: "Could it not travel on the road where Joyce, Eliot, Borges and Perec have already arrived?"[33] While Greenaway is right to direct filmmakers to more innovative literary narratives, new media artists working on the database-problem can learn from cinema "as it is." For cinema already exists right at the intersection between database and narrative. We can think of all the material accumulated during shooting as forming a database, especially since the shooting schedule usually does not follow the narrative of the film but is determined by production logistics. During editing, the editor constructs a film narrative out of this database, creating a unique trajectory through the conceptual space of all possible films that could have been constructed. From this perspective, every filmmaker

---

33. Peter Greenaway, *The Stairs—Munich—Projection 2* (London: Merrell Holberton Publishers, 1995), 21.

engages with the database-narrative problem in every film, although only a few have done so self-consciously.

One exception is Greenaway himself. Throughout his career, he has been working on the problem of how to reconcile database and narrative forms. Many of his films progress by recounting a list of items, a catalog without any inherent order (for example, the different books in *Prospero's Books*). Working to undermine a linear narrative, Greenaway uses different systems to order his films. He wrote about this approach: "If a numerical, alphabetic color-coding system is employed, it is done deliberately as a device, a construct, to counteract, dilute, augment or complement the all-pervading obsessive cinema interest in plot, in narrative, in the 'I'm now going to tell you a story' school of film-making."[34] His favorite system is numbers. The sequence of numbers acts as a narrative shell that "convinces" the viewer that she is watching a narrative. In reality, the scenes that follow one another are not connected in any logical way. By using numbers, Greenaway "wraps" a minimal narrative around a database. Although Greenaway's database logic was already present in his "avant-garde" films such as *The Falls* (1980), it has also structured his "commercial" films. The *Draughtsman's Contract* (1982) is centered around twelve drawings in the process of being made by a draftsman. They do not form any order; Greenaway emphasizes this by having the draftsman work on a few drawings at once. Eventually, Greenaway's desire to take "cinema out of cinema" led to his work on a series of installations and museum exhibitions in the 1990s. No longer obliged to conform to the linear medium of film, the elements of a database are spatialized within a museum or even a whole city. This move can be read as the desire to create a database in its most pure form—as a set of elements not ordered in any way. If the elements exist in one dimension (the time of a film, the list on a page), they will inevitably be ordered. So the only way to create a pure database is to spatialize it, distributing the elements in space. This is exactly the path that Greenaway took. Situated in a three-dimensional space that does not have an inherent narrative logic, the 1992 installation "100 Objects to Represent the World" by its very title proposes that the world should be under-

---

34. Quoted in David Pascoe, *Peter Greenaway: Museums and Moving Images* (London: Reaktion Books, 1997), 9–10.

stood through a catalog rather than a narrative. At the same time, Greenaway does not abandon narrative; he continues to investigate how database and narrative can work together. Having presented "100 Objects" as an installation, Greenaway next turned it into an opera set. In the opera, the narrator Thrope uses the objects to conduct Adam and Eve through the whole of human civilization, thus turning one hundred objects into a sequential narrative.[35] In another installation, "The Stairs, Munich, Projection" (1995), Greenaway put up a hundred screens—each representing one year in the history of cinema—throughout Munich. Again, Greenaway presents us with a spatialized database—but also with a narrative. By walking from one screen to another, one follows cinema's history. The project uses Greenaway's favorite principle of organization by numbers, pushing it to the extreme: The projections on the screens contain no figuration, just numbers. The screens are numbered from 1895 to 1995, one screen for each year of cinema's history. Along with numbers, Greenaway introduces another line of development: Each projection is slightly different in color.[36] The hundred colored squares form an abstract narrative of their own that runs in parallel to the linear narrative of cinema's history. Finally, Greenaway superimposes yet a third narrative by dividing the history of cinema into five sections, each section staged in a different part of the city. The apparent triviality of the basic narrative of the project—one hundred numbers, standing for one hundred years of cinema's history—"neutralizes" the narrative, forcing the viewer to focus on the phenomenon of the projected light itself, which is the actual subject of this project.

Along with Greenaway, Dziga Vertov can be thought of as a major "database filmmaker" of the twentieth century. *Man with a Movie Camera* is perhaps the most important example of a database imagination in modern media art. In one of the key shots, repeated a few times throughout the film, we see an editing room with a number of shelves used to keep and organize the shot material. The shelves are marked "machines," "club," "the movement of a city," "physical exercise," "an illusionist," and so on. This is the database of the recorded material. The editor, Vertov's wife, Elizaveta Svilova, is shown

---

35. http://www.tem-nanterre.com/greenaway-100objects/.
36. Greenaway, *The Stairs, Munich, Projection 2*, 47–53.

working with this database—retrieving some reels, returning used reels, adding new ones.

Although I pointed out that film editing in general can be compared to creating a trajectory through a database, this comparison in the case of *Man with a Movie Camera* constitutes the very method of the film. Its subject is the filmmaker's struggle to reveal (social) structure among the multitude of observed phenomena. Its project is a brave attempt at an empirical epistemology that has but one tool—perception. The goal is to decode the world purely through the surfaces visible to the eye (natural sight enhanced, of course, by a movie camera). This is how the film's coauthor Mikhail Kaufman describes it:

An ordinary person finds himself in some sort of environment, gets lost amidst the zillions of phenomena, and observes these phenomena from a bad vantage point. He registers one phenomenon very well, registers a second and a third, but has no idea of where they may lead. . . . But the man with a movie camera is infused with the particular thought that he is actually seeing the world for other people. Do you understand? He joins these phenomena with others, from elsewhere, which may not even have been filmed by him. Like a kind of scholar he is able to gather empirical observations in one place and then in another. And that is actually the way in which the world has come to be understood.[37]

Therefore, in contrast to standard film editing that consists of selection and ordering of previously shot material according to a preexistent script, here the process of relating shots to each other, ordering, and reordering them to discover the hidden order of the world constitutes the film's method. *Man with a Movie Camera* traverses its database in a particular order to construct an argument. Records drawn from a database and arranged in a particular order become a picture of modern life—but simultaneously an argument about this life, an interpretation of what these images, which we encounter every day, every second, actually mean.[38]

Was this brave attempt successful? The overall structure of the film is quite complex, and at first glance seems to have little to do with a database.

---

37. Mikhail Kaufman, "An Interview," *October* 11 (Winter 1979): 65.

38. It can be said that Vertov uses "the Kuleshov's effect" to give meaning to the database records by placing them in a particular order.

Just as new media objects contain a hierarchy of levels (interface—content, operating system—application, Web page—HTML code, high-level programming language—assembly language—machine language), Vertov's film contains at least three levels. One level is the story of a cameraman shooting material for the film. The second level consists of the shots of the audience watching the finished film in a movie theater. The third level is the film itself, which consists of footage recorded in Moscow, Kiev, and Riga, arranged according to the progression of a single day: waking up—work—leisure activities. If this third level is a text, the other two can be thought of as its metatexts.[39] Vertov goes back and forth between the three levels, shifting between the text and its metatexts—between the production of the film, its reception, and the film itself. But if we focus on the film within the film (i.e., the level of the text) and disregard the special effects used to create many of the shots, we discover almost a linear printout, so to speak, of a database—a number of shots showing machines, followed by a number of shots showing work activities, followed by different shots of leisure, and so on. The paradigm is projected onto the syntagm. The result is a banal, mechanical catalog of subjects that one could expect to find in the city of the 1920s—running trams, city beach, movie theaters, factories . . .

Of course, watching *Man with a Movie Camera* is anything but a banal experience. Even after the 1990s, when designers and video-makers systematically had exploited every avant-garde device, the original still looks striking. What makes its striking is not its subjects and the associations Vertov tries to establish between them to impose "the communist decoding of the world," but rather the most amazing catalog of film techniques contained within it. Fades and superimpositions, freeze-frames, acceleration, split screens, various types of rhythm and intercutting, different montage techniques[40]—what

---

39. Linguistics, semiotics, and philosophy use the concept of metalanguage. Metalanguage is the language used for the analysis of object language. Thus a metalanguage may be thought of as a language about another language. A metatext is a text in metalanguage about a text in object language. For instance, an article in a fashion magazine is a metatext about the text of clothes. Or an HTML file is a metatext that describes the text of a Web page.

40. We should remember that various temporal montage techniques were still a novelty in the 1920s; they had the same status for viewers then as "special effects" such as 3-D characters have for viewers today. The original viewers of Vertov's film probably experienced it as one long special-effects sequence.

film scholar Annette Michelson has called "a summation of the resources and techniques of the silent cinema"[41]—and of course, a multitude of unusual, "constructivist" points of view are strung together with such density that the film cannot simply be labeled "avant-garde." If a "normal" avant-garde film still proposes a coherent language different from the language of mainstream cinema, that is, a small set of techniques that are repeated, *Man with a Movie Camera* never arrives at anything like a well-defined language. Rather, it proposes an untamed, and apparently endless, unwinding of techniques, or, to use contemporary language, "effects," as cinema's new way of speaking.

Traditionally, a personal artistic language or a style common to a group of cultural objects or a period requires a stability of paradigms and consistent expectations as to which elements of paradigmatic sets may appear in a given situation. For example, in the case of classic Hollywood style, a viewer may expect that a new scene will begin with an establishing shot or that a particular lighting convention such as high key or low key will be used throughout the film. (David Bordwell defines a Hollywood style in terms of paradigms ranked in terms of probabilities.)[42]

The endless new possibilities provided by computer software hold the promise of new cinematic languages, but at the same time they prevent such languages from coming into being. (I am using the example of film, but the same logic applies to all other areas of computer-based visual culture.) Since every software comes with numerous sets of transitions, 2-D filters, 3-D transformations, and other effects and "plug-ins," the artist, especially the beginner, is tempted to use many of them in the same work. In such a case, a paradigm becomes the syntagm; that is, rather than making singular choices from the sets of possible techniques, or, to use the term of Russian formalists, devices, and then repeating them throughout the work (for instance, using only cuts, or only cross-dissolves), the artist ends up using many options in the same work. Ultimately, a digital film becomes a list of different effects, which appear one after another. Whitney's *Catalog* is the extreme expression of this logic.

---

41. Ibid., 55.

42. David Bordwell, "Classical Hollywood Film," in Philip Rosen, ed., *Narrative, Apparatus, Ideology: Film Theory Reader* (New York: Columbia University Press, 1987).

The possibility of creating a stable new language is also subverted by the constant introduction of new techniques over time. Thus the new media paradigms not only contain many more options than old media paradigms, but they also keep growing. And in a culture ruled by the logic of fashion, that is, the demand for constant innovation, artists tend to adopt newly available options while simultaneously dropping already familiar ones. Every year, every month, new effects find their way into media works, displacing previously prominent ones and destabilizing any stable expectations that viewers might have begun to form.

And this is why Vertov's film has particular relevance to new media. It proves that it is possible to turn "effects" into a meaningful artistic language. Why is it that in Whitney's computer films and music videos effects are just effects, whereas in the hands of Vertov they acquire meaning? Because in Vertov's film they are motivated by a particular argument, which is that the new techniques of obtaining images and manipulating them, summed up by Vertov in his term "kino-eye," can be used to decode the world. As the film progresses, straight footage gives way to manipulated footage; newer techniques appear one after another, reaching a roller-coaster intensity by the film's end—a true orgy of cinematography. It is as though Vertov restages his discovery of the kino-eye for us, and along with him, we gradually realize the full range of possibilities offered by the camera. Vertov's goal is to seduce us into his way of seeing and thinking, to make us share his excitement, as he discovers a new language for film. This gradual process of discovery is film's main narrative, and it is told through a catalog of discoveries. Thus in the hands of Vertov, the database, this normally static and "objective" form, becomes dynamic and subjective. More important, Vertov is able to achieve something that new media designers and artists still have to learn—how to merge database and narrative into a new form.

Navigable Space

Doom and *Myst*

Looking at the first decade of new media—the 1990s—one can point at a number of objects that exemplify new media's potential to give rise to genuinely original and historically unprecedented aesthetic forms. Among them, two stand out. Both are computer games. Both were published in the same year, 1993. Each became a phenomenon whose popularity has extended beyond the hard-core gaming community, spilling into sequels, books, TV, films, fashion, and design. Together, they define the new field and its limits. These games are *Doom* (id Software, 1993) and *Myst* (Cyan, 1993).

In a number of ways, *Doom* and *Myst* are completely different. *Doom* is fast paced; *Myst* is slow. In *Doom* the player runs through the corridors trying to complete each level as soon as possible, and then moves to the next one. In *Myst,* the player moves through the world literally one step at a time, unraveling the narrative along the way. *Doom* is populated with numerous demons lurking around every corner, waiting to attack; *Myst* is completely empty. The world of *Doom* follows the convention of computer games: It consists of a few dozen levels. Although *Myst* also contains four separate worlds, each is more like a self-contained universe than a traditional computer game level. While in most games levels are quite similar to each other in structure and look, the worlds of *Myst* are distinctly different.

Another difference lies in the aesthetics of navigation. In *Doom*'s world, defined by rectangular volumes, the player moves in straight lines, abruptly turning at right angles to enter a new corridor. In *Myst,* the navigation is more free-form. The player, or more precisely, the visitor, slowly explores the environment: She may look around for a while, go in circles, return to the same place over and over, as though performing an elaborate dance.

Finally, the two objects exemplify two different types of cultural economy. With *Doom,* id software pioneered the new economy that critic of computer games J. C. Herz summarizes as follows: "It was an idea whose time had come. Release a free, stripped-down version through shareware channels, the Internet, and online services. Follow with a spruced-up, registered retail version of the software." Fifteen million copies of the original *Doom* game were downloaded around the world.[43] By releasing detailed descriptions of game formats and a game editor, id software also encouraged the players to expand the game, creating new levels. Thus hacking and adding to the game became an essential part of the game, with new levels widely available on the Internet for anyone to download. Here was a new cultural economy that transcended the usual relationship between producers and consumers or between "strategies" and "tactics" (de Certeau): *The producers define the basic structure of an object, and release a few examples as well as tools to allow consumers to build their own versions, to be shared with other consumers.* In contrast, the creators of *Myst* followed an older model of cultural economy. Thus *Myst* is more similar to a traditional artwork than to a piece of software—something to behold and admire rather than take apart and modify. To use the terms of the software industry, it is a closed, or proprietary, system, something that only the original creators can modify.

Despite all these differences in cosmogony, gameplay, and underlying economic model, the two games are similar in one key respect. Both are spatial journeys. Navigation though 3-D space is an essential, if not the key, component of the gameplay. *Doom* and *Myst* present the user with a space to be traversed, to be mapped out by moving through it. Both begin by dropping the player somewhere in this space. Before reaching the end of the game narrative, the player must visit most of it, uncovering its geometry and topology, learning its logic and its secrets. In *Doom* and *Myst*—and in a great many other computer games—narrative and time itself are equated with movement through 3-D space, progression through rooms, levels, or words. In contrast to modern literature, theater, and cinema, which are built around psychological tensions between characters and movement in psychological

---

43. J. C. Hertz, *Joystick Nation,* 90, 84.

space, these computer games return us to ancient forms of narrative in which the plot is driven by the spatial movement of the main hero, traveling through distant lands to save the princess, to find the treasure, to defeat the dragon, and so on. As J. C. Herz writes about the experience of playing the classic text-based adventure game *Zork,* "You gradually unlocked a world in which the story took place, and the receding edge of this world carried you through to the story's conclusion."[44] Stripping away the representation of inner life, psychology, and other modernist nineteenth-century inventions, these are the narratives in the original ancient Greek sense, for, as Michel de Certeau reminds us, "in Greek, narration is called 'diagesis': it establishes an itinerary (it 'guides') and it passes through (it 'transgresses.')"[45]

In the introduction to this chapter, I invoked the opposition between narration and description in narratology. As noted by Mieke Bal, the standard theoretical premise of narratology is that "descriptions interrupt the line of fabula."[46] For me, this opposition, in which description is defined negatively as absence of narration, has always been problematic. It automatically privileges certain types of narrative (myths, fairy tales, detective stories, classical Hollywood cinema), while making it difficult to think about other forms in which the actions of characters do not dominate the narrative (for instance, films by Andrey Tarkovskiy, or Hirokazu Kore-eda, the director of *Maborosi* and *After Life*).[47] Games structured around first-person navigation through space further challenge the narration-description opposition.

---

44. Ibid., 150.

45. Michel de Certeau, *The Practice of Everyday Life,* trans. Steven Rendall (Berkeley: University of California Press, 1984), 129.

46. Bal, *Narratology,* 130. Bal defines *fabula* as "a series of logically and chronologically related events that are caused or experienced by actors" (5).

47. In *Understanding Comics,* Scott McLoud notes how, in contrast to Western comics, Japanese comics spend much more time on "description" not directly motivated by the narrative development. The same opposition holds between the language of classical Hollywood cinema and many films from the "east," such as the works of Tarkovsky and Kore-eda. Although I recognize the danger of such a generalization, it is tempting to connect the narration–description opposition to a much larger opposition between traditionally Western and Eastern ways of existence and philosophies—the drive of the Western subject to know and conquer the world outside versus the Buddhist emphasis on meditation and stasis. Scott McLoud, *Understanding Comics: The Invisible Art* (Harper Perennial, 1994).

Instead of narration and description, we may be better off thinking about games in terms of *narrative actions* and *exploration.* Rather than being narrated to, the player herself has to perform actions to move narrative forward— talking to other characters she encounters in the game world, picking up objects, fighting enemies, and so on. If the player does nothing, the narrative stops. From this perspective, movement through the game world is one of the main narrative actions. But this movement also serves the self-sufficient goal of exploration. Exploring the game world, examining its details and enjoying its images, is as important for the success of games such as *Myst* and its followers as progressing through the narrative. Thus, while from one point of view, game narratives can be aligned with ancient narratives that are also structured around movement through space, from another perspective they are exact opposites. Movement through space allows the player to progress through the narrative, but it is also valuable in itself. It is a way for the player to explore the environment.

Narratology's analysis of description can be a useful start in thinking about exploration of space in computer games and other new media objects. Bal states that descriptive passages in fiction are motivated by speaking, looking, and acting. Motivation by looking works as follows: "A character sees an object. The description is the reproduction of what it sees." Motivation by acting means that "the actor carries out an action with an object. The description is then made fully narrative. The example of this is the scene in Zola's *La Bête* in which Jacques polishes [strokes] every individual component of his beloved locomotive."[48]

In contrast to the modern novel, action-oriented games do not have that much dialog, but looking and acting are indeed the key activities performed by a player. And if in modern fiction looking and acting are usually separate activities, in games they more often than not occur together. As the player comes across a door leading to another level, a new passage, ammunition for his machine gun, an enemy, or a "health potion," he immediately acts on these objects—opens a door, picks up ammunition or "health potion," fires at the enemy. Thus narrative action and exploration are closely linked together.

The central role of navigation through space, both as a tool of narration and of exploration, is acknowledged by the games' designers themselves.

---

48. Bal, *Narratology,* 130–132.

According to Robyn Miller, one of the two codesigners of *Myst,* "We are creating environments to just wander around inside of. People have been calling it a game for lack of anything better, and we've called it a game at times. But that's not what it really is; it's a world."[49] Richard Garriott, designer of the classic RPG *Ultima* series, contrasts game design and fiction writing: "A lot of them [fiction writers] develop their individual characters in detail, and they say what is their problem in the beginning, and what they are going to grow to learn in the end. That's not the method I've used . . . I have the world. I have the message. And then the characters are there to support the world and the message."[50]

Structuring the game as a navigation through space is common to games across all genres. This includes adventure games (for instance, *Zork, 7th Level, The Journeyman Project, Tomb Raider, Myst*); strategy games (*Command and Conquer*); role-playing games (*Diablo, Final Fantasy*); flying, driving, and other simulators (*Microsoft Flight Simulator*); action games (*Hexen, Mario*); and, of course, first-person shooters following in *Doom's* steps (*Quake, Unreal*). These genres obey different conventions. In adventure games, the user explores a universe, gathering resources. In strategy games, the user engages in allocating and moving resources and in risk management. In RPGs (role-playing games), the user builds a character and acquires skills; the narrative is one of self-improvement. The genre conventions by themselves do not make it necessary for these games to employ a navigable space interface. The fact that they all consistently do, therefore, suggests to me that navigable space represents a larger cultural form. In other words, it is something that transcends computer games and in fact, as we will see later, computer culture as well. Just like a database, navigable space is a form that existed before computers, even if the computer becomes its perfect medium.

Indeed, the use of navigable space is common to all areas of new media. During the 1980s, numerous 3-D computer animations were organized around a single, uninterrupted camera move through a complex and extensive set. In a typical animation, a camera would fly over mountain terrain, or move through a series of rooms, or maneuver past geometric shapes. In con-

---

49. McGoman and McCullaugh, *Entertainment in the Cyber Zone,* 120.

50. Quoted in J. C. Hertz, *Joystick Nation,* 155–156.

trast to both ancient myths and computer games, this journey had no goal, no purpose. In short, there was no narrative. Here was the ultimate "road movie," where navigation through space was sufficient in itself.

In the 1990s, these 3-D fly-throughs have come to constitute the new genre of postcomputer cinema and location-based entertainment—the motion simulator.[51] By using first-person point of view and by synchronizing the movement of the platform housing the audience with the movement of a virtual camera, motion simulators recreate the experience of traveling in a vehicle. Thinking about the historical precedents of a motion simulator, we begin to uncover some places where the form of navigable space has already manifested itself. They include *Hale's Tours and Scenes of the World,* a popular film-based attraction that debuted at the St. Louis Fair in 1904; roller-coaster rides; flight, vehicle, and military simulators, which have used a moving base since the early 1930s; and the fly-through sequences in *2001: A Space Odyssey* (Kubrick, 1968) and *Star Wars* (Lucas, 1977). Among these, *A Space Odyssey* plays a particularly important role; Douglas Trumbull, who since the late 1980s has produced some of the best-known motion-simulator attractions and was the key person behind the rise of the motion-simulator phenomenon, began his career by creating ride sequences for this film.

Along with providing a key foundation for new media aesthetics, navigable space has also become a new tool of labor. It is now a common way to visualize and work with any data. From scientific visualization to walk-throughs of architectural designs, from models of a stock market performance to statistical datasets, the 3-D virtual space combined with a camera model is the accepted way to visualize all information. It is as accepted in computer culture as charts and graphs were in a print culture.[52]

Since navigable space can be used to represent both physical spaces and abstract information spaces, it is only logical that it has also emerged as an important paradigm in human-computer interfaces. Indeed, on one level, HCI can be

---

51. For a critical analysis of the motion simulator phenomenon, see Erkki Huhtamo, "Phantom Train to Technopia," in Minna Tarkka, ed., *ISEA '94: The 5th International Symposium on Electronic Art Catalogue* (Helsinki: University of Art and Design, 1994); "Encapsulated Bodies in Motion: Simulators and the Quest for Total Immersion," in Simon Penny, ed., *Critical Issues in Electronic Media.*

52. See www.cybergeography.com.

seen as a particular case of data visualization, the data being computer files rather than molecules, architectural models, or stock market figures. Examples of 3-D navigable space interfaces are the Information Visualizer (Xerox Parc), which replaces a flat desktop with 3-D rooms and planes rendered in perspective;[53] T_Vision (ART+COM), which uses a navigable 3-D representation of the earth as its interface;[54] and The Information Landscape (Silicon Graphics), in which the user flies over a plane populated by data objects.[55]

The original (i.e., the 1980s) vision of cyberspace called for a 3-D space of information to be traversed by a human user or, to use the term of William Gibson, a "data cowboy."[56] Even before Gibson's fictional descriptions of cyberspace were published, cyberspace was visualized in the film *Tron* (Disney, 1982). Although *Tron* takes place inside a single computer rather than a network, its vision of users zapping through immaterial space defined by lines of light is remarkably similar to the one articulated by Gibson in his novels. In an article that appeared in the 1991 anthology *Cyberspace: First Steps,* Marcos Novak still defined *cyberspace* as "a completely spatialized visualization of all information in global information processing systems."[57] In the first part of the 1990s, this vision has survived among the original designers of VRML. In designing the language, they aimed to "create a unified conceptualization of space spanning the entire Internet, a spatial equivalent of WWW."[58] They saw VRML as a natural stage in the evolution of the Net from an abstract data network toward a "'perceptualized' Internet where the data has been sensualized," that is, represented in three dimensions.[59]

---

53. Stuart Card, George Robertson, and Jock Mackingly, "The Information Visualizer, an Information Workplace," in *CHI '91: Human Factors in Computing Systems Conference Proceedings* (New York: ACM, 1991), 181–186; available online at http://www.acm.org/pubs/articles/proceedings/chi/108844/p181-card/p181-card.pdf.

54. http://www.artcom.de/projects/t_vision/.

55. http://www.acm.org/sigchi/chi95/proceedings/panels/km_bdy.htm.

56. William Gibson, *Neuromancer* (New York: Ace Books, 1984).

57. Marcos Novak, "Liquid Architecture in Cyberspace," in Michael Benedikt, ed., *Cyberspace: First Steps* (Cambridge, Mass.: MIT Press, 1991), 225–254.

58. Mark Pesce, Peter Kennard, and Anthony Parisi, "Cyberspace," 1994, http://www.hyperreal.org/~mpesce/www.html.

59. Ibid.

The term *cyberspace* is derived from another term—*cybernetics.* In his 1947 book *Cybernetics,* mathematician Norbert Wiener defined it as "the science of control and communications in the animal and machine." Wiener conceived of cybernetics during World War II when he was working on problems concerning gunfire control and automatic missile guidance. He derived the term *cybernetics* from the ancient Greek word *kybernetikos,* which refers to the art of the steersman and can be translated as "good at steering." Thus the idea of navigable space lies at the very origins of the computer era. The steersman navigating the ship and the missile traversing space on its way to a target have given rise to a whole number of new figures—the heroes of William Gibson, "data cowboys" moving through the vast terrains of cyberspace; "drivers" of motion simulators; computer users navigating through scientific data sets and computer data structures, molecules and genes, the earth's atmosphere and the human body; and last but not least, players of *Doom, Myst,* and their endless imitations.

From one point of view, navigable space can legitimately be seen as a particular kind of an interface to a database, and thus something that does not deserve special focus. I would like, however, to think of it also as a cultural form in its own right, not only because of its prominence across the new media landscape and, as we will later see, its persistence in new media history, but also because, more than a database, it is a new form that may be unique to new media. Of course, both the organization of space and its use to represent or visualize something else have always been a fundamental part of human culture. Architecture and ancient mnemonics, city planning and diagramming, geometry and topology, are just some of the disciples and techniques that were developed to harness space's symbolic and economic capital.[60] Spatial constructions in new media draw on all these existing traditions—but they are also fundamentally different in one key respect. For the first time, *space becomes a media type.* Just as other media types—audio, video, stills, and text—it can now be instantly transmitted, stored, and retrieved; compressed, reformatted, streamed, filtered, com-

---

60. Michael Benedikt explores the relevance of some of these disciplines to the concept of cyberspace in the introduction to his groundbreaking anthology *Cyberspace: First Steps,* which remains one of the best books on the topic of cyberspace.

puted, programmed, and interacted with. In other words, all operations that are possible with media as a result of its conversion to computer data can also now apply to representations of 3-D space.

Recent cultural theory has paid increasing attention to the category of space. Examples are Henri Lefebvre's work on the politics and anthropology of everyday space, Michel Foucault's analysis of the Panopticon's topology as a model of modern subjectivity, the writings of Fredric Jameson and David Harvey on the postmodern space of global capitalism, and Edward Soja's work on political geography.[61] At the same time, new media theoreticians and practitioners have come forward with many formulations of how cyberspace should be structured and how computer-based spatial representations might be used in new ways.[62] What has received little attention, however, both in cultural theory and in new media theory, is the particular category of *navigation through space*. And yet, this category characterizes new media as it actually exists; in other words, new media spaces are always spaces of navigation. At the same time, as we will see later in this section, this category also fits a number of developments in other cultural fields such as anthropology and architecture.

To summarize, along with a database, navigable space is another key form of new media. It is already an accepted way of interacting with any kind of data, a familiar interface in computer games and motion simulators, and a possible form for nearly any computing practice. Why does computer culture spatialize all representations and experiences (the library is replaced by cyberspace; narrative is equated with traveling through space; all kinds of data are rendered in three dimensions through computer visualization)? Shall we try to oppose this spatialization (i.e., what about time in new

---

61. Henri Lefebvre, *The Production of Space* (Oxford: Blackwell, 1991); Michel Foucault, *Discipline and Punish: The Birth of the Prison* (New York: Pantheon Books, 1977); Fredric Jameson, *The Geopolitical Aesthetic: Cinema and Space in the World System* (Bloomington: Indiana University Press, 1992); David Harvey, *The Condition of Postmodernity* (Oxford: Blackwell, 1989); Edward Soja, *Postmodern Geographies: The Reassertion of Space in Critical Social Theory* (London: Verso, 1989).

62. See, for instance, Benedikt, *Cyberspace: First Steps* and the articles of Marcos Novak (http://www.aud.ucla.edu/~marcos).

media?) And, finally, what are the aesthetics of navigation through virtual space?

Computer Space

The very first coin-op arcade game was called *Computer Space.* The game simulated a dogfight between a spaceship and a flying saucer. Released in 1971, it was a remake of the first computer game, *Spacewar,* programmed on PDP-1 at MIT in 1962.[63] Both of these legendary games included the word *space* in their titles; and appropriately, space was one of the main characters in each of them. In the original *Spacewar,* the players navigated two spaceships around the screen while shooting torpedoes at one another. The player also had to be careful in maneuvering the ships to make sure they would not get too close to the star in the center of the screen that pulled them toward it. Thus along with the spaceships, the player had to interact with space itself. And although, in contrast to such films as *2001, Star Wars,* and *Tron,* the space of *Spacewar* and *Computer Space* was not navigable—one could not move through it—the simulation of gravity made it a truly active presence. Just as the player had to engage with the spaceships, he also had to engage with space itself.

This active treatment of space is the exception rather than the rule in new media. Although new media objects favor the use of space for representations of all kinds, virtual spaces are most often not true spaces but collections of separate objects. Or, to put this in a slogan: There is no space in cyberspace.

To explore this thesis further, we can borrow categories developed by art historians early in this century. Alois Riegl, Heinrich Wölfflin, and Erwin Panofsky, the founders of modern art history, defined their field as the history of the representation of space. Working within the paradigm of cyclic cultural development, they related the representation of space in art to the spirit of entire epochs, civilizations, and races. In his 1901 *Die Spätrömische Kunstindustrie* (The late-Roman art industry), Riegl characterized mankind's cultural development as the oscillation between two ways of understanding space, which he called "haptic" and "optic." Haptic perception isolates the object in the field as a discrete entity, whereas optic perception unifies

---

63. http://icwhen.com/the70s/1971.html.

objects in a spatial continuum. Riegl's contemporary, Heinrich Wölfflin, similarly proposed that the temperament of a period or a nation expresses itself in a particular mode of seeing and representing space. Wölfflin's *Principles of Art History* (1913) plotted the differences between Renaissance and baroque styles along five axes: linear/painterly; plane/recession; closed form/open form; multiplicity/unity; and clearness/unclearness.[64] Erwin Panofsky, another founder of modern art history, contrasted the "aggregate" space of the Greeks with the "systematic" space of the Italian Renaissance in his famous essay *Perspective as Symbolic Form* (1924–1925).[65] Panofsky established a parallel between the history of spatial representation and the evolution of abstract thought. The former moves from the space of individual objects in antiquity to the representation of space as continuous and systematic in modernity. Correspondingly, the evolution of abstract thought progresses from ancient philosophy's view of the physical universe as discontinuous and "aggregate," to the post-Renaissance understanding of space as infinite, homogeneous, isotropic, and with ontological primacy in relation to objects—in short, as systematic.

We do not have to believe in grand evolutionary schemes in order to usefully retain such categories. What kind of space is virtual space? At first glance, the technology of 3-D computer graphics exemplifies Panofsky's concept of systematic space, which exists prior to the objects in it. Indeed, the Cartesian coordinate system is built into computer graphics software and often into the hardware itself.[66] A designer launching a modeling program is typically presented with an empty space defined by a perspectival grid; the space will be gradually filled by the objects created. If the built-in message of a music synthesizer is a sine wave, the built-in world of computer graphics is an empty Renaissance space—the coordinate system itself.

Yet computer-generated worlds are actually much more haptic and aggregate than optic and systematic. The most commonly used computer-

64. Heinrich Wölfflin, *Principles of Art History,* trans. M. D. Hottinger (New York: Dover Publications, 1950).

65. Erwin Panofsky, *Perspective as Symbolic Form,* trans. Christopher S. Wood (New York: Zone Books, 1991).

66. See my article "Mapping Space: Perspective, Radar, and Computer Graphics."

graphics technique of creating 3-D worlds is polygonal modeling. The virtual world created with this technique is a vacuum containing separate objects defined by rigid boundaries. What is missing from computer space is space in the sense of medium—an environment in which objects are embedded and the effect of these objects on each other, what Russian writers and artists call *prostranstvennaya sreda.* Pavel Florensky, a legendary Russian philosopher and art historian, described it in the following way in the early 1920s: "The space-medium is objects mapped onto space . . . We have seen the inseparability of Things and space, and the impossibility of representing Things and space by themselves."[67] This understanding of space also characterizes a particular tradition of modern painting that stretches from Seurat to Giacometti and de Kooning. These painters tried to eliminate the notions of a distinct object and empty space as such. Instead they depicted a dense field that occasionally hardens into something that we can read as an object. Following the example of Gilles Deleuze's analysis of cinema as an activity of articulating new concepts akin to philosophy,[68] it can be said that modern painters belonging to this tradition worked to articulate a particular philosophical concept in their painting—that of space-medium. This concept is something mainstream computer graphics still has to discover.

Another basic technique used in creating virtual worlds also leads to aggregate space. It involves superimposing animated characters, still images, digital movies, and other elements over a separate background. Traditionally, this technique was used in video and computer games. Responding to the limitations of the available computers, the designers of early games would limit animation to a small part of a screen. 2-D animated objects and characters called "sprites" were drawn over a static background. For example, in *Space Invaders* the abstract shapes representing the invaders would fly over a blank background, while in *Pac-Man* the tiny character moved across the picture of a maze. The sprites were essentially animated 2-D cutouts thrown over the background image at game time, so no real interaction

---

67. Quoted in Alla Efimova and Lev Manovich, "Object, Space, Culture: Introduction," in *Tekstura: Russian Essays on Visual Culture,* eds. Alla Efimova and Lev Manovich (Chicago: University of Chicago Press, 1993), xxvi.

68. Gilles Deleuze, *Cinema* (Minneapolis: University of Minnesota Press, 1986–1989).

between them and the background took place. In the second half of the 1990s, much faster processors and 3-D graphics cards made it possible for games to switch to real-time 3-D rendering. This allowed for modeling of visual interactions between objects and the space in which they were located, such as reflections and shadows. Consequently, the game space became more of a coherent, true 3-D space, rather than a set of 2-D planes unrelated to each other. However, the limitations of earlier decades returned in another area of new media—online virtual worlds. Because of the limited bandwidth of the 1990s Internet, virtual world designers have to deal with constraints similar to and sometimes even more severe than those faced by game designers two decades earlier. In online virtual worlds, a typical scenario may involve an avatar animated in real time in response to the user's commands. The avatar is superimposed on a picture of a room in the same way as in video games sprites are superimposed on backgrounds. The avatar is controlled by the user; the picture of the room is provided by a virtual-world operator. Because the elements come from different sources and are put together in real time, the result is a series of 2-D planes rather than a real 3-D environment. Although the image depicts characters in a 3-D space, it is an illusion since the background and the characters do not "know" about each other, and no interaction between them is possible.

Historically, we can connect the technique of superimposing animated sprites on backgrounds to traditional cell animation. To save labor, animators similarly divided an image between a static background and animated characters. In fact, the sprites of computer games can be thought of as reincarnated animation characters. Yet the use of this technique did not prevent Fleischer and Disney animators from thinking of space as a space-medium (to use Florensky's term), although they created this space-medium in a different way than did modern painters. (Thus while the masses run away from serious and "difficult" abstract art to enjoy the funny and figurative images of cartoons, what they saw was not that different from Giacometti's and de Kooning's canvases.) Although all objects in cartoons have hard edges, the total anthropomorphism of the cartoon universe breaks distinctions both between subjects and objects and objects and space. Everything is subjected to the same laws of stretch and squash, everything moves and twists in the same way, everything is alive to the same extent. It is as though everything—the character's body, chairs, walls, plates, food, cars, and so on—is made from the same bio-material. This monism of the cartoon worlds stands in opposition to the binary ontology of computer worlds in which the space and the sprites/characters appear to be made from two fundamentally different substances.

In summary, although 3-D computer-generated virtual worlds are usually rendered in linear perspective, they are really collections of separate objects, unrelated to each other. In view of this, the common argument that 3-D computer simulations return us to Renaissance perspective and therefore, from the viewpoint of twentieth-century abstraction, should be considered regressive, turns out to be ungrounded. If we are to apply the evolutionary paradigm of Panofsky to the history of virtual computer space, we must conclude that it has not yet reached its Renaissance stage. It is still at the level of ancient Greece, which could not conceive of space as a totality.

Computer space is also aggregate yet in another sense. As I already noted, using the example of *Doom,* traditionally the world of a computer game is not a continuous space but a set of discrete levels. In addition, each level is also discrete—it is a sum of rooms, corridors, and arenas built by the designers. Thus rather than conceiving space as a totality, one is dealing with a set of separate places. The convention of levels is remarkably stable, persisting across genres and numerous computer platforms.

If the World Wide Web and the original VRML are any indications, we are not moving any closer toward systematic space; instead, we are embracing aggregate space as a new norm, both metaphorically and literally. The space of the Web, in principle, cannot be thought of as a coherent totality: It is, rather, a collection of numerous files, hyperlinked but without any overall perspective to unite them. The same holds for actual 3-D spaces on the Internet. A 3-D scene as defined by a VRML file is a list of separate objects that may exist anywhere on the Internet, each created by a different person or a different program. A user can easily add or delete objects without taking into account the overall structure of the scene.[69] Just as in the case of a database, the narrative is replaced by a list of items; a coherent 3-D scene becomes a list of separate objects.

With its metaphors of navigation and homesteading, the web has been compared to the American Wild West. The spatialized Web envisioned by VRML (itself a product of California) reflects the treatment of space in

---

69. John Hartman and Josie Wernecke, *The VRML 2.0 Handbook.*

American culture generally, in its lack of attention to any zone that is not functionally used. The marginal areas that exist between privately owned houses, businesses, and parks are left to decay. The VRML universe, as defined by software standards and the default settings of software tools, pushes this tendency to the limit: It does not contain space as such but only objects that belong to different individuals. Obviously, the users can modify the default settings and use the tools to create the opposite of what the default values suggest. In fact, the actual muti-user spaces built on the Web can be seen precisely as a reaction against the anticommunal and discrete nature of American society, an attempt to compensate for the much discussed disappearance of traditional community by creating virtual ones. (Of course, if we follow the nineteenth-century sociologist Ferdinand Tönnies, the shift from traditional close-knit scale community to modern impersonal society had already taken place in the nineteenth century and was an inevitable side-effect as well as prerequisite for modernization.)[70] However, it is important that the ontology of virtual space as defined by software itself is fundamentally aggregate, a set of objects without a unifying point of view.

Art historians and literary and film scholars have traditionally analyzed the structure of cultural objects as reflecting larger cultural patterns (for instance, Panofsky's reading of perspective); in the case of new media, we should look not only at the finished objects but first of all at the software tools, their organization and default settings.[71] This is particularly important because in new media the relation between production tools and media objects is one of continuity; in fact, it is often hard to establish the boundary between them. Thus we may connect the American ideology of democracy with its paranoid fear of hierarchy and centralized control with the flat structure of the Web, where every page exists on the same level of importance as any other and where any two sources connected through hyperlinking have equal weight. Similarly, in the case of virtual 3-D spaces on the Web, the lack of a unifying perspective in U.S. culture, whether in the space of an Ameri-

70. See Ferdinand Tönnies, *Community and Society,* trans. Charles P. Loomis (East Lansing: Michigan State University Press, 1957).

71. One important exception was the apparatus theory developed by film theoreticians in the 1970s.

can city or in the space of an increasingly fragmented public discourse, can be correlated with the design of VRML, which substitutes a collection of objects for a unified space.

The Poetics of Navigation

In order to analyze computer representations of 3-D space, I have used theories from early art history, but it would not be hard to find other theories that could work as well. Navigation through space, however, is a different matter. While art history, geography, anthropology, sociology, and other disciplines have come up with many approaches to analyze space as a static, objectively existing structure, we do not have the same wealth of concepts to help us think about the poetics of navigation through space. And yet, if I am right to claim that the key feature of computer space is its navigability, we need to be able to address this feature theoretically.

As a way to begin, we may take a look at some of the classic navigable computer spaces. The 1978 project *Aspen Movie Map,* designed at the MIT Architecture Machine Group, headed by Nicholas Negroponte (the group later expanded into the MIT Media Laboratory), is acknowledged as the first interactive virtual navigable space, and also as the first hypermedia program to be shown publicly. The program allowed the user to "drive" through the city of Aspen, Colorado. At each intersection the user was able to select a new direction using a joystick. To construct this program, the MIT team drove through Aspen in a car taking pictures every three meters. The pictures were then stored on a set of videodiscs. Responding to the information from the joystick, the appropriate picture or sequence of pictures was displayed on the screen. Inspired by a mockup of an airport used by Israeli commandos to train for the Entebbe hostage-freeing raid of 1973, *Aspen Movie Map* was a simulator and, therefore, its navigation modeled the real-life experience of moving in a car with all its limitations.[72] Yet its realism also opened up a new set of aesthetic possibilities, which, unfortunately, later designers of navigable spaces did not explore further. They relied on interactive 3-D computer graphics to construct their spaces. In contrast, the designers of *Aspen Movie Map* utilized a set of photographic images; in addition, because the images

---

72. Stewart Brand, *The Media Lab* (New York: Penguin Books, 1988), 141.

were taken every three meters, the result was an interesting sampling of three-dimensional space. Although in the 1990s Apple's QuickTime VR technology made this technique quite accessible, the idea of constructing a large-scale virtual space from photographs or a video of a real space was never systematically attempted again, despite the fact that it opens up unique aesthetic possibilities not available with 3-D computer graphics.

Jeffrey Shaw's *Legible City* (1988–1991), another well-known and influential computer navigable space, is also based on an existing city.[73] As in *Aspen Movie Map,* the navigation also simulates a real, physical situation, in this case, riding a bicycle. Its virtual space, however, is not tied to the simulation of physical reality: it is an imaginary city made from 3-D letters. In contrast to most navigable spaces whose parameters are chosen arbitrarily, every value of virtual space in *Legible City* (Amsterdam and Karlsruhe versions) is derived from the actual existing physical space it replaces. Each 3-D letter in the virtual city corresponds to an actual building in a physical city; the letter's proportions, color, and location are derived from the building it replaces. By navigating through the space, the user reads the texts composed by the letters; these texts are drawn from the archive documents describing the city's history. Through this mapping, Shaw foregrounds, or, more precisely, "stages," one of the fundamental problematics of new media and the computer age as a whole—the relation between the virtual and the real. In his other works Shaw has systematically "staged" other key aspects of new media such as the interactive relation between the viewer and the image, or the discrete quality of all computer-based representations. *Legible City* functions not only as a unique navigable virtual space of its own, but also as a comment on all the other navigable spaces. It suggests that instead of creating virtual spaces that have nothing to do with actual physical spaces, or spaces that are closely modeled after existing physical structures, such as towns or shopping malls (this holds for most commercial virtual worlds and VR works), we may take a middle road. In *Legible City,* the memory of the real city is carefully preserved without succumbing to illusionism; the vir-

---

73. Manuela Abel, ed., *Jeffrey Shaw—A User's Manual* (Karlsruhe, Germany: ZKM, 1997), 127–129. Three different versions of Legible City were created based on the plans of Manhattan, Amsterdam, and Karlsruhe.

tual representation encodes the city's genetic code, its deep structure rather than its surface. Through this mapping Shaw proposes an ethics of the virtual. Shaw suggests that the virtual can at least preserve the memory of the real it replaces, encoding its structure, if not its aura, in a new form.

Although *Legible City* was a landmark work in that it presented a symbolic rather than illusionistic space, its visual appearance in many ways reflected the default real-time graphics capability of SGI workstations on which it was running: flat-shaded shapes attenuated by a fog. Char Davies and her development team at SoftImage have consciously addressed the goal of creating a different, more painterly aesthetic for the navigable space in their interactive VR installation *Osmose* (1994–1995).[74] From the point of view of the history of modern art, the result hardly represented something new. *Osmose* simply replaced the usual hard-edge, polygonal, Cézanne-like look of 3-D computer graphics with a softer, more atmospheric, Renoir- or late Monet-like environment made of translucent textures and flowing particles. Yet, in the context of other 3-D virtual worlds, it was an important advance. The "soft" aesthetic of *Osmose* is further supported through the use of slow cinematic dissolves between its dozen or so worlds. Like in *Aspen Movie Map* and *Legible City,* the navigation in *Osmose* is modeled on a real-life experience, in this case, scuba diving. The "immersant" controls navigation by breathing: Breathing in sends the body upward, while breathing out makes it fall. The resulting experience, according to the designers, is one of floating, rather than flying or driving, typical of virtual worlds. Another important aspect of *Osmose*'s navigation is its collective character. While only one person can be "immersed" at a time, the audience can witness her or his journey through the virtual worlds as it unfolds on a large projection screen. At the same size, another translucent screen enables the audience to observe the body gestures of the "immersant" as a shadow-silhouette. The "immersant" thus becomes a kind of ship captain, taking the audience along on a journey; like a captain, she occupies a visible and symbolically marked position, being responsible for the audience's aesthetic experience.

Tamás Waliczky's *The Forest* (1993) liberated the virtual camera from its enslavement to the simulation of humanly possible navigation—walking,

---

74. http://www.softimage.com/Projects/Osmose/.

driving a car, pedaling a bicycle, scuba diving. In *The Forest* the camera slides through the endless black-and-white forest in a series of complex and melancholic moves. If modern visual culture exemplified by MTV can be thought of as a mannerist stage of cinema, its perfected techniques of cinematography, mise-en-scène, and editing self-consciously displayed and paraded for its own sake, Waliczky's film presents an alternative response to cinema's classical age, which is now behind us. In this metafilm, the camera, part of cinema's apparatus, becomes the main character (and in this respect, we can connect *The Forest* to another metafilm, *Man with a Movie Camera*). On first glance, the logic of camera movements can be identified as the quest of a human being trying to escape from the forest (which, in reality, is just a single picture of a tree repeated over and over). Yet just as in some of the animated films of the Brothers Quay, such as *The Street of Crocodiles,* the virtual camera of *The Forest* neither simulates natural perception nor does it follow the standard grammar of cinema's camera; instead, it establishes a distinct system of its own. In *The Street of Crocodiles,* the camera suddenly takes off, rapidly moving in a straight line parallel to an image plane, as though mounted on some robotic arm, and just as suddenly stops to frame a new corner of the space. The logic of these movements is clearly non-human; this is the vision of some alien creature. In contrast, the camera never stops at all in *The Forest,* the whole film being one uninterrupted camera trajectory. The camera system of *The Forest* can be read as a commentary on the fundamentally ambiguous nature of computer space. On the one hand, while not indexically tied to physical reality or the human body, computer space is isotropic. In contrast to human space, in which the verticality of the body and the direction of the horizon are two dominant directions, computer space does not privilege any particular axis. In this way it is similar to the space of El Lissitzky's *Prouns* and Kazimir Malevich's suprematist compositions—an abstract cosmos, unencumbered by either earth's gravity or the weight of a human body. (Thus the game *Spacewar* with its simulated gravity got it wrong!) William Gibson's term "matrix," which he used in his novels to refer to cyberspace, captures well this isotropic quality. But, on the other hand, computer space is also the space of a human dweller, something used and traversed by a user, who brings her own anthropological framework of horizontality and verticality along with her. The camera system of *The Forest* foregrounds this double character of computer space. While no human figures or avatars appear in the film and we are never shown either the ground or the sky, it is centered around a stand-in for the human subject—a tree. The constant movements of the camera along the vertical dimension throughout the film—sometimes getting closer to where we imagine the ground plane is located, sometimes moving toward (but again, never actually showing) the sky—can be interpreted as an attempt to negotiate between isotropic space and the space of human anthropology, with its horizontality of the ground plane and the horizontal and vertical dimension of human bodies. The navigable space of *The Forest* thus mediates between human subjectivity and the very different and ultimately alien logic of a computer—the ultimate and omnipresent Other of our age.

While the works discussed so far all create virtual navigable spaces, George Legrady's interactive computer installation *Transitional Spaces* (1999) moves from the virtual back to the physical. Legrady locates an already existing architectural navigable space (the Siemens headquarters building in Munich) and makes it into an "engine" that triggers three cinematic projections. As regular office employees and visitors move through the main entrance section and second-level entrance/exit passageways, their motions are picked up by cameras and are used to control the projections. Legrady writes in his installation proposal:

As the speed, location, timing, and number of individuals in the space control the sequence and timing of projection sequences, the audience will have the opportunity to "play" the system, that is, engage consciously by interacting with the camera sensing to control the narrative flow of the installation.

All three projections will comment on the notion of "transitional space" and narrative development. Image sequences will represent transitional states: from noise covered to clear, from empty to full, from open to closed, from dark to light, from out of focus to in-focus.[75]

Legrady's installation begins to explore one element in the "vocabulary" of the navigable space "alphabet"—the transition from one state to another. (Other potential elements of this alphabet include the character of a trajectory; the pattern of the user's movement—for instance, rapid geometric

---

75. George Legrady, *Transitional Spaces* (Munich: Siemens Kultur Programm, 1999), 5.

movement in *Doom* versus wandering in *Myst;* possible interactions between the user and the space, such as the character acting as a center of perspective in Waliczky's *The Garden* (1992); and, of course, the architecture of space itself.) Earlier I invoked a definition of narrative by Bal that may be too restrictive in relation to new media. Legrady quotes another, much broader definition by literary theorist Tzvetan Todorov, according to whom minimal narrative involves the passage from "one equilibium to another" (or, in different words, from one state to another). Legrady's installation suggests that we can think of a subject's movement from one "stable" point in space to another (for instance, moving from a lobby to a building to an office) like a narrative; by analogy, we may also think of a transition from one state of a new media object to another (for instance, from a noisy image to a noise-free image) as a minimal narrative. For me, the second analogy is more problematic than the first, because, in contrast to a literary narrative, it is hard to say what constitutes a "state of equilibrium" in a typical new media object. Nevertheless, rather than concluding that Legrady's installation does not really create narratives, we should recognize it instead as an important example of a whole trend among new media artists—exploration of the minimal condition of a narrative in new media.

Each of the computer spaces just discussed, from *Aspen Movie Map* to *Forest,* establishes a distinct aesthetic of its own. However, the majority of navigable virtual spaces mimic existing physical reality without proposing any coherent aesthetic program. What artistic and theoretical traditions can the designers of navigable spaces draw upon to make them more interesting? One obvious candidate is modern architecture. From Melnikov, Le Corbusier, and Frank Lloyd Wright to *Archigram* and Bernard Tschumi, modern architects have elaborated a variety of schemes for structuring and conceptualizing space to be navigated by users: We can look, for instance, at the 1925 USSR Pavilion (Melnikov), Villa Savoye (Le Corbusier), Walking City (Archigram), and Parc de la Villette (Tschumi).[76] Even more relevant is the tradition of "paper architecture"—designs that were not intended to be built and whose authors therefore felt unencumbered by the limitations of mate-

---

76. For a discussion of the Archigram group in the context of computer-based virtual spaces, see Hans-Peter Schwarz, *Media-Art-History: Media Museum* (Munich: Prestel, 1997), 74–76.

rials, gravity, and budgets.[77] Another highly relevant tradition is film architecture.[78] As discussed in the "Language of Cultural Interfaces" section, the standard interface to computer space is the virtual camera modeled after the film camera rather than a simulation of unaided human sight. After all, film architecture is architecture designed for navigation and exploration by a film camera.

Along with different architectural traditions, designers of navigable spaces can find a wealth of relevant ideas in modern art. They may consider, for instance, the works of modern artists situated between art and architecture, which, like the projects of paper architects, display a spatial imagination freed from the questions of utility and economy—the warped worlds of Jean Dubuffet, mobiles by Alexander Calder, earth works by Robert Smithson, moving-text spaces by Jenny Holzer. While many modern artists felt compelled to create 3-D structures in real spaces, others were satisfied with painting virtual worlds: Think, for, instance, of the melancholic cityscapes of Giorgio de Chirico, the biomorphic worlds of Yves Tanguy, the economical wireframe structures of Alberto Giacometti, and the existential landscapes of Anselm Kiefer. Besides providing us with many examples of imaginative spaces, both abstract and figurative, modern painting is relevant to the design of virtual navigable spaces in two additional ways. First, given that new media are most often experienced, like paintings, via a rectangular frame, virtual architects can study how painters organized their spaces within the constraints of a rectangle. Second, modern painters who belong to what I call the "space-medium tradition" elaborated the concept of space as a homogeneous, dense field, where everything is made from the same "stuff"—in contrast to architects who always have to work with the basic dichotomy between built structure and empty space. And although the virtual spaces that have thus far been realized, with the possible exception of *Osmose*, accept the same dichotomy between rigid objects and the void between

---

77. See, for instance, *Visionary Architects: Boullee, Ledoux, Lequeu* (Houston: University of St. Thomas, 1968); Heinrich Klotz, ed., *Paper Architecture: New Projects from the Soviet Union* (Frankfurt: Deutsches Architekturmuseum, 1988).

78. See, for instance, Dietrich Neumann, ed., *Film Architecture: Set Designs from Metropolis to Blade Runner* (Munich: Prestel, 1996).

them, on the level of material organization they are intrinsically related to the monistic ontology of modern painters such as Matta, Giacometti, or Pollock, for everything in them is also made from the same material—pixels, on the level of surface; polygons or voxels, on the level of 3-D representation. Thus virtual computer space is structurally closer to modern painting than it is to architecture.

Along with painting, a genre of modern art with particular relevance to the design of navigable virtual spaces is installation. Seen in the context of new media, many installations can be thought of as dense multimedia information spaces. They combine images, video, texts, graphics, and 3-D elements within a spatial layout. While most installations leave it up to the viewer to determine the order of "information access" to their elements, one of the most well-known installation artists, Ilya Kabakov, elaborated a system of strategies to structure the viewer's navigation through his spaces.[79] In most installations, according to Kabakov, "the viewer is completely free because the space surrounding her and the installation remain completely indifferent to the installation it encloses."[80] In contrast, by creating a separate, enclosed space with carefully chosen proportions, colors, and lighting within the larger space of a museum or a gallery, Kabakov aims to completely "immerse" the viewer inside his installation. He calls this installation type a "total installation."

For Kabakov, a "total" installation has a double identity. On the one hand, it belongs to the plastic arts designed to be viewed by an immobile spectator—painting, sculpture, architecture. On the other hand, it also belongs to time-based arts such as theater and cinema. We can say the same about virtual navigable spaces. Another concept of Kabakov directly applicable to virtual space design is his distinction between the spatial structure of an installation and its dramaturgy, that is, the time-space structure created by the movement of a viewer through an installation.[81] Kabakov's strategies of dramaturgy include dividing the total space of an installation into two or more connected spaces and creating a well-defined path through the space

---

79. Ilya Kabakov, *On the "Total Installation"* (Bonn: Cantz Verlag, 1995).

80. Ibid., 125. This and the following translations from the Russian text of Kabakov are mine.

81. Ibid., 200.

that does not preclude the viewer from wandering on her own, yet prevents her from feeling lost and bored. To make such a path, Kabakov constructs corridors and abrupt openings between objects; he also places objects in strange places to obstruct passage. Another strategy of the "total installation" is the choice of particular kinds of narratives that in and of themselves lead to spatialization. These are narratives that take place around a main event that becomes the center of an installation: "The beginning [of the installation] leads to the main event [of the narrative] while the last part exists after the event took place." Yet another strategy involves the positioning of text within the space of an installation as a way to orchestrate the attention and navigation of the viewer. For instance, placing two to three pages of text at a particular point in the space creates a deliberate stop in the navigation rhythm.[82] Finally, Kabakov "directs" the viewer to keep alternating between focusing her attention on particular details and the installation as a whole. He describes these two kinds of spatial attention (which we can correlate with haptic and optic perception as theorized by Riegl and others) as follows: "wandering, total ("summarnaia") orientation in space—and active, well-aimed 'taking in' of the partial, the small, the unexpected."[83]

All these strategies can be directly applied to the design of virtual navigable spaces (and interactive multimedia in general). In particular, Kabakov is very successful at making viewers of his installations read carefully the significant amounts of text included in them—something that represents a constant challenge for new media designers. His constant concern is the viewer's attention and reaction to what she will encounter: "The reaction of the viewer during her movement through the installation is the main concern of the designer . . . The loss of the viewer's attention is the end of the installation."[84] This focus on the viewer offers an important lesson for new media designers, who often forget that what they are designing is not an object in itself but a viewer's experience in time and space.

I have purposefully used the word *strategy* to refer to Kabakov's techniques. To evoke the terminology of Michel de Certeau's *The Practice of*

---

82. Ibid., 200–208.

83. Ibid., 162.

84. Ibid., 162.

Everyday Life, Kabakov uses strategies to impose a particular matrix of space, time, experience, and meaning on his viewers; they, in turn, use "tactics" to create their own trajectories (this is a term actually used by de Certeau) within this matrix. If Kabakov is perhaps the most accomplished architect of navigable spaces, de Certeau could very well be their best theoretician. Like Kabakov, he never deals with computer media directly, and yet *The Practice of Everyday Life* contains a multitude of ideas directly applicable to new media. His analysis of the ways in which people employ "tactics" to create their own trajectories through the spaces defined by others (both metaphorically and in the case of spatial tactics, literally) offers a good model for thinking about the ways in which computer users navigate through computer spaces they did not design:

> Although they are composed with the vocabularies of established languages (those of television, newspapers, supermarkets of established sequences) and although they remain subordinated to prescribed syntactical forms (temporal modes of schedules, paradigmatic orders of spaces, etc.), the trajectories trace out the rules of other interests and desires that are neither determined, nor captured by, the system in which they develop.[85]

The Navigator and the Explorer

Why is navigable space such a popular construct in new media? What are the historical origins and precedents of this form?

In his famous 1863 essay "The Painter of Modern Life," Charles Baudelaire documented the new modern male urban subject—the flâneur.[86] (Recent writings on visual culture, film theory, cultural history, and cyberculture have invoked the figure of the flâneur much too often; my justification for invoking it once again here is that I hope to use it in new ways.) An anonymous observer, the flâneur navigates through the space of a Parisian crowd, mentally recording and immediately erasing the faces and figures of passersby. From time to time, his gaze meets the gaze of a passing woman,

---

85. De Certeau, *The Practice of Everyday Life,* xviii.

86. Charles Baudelaire, "The Painter of Modern Life," in *My Heart Laid Bare and Other Prose Writings* (London: Soho Book Company, 1986).

engaging her in a split-second virtual affair, only to be unfaithful to her with the next female passerby. The flâneur is only truly at home in one place—moving through the crowd. Baudelaire writes: "To the perfect spectator, the impassioned observer, it is an immense joy to make his domicile amongst numbers, amidst fluctuation and movement, amidst the fugitive and infinite . . . To be away from home, and yet to feel at home; to behold the world, to be in the midst of the world and yet to remain hidden from the world." There is a theory of navigable virtual spaces hidden here, and we can turn to Walter Benjamin to help us in articulating it. According to Benjamin, the flâneur's navigation transforms the space of the city: "The Crowd is the veil through which the familiar city lures the flâneur like a phantasmagoria. In it the city is now a landscape, now a room."[87] The navigable space is thus a subjective space, its architecture responding to the subject's movement and emotion. In the case of the flâneur moving through the physical city, this transformation, of course, only happens in the flâneur's perception, but in the case of navigation through a virtual space, the space can literally change, becoming a mirror of the user's subjectivity. The virtual spaces built on this principle can be found in Waliczky's *The Garden* and also in the commercial film *Dark City* (Proyas, 1998).

Following European tradition, the subjectivity of the flâneur is determined by his interaction with a group—even though it is a group of strangers. In place of the close-knit community of the small-scale traditional society (Gemeinschaft), we now have the anonymous associations of modern society (Gesellschaft).[88] We can interpret the flâneur's behavior as a response to this historical shift. It is as though he is trying to compensate for the loss of a close relationship with his group by inserting himself into the anonymous crowd. He thus exemplifies the historical shift from Gemeinschaft to Gesellshaft, and the fact that he only feels at home in a crowd of strangers shows the psychological price paid for modernization. Still, the subjectivity of the flâneur is, in essence, intersubjectivity—an exchange of glances between him and other human beings.

---

87. Walter Benjamin, "Paris, Capital of the Nineteenth Century," in *Reflections* (New York: Schocken Books, 1986), 156.

88. The distinction between Gemeinschaft and Gesellshaft was developed by Tönnies in *Community and Society*.

A very different image of navigation through space—and of subjectivity—is presented in the novels of nineteenth-century American writers such as James Fenimore Cooper (1789–1851) and Mark Twain (1835–1910). The main character of Cooper's novels, the wilderness scout Natty Bumppo, alias Leatherstocking, navigates through spaces of nature rather than culture. Similarly, in Twain's *Huckleberry Finn,* the narrative is organized around the voyage of the two boy heroes down the Mississippi River. Instead of the thickness of the urban human crowd, the milieu of a Parisian flâneur, the heroes of these American novels are most at home in the wilderness, away from the city. They navigate forests and rivers, overcoming obstacles and fighting enemies. Subjectivity is constructed through conflicts between the subject and nature, and between the subject and his enemies, rather than through interpersonal relations within a group. This structure finds its ultimate expression in the unique American form, the Western, and its hero, the cowboy—a lonely explorer who only occasionally shows up in town to get a drink at the saloon. Rather than providing a home for the cowboy, as it does for the flâneur, the town is a hostile place, full of conflict which eventually erupts into the inevitable showdown.

Both the flâneur and the explorer find their expression in different subject positions, or phenotypes, of new media users. Media theoretician and activist Geert Lovink describes the figure of the present-day media user and Net surfer, whom he calls "the Data Dandy." Although Lovink's reference is Oscar Wilde rather than Baudelaire, his Data Dandy exhibits behaviors that also qualify him to be called a "Data Flâneur." "The Net is to the electronic dandy what the metropolitan street was for the historical dandy."[89] A perfect aesthete, the Data Dandy loves to display his private and totally irrelevant collection of data to other Net users. "Wrapped in the finest facts and the most senseless gadgets, the new dandy deregulates the time economy of the info = money managers . . . if the anonymous crowd in the streets was the audience of the Boulevard dandy, the logged-in Net-users are that of the data dandy."[90] While displaying his dandyism, the data dandy does not want to be above the crowd; like Baudelaire's flâneur, he wants to lose himself in its

---

89. Adilkno, *The Media Archive* (Brooklyn, New York: Autonomedia, 1998), 99.
90. Ibid., 100.

mass, to be moved by the semantic vectors of mass media icons, themes, and trends. As Lovink points out, a data dandy "can only play with the rules of the Net as a non-identity. What is exclusivity in the age of differentiation? . . . Data dandyism is born of an aversion to being exiled into a subculture of one's own."[91] Although Lovink positions the Data Dandy exclusively in data space ("Cologne and pink stockings have been replaced by precious Intel"), the Data Dandy does have a dress code of his own. This look was popular with new media artists of the 1990s—no labels, no distinct design, no bright colors or extravagant shapes—a non-identity that is nevertheless paraded as style and, in fact, is carefully constructed (as I learned while shopping in Berlin in 1997 with Russian net.artist Alexei Shulgin). The designers who best exemplify this style in the 1990s are Hugo Boss and Prada, whose restrained no-style style contrasts with the opulence of Versace and Gucci, the stars of the 1980s era of exess. The new style of non-identity corresponds perfectly to the rise of the Net, where endless mailing lists, newsgroups, and sites delude any single topic, image, or idea: "On the Net, the only thing which appears as a mass is information itself. . . . Today's new theme is tomorrow's 23 newsgroups."[92]

If the Net surfer, who keeps posting to mailing lists and newsgroups and accumulating endless data, is a reincarnation of Baudelaire's flâneur, the user navigating a virtual space assumes the position of the nineteenth-century explorer, a character from Cooper or Twain. This is particularly true for the navigable spaces of computer games. The dominance of spatial exploration in games exemplifies the classical American mythology in which the individual discovers his identity and builds character by moving through space. Correspondingly, in many American novels and short stories (O. Henry, Hemingway), narrative is driven by the character's movements in the outside space. In contrast, nineteenth-century European novels do not feature much movement in physical space because the action takes place in a psychological space. From this perspective, most computer games follow the logic of American rather than European narratives. Their heroes are not developed, and their psychology is not represented. But as these heroes move

---

91. Ibid.
92. Ibid.

through space, defeating enemies, acquiring resources, and, more importantly, skill, they are "building character." This is particularly true for Role Playing Games (RPG), whose narrative is one of self-improvement. But it also holds true for other game genres (action, adventure, simulators) that put the user in command of a character (*Doom, Mario, Tomb Raider*). As the character progresses through the game, the game player acquires new skills and knowledge. She learns how to outwit the mutants lurking in the levels of *Doom,* how to defeat the enemies with just a few kicks in *Tomb Raider,* how to solve the secrets of the playful world in *Mario,* and so on.[93]

While movement through space as a means of building character is one theme of American frontier mythology, another is exploring and "culturing" unknown space. This theme is also reflected in the structure of computer games. A typical game begins at some point in a large, unknown space; in the course of the game, the player has to explore this space, mapping out its geography and unraveling its secrets. In the case of games organized into discrete levels such as *Doom,* the player has to investigate systematically all the spaces of a given level before he can move to the next level. In other games taking place in one large territory, the game play gradually involves larger and larger parts of this territory (*Adventure, War Craft*).

Although I focus in this section on navigating a space in a literal sense, that is, moving through a 3-D virtual space, this concept is also a key metaphor in the conceptualization of new media. From the 1980s concept of cyberspace to 1990s software such as Netscape Navigator, interacting with computerized data and media has been consistently framed in spatial terms. Computer scientists adopted this metaphor as well: They use the term *navigation* to refer to different methods of organizing and accessing hypermedia, even though a 3-D virtual space interface is not at all the most common method. For instance, in his *Elements of Hypermedia Design,* Peter Gloor lists "seven design concepts for navigation in dataspace": linking, searching, sequentialization, hierarchy, similarity, mapping, guides and agents.[94] Thus, "navigating the Internet" includes following hyperlinks, using menus

---

93. This narrative of maturation can also be seen as a particular case of an initiation ceremony, something traditionally a part of every human society.

94. Peter Gloor, *Elements of Hypermedia Design* (Boston: Birkhäuser, 1997).

commonly provided by Web sites, as well as using search engines. If we accept this spatial metaphor, both the nineteenth-century European flâneur and the American explorer find their reincarnation in the figure of the net surfer. We may even correlate these two historical figures with the names of the two most popular Web browsers: the flâneur of Baudelaire—Netscape Navigator; the explorer of Cooper, Twain, and Hemingway—Internet Explorer. Of course, names apart, these two browsers are functionally quite similar. However, given that they both focus on a single user navigating through Web sites rather than more communal experiences, such as newsgroups, mailing lists, text-based chat, and IRC, we can say that they privilege the explorer rather than the flâneur—a single user navigating through an unknown territory rather than a member of a group, even if this group is a crowd of strangers. And although different software solutions have been developed to make Internet navigation more of a social experience—for instance, allowing remote users to navigate the same Web site together, simultaneously, or allowing the user to see who has already accessed a particular document—individual navigation through "history-free" data was still the norm at the end of the 1990s.

Kino-Eye and Simulators

I have presented two historical trajectories: from flâneur to Net surfer, and from nineteenth-century American explorer to the explorer of navigable virtual space. It is also possible to construct another trajectory, leading from the Parisian flanerie to navigable computer spaces. In *Window Shopping,* film historian Anne Friedberg presents an archeology of a mode of perception that, according to her, characterizes modern cinematic, televisual, and cyber cultures. This mode, which she calls a "mobilized virtual gaze,"[95] combines two conditions: "a received perception mediated through representation" and travel "in an imaginary flanerie through an imaginary elsewhere and an imaginary elsewhen."[96] According to Friedberg's archeology, this mode emerged when a new nineteenth-century technology of virtual representation—photography—merged with the mobilized gaze of

---

95. Friedberg, *Window Shopping,* 2.
96. Ibid.

tourism, urban shopping, and flanerie.[97] As can be seen, Friedberg connects Baudelaire's flâneur with a range of other modern practices: "The same impulses which send flâneurs through the arcades, traversing the pavement and wearing thin their shoe leather, sent shoppers into the department stores, tourists to exhibitions, spectators into the panorama, diaroma, wax museum, and cinema."[98] The flâneur occupies a privileged position among these nineteenth-century subjects because he embodied most strongly the desire to combine perception with motion through a space. All that remained in order to arrive at the "mobilized virtual gaze" was to virtualize this perception—something that cinema accomplished in the last decade of the nineteenth century.

Although Friederg's account ends with television and does not consider new media, the form of navigable virtual space fits well in her historical trajectory. Navigation through a virtual space, whether in a computer game, motion simulator, data visualizations, or 3-D human-computer interface, follows the logic of the "virtual mobile gaze." Instead of Parisian streets, shopping windows, and the faces of the passersby, the virtual flâneur travels through virtual streets, highways, and planes of data; the eroticism of a split-second virtual affair with a passerby of the opposite sex is replaced with the excitement of locating and opening a particular file or zooming into the virtual object. Like Baudelaire's flâneur, the virtual flâneur is happiest on the move, clicking from one object to another, traversing room after room, level after level, data volume after data volume.

Thus just as a database form can be seen as an expression of a "database complex," an irrational desire to preserve and store everything, navigable space is not just a purely functional interface. It is also an expression and gratification of a psychological desire, a state of being, a subject position—or rather, a subject's trajectory. If the subject of modern society looked for refuge from the chaos of the real world in the stability and balance of the static composition of a painting, and later in the cinematic image, the subject of the information society finds peace in the knowledge that she can slide over endless fields of data, locating any morsel of information with the click of a button, zooming through file systems and networks. She is comforted

---

97. Ibid., 184.
98. Ibid., 94.

not by an equilibrium of shapes and colors, but by the variety of data manipulation operations at her control.

Does this mean that we have reached the end of the trajectory described by Friedberg? While still enjoying a privileged place in computer culture, flanerie now shows its age. Here we can make an analogy with the history of the GUI (Graphical User Interface). Developed at Xerox PARC in the 1970s and commercialized by Apple in the early 1980s, it was appropriate when a typical user's hard drive contained dozens or even hundreds of files. But for the next stage of Net-based computing, in which the user is accessing millions of files, it is no longer sufficient.[99] Bypassing the ability to display and navigate files graphically, the user resorts to a text-based search engine. Similarly, while the "mobilized virtual gaze" described by Friedberg was a significant advancement over earlier more static methods of data organization and access (static image, text, catalog, library), its "bandwidth" is too limited in the information age. Moreover, a simple simulation of movement through a physical space defeats the computer's new capabilities of data access and manipulation. Thus for the virtual flâneur, such operations as search, segmentation, hyperlinking, visualization, and data mining are more satisfying than just navigating through a simulation of a physical space.

In the 1920s Dziga Vertov already understood this very well. *Man with a Movie Camera* is an important point in the trajectory that leads from Baudelaire's flanerie to *Aspen Movie Map, Doom,* and VRML worlds, not simply because Vertov's film is structured around the camera's active exploration of city spaces, and not only because it fetishizes the camera's mobility. Vertov wanted to overcome the limits of human vision and human movement through space to arrive at more efficient means of data access. However, the data with which he worked is raw visible reality—not reality digitized and stored in a computer's memory as numbers. Similarly, his interface was a film camera, that is, an anthropomorphic simulation of human vision—not computer algorithms. Thus, *Vertov stands halfway between Baudelaire's flâneur and today's computer user: No longer just a pedestrian walking down a street, but not yet Gibson's data cowboy who zooms through pure data armed with data-mining algorithms.*

---

99. See Don Gentner and Jakob Nielson, "The Anti-Mac Interface," *Communications of the ACM* 39, no. 8 (August 1996): 70–82. Available online at http://www.acm.org/cacm/AUG96/antimac.htm.

In his research on what can be called the "kino-eye interface," Vertov systematically tried different ways to overcome what he thought were the limits of human vision. He mounted cameras on the roof of a building and a moving automobile; he slowed and sped up film speed; he superimposed a number of images together in time and space (temporal montage and montage within a shot). *Man with a Movie Camera* is not only a database of city life in the 1920s, a database of film techniques, and a database of new operations of visual epistemology, but also a database of new interface operations that together aim to go beyond simple human navigation through physical space.

Along with *Man with a Movie Camera,* another key point in the trajectory from the navigable space of a nineteenth-century city to the virtual navigable computer space is flight simulators. At the same time as Vertov was working on his film, young American engineer E. A. Link, Jr. developed the first commercial flight simulator. Significantly, Link's patent for his simulator filed in 1930 refers to it as a "Combination Training Device for Student Aviators and Entertainment Apparatus."[100] Thus, rather than being an afterthought, the adaptation of flight simulator technology to consumer entertainment that took place in the 1990s was already envisioned by its inventor. Link's design was a simulation of a pilot's cockpit with all the controls, but, in contrast to a modern simulator, it had no visuals. In short, it was a motion ride without a movie. In the 1960s, visuals were added by using new video technology. A video camera was mounted on a movable arm positioned over a room-size model of an airport. The movement of the camera was synchronized with the simulator controls; its image was transmitted to a video monitor in the cockpit. While useful, this approach was limited because it was based on the physical reality of an actual model set. As we saw in the "Compositing" section, a filmed and edited image is a better simulation technology than a physical construction; and a virtual image controlled by a computer is better still. Not surprisingly, soon after interactive 3-D computer graphics technology was developed, it was applied to produce visuals for the simulators by one of its developers. In 1968, Ivan Sutherland, who had already pioneered interactive computer-aided design ("Sketchpad,"

---

100. Benjamin Wooley, *Virtual Worlds* (Oxford: Blackwell, 1992), 39, 43.

1962) and virtual reality (1967), formed a company to produce computer-based simulators. In the 1970s and 1980s simulators were one of the main applications of real-time 3-D computer graphics technology, thus determining to a significant degree the way this technology was developed. For instance, simulation of particular landscape features typically seen by a pilot, such as flat terrain, mountains, sky with clouds, and fog, all became important research problems.[101] The application of interactive graphics to simulators has also shaped the imagination of researchers regarding how this technology can be used. It naturalized a particular idiom—flying through a simulated spatial environment.

Thus, one of the most common forms of navigation used today in computer culture—flying through spatialized data—can be traced back to 1970s military simulators. From Baudelaire's flâneur strolling through physical streets, we move to Vertov's camera mounted on a moving car and then to the virtual camera of a simulator that represents the viewpoint of a military pilot. Although it was not an exclusive factor, the end of the Cold War played an important role in the extension of the military mode of perception into general culture. Until 1990, such companies as Evans and Sutherland, Boeing, and Lockheed were busy developing multi-million-dollar simulators, but as military orders dried up, they were forced to look for consumer applications of their technology. During the 1990s, these and other companies converted their expensive simulators into arcade games, motion rides, and other forms of location-based entertainment. By the end of the decade, Evans and Sutherland's list of products included image-generators for use in military and aviation simulators; a virtual set technology for use in television production; Cyber Fighter, a system of networked game stations modeled after networked military simulators; and Virtual Glider, an immersive, location-based entertainment station.[102] As military budgets continued to diminish and entertainment budgets soared, the entertainment industry and the military often came to share the same technologies and employ the same visual forms. Probably the most graphic example

---

101. For more on the history of 3-D computer graphics, see my article "Mapping Space: Perspective, Radar, and Computer Graphics."

102. http://www.es.com/product_index.html.

of the ongoing circular transfer of technology and imagination between the military and the civilian sector in new media is *Doom.* Originally developed and released over the Internet as a consumer game in 1993 by id software, it was soon picked up by the U.S. Marine Corps, which customized it into a military simulator for group-combat training.[103] Instead of using multi-million-dollar simulators, the Army could now train soldiers on a fifty-dollar game. The Marines, who were involved in the modifications, then went on to form their own company in order to market the customized *Doom* as a commercial game.

The discussion of the military origins of the navigable space form would be incomplete without acknowledging the pioneering work of Paul Virilio. In his brilliant 1984 book *War and Cinema,* Virilio documented numerous parallels between the military and film cultures of the twentieth century, including the use of a mobile camera moving through space in military aerial surveillance and in cinematography.[104] Virilio went on to suggest that, whereas space was the main category of the nineteenth century, the main category of the twentieth century was time. As I already discussed, tele-communication technology for Virilio eliminates the category of space altogether as it makes every point on Earth as accessible as any other—at least in theory. This technology also leads to a real-time politics, which requires instant reactions to events transmitted at the speed of light and, ultimately, can only be handled efficiently by computers responding to each other without human intervention. From a post-Cold War perspective, Virilio's theory can be seen as another example of the imagination transfer from the military to the civilian sector. In this case, the techno-politics of the Cold War nuclear arms equilibrium between the two superpowers capable of striking each other or any point on Earth at any moment is seen as a fundamentally new stage of culture, in which real time triumphs over space.

Although Virilio did not write on computer interfaces, the logic of his books suggests that the ideal computer interface for a culture of real-time politics would be the War Room in *Dr. Strangelove or: How I Learned to Stop*

---

103. Elizabeth Sikorovsky, "Training Spells Doom for Marines," *Federal Computer Week,* 15 July 1996, available online at http://www.fcm.com/pubs/fcw/0715/guide.htm.

104. Paul Virilio, *War and Cinema* (London: Verso, 1989).

Worrying and Love the Bomb (Kubrick, 1964), with its direct lines of communication between the generals and the pilots; or DOS command lines, with their military economy of command and response, rather than the more spectacular but inefficient VRML worlds. Uneconomical and inefficient as it may be, the navigable space interface is nevertheless thriving in all areas of new media. How can we explain its popularity? Is it simply a result of cultural inertia? A leftover from the nineteenth century? A way to make the ultimately alien space of a computer compatible with humans by anthropomorphizing it, superimposing a simulation of a Parisian flanerie over abstract data? A relic of Cold War culture?

While all these answers make sense, it would be unsatisfactory to see navigable space as merely the end of a historical trajectory; it is also a new beginning. The few computer spaces discussed here point toward some of the aesthetic possibilities of this form; more possibilities are contained in the works of modern painters, installation artists, and architects. Theoretically as well, navigable space represents a new challenge. Rather than considering only the topology, geometry, and logic of a static space, we need to take into account the new way in which space functions in computer culture—as something traversed by a subject, as a trajectory rather than an area. But computer culture is not the only field where the use of the category of navigable space makes sense. I will now briefly look at two other fields— anthropology and architecture—in which we find more examples of "navigable space imagination."

In his book *Non-places: Introduction to an Anthropology of Supermodernity,* French anthropologist Marc Auge advances the hypothesis that "supermodernity produces non-places, meaning spaces which are not themselves anthropological places and which, unlike Baudelairean modernity, do not integrate with earlier places."[105] Place is what anthropologists have studied traditionally; it is characterized by stability, and it supports stable identity, relations, and history.[106] Auge's main source for his distinction between place and space, or non-place, is Michel de Certeau: "Space, for him, is a

---

105. Marc Auge, *Non-places: Introduction to an Anthropology of Supermodernity,* trans. John Howe (London: Verso, 1995), 78.
106. Ibid., 53–53.

'frequent place,' 'an intersection of moving bodies': it is the pedestrians who transform a street (geometrically defined as a place by town planners) into a space"; it is an animation of a place by the motion of a moving body.[107] Thus from one perspective we can understand place as a product of cultural producers, while non-places are created by users; in other words, non-place is an individual trajectory through a place. From another perspective, in supermodernity, traditional places are replaced by equally institutionalized non-places, a new architecture of transit and impermanence: hotel chains and squats, holiday clubs and refugee camps, supermarkets, airports, and highways. Non-place becomes the new norm, the new way of existence.

It is interesting that Auge chooses the counterpart of the pilot or the user of the flight simulator—the airline passenger—as the subject who exemplifies the condition of supermodernity. "Alone, but one of many, the user of a non-place has contractual relations with it." This contract relieves the person of his usual determinants. "He becomes no more than what he does or experiences in the role of passenger, customer or driver."[108] Auge concludes that "as anthropological places create the organically social, so non-places create solitary contractuality," the very opposite of the traditional object of sociology: "Try to imagine a Durkheimian analysis of a transit lounge at Roissy!"[109]

Architecture by definition stands on the side of order, society, and rules; it is thus a counterpart of sociology as it deals with regularities, norms, and "strategies" (to use de Certeau's term). Yet the very awareness of these assumptions underlying architecture led many contemporary architects to focus their attention on the activities of users who through their "speech acts" "reappropriate the space organized by the techniques of sociocultural production" (de Certeau).[110] Architects come to accept that the structures they design will be modified by users' activities, and that these modifications represent an essential part of architecture. They also took up the challenge of "a Durkheimian analysis of a transit lounge at Roissy," putting their energy and

---

107. Ibid., 79–80.
108. Ibid., 101, 103.
109. Ibid., 94.
110. De Certeau, *The Practice of Everyday Life,* xiv.

imagination into the design of non-places such as airports (Kansai International Airport in Osaka by Renzo Piano), train terminals (Waterloo International Terminal in London by Nicholas Grimshaw) and highway control stations (Steel Cloud or Los Angeles West Coast Gateway by Asymptote Architecture group).[111] Probably the ultimate in non-place architecture is the one-million-square-meter Euralille project, which redefined the city of Lille, France as the transit zone between the Continent and London. The project attracted some of the most interesting contemporary architects—Rem Koolhaas designed the masterplan, and Jean Nouvel built Centre Euralille, which contains a shopping center, school, hotel, and apartments next to the train terminal. Centered around the entrance to the Chunnel, the underground tunnel for cars that connects the Continent and England, and the terminal for the high-speed train that travels between Lille, London, Brussels, and Paris, Euralille is a space of navigation par excellence, a mega-non-place. Like the network players of *Doom,* Euralille users emerge from trains and cars to temporarily inhabit a zone defined through their trajectories, an environment "to just wander around inside of" (Robyn Miller), "an intersection of moving bodies" (de Certeau).

EVE and *Place*

We have come a long way since *Spacewar* (1962) and *Computer Space* (1971)—at least in terms of graphics. The images of these early computer games seem to have more in common with the abstract paintings of Malevich and Mondrian than with the photorealistic renderings of *Quake* (1996) and *Unreal* (1997). Whether this evolution in graphics was also accompanied by a conceptual evolution is another matter. Compared to the richness of modern concepts of space developed by artists, architects, filmmakers, art historians, and anthropologists, our computer spaces have a long way to go.

Often the way to go forward is to go back. As this section has suggested, designers of virtual spaces may find a wealth of relevant ideas by looking at twentieth-century art, architecture, film, and other arts. Similarly, some of the earliest computer spaces, such as *Spacewar* and *Aspen Movie Map,* con-

---

111. Jean-Claude Dubost and Jean-François Gonthier, eds., *Architecture for the Future* (Paris: Éditions Pierre Terrail, 1996), 171.

tained aesthetic possibilities that are still waiting to be explored. In conclusion, I will discuss two more works by Jeffrey Shaw, who probably draws on various cultural traditions of space construction and representation more systematically than any other new media artist.

While Friedberg's concept of the virtual mobile gaze is useful in allowing us to see the connections between a number of technologies and practices of spatial navigation, such as panorama, cinema, and shopping, it can also make us blind to the important differences between them. In contrast, Shaw's *EVE* (1993–present) and *Place: A User's Manual* (1995) emphasize both the similarities and differences between various technologies of navigation.[112] In these works, Shaw evokes the navigation methods of panorama, cinema, video, and VR. But rather than collapsing different technologies into one, he "layers" them side by side; that is, he literally encloses the interface of one technology within the interface of another. For instance, in the case of *EVE,* visitors find themselves inside a large semisphere reminiscent of the nineteenth-century panorama. The projectors located in the middle of the sphere throw a rectangular image on the inside surface of the semisphere. In this way, the interface of cinema (an image enclosed by a rectangular frame) is placed inside the interface of panorama (a semispherical enclosed space). In *Place: A User's Manual,* a different "layering" takes place: A panorama interface is placed inside a typical computer-space interface. The user navigates a virtual landscape using a first-person perspective characteristic of VR, computer games, and navigable computer spaces in general. Inside this landscape are eleven cylinders with photographs mapped on them. Once the user moves inside one of these cylinders, she switches to a mode of perception typical of the panorama tradition.

By placing interfaces of different technologies next to one other within a single work, Shaw foregrounds the unique logic of seeing, spatial access, and user behavior characteristic of each. The tradition of the framed image, that is, a representation that exists within the larger physical space that contains the viewer (painting, cinema, computer screen), meets the tradition of "total" simulation, or "immersion," that is, a simulated space that encloses the viewer (panorama, VR).

Another historical dichotomy staged for us by Shaw is that between the traditions of collective and individualized viewing in screen-based arts. The

---

112. Abel, *Jeffrey Shaw,* 138–139, 142–145.

first tradition spans from magic-lantern shows to twentieth-century cinema. The second passes from the camera obscura, stereoscope, and kinescope to head-mounted displays of VR. Both have their dangers. In the first tradition, the individual's subjectivity can be dissolved in a mass-induced response. In the second, subjectivity is defined through the interaction of an isolated subject with an object at the expense of intersubjective dialogue. In the case of viewers' interactions with computer installations, as I noted when discussing *Osmose,* something quite new begins to emerge—a combination of individualized and collective spectatorship. The interaction of one viewer with the work (via a joystick, mouse, or head-mounted sensor) becomes in itself a new text for other viewers, situated within the work's arena, so to speak. This affects the behavior of this viewer, who acts as a representative for the desires of others, and who is now oriented both to them and to the work.

EVE rehearses the whole Western history of simulation, functioning as a kind of Plato's cave in reverse: Visitors progress from the real world into the space of simulation, where instead of mere shadows they are presented with technologically enhanced (via stereo) images, which look more real than their normal perceptions.[113] At the same time, *EVE*'s enclosed round shape refers us back to the fundamental modern desire to construct a perfect, self-sufficient utopia, whether visual (the nineteenth-century panorama) or social. (For instance, after 1917, Russian architect G. I. Gidoni designed a monument to the revolution in the form of a semitransparent globe that could hold several thousand spectators.) Yet rather than being presented with a simulated world that has nothing to do with the real space of the viewer (as in typical VR), visitors who enter *EVE*'s enclosed space discover that *EVE*'s apparatus shows the outside reality they ostensibly just left behind. Moreover, instead of being fused in a single collective vision (Gesamtkunstwerk, cinema, mass society), visitors are confronted with a subjective and partial view. Visitors see only what one person who wears a head-mounted sensor chooses to show them; that is, they are literally limited by this person's point of view. In addition, instead of a 360-degree view, they see a small rectangular image—a mere sample of the world outside. The one visitor wearing a sensor, who thus literally acts as an eye for the rest of

---

113. Here I am describing the particular application of EVE that I saw at the "Multimediale 4" exhibition, Karlsruhe, Germany, May 1995.

the audience, occupies many positions at once—master subject, visionary who shows the audience what is worth seeing, and (at the same time) mere object, an interface between them and outside reality, that is, a tool for others; a projector, light, and reflector, all at once.

Having examined the two key forms of new media—database and navigable space—one is tempted to see their privileged role in computer culture as a sign of a larger cultural change. If we use Auge's distinction between modernity and supermodernity, the following scheme can be established:

1. modernity—"supermodernity,"
2. narrative (= hierarchy)—database, hypermedia, network (= flattening of hierarchy),
3. objective space—navigable space (trajectory through space),
4. static architecture—"liquid architecture,"[114] and
5. geometry and topology as theoretical models for cultural and social analysis—trajectory, vector, and flow as theoretical categories.

As can be seen from this scheme, the two "supermodern" forms of database and navigable space are complementary in their effects on the forms of modernity. On the one hand, a narrative is "flattened" into a database. A trajectory through events and/or time becomes a flat space. On the other hand, a flat space of architecture or topology is narrativized, becoming a support for individual users' trajectories.

But this is only one possible scheme. What is clear, however, is that we have left modernity for something else. We are still searching for names to describe it. Yet the names that we have come up with—"supermodernity," "transmodernity," "second modern"—all seem to reflect the sense of the continuity of this new stage with the old. If the 1980s' concept of "postmodernism" implied a break with modernity, we now seem to prefer to think of cultural history as a continuous trajectory through a single conceptual and aesthetic space. Having lived through the twentieth century, we learned all too well the human price of "breaking with the past," "building from scratch," "making new," and other similar claims—whether involving aes-

---

114. See Novak, "Liquid Architectures in Cyberspace."

thetic, moral, or social systems. The claim that new media should be totally new is only one in the long list of such claims.

Such a notion of a continuous trajectory is more compatible with human anthropology and phenomenology. Just as a human body moves through physical space in a continuous trajectory, the notion of history as a continuous trajectory is, in my view, preferable to the one that postulates epistemological breaks or paradigm shifts from one era to the next. This notion, articulated by Michel Foucault and Thomas Kuhn, in the 1960s, fits with the aesthetics of modernist montage of Eisenstein and Godard—rather than our own aesthetics of continuity as exemplified by compositing, morphing, and navigable spaces.[115]

These thinkers also seem to have projected onto a diachronic plane of history the traumatic synchronic division of their time—the split between the capitalist West and the communist East. But with the official (although not necessarily actual) collapse of this split in the 1990s, we have seen how history has reasserted its continuity in powerful and dangerous ways. The return of nationalism and religion and the desire to erase everything associated with the Communist regime and return to the past—pre-1917 Russia and pre-1945 Eastern Europe—are only some of the more dramatic signs of this process. A radical break with the past has a price. Despite the interruption, the historical trajectory keeps accumulating potential energy until one day it reasserts itself with new force, breaking out into the open and crushing whatever new has been created in the meantime.

In this book, I have chosen to emphasize the continuities between the new media and the old, the interplay between historical repetition and innovation. I wanted to show how new media appropriate old forms and conventions of different media, in particular, cinema. Like a river, cultural history can not suddenly change its course; its movement is that of a spline rather than a set of straight lines between points. In short, I wanted to create trajectories through the space of cultural history that would pass through new media, thus grounding it in what came before.

---

115. Another notion that belongs to this paradigm of discontinuity is René Thom's catastrophe theory. See his *Structural Stability and Morphogenesis* (Reading, Mass.: W. A. Benjamin, 1975).

6

What Is Cinema?

It is useful to think about the relations between cinema and new media in terms of two vectors. The first vector goes from cinema to new media, and it constitutes the backbone of this book. Chapters 1–5 uses the history and theory of cinema to map out the logic driving the technical and stylistic development of new media. I also trace the key role played by cinematic language in new media interfaces—both the traditional HCI (the interface of the operating system and software applications) and what I call "cultural interfaces"—interfaces between the human user and cultural data.

The second vector goes in the opposite direction—from computers to cinema. How does computerization affect our very concept of moving images? Does it offer new possibilities for film language? Has it led to the development of totally new forms of cinema? This last chapter is devoted to these questions. In part I started to address them in the "Compositing" section and the "Illusion" chapter. The main part of that chapter focuses on the new identity of the computer-generated image; it is logical that we now extend our inquiry to include moving images.

Before proceeding, I would like to offer two lists. My first list summarizes the effects of computerization on cinema proper:

1. Use of computer techniques in traditional filmmaking:
    1.1   3-D computer animation/digital composing. Examples: *Titanic* (James Cameron, 1997), *The City of Lost Children* (Marc Caro and J. P. Jeunet, 1995).
    1.2   Digital painting. Example: *Forrest Gump* (Robert Zemeckis, 1994).
    1.3   Virtual sets. Example: *Ada* (Lynn Hershman, 1997).
    1.4   Virtual actors/motion capture. Example: *Titanic.*

2. New forms of computer-based cinema:
    2.1   Motion rides/location-based entertainment. Example: rides produced by Douglas Trumbull.
    2.2   Motion graphics, or what I might call *typographic cinema:* film + graphic design + typography. Example: film title sequences.
    2.3   Net.cinema: films designed exclusively for Internet distribution. Example: New Venue, one of the first onlines sites devoted to

showcasing short digital films. In 1998 it accepted only Quick-Time files under five Mb.

2.4 Hypermedia interfaces to a film that allows nonlinear access at different scales. Examples: *WaxWeb* (David Blair, 1994–1999), Stephen Mamber's database interface to Hitchcock's *Psycho* (Mamber, 1996–).

2.5 Interactive movies and games structured around film-like sequences. These sequences can be created using traditional film techniques (example: the *Johnny Mnemonic* game) or computer animation (example: the *Blade Runner* game). (The pioneer of interactive cinema is experimental filmmaker Grahame Weinbren, whose laserdisks *Sonata* and *The Erl King* are the true classics of this new form.) Note that it is hard to draw a strict line between such interactive movies and many other games that may not use traditional film sequences yet follow many other conventions of film language in their structure. From this perspective, the majority of the computer games of the 1990s can actually be considered interactive movies.

2.6 Animated, filmed, simulated, or hybrid sequences that follow film language, and appear in HCI, Web sites, computer games, and other areas of new media. Examples: transitions and Quick-Time movies in *Myst,* FMV (full motion video) openings in *Tomb Raider* and many other games.

3. Filmmakers' reactions to the increasing reliance of cinema on computer techniques in postproduction:

3.1 Films by Dogme 95 movement. Example: *Celebration* (Vinterberg, 1998).

3.2 Films that focus on the new possibilities offered by inexpensive DV (Digital Video) cameras. Example: *Time Code* (Figgis, 2000).

4. Filmmakers' reactions to the conventions of new media:

4.1 Conventions of a computer screen. Example: *Prospero's Books* (Greenaway).

4.2 Conventions of game narratives. Examples: *Run, Lola, Run* (Tykwer, 1999), *Sliding Doors* (Howitt, 1998).

The first section of this chapter, "Digital Cinema and the History of a Moving Image," will focus on 1.1–1.3. The second section, "New Language of Cinema," will use examples drawn from 2.3–2.6.[1]

Note that I do not include on this list new distribution technologies such as digital film projection or network film distribution, which by 1999 was already used in Hollywood on a experimental basis, nor do I mention the growing number of Web sites devoted to distribution of films.[2] Although all these developments will undoubtedly have an important effect on the economics of film production and distribution, they do not appear to have a direct effect on film language, which is my main concern here.

My second, and highly tentative, list summarizes some of the distinct qualities of a computer-based image. This list pulls together arguments presented throughout the book so far. As I noted in chapter 1, I feel that it is important to pay attention not only to the new properties of a computer image that can be logically deduced from its new "material" status, but also to how images are actually used in computer culture. Therefore, the number of properties on this list reflects the typical usage of images rather than some "essential" properties it may have due to its digital form. It is also legitimate to think of some of these qualities as particular consequences of the oppositions that define the concept of representation, as summarized in the Introduction:

1. The computer-based image is discrete, because it is broken into pixels. This makes it more like a human language (but not in the semiotic sense of having distinct units of meaning).

2. The computer-based image is modular, because it typically consists of a number of layers whose contents often correspond to meaningful parts of the image.

3. The computer-based image consists of two levels, a surface appearance and the underlying code (which may be the pixel values, a mathematical function, or HTML code). In terms of its "surface," an image participates in dialog with other cultural objects. In terms of its code, an image exists on the same conceptual plane as other computer objects. (Surface–code can be

---

1. The phenomenon of motion rides has already been discussed in detail by Finnish new media theoretician and historian Erkki Huhtamo.

2. For a list of some of these sites as of October 1999, see "Small-Screen Multiplex," *Wired* 7.10 (October 1999), http://www.wired.com/archive/7.10/multiplex.html.

related to other pairs: signifier—signified, base—superstructure, unconscious—conscious. So just as a signifier exists in a structure with other sig-
nifiers of a language, the "surface" of an image, that is, its "contents," enters
into dialog with all other images in a culture.)

4.   Computer-based images are typically compressed using lossy compression techniques, such as JPEG. Therefore, the presence of noise (in the sense
of undesirable artifacts and loss of original information) is its essential,
rather than accidental, quality.

5.   An image acquires the new role of an interface (for instance, imagemaps
on the Web, or the image of a desktop as a whole in GUI). Thus, image becomes image-interface. In this role it functions as a portal into another
world, like an icon in the Middle Ages or a mirror in modern literature and
cinema. Rather than staying on its surface, we expect to go "into" the image.
In effect, every computer user becomes Carroll's Alice. The image can function as an interface because it can be "wired" to programming code; thus
clicking on the image activates a computer program (or its part).

6.   The new role of an image as image-interface competes with its older role
as representation. Therefore, conceptually, a computer image is situated between two opposing poles—an illusionistic window into a fictional universe
and a tool for computer control. The task of new media design and art is to
learn how to combine these two competing roles of an image.

7.   Visually, this conceptual opposition translates into the opposition between depth and surface, between a window into a fictional universe and a
control panel.

8.   Along with functioning as image-interfaces, computer images also
function as image-instruments. If an image-interface controls a computer, an
image-instrument allows the user to remotely affect physical reality in real
time. This ability not only to act but to "teleact" distinguishes the new computer-based image-instrument from its predecessors. In addition, if old image-instruments such as maps were clearly distinguished from illusionistic
images such as paintings, computer images often combine both functions.

9.   A computer image is frequently hyperlinked to other images, texts, and
other media elements. Rather than being a self-enclosed entity, it points,
leads to, and directs the user outside itself toward something else. A moving
image may also include hyperlinks (for instance, in QuickTime format.) We
can say that a hyperlinked image, and hypermedia in general, "externalizes"
Pierce's idea of infinite semiosis and Derrida's concept of infinite deferral of
meaning—although this does not mean that this "externalization" automat-

ically legitimizes these concepts. Rather than celebrating "the convergence of technology and critical theory," we should use new media technology as an opportunity to question our accepted critical concepts and models.

10.   Variability and automation, these general principles of new media, also apply to images. For example, a designer using a computer program can automatically generate infinite versions of the same image, which can vary in size, resolution, colors, composition, and so on.

11.   From a single image that represents the "cultural unit" of a previous period, we move to a database of images. Thus if the hero of Antonioni's *Blow-Up* (1966) was looking for truth within a single photographic image, the equivalent of this operation in a computer age is to work with a whole database of many images, searching and comparing them with each other. (Although many contemporary films include scenes of image search, none of them makes it a subject in the way *Blow-Up* does by zooming into a photograph. From this perspective, it is interesting that fifteen years after *Blow-Up, Blade Runner* still applies "old" cinematic logic in relation to the computer-based image. In a well-known scene, the hero uses voice commands to direct a futuristic computer device to pan and zoom into a *single* image. In reality, the military has used various computer techniques that rely on *databases* of images to automatically identify objects represented in a single image, detect changes in images over time, and so forth, since the 1950s.)[3] Any unique image that you desire probably already exists on the Internet or in some database. As I have already noted, the problem today is no longer how to create the right image, but how to find an already existing one.

Since a computer-based moving image, like its analog predecessor, is simply a sequence of still images, all these properties apply to it as well. To delineate the new qualities of a computer-based still image, I have compared it with other types of modern images commonly used before it—drawings, maps, paintings, and most importantly, still photographs. It would be logical to begin discussion of the computer-based moving image by also relating it to the two most common types of moving images it replaces in turn—the film image and the animated image. In the first section, "Digital Cinema and

---

3. On the history of computer-based image analysis, see my article "Automation of Sight from Photography to Computer Vision."

the History of a Moving Image," I attempt precisely this. I ask how the shift to computer-based representation and production processes redefines the identity of the moving image and the relationship between cinema and animation. This section also deals with the question of computer-based illusionism, considering it in relation to animation, analog cinema, and digital cinema. The following section, "The New Language of Cinema," presents examples of some new directions for film language—or, more generally, the language of moving images—opened up by computerization. My examples come from different areas in which computer-based moving images are used—digital films, net.films, self-contained hypermedia, and Web sites.

Digital Cinema and the History of a Moving Image

Cinema, the Art of the Index

Most discussions of cinema in the computer age have focused on the possibilities of interactive narrative. It is not hard to understand why: Since the majority of viewers and critics equate cinema with storytelling, computer media is understood as something that will let cinema tell its stories in a new way. Yet as exciting as the idea of a viewer participating in a story, choosing different paths through the narrative space, and interacting with characters may be, it addresses only one aspect of cinema that is neither unique nor, as many will argue, essential to it—narrative.

The challenge that computer media pose to cinema extends far beyond the issue of narrative. Computer media redefine the very identity of cinema. In a symposium that took place in Hollywood in the spring of 1996, one of the participants provocatively referred to movies as "flatties" and to human actors as "organics" and "soft fuzzies."[4] As these terms accurately suggest, what used to be cinema's defining characteristics are now just default options, with many others available. Now that one can "enter" a virtual three-dimensional space, viewing flat images projected on a screen is no longer the

---

4. Scott Billups, presentation during the "Casting from Forest Lawn (Future of Performers)" panel at "The Artists Rights Digital Technology Symposium '96," Los Angeles, Directors Guild of America, 16 February 1996. Billups was a major figure in bringing together Hollywood and Silicon Valley by way of the American Film Institute's Apple Laboratory and Advanced Technologies Programs in the late 1980s and early 1990s. See Paula Parisi, "The New Hollywood Silicon Stars," *Wired* 3.12 (December 1995), 142–145, 202–210.

only option. Given enough time and money, almost everything can be simulated on a computer; filming physical reality is but one possibility.

This "crisis" of cinema's identity also affects the terms and categories used to theorize cinema's past. French film theorist Christian Metz wrote in the 1970s that "most films shot today, good or bad, original or not, 'commercial' or not, have as a common characteristic that they tell a story; in this measure they all belong to one and the same genre, which is, rather, a sort of 'super-genre' [sur-genre]."[5] In identifying fictional film as a "super-genre" of twentieth-century cinema, Metz did not bother to mention another characteristic of this genre because at that time it was too obvious: Fictional films are *live-action* films; that is, they largely consist of unmodified photographic recordings of real events that took place in real, physical space. Today, in the age of photorealistic 3-D computer animation and digital compositing, invoking this characteristic becomes crucial in defining the specificity of twentieth-century cinema. From the perspective of a future historian of visual culture, the differences between classical Hollywood films, European art films, and avant-garde films (apart from abstract ones) may appear less significant than this common feature—their reliance on lens-based recordings of reality. This section is concerned with the effect of computerization on cinema as defined by its "super-genre," fictional live-action film.[6]

During cinema's history, a whole repertoire of techniques (lighting, art direction, the use of different film stocks and lenses, etc.) was developed to modify the basic record obtained by a film apparatus. Yet behind even the most stylized cinematic images, we can discern the bluntness, sterility, and banality of early nineteenth-century photographs. No matter how complex its stylistic innovations, the cinema has found its base in these deposits of reality, these samples obtained by a methodical and prosaic process. Cinema emerged out of the same impulse that engendered naturalism, court stenog-

---

5. Christian Metz, "The Fiction Film and Its Spectator," 402.

6. Cinema as defined by its "super-genre" of fictional live-action film belongs to the media arts, which, in contrast to traditional arts, rely on recordings of reality as their basis. Another term not as popular as "media arts" but perhaps more precise is "recording arts." For the use of this term, see James Monaco, *How to Read a Film,* rev. ed. (New York: Oxford University Press, 1981), 7.

raphy, and wax museums. Cinema is the art of the index; it is an attempt to make art out of a footprint.

Even for director Andrey Tarkovsky, film-painter par excellence, cinema's identity lies in its ability to record reality. Once, during a public discussion in Moscow sometime in the 1970s, he was asked whether he was interested in making abstract films. He replied that there can be no such thing. Cinema's most basic gesture is to open the shutter and to start the film rolling, recording whatever happens to be in front of the lens. For Tarkovsky, an abstract cinema is thus impossible.

But what happens to cinema's indexical identity if it is now possible to generate photorealistic scenes entirely on a computer using 3-D computer animation; modify individual frames or whole scenes with the help a digital paint program; cut, bend, stretch, and stitch digitized film images into something with perfect photographic credibility, even though it was never actually filmed?

This section will address the meaning of these changes in the filmmaking process from the point of view of the larger cultural history of the moving image. Seen in this context, the manual construction of images in digital cinema represents a return to the pro-cinematic practices of the nineteenth century, when images were hand-painted and hand-animated. At the turn of the twentieth century, cinema was to delegate these manual techniques to animation and define itself as a recording medium. As cinema enters the digital age, these techniques are again becoming commonplace in the filmmaking process. Consequently, cinema can no longer be clearly distinguished from animation. It is no longer an indexical media technology but, rather, a subgenre of painting.

This argument will be developed in two stages. I will first follow a historical trajectory from nineteenth-century techniques for creating moving images to twentieth-century cinema and animation. Next I will arrive at a definition of digital cinema by abstracting the common features and interface metaphors of a variety of computer software and hardware that are currently replacing traditional film technology. Seen together, these features and metaphors suggest the distinct logic of a digital moving image. This logic subordinates the photographic and the cinematic to the painterly and the graphic, destroying cinema's identity as a media art. In the beginning of the next section, "New Language of Cinema," I will examine different production contexts that already use digital moving images—Hollywood films, music videos, CD-ROM–based games, and other stand-alone hypermedia—to see if and how this logic has begun to manifest itself.

A Brief Archeology of Moving Pictures

As testified by its original names (kinetoscope, cinematograph, moving pictures), cinema was understood from its birth as the art of motion, the art that finally succeeded in creating a convincing illusion of dynamic reality. If we approach cinema in this way (rather than as the art of audio-visual narrative, or the art of the projected image, or the art of collective spectatorship, etc.), we can see how it superseded earlier techniques for creating and displaying moving images.

These earlier techniques share a number of common characteristics. First, they all relied on hand-painted or hand-drawn images. Magic-lantern slides were painted at least until the 1850s, as were the images used in the Phenakistiscope, the Thaumatrope, the Zootrope, the Praxinoscope, the Choreutoscope, and numerous other nineteenth-century pro-cinematic devices. Even Muybridge's celebrated Zoopraxiscope lectures of the 1880s featured not actual photographs but colored drawings painted from photographs.[7]

Not only were the images created manually, they were also manually animated. In Robertson's *Phantasmagoria,* which premiered in 1799, magic-lantern operators moved behind the screen to make projected images appear to advance and withdraw.[8] More often an exhibitor used only his hands, rather than his whole body, to put the images in motion. One animation technique involved using mechanical slides consisting of a number of layers. An exhibitor would slide the layers to animate the image.[9] Another technique was to move a long slide containing separate images slowly in front of a magic lantern lens. Nineteenth-century optical toys enjoyed in private homes also required manual action to create movement—twirling the strings of the Thaumatrope, rotating the Zootrope's cylinder, turning the Viviscope's handle.

It was not until the last decade of the nineteenth century that the automatic generation of images and automatic projection were finally combined.

---

7. Musser, *The Emergence of Cinema,* 49–50.

8. Musser, *The Emergence of Cinema,* 25.

9. C. W. Ceram, *Archeology of the Cinema,* 44–45.

A mechanical eye was coupled with a mechanical heart; photography met the motor. As a result, cinema—a very particular regime of the visible—was born. Irregularity, nonuniformity, the accident, and other traces of the human body that previously had inevitably accompanied moving-image exhibitions, were replaced by the uniformity of machine vision.[10] A machine, like a conveyer belt, now spat out images, all sharing the same appearance and the same size, all moving at the same speed, like a line of marching soldiers.

Cinema also eliminated the discrete character of both space and movement in moving images. Before cinema, the moving element was visually separated from the static background, as with a mechanical slide show or Reynaud's Praxinoscope Theater (1892).[11] The movement itself was limited in range and affected only a clearly defined figure rather than the whole image. Thus, typical actions would include a bouncing ball, a raised hand or raised eyes, a butterfly moving back and forth over the heads of fascinated children—simple vectors charted across still fields.

Cinema's most immediate predecessors share something else. As the nineteenth-century obsession with movement intensified, devices that could animate more than just a few images became increasingly popular. All of them—the Zootrope, Phonoscope, Tachyscope, and Kinetoscope—were based on loops, sequences of images featuring complete actions that can be played repeatedly. Throughout the nineteenth-century, the loops grew progressively longer. The Thaumatrope (1825), in which a disk with two different images painted on each face was rapidly rotated by twirling strings attached to it, was, in essence, a loop in its most minimal form—two elements replacing one another in succession. In the Zootrope (1867) and its numerous variations, approximately a dozen images were arranged around

---

10. The birth of cinema in the 1890s is accompanied by an interesting transformation: While the body as the generator of moving pictures disappears, it simultaneously becomes their new subject. Indeed, one of the key themes of early films produced by Edison is a human body in motion—a man sneezing, the famous bodybuilder Sandow flexing his muscles, an athlete performing a somersault, a woman dancing. Films of boxing matches play a key role in the commercial development of Kinetoscope. See Musser, *The Emergence of Cinema,* 72–79, and David Robinson, *From Peep Show to Palace: The Birth of American Film* (New York: Columbia University Press, 1996), 44–48.

11. Robinson, *From Peep Show to Palace,* 12.

the perimeter of a circle.[12] The Mutoscope, popular in America throughout the 1890s, increased the duration of the loop by placing a larger number of images radially on an axle.[13] Even Edison's Kinetoscope (1892–1896), the first modern cinematic machine to employ film, continued to arrange images in a loop.[14] Fifty feet of film translated to an approximately twenty-second-long presentation—a genre whose potential development was cut short when cinema adopted a much longer narrative form.

From Animation to Cinema

Once the cinema was stabilized as a technology, it cut all references to its origins in artifice. Everything that characterized moving pictures before the twentieth century—the manual construction of images, loop actions, the discrete nature of space and movement—was delegated to cinema's bastard relative, its supplement and shadow—animation. Twentieth-century animation became a depository for nineteenth-century moving-image techniques left behind by cinema.

The opposition between the styles of animation and cinema defined the culture of the moving image in the twentieth century. Animation foregrounds its artificial character, openly admitting that its images are mere representations. Its visual language is more aligned to the graphic than to the photographic. It is discrete and self-consciously discontinuous—crudely rendered characters moving against a stationary and detailed background, sparsely and irregularly sampled motion (in contrast to the uniform sampling of motion by a film camera—recall Jean-Luc Godard's definition of cinema as "truth 24 frames per second"), and finally space constructed from separate image layers.

In contrast, cinema works hard to erase any traces of its own production process, including any indication that the images that we see could have been constructed rather than simply recorded. It denies that the reality it shows often does not exist outside the film image, an image arrived at by photographing an already impossible space, itself put together with the use of models, mirrors,

---

12. This arrangement was previously used in magic lantern projections; it is described in the second edition of Althanasius Kircher's *Ars magna* (1671). See Musser, *The Emergence of Cinema*, 21–22.

13. Ceram, *Archeology of the Cinema*, 140.

14. Musser, *The Emergence of Cinema*, 78.

and matte paintings, and then combined with other images through optical printing. It pretends to be a simple recording of an already existing reality—both to the viewer and to itself.[15] Cinema's public image stressed the aura of reality "captured" on film, thus implying that cinema was about photographing what existed before the camera rather than creating the "never-was" of special effects.[16] Rear-projection and blue-screen photography, matte paintings and glass shots, mirrors and miniatures, push development, optical effects, and other techniques that allowed filmmakers to construct and alter moving images, and thus could reveal that cinema was not really different from animation, were pushed to cinema's periphery by its practitioners, historians, and critics.[17]

---

15. The extent of this lie is made clear by the films of Andy Warhol from the early 1960s—perhaps the only real attempt to create cinema without language.

16. I have borrowed this definition of special effects from David Samuelson, *Motion Picture Camera Techniques* (London: Focal Press, 1978).

17. The following examples illustrate this disavowal of special effects; other examples can be easily found. The first example is from popular discourse on cinema. A section entitled "Making the Movies" in Kenneth W. Leish's *Cinema* (New York: Newsweek Books, 1974) contains short stories from the history of the movie industry. The heroes of these stories are actors, directors, and producers; special effects artists are mentioned only once. The second example is from an academic source: The authors of the authoritative *Aesthetics of Film* state, "The goal of our book is to summarize from a synthetic and didactic perspective the diverse theoretical attempts at examining these empirical notions [terms from the lexicon of film technicians], including ideas like frame vs. shot, terms from production crews' vocabularies, the notion of identification produced by critical vocabulary, etc." The fact that the text never mentions special effects techniques reflects the general lack of any historical or theoretical interest in the topic by film scholars. Bordwell and Thompson's *Film Art: An Introduction,* which is used as a standard textbook in undergraduate film classes, is a little better as it devotes three of its five hundred pages to special effects. Finally, a relevant statistic: A library of the University of California, San Diego, contains 4,273 titles catalogued under the subject "motion pictures" and only sixteen titles under "special effects cinematography." For the few important works addressing the larger cultural significance of special effects by film theoreticians, see Vivian Sobchack and Scott Bukatman. Norman Klein is currently working on a history of special effects environments. Kenneth W. Leish, *Cinema* (New York: Newsweek Books, 1974); Jacques Aumont, Alain Bergala, Michel Marie, and Marc Vernet, *Aesthetics of Film,* trans. Richard Neupert (Austin: University of Texas Press, 1992), 7; Bordwell and Thompson, *Film Art;* Vivian Sobchack, *Screening Space: The American Science Fiction Film,* 2d ed. (New York: Ungar, 1987); Scott Bukatman, "The Artificial Infinite," in *Visual Display,* eds. Lynne Cooke and Peter Wollen (Seattle: Bay Press, 1995).

In the 1990s, with the shift to computer media, these marginalized techniques moved to the center.

Cinema Redefined

A visible sign of this shift is the new role that computer-generated special effects have come to play in the Hollywood industry in the 1990s. Many blockbusters have been driven by special effects; feeding on their popularity, Hollywood has even created a new minigenre of "The Making of . . . ," videos and books that reveal how special effects are created.

I will use special effects from 1990s' Hollywood films as illustrations of some of the possibilities of digital filmmaking. Until recently, Hollywood studios were the only ones who had the money to pay for digital tools and for the labor involved in producing digital effects. However, the shift to digital media affects not just Hollywood, but filmmaking as a whole. As traditional film technology is universally being replaced by digital technology, the logic of the filmmaking process is being redefined. What I describe below are the new principles of digital filmmaking that are equally valid for individual or collective film productions, regardless of whether they are using the most expensive professional hardware and software or amateur equivalents.

Consider, the following principles of digital filmmaking:

1. Rather than filming physical reality, it is now possible to generate film-like scenes directly on a computer with the help of 3-D computer animation. As a result, live-action footage is displaced from its role as the only possible material from which a film can be constructed.

2. Once live-action footage is digitized (or directly recorded in a digital format), it loses its privileged indexical relationship to prefilmic reality. The computer does not distinguish between an image obtained through a photographic lens, an image created in a paint program, or an image synthesized in a 3-D graphics package, since they are all made from the same material—pixels. And pixels, regardless of their origin, can be easily altered, substituted one for another, and so on. Live-action footage is thus reduced to just another graphic, no different than images created manually.[18]

---

18. For a discussion of the subsumption of the photographic by the graphic, see Peter Lunenfeld, "Art Post-History: Digital Photography and Electronic Semiotics," *Photography after Pho-*

3. If live-action footage were left intact in traditional filmmaking, now it functions as raw material for further compositing, animating, and morphing. As a result, while retaining the visual realism unique to the photographic process, film obtains a plasticity that was previously only possible in painting or animation. To use the suggestive title of a popular morphing software, digital filmmakers work with "elastic reality." For example, the opening shot of *Forrest Gump* (Zemeckis, Paramount Pictures, 1994; special effects by Industrial Light and Magic) tracks an unusually long and extremely intricate flight of a feather. To create the shot, the real feather was filmed against a blue background in different positions; this material was then animated and composited against shots of a landscape.[19] The result: a new kind of realism, which can be described as "something which looks exactly as if it could have happened, although it really could not."

4. In traditional filmmaking, editing and special effects were strictly separate activities. An editor worked on ordering sequences of images; any intervention within an image was handled by special-effects specialists. The computer collapses this distinction. The manipulation of individual images via a paint program or algorithmic image-processing becomes as easy as arranging sequences of images in time. Both simply involve "cut and paste." As this basic computer command exemplifies, modification of digital images (or other digitized data) is not sensitive to distinctions of time and space or to differences in scale. So, reordering sequences of images in time, compositing them together in space, modifying parts of an individual image, and changing individual pixels become the same operation, conceptually and practically.

Given the preceding principles, we can define digital film in this way:

> digital film = live action material + painting + image processing + compositing + 2-D computer animation + 3-D computer animation

---

tography, eds. Hubertus von Amelunxen, Stefan Iglhaut, and Florian Rötzer, 58–66 (Munich: Verlag der Kunst, 1995).

19. For a complete list of people at ILM who worked on this film, see *SIGGRAPH '94 Visual Proceedings* (New York: ACM SIGGRAPH, 1994), 19.

Live-action material can either be recorded on film or video or directly in a digital format.[20] Painting, image processing, and computer animation refer to the processes of modifying already existent images as well as creating new ones. In fact, the very distinction between creation and modification, so clear in film-based media (shooting versus darkroom processes in photography, production versus postproduction in cinema), no longer applies to digital cinema, given that each image, regardless of its origin, goes through a number of programs before making it into the final film.[21]

Let us summarize these principles. Live-action footage is now only raw material to be manipulated by hand—animated, combined with 3-D computer generated scenes, and painted over. The final images are constructed manually from different elements, and all the elements are either created entirely from scratch or modified by hand. Now we can finally answer the question "What is digital cinema?" *Digital cinema is a particular case of animation that uses live-action footage as one of its many elements.*

This can be reread in view of the history of the moving image sketched earlier. Manual construction and animation of images gave birth to cinema and slipped into the margins . . . only to reappear as the foundation of digital cinema. The history of the moving image thus makes a full circle. *Born from animation, cinema pushed animation to its periphery, only in the end to become one particular case of animation.*

The relationship between "normal" filmmaking and special effects is similarly reversed. Special effects, which involved human intervention into ma-

---

20. In this respect, 1995 can be called the last year of digital media. At the 1995 National Association of Broadcasters convention, Avid showed a working model of a digital video camera that records not on a videocassette but directly onto a hard drive. Once digital cameras become widely used, we will no longer have any reason to talk about digital media since the process of digitization will have been eliminated.

21. Here is another, even more radical definition: Digital film = $f(x, y, t)$. This definition would be greeted with joy by the proponents of abstract animation. Since a computer breaks down every frame into pixels, a complete film can be defined as a function that, given the horizontal, vertical, and time location of each pixel, returns its color. This is actually how a computer represents a film, a representation that has a surprising affinity with a certain well-known avant-garde vision of cinema! For a computer, a film is an abstract arrangement of colors changing in time, rather than something structured by "shots," "narrative," "actors," and so on.

chine-recorded footage and which were therefore delegated to cinema's periphery throughout its history, become the norm of digital filmmaking.

The same logic applies to the relationship between production and postproduction. Cinema traditionally involved arranging physical reality to be filmed through the use of sets, models, art direction, cinematography, and so forth. Occasional manipulation of recorded film (for instance, through optical printing) was negligible compared to the extensive manipulation of reality in front of the camera. In digital filmmaking, shot footage is no longer the final point, it is merely raw material to be manipulated on a computer, where the real construction of a scene will take place. In short, production becomes just the first stage of postproduction.

The following example illustrates this new relationship between different stages of the filmmaking process. Traditional on-set filming for *Stars Wars: Episode 1—The Phantom Menace* (Lucas, 1999) was done in just sixty-five days. The postproduction, however, stretched over two years, since ninety-five percent of the film (approximately two thousand shots out of the total 2,200) was constructed on a computer.[22]

Here are two further examples illustrating the shift from rearranging reality to rearranging its images. From the analog era: for a scene in *Zabriskie Point* (1970), Michaelangelo Antonioni, trying to achieve a particularly saturated color, ordered a field of grass to be painted. From the digital era: To create the launch sequence in *Apollo 13* (Howard, 1995; special effects by Digital Domain), the crew shot footage at the original location of the launch at Cape Canaveral. The artists at Digital Domain scanned the film and altered it on computer workstations, removing recent building construction, adding grass to the launch pad and painting the skies to make them more dramatic. This altered film was then mapped onto 3-D planes to create a virtual set that was animated to match a 180-degree dolly movement of a camera following a rising rocket.[23]

The last example brings us to another conceptualization of digital cinema—as painting. In his study of digital photography, Mitchell focuses our

22. Paula Parisi, "Grand Illusion," *Wired* 7.05 (May 1999), 137.

23. See Barbara Robertson, "Digital Magic: Apollo 13," *Computer Graphics World* (August 1995), 20.

attention on what he calls the inherent mutability of the digital image: "The essential characteristic of digital information is that it can be manipulated easily and very rapidly by computer. It is simply a matter of substituting new digits for old . . . Computational tools for transforming, combining, altering, and analyzing images are as essential to the digital artist as brushes and pigments to a painter."[24] As Mitchell points out, this inherent mutability erases the difference between a photograph and a painting. Since a film is a series of photographs, it is appropriate to extend Mitchell's argument to digital film. Given that an artist is easily able to manipulate digitized footage either as a whole or frame by frame, a film in a general sense becomes a series of paintings.[25]

Hand-painting digitized film frames, made possible by a computer, is probably the most dramatic example of the new status of cinema. No longer strictly locked in the photographic, cinema opens itself toward the painterly. Digital hand-painting is also the most obvious example of the return of cinema to its nineteenth-century origins—in this case, the hand-crafted images of magic lantern slides, the Phenakistiscope, and Zootrope.

We usually think of computerization as automation, but here the result is the reverse: What was previously recorded by a camera automatically now has to be painted one frame at a time. And not just a dozen images, as in the nineteenth century, but thousands and thousands. We can draw another parallel with the practice of manually tinting film frames in different colors according to a scene's mood, a practice common in the early days of silent cinema.[26] Today, some of the most visually sophisticated digital effects are often achieved using the same simple method: painstakingly altering thousands of frames by hand. The frames are painted over either to create mattes ("hand-drawn matte extraction") or to change the images directly, as, for instance, in *Forrest Gump,* where President Kennedy is made to speak new sentences by altering the shape of his lips, one frame at a

---

24. Mitchell, *The Reconfigured Eye,* 7.

25. The full advantage of mapping time into 2-D space, already present in Edison's first cinema apparatus, is now realized: One can modify events in time by literally painting on a sequence of frames, treating them as a single image.

26. See Robinson, *From Peep Show to Palace,* 165.

time.[27] In principle, given enough time and money, one can create what will be the ultimate digital film: 129,600 frames (ninety minutes) completely painted by hand from scratch, but indistinguishable in appearance from live photography.

The concept of digital cinema as painting can also be developed in a different way. I would like to compare the shift from analog to digital filmmaking to the shift from fresco and tempera to oil painting in the early Renaissance. A painter making a fresco has limited time before the paint dries, and once it has dried, no further changes to the image are possible. Similarly, a traditional filmmaker has limited means of modifying images once they are recorded on film. Medieval tempera painting, can be compared to the practice of special effects during the analog period of cinema. A painter working with tempera could modify and rework the image, but the process was painstaking and slow. Medieval and early Renaissance masters would spend up to six months on a painting only a few inches tall. The switch to oils greatly liberated painters by allowing them to quickly create much larger compositions (think, for instance, of the works by Veronese and Titian) as well as to modify them as long as necessary. This change in painting technology led the Renaissance painters to create new kinds of compositions, new pictorial space, and new narratives. Similarly, by allowing a filmmaker to treat a film image as an oil painting, digital technology redefines what can be done with cinema.

If digital compositing and digital painting can be thought of as an extension of cell animation techniques (since composited images are stacked in depth parallel to each other, as cells on a animation stand), the newer method of computer-based postproduction makes filmmaking a subset of animation in a different way. In this method, the live-action photographic stills and/or graphic elements are positioned in a 3-D virtual space, thus giving the director the ability to move the virtual camera freely through this space, dollying and panning. Thus cinematography is subordinated to 3-D computer animation. We may think of this method as an extension of the multiplane animation camera. However, if the camera mounted over a multiplane stand

---

27. See "Industrial Light and Magic Alters history with MATADOR," promotion material by Parallax Software, SIGGRAPH 95 Conference, Los Angeles, August 1995.

could only move perpendicular to the images, now it can move in an arbitrary trajectory. An example of a commercial film that relies on this newer method, which one day may become the standard of filmmaking (because it gives the director the most flexibility), is Disney's *Aladdin;* an example of an independent work that fully explores the new aesthetic possibilities of this method without subordinating it to traditional cinematic realism is Waliczky's *The Forest.*

In the "Compositing" section, I pointed out that digital compositing can be thought off as an intermediary step between 2-D images and 3-D computer representation. The newer postproduction method represents the next logical step toward completely computer-generated 3-D representations. Instead of the 2-D space of "traditional" composite, we now have layers of moving images positioned in a virtual 3-D space.

The reader who has followed my analysis of the new possibilities of digital cinema may wonder why I have stressed the parallels between digital cinema and the pro-cinematic techniques of the nineteenth century, but have not mentioned twentieth-century avant-garde filmmaking. Did not the avant-garde filmmakers already explore many of these new possibilities? To take the notion of cinema as painting, Len Lye, one of the pioneers of abstract animation, was painting directly on film as early as 1935; he was followed by Norman McLaren and Stan Brackage, the latter extensively covering shot footage with dots, scratches, splattered paint, smears, and lines in an attempt to turn his films into equivalents of Abstract Expressionist paintings. More generally, one of the major impulses in all avant-garde filmmaking from Leger to Godard was to combine the cinematic, the painterly, and the graphic—by using live-action footage and animation within one film or even a single frame, by altering this footage in a variety of ways, or by juxtaposing printed texts and filmed images.

When the avant-garde filmmakers collaged multiple images within a single frame, or painted and scratched film, or revolted against the indexical identity of cinema in other ways, they were working against "normal" filmmaking procedures and the intended uses of film technology. (Film stock was not designed to be painted on.) Thus they operated on the periphery of commercial cinema not only aesthetically but also technically.

One general effect of the digital revolution is that avant-garde aesthetic strategies came to be embedded in the commands and interface metaphors of computer software.[28] In short, *the avant-garde became materialized in a computer.* Digital-cinema technology is a case in point. The avant-garde strategy of collage reemerged as the "cut-and-paste" command, the most basic operation one can perform on digital data. The idea of painting on film became embedded in the paint functions of film-editing software. The avant-garde move to combine animation, printed texts, and live-action footage is repeated in the convergence of animation, title generation, paint, compositing, and editing systems into all-in-one packages. Finally, the move to combine a number of film images within one frame (for instance, in Leger's 1924 *Ballet Mechanique* or in *Man with a Movie Camera*) also becomes legitimized by technology, given that all editing software, including Photoshop, Premiere, After Effects, Flame, and Cineon, assume by default that a digital image consists of a number of separate image layers. All in all, what used to be exceptions for traditional cinema have become the normal, intended techniques of digital filmmaking, embedded in technology design itself.[29]

From Kino-Eye to Kino-Brush

In the twentieth century, cinema played two roles at once. As a media technology, its role was to capture and store visible reality. The difficulty of modifying images once recorded was precisely what lent it value as a document, assuring its authenticity. This same rigidity has defined the limits of cinema as a "super-genre" of *live-action* narrative. Although cinema includes within itself a variety of styles—the result of the efforts of numerous directors, designers, and cinematographers—these styles share a strong family resemblance. They are all children of a recording process that uses lenses, regular sampling of time, and photographic media. They are all children of a machine vision.

The mutability of digital data impairs the value of cinema recordings as documents of reality. In retrospect, we can see that twentieth-century cinema's regime of visual realism, the result of automatically recording

---

28. See my "Avant-Garde as Software" (http://visarts.ucsd.edu/~manovich).

29. For the experiments in painting on film by Lye, McLaren, and Brackage, see Robert Russett and Cecile Starr, *Experimental Animation* (New York: Van Nostrand Reinhold, 1976), 65–71, 117–128; P. Adams Smith, *Visionary Film,* 2d ed. (Oxford: Oxford University Press), 230, 136–227.

visual reality, was only an exception, an isolated accident in the history of visual representation, which has always involved, and now again involves, the manual construction of images. Cinema becomes a particular branch of painting—painting in time. No longer a kino-eye, but a kino-brush.[30]

The privileged role played by the manual construction of images in digital cinema is one example of a larger trend—the return of pro-cinematic moving-image techniques. Although marginalized by the twentieth-century institution of live-action, narrative cinema, which relegated them to the realms of animation and special effects, these techniques are reemerging as the foundation of digital filmmaking. What was once supplemental to cinema becomes its norm; what was at the periphery comes into the center. Computer media return to us the repressed of the cinema.

As the examples in this section suggest, directions that were closed off at the turn of the century when cinema came to dominate the modern moving-image culture are now again beginning to be explored. The moving-image culture is being redefined once again; cinematic realism is being displaced from the dominant mode to merely one option among many.

---

30. Dziga Vertov coined the term "kino-eye" in the 1920s to describe the cinematic apparatus's ability "to record and organize the individual characteristics of life's phenomena into a whole, an essence, a conclusion." For Vertov, it was the presentation of film "facts," based as they were on materialist evidence, that defined the very nature of the cinema. See *Kino-Eye: The Writings of Dziga Vertov,* ed. Annette Michelson, trans. Kevin O'Brien (Berkeley: University of California Press, 1984). The quotation above is from "Artistic Drama and Kino-Eye," originally published in 1924, 47–49, 47.

The New Language of Cinema

Cinematic and Graphic: Cinegratography

3-D animation, compositing, mapping, paint retouching: In commercial cinema, these radical new techniques are used mostly to solve technical problems while traditional cinematic language is preserved unchanged. Frames are hand-painted to remove wires that supported an actor during shooting; a flock of birds is added to a landscape; a city street is filled with crowds of simulated extras. Although most Hollywood releases now involve digitally manipulated scenes, the use of computers is always carefully hidden.[31] Appropriately, in Hollywood the practice of simulating traditional film language has received a name—"invisible effects," defined as "computer-enhanced scenes that fool the audience into believing the shots were produced with live actors on location, but are really composed of a mélange of digital and live action footage."[32]

Commercial narrative cinema continues to hold on to the classical realist style in which images function as unretouched photographic records of events that took place in front of the camera. So when Hollywood cinema uses computers to create a fantastic, impossible reality, it is done through

---

31. Reporting in the December 1995 issue of *Wired,* Parisi writes: "A decade ago, only an intrepid few, led by George Lucas's Industrial Light and Magic, were doing high-quality digital work. Now computer imaging is considered an indispensable production tool for all films, from the smallest drama to the largest visual extravaganza" (Parisi, "The New Hollywood Silicon Stars," 144.)

32. Mark Frauenfelder, "Hollywood's Head Case," *Wired* 7.08 (August 1999), 112.

the introduction of various nonhuman characters such as aliens, mutants, and robots. We never notice the pure arbitrariness of their colorful mutating bodies, the beams of energy radiating from their eyes, the whirlpools of particles emanating from their wings, because they are perceptually consistent with the set; that is, they look like something that could have existed in a three-dimensional space and, therefore, could have been photographed.

But how do filmmakers justify turning a familiar reality such as a human body or landscape into something physically impossible in our world? Such transformations are motivated by the movie's narrative. The shiny, metallic body of the Terminator in *Terminator 2* is possible because the Terminator is a cyborg sent from the future; the rubbery body of Jim Carrey in *The Mask* (Russell, 1994) is possible because his character wears a mask with magical powers. Similarly, in *What Dreams May Come* (Ward, special effects by Mass.Illusions and others, 1998) the fantastic landscape made of swirling brushstrokes to which the main hero is transported after his death is motivated by the unique status of this location.

While embracing computers as a productivity tool, cinema refuses to give up its unique cinema-effect, an effect which, according to Christian Metz's penetrating analysis made in the 1970s, depends upon narrative form, the reality effect, and cinema's architectural arrangement all working together.[33] Toward the end of his essay, Metz wonders whether in the future nonnarrative films may become more numerous; if this happens, he suggests, cinema will no longer need to manufacture its reality effect. Electronic and digital media have already brought about this transformation. Beginning in the 1980s, we see the emergence of new cinematic forms that are not linear narratives, that are exhibited on a television or computer screen rather than in a movie theater—and that simultaneously give up cinematic realism.

What are these forms? First, there is the music video. Probably not by accident, the genre of the music video came into existence precisely at the time when electronic video-effects devices were entering editing studios. Importantly, just as music videos often incorporate narratives within them but are not linear narratives from start to finish, they rely on film (or video) images but change them beyond the norms of traditional cinematic realism. The

---

33. Metz, "The Fiction Film and Its Spectator."

manipulation of images through hand-painting and image processing, hidden techniques in Hollywood cinema, is brought into the open on a television screen. Similarly, the construction of an image from heterogeneous sources is not subordinated to the goal of photorealism, but functions as an aesthetic strategy. The genre of music video has served as a laboratory for exploring numerous new possibilities of manipulating photographic images made possible by computers—the numerous points that exist in the space between the 2-D and the 3-D, cinematography and painting, photographic realism and collage. In short, it is a living and constantly expanding textbook for digital cinema.

A detailed analysis of the evolution of music video imagery (or, more generally, broadcast graphics in the electronic age) deserves a separate treatment, and I will not try to take it up here. Instead, I will discuss another new cinematic non-narrative form, CD-ROM-based games, which, in contrast to the music video, has relied on the computer for storage and distribution from the very beginning. And unlike music video designers, who were consciously pushing traditional film or video images into something new, the designers of CD-ROMs arrived at a new visual language unintentionally while attempting to emulate traditional cinema.

In the late 1980s, Apple began to promote the concept of computer multimedia, and in 1991 it released QuickTime software to enable an ordinary personal computer to play movies. During the first few years the computer did not perform its new role very well. First, CD-ROMs could not hold anything close to the length of a standard theatrical film. Second, the computer could not smoothly play a movie larger than the size of a stamp. Finally, the movies had to be compressed, degrading their visual appearance. Only in the case of still images was the computer able to display photographic-like detail at full-screen size.

Because of these particular hardware limitations, the designers of CD-ROMs had to invent a different kind of cinematic language in which a range of strategies, such as discrete motion, loops, and superimposition—previously used in nineteenth-century moving-image presentations, twentieth-century animation, and the avant-garde tradition of graphic cinema—were applied to photographic or synthetic images. This language synthesized cinematic illusionism and the aesthetics of graphic collage, with its characteristic heterogeneity and discontinuity. The photographic and the graphic, divorced when cinema and animation went their separate ways, met again on the computer screen.

The graphic also met the cinematic. The designers of CD-ROMs were aware of the techniques of twentieth-century cinematography and film editing, but they had to adapt these techniques both to an interactive format and to hardware limitations. As a result, the techniques of modern cinema and of nineteenth-century moving-image presentations merged in a new hybrid language that can be called "cinegratography."

We can trace the development of this language by analyzing a few well-known CD-ROM titles. The best-selling game *Myst* unfolds its narrative strictly through still images, a practice that takes us back to magic-lantern shows (and to Chris Marker's *La Jetée*).[34] But in other ways *Myst* relies on the techniques of twentieth-century cinema. For instance, the CD-ROM uses simulated camera turns to switch from one image to the next. It also employs the basic technique of film editing to subjectively speed up or slow down time. In the course of the game, the user moves around a fictional island by clicking on a mouse. Each click advances a virtual camera forward, revealing a new view of the 3-D environment. When the user begins to descend into the underground chambers, the spatial distance between the points of view of each two consecutive views sharply decreases. If before, the user was able to cross a whole island with just a few clicks, now it takes a dozen clicks to get to the bottom of the stairs! In other words, just as in traditional cinema, *Myst* slows down time to create suspense and tension.

In *Myst,* miniature animations are sometimes embedded within the still images. In the next best-selling CD-ROM, *7th Guest* (Virgin Games, 1993), the user is presented with video clips of live actors superimposed over static backgrounds created with 3-D computer graphics. The clips are looped, and the moving human figures clearly stand out against the backgrounds. Both of these features connect the visual language of *7th Guest* to nineteenth-century pre-cinematic devices and twentieth-century cartoons rather than to cinematic verisimilitude. But like *Myst, 7th Guest* also evokes distinctly modern cinematic codes. The environment where all the action takes place (an interior of a house) is rendered using a wide angle lens; to move from one

---

34. This twenty-eight-minute film, made in 1962, is composed almost exclusively of still frames. For documentation, see Chris Marker, *La Jetée: Ciné-roman* (New York: Zone Books, 1992).

view to the next, a camera follows a complex curve, as though mounted on a virtual dolly.

Next, consider the CD-ROM *Johnny Mnemonic* (Sony Imagesoft, 1995). Produced to complement the fiction film of the same title, marketed not as a "game" but as an "interactive movie," and featuring full-screen video throughout, *Johnny Mnemonic* comes closer to cinematic realism than the previous CD-ROMs—yet it is still quite distinct from it. With all action shot against a green screen and then composited with graphic backgrounds, its visual style exists within the space between cinema and collage.

It would not be entirely inappropriate to read this short history of the digital moving image as a teleological development that replays the emergence of cinema a hundred years earlier. Indeed, as the speed of computers keeps increasing, CD-ROM designers have been able to go from a slide-show format to the superimposition of small moving elements over static backgrounds and finally to full-frame moving images. This evolution repeats the nineteenth-century progression—from sequences of still images (magic-lantern slide presentations) to moving characters over static backgrounds (as in, for instance, Reynaud's Praxinoscope Theater) to full motion (the Lumières' cinematograph). Moreover, the introduction of QuickTime in 1991 can be compared to the introduction of the Kinetoscope in 1892: Both were used to present short loops, both featured images approximately two by three inches in size, both called for private viewing rather than collective exhibition. The two technologies even appear to play a similar cultural role. If in the early 1890s the public patronized Kinetoscope parlors where peep-hole machines presented them with the latest marvel—tiny, moving photographs arranged in short loops— exactly a hundred years later, computer users were equally fascinated with tiny QuickTime movies that turned a computer in a film projector, however imperfect.[35] Finally, the Lumières' first film screenings of 1895 that shocked their audiences with huge moving images found their parallel in 1995 CD-ROMs in which the moving image finally fills the entire computer screen (for instance, *Johnny Mnemonic.*) Thus, exactly a hundred years after cinema was officially "born," it was reinvented on a computer screen.

---

35. These parallels are further investigated in my "Little Movies" (http://visarts.ucsd.edu/~manovich/little-movies).

But this is only one reading. We no longer think of the history of cinema as a linear march toward one language, or as a progression toward increasingly accurate verisimilitude. Rather, we have come to see it as a succession of distinct and equally expressive languages, each with its own aesthetic variables, each new language closing off some of the possibilities of the previous one—a cultural logic not dissimilar to Kuhn's analysis of scientific paradigms.[36] Similarly, instead of dismissing the visual strategies of early multimedia titles as the result of technological limitations, we may want to think of them as an alternative to traditional cinematic illusionism, as the beginning of digital cinema's new language.

For the computer/entertainment industries, these strategies represent only a temporary limitation, an annoying drawback that needs to be overcome. This is one important difference between the situation at the end of the nineteenth century and the situation at the end of the twentieth century: If cinema was developing toward a still open horizon of many possibilities, the development of commercial multimedia, and of corresponding computer hardware (compression boards, storage formats such as DVD), was driven by a clearly defined goal—the exact duplication of cinematic realism. So if the computer screen increasingly emulates cinema's screen, this is not an accident, but the result of conscious planning by the computer and entertainment industries. But this drive to turn new media into a simulation of classical film language, which parallels the encoding of cinema's techniques in software interfaces and in the hardware itself, as described in the "Cultural Interfaces" section, is just one direction for new media development among numerous others. I will next examine a number of new media and old media objects that point toward other possible trajectories.

The New Temporality: The Loop as a Narrative Engine

One of the underlying assumptions of this book is that, by looking at the history of visual culture and media, in particular, cinema, we can find many strategies and techniques relevant to new media design. Put differently, to develop a new aesthetics of new media, we should pay as much attention to cultural history as to the computer's unique new possibilities to generate, organize, manipulate, and distribute data.

---

36. Kuhn, *The Structure of Scientific Revolutions.*

As we scan cultural history (which includes the history of new media up until the time of research), three kinds of situations will be particularly relevant for us:

- An interesting strategy or technique is abandoned or forced "underground" without fully developing its potential.
- A strategy can be understood as a response to technological constraints (I am purposefully using this more technical term instead of the more ideologically loaded "limitations") similar to those of new media.
- A strategy is used in a situation similar to that faced by new media designers. For instance, montage was a strategy for dealing with the modularity of film (how do you join separate shots?) as well as the problem of coordinating different media types such as images and sound. Both of these situations are being faced once again by new media designers.

I have already used these principles in discussing the parallels between nineteenth-century pro-cinematic techniques and the language of new media; they have also guided me in thinking about animation (the "underground" of twentieth-century cinema) as the basis for digital cinema. I will now use a particular parallel between early cinematic and new media technology to highlight another older technique useful to new media—the loop. Characteristically, many new media products, whether cultural objects (such as games) or software (various media players such as QuickTime Player) use loops in their design, while treating them as temporary technological limitations. I, however, want to think about them as a source of new possibilities for new media.[37]

As already mentioned in the previous section, all nineteenth-century pro-cinematic devices, up through Edison's Kinetoscope, were based on short loops. As "the seventh art" began to mature, it banished the loop to the low-art realms of the instructional film, pornographic peep-show, and animated cartoon. In contrast, narrative cinema avoids repetitions; like modern Western fictional

---

37. My own "Little Movies" explores the aesthetics of digital cinema and draws parallels between the early cinema of the 1890s, the structuralist filmmaking of the 1960s, and the new media of the 1990s.

forms in general, it puts forward a notion of human existence as a linear progression through numerous unique events.

Cinema's birth from a loop form was reenacted at least once during its history. In one of the sequences of *Man with a Movie Camera,* Vertov shows us a cameraman standing in the back of a moving automobile. As he is being carried forward by the automobile, he cranks the handle of his camera. A loop, a repetition, created by the circular movement of the handle, gives birth to a progression of events—a very basic narrative that is also quintessentially modern—a camera moving through space recording whatever is in its way. In what seems to be a reference to cinema's primal scene, these shots are intercut with the shots of a moving train. Vertov even restages the terror that the Lumières' film supposedly provoked in its audience; he positions his camera right along the train track so the train runs over our point of view a number of times, crushing us again and again.

Early digital movies shared the same limitations of storage as nineteenth-century pro-cinematic devices. This is probably why the loop playback function was built into the QuickTime interface, giving it the same weight as the VCR-style "play" function. So, in contrast to films and videotapes, Quick-Time movies were supposed to be played forward, backward, or looped. Computer games also heavily relied on loops. Since it was not possible to animate every character in real time, designers stored short loops of a character's motions—for instance, an enemy soldier or a monster walking back and forth—that would be recalled at appropriate times in the game. Internet pornography also heavily relied on loops. Many sites featured numerous "channels" that were supposed to stream either feature-length feature films or "live feeds"; in reality, they would usually play short loops (a minute or so) over and over. Sometimes a few films would be cut into a number of short loops that would become the content of one hundred, five hundred, or one thousand channels.[38]

The history of new media tells us that hardware limitations never go away: They disappear in one area only to come back in another. One example I have already noted is the hardware limitations of the 1980s in the area of 3-D computer animation. In the 1990s they returned in a new

---

38. http://www.danni.com.

area—Internet-based real-time virtual worlds. What used to be the slow speed of CPUs became slow bandwidth. As a result, the VRML worlds of the 1990s look like the prerendered animations done ten years earlier.

A similar logic applies to loops. Early QuickTime movies and computer games relied heavily on loops. As the CPU speed increased and larger storage media such as CD-ROM and DVD became available, the use of loops in stand-alone hypermedia declined. However, online virtual worlds such as Active Worlds came to use loops extensively, as they provide a cheap (in terms of bandwidth and computation) means of adding some signs of "life" to their geometric-looking environments.[39] Similarly, we may expect that when digital videos appear on small displays in our cellular phones, personal managers such as Palm Pilot, or other wireless communication devices, they will once again be arranged in short loops because of bandwidth, storage, or CPU limitations.

Can the loop be a new narrative form appropriate for the computer age?[40] It is relevant to recall that the loop gave birth not only to cinema but also to computer programming. Programming involves altering the linear flow of data through control structures, such as "if/then" and "repeat/while"; the loop is the most elementary of these control structures. Most computer programs are based on repetitions of a set number of steps; this repetition is controlled by the program's main loop. So if we strip the computer from its usual interface and follow the execution of a typical computer program, the computer will reveal itself to be another version of Ford's factory, with the loop as its conveyer belt.

As the practice of computer programming illustrates, the loop and the sequential progression do not have to be considered mutually exclusive. A computer program progresses from start to finish by executing a series of loops. Another illustration of how these two temporal forms can work together is Möbius House by the Dutch team UN Studio/Van Berkel & Bos.[41]

---

39. http://www.activeworlds.com.

40. Natalie Bookchin's CD-ROM *Databank of the Everyday* (1996) investigates the loop as a structure of everyday life. Because I did the majority of the cinematography and some interface design for this project, I do not discuss it in the main text.

41. Riley, *The Un-private House.*

In this house a number of functionally different areas are arranged one after another in the form of a Möbius strip, thus forming a loop. As the narrative of the day progresses from one activity to the next, the inhabitants move from area to area.

Traditional cell animation similarly combines a narrative and a loop. In order to save labor, animators arrange many actions, such as movements of characters' legs, eyes, and arms, into short loops and repeat them over and over. Thus, as already mentioned in the previous section, in a typical twentieth-century cartoon, a large proportion of motions involves loops. This principle is taken to the extreme in Rybczynski's *Tango*. Subjecting live-action footage to the logic of animation, Rybczynski arranges the trajectory of each character through space as a loop. These loops are further composited, resulting in a complex and intricate time-based structure. At the same time, the overall "shape" of this structure is governed by a number of narratives. The film begins in an empty room; next, the loops of a character's trajectories through this room are added, one by one. The end of the film mirrors its beginning as the loops are "deleted" in reverse order, one by one. This metaphor for the progression of a human life (we are born alone, gradually form relations with other humans, and eventually die alone) is also supported by another narrative: The first character to appear in the room is a young boy; the last, an old woman.

The concept of a loop as an "engine" that puts the narrative in motion becomes the foundation of a brilliant interactive TV program *Akvaario* (Aquarium) by a number of graduate students at Helsinki's University of Art and Design (director Teijo Pellinen, 1999).[42] In contrast to many new media objects that combine the conventions of cinema, print, and HCI, *Akvaario* aims to preserve the continuous flow of traditional cinema, while adding interactivity to it. Along with an earlier game *Johnny Mnemonic* (SONY, 1995), as well as the pioneering interactive, laserdisk computer installations by Graham Weinbren done in the 1980s, this project is a rare example of a new media narrative that does not rely on the oscillation between noninteractive and interactive segments.

Using the already familiar convention of games such as Tamagotchi (1996–), the program asks TV viewers to "take charge" of a fictional human

---

42. http://www.mlab.uiah.fi/.

character.[43] Most shots show this character engaged in different activities in his apartment—eating dinner, reading a book, staring into space. The shots replace each other following standard conventions of film and TV editing. The result is something that looks at first like a conventional, although very long, movie (the program was projected to run for three hours every day over the course of a few months), even though the shots are selected in real time by a computer program from a database of a few hundred different shots.

By choosing from one of four buttons always present at the bottom of the screen, the viewer controls the character's motivation. When a button is pressed, a computer program selects a sequence of particular shots to follow the shot currently playing. Because of the visual, spatial, and referential discontinuity between shots typical of standard editing, the result is something that the viewer interprets as a conventional narrative. A film or television viewer does not expect two consecutive shots to necessarily display the same space or subsequent moments of time. Therefore in *Akvaario* a computer program can "weave" an endless narrative by choosing from a database of different shots. What gives the resulting "narrative" a sufficient continuity is that almost all the shots show the same character.

Akvaario is one of the first examples of what in a previous chapter I called a "database narrative." It is, in other words, a narrative that fully utilizes many features of the database organization of data. It relies on our abilities to classify database records according to different dimensions, sort through records, quickly retrieve any record, as well as "stream" a number of different records continuously one after another.

In *Akvaario* the loop becomes the way to bridge linear narrative and interactive control. When the program begins, a few shots keep following each other in a loop. After the user chooses the character's motivation by pressing a button, this loop becomes a narrative. Shots stop repeating, and a sequence of new shots is displayed. If no button is pressed again, the narrative turns back into a loop; that is, a few shots start repeating over and over. In *Akvaario* a narrative is born from a loop, and it returns back to a loop. The historical birth of modern fictional cinema out of the loop returns as a condition of

---

43. My analysis is based on a project prototype that I saw in October of 1999. The completed project is projected to have a male and a female character.

cinema's rebirth as an interactive form. Rather than being an archaic leftover, a reject from cinema's evolution, the use of the loop in *Akvaario* suggests a new temporal aesthetics for computer-based cinema.

Jean-Louis Boissier's *Flora petrinsularis* realizes some of the possibilities contained in the loop form in a different way.[44] This CD-ROM is based on Rousseau's *Confessions*. It opens with a white screen, containing a numbered list. Clicking on each item leads us to a screen containing two windows, positioned side by side. Both windows show the same video loop made from a few different shots. The two loops are offset from each other in time. Thus the images appearing in the left window reappear in a moment on the right and vice versa, as though an invisible wave is running through the screen. This wave soon becomes materialized—when we click inside the windows, we are taken to a new screen that also contains two windows, each showing the loop of a rhythmically vibrating water surface. The loops of water surfaces can be thought of as two sine waves offset in phase. This structure, then, functions as a metatext of the structure in the first screen. In other words, the loops of a water surface act as a diagram of the loop structure that controls the correlations between shots in the first screen, similar to how Marey and the Gibsons diagrammed human motion in their film studies at the beginning of the twentieth century.

As each mouse click reveals another loop, the viewer becomes an editor, but not in the traditional sense. Rather than constructing a singular narrative sequence and discarding material not used, here the viewer brings to the forefront, one by one, numerous layers of looped actions that seem to be taking place all at once, a multitude of separate but coexisting temporalities. The viewer is not cutting but reshuffling. In a reversal of Vertov's sequence in which a loop generates a narrative, the viewer's attempt to create a story in *Flora petrinsularis* leads to a loop.

It is useful to analyze the loop structure of *Flora petrinsularis* in terms of montage theory. From this perspective, the repetition of images in two adjoining windows can be interpreted as an example of what Eisenstein called

---

44. *Flora petrinsularis* (1993) is included in the compilation CD-ROM, *Artintact 1* (Karlsruhe, Germany: ZKM/Center for Art and Media, 1994). That and other ZKM publications are available from http://www.zkm.de.

"rhythmical montage." At the same time, Boissier takes montage apart, so to speak. Shots that in traditional temporal montage would follow each in time here appear next to one other in space. In addition, rather than being "hard-wired" by an editor in only one possible structure, here the shots can appear in different combinations since they are activated by a user moving a mouse across the windows.

It is also possible to find other examples of traditional temporal montage in this work as well—for instance, the move from the first screen, which shows a close-up of a woman, to a second screen, which shows water surfaces, and back to the first screen. This move can be interpreted as traditional parallel editing. In cinema, parallel editing involves alternating between two subjects. For instance, a chase sequence may go back and forth between the images of two cars, one pursuing another. However, in our case the water images are always present "underneath" the first set of images. So the logic here again is coexistence rather than replacement.

The loop that structures *Flora petrinsularis* on a number of levels becomes a metaphor for human desire that can never achieve resolution. It can also be read as a comment on cinematic realism. What are the minimal conditions necessary to create the impression of reality? In the case of a field of grass, or a close-up of a plant or stream, just a few looped frames, as Boissier demonstrates, is sufficient to produce the illusion of life and of linear time.

Steven Neale describes how early film demonstrated its authenticity by representing moving nature: "What was lacking [in photographs] was the wind, the very index of real, natural movement. Hence the obsessive contemporary fascination, not just with movement, not just with scale, but also with waves and sea spray, with smoke and spray."[45] What for early cinema was its biggest pride and achievement—a faithful documentation of nature's movement—becomes for Boissier a subject of ironic and melancholic simulation. As the few frames are looped over and over, we see blades of grass shifting slightly back and forth, rhythmically responding to a nonexistent wind, almost approximated by the noise of a computer reading data from a CD-ROM.

Something else is being simulated here as well, perhaps unintentionally. As you watch the CD-ROM, the computer periodically staggers, unable to

---

45. Neale, *Cinema and Technology,* 52.

maintain consistent data rate. As a result, the images on the screen move in uneven bursts, slowing and speeding up with human-like irregularity. It is as though they are brought to life not by a digital machine but by a human operator, cranking the handle of the Zootrope a century and a half ago . . .

Spatial Montage and Macrocinema

Along with taking on a loop, *Flora petrinsularis* can also be seen as a step toward what I will call *spatial montage.* Instead of the traditional singular frame of cinema, Boissier uses two images at once, positioned side by side. This can be thought of as the simplest case of spatial montage. In general, spatial montage could involve a number of images, potentially of different sizes and proportions, appearing on the screen at the same time. This juxtaposition by itself of course does not result in montage; it is up to the filmmaker to construct a logic that determines which images appear together, when they appear, and what kind of relationships they enter into with one other.

Spatial montage represents an alternative to traditional cinematic temporal montage, replacing its traditional sequential mode with a spatial one. Ford's assembly line relied on the separation of the production process into sets of simple, repetitive, and sequential activities. The same principle made computer programming possible: A computer program breaks a task into a series of elemental operations to be executed one at a time. Cinema followed this logic of industrial production as well. It replaced all other modes of narration with a sequential narrative, an assembly line of shots that appear on the screen one at a time. This type of narrative turned out to be particularly incompatible with the spatial narrative that had played a prominent role in European visual culture for centuries. From Giotto's fresco cycle at Capella degli Scrovegni in Padua to Courbet's *A Burial at Ornans,* artists presented a multitude of separate events within a single space, whether the fictional space of a painting or the physical space that can be taken in by the viewer all at once. In the case of Giotto's fresco cycle and many other fresco and icon cycles, each narrative event is framed separately, but all of them can be viewed together in a single glance. In other cases, different events are represented as taking place within a single pictorial space. Sometimes, events that form one narrative but are separated by time are depicted within a single painting. More often, the painting's subject becomes an excuse to show a number of separate "micronarratives" (for instance, works by Hiëronymous Bosch and Peter Bruegel). All in all, in contrast to cinema's sequential narrative, all the "shots" in spatial narrative are accessible to the viewer at once. Like nineteenth-century animation, spatial narrative did not disappear completely in the twentieth century, but rather, like animation, came to be delegated to a minor form of Western culture—comics.

It is not accidental that the marginalization of spatial narrative and the privileging of the sequential mode of narration coincided with the rise of the historical paradigm in human sciences. Cultural geographer Edward Soja has argued that the rise of history in the second half of the nineteenth century coincided with a decline in spatial imagination and a spatial mode of social analysis.[46] According to Soja, it is only in the last decades of the twentieth century that this mode has made a powerful comeback, as exemplified by the growing importance of such concepts as "geopolitics" and "globalization" as well as by the key role that analysis of space plays in theories of postmodernism. Indeed, although some of the best thinkers of the twentieth century, including Freud, Panofsky, and Foucault, were able to combine historical and spatial modes of analysis in their theories, they probably represent exceptions rather than the norm. The same holds for film theory, which, from Eisenstein in the 1920s to Deleuze in the 1980s, focuses on temporal rather than spatial structures of film.

Twentieth-century film practice has elaborated complex techniques of montage with different images replacing each other in time, but the possibility of what can be called a "spatial montage" of simultaneously coexisting images has not been explored as systematically. (Thus, cinema is also given to historical imagination at the expense of spatial imagination.) Notable exceptions include the use of a split screen by Abel Gance in *Napoléon* in the 1920s and also the American experimental filmmaker Stan Van der Beek in the 1960s; some of the works, or rather events, of the "expanded cinema" movement of the 1960s, and, last but not least, the legendary multi-image multimedia presentation shown in the Czech Pavilion at the 1967 World Expo. Emil Radok's *Diapolyeran* consisted of 112 separate cubes. One hundred and sixty different images could be projected onto each cube. Radok was able to "direct" each cube separately. To the best of my knowledge, no

---

46. Edward Soja, keynote lecture at the "History and Space" conference, University of Turku, Turku, Finland, October 2, 1999.

one has since attempted to create a spatial montage of this complexity in any technology.

Traditional film and video technology was designed to fill a screen completely with a single image; thus to explore spatial montage a filmmaker had to work "against" the technology. This in part explains why so few have attempted it. But when, in the 1970s, the screen became a bit-mapped computer display, with individual pixels corresponding to memory locations that could be dynamically updated by a computer program, the one image/ one screen logic was broken. Since the development of the Xerox PARC Alto workstation, GUI has used multiple windows. It would be logical to expect that cultural forms based on moving images will eventually adopt similar conventions. In the 1990s some computer games such as *Goldeneye* (Nintendo/Rare, 1997) already used multiple windows to present the same action simultaneously from different viewpoints. We may expect that computer-based cinema will eventually go in the same direction—especially once the limitations of communication bandwidth disappear and the resolution of displays significantly increases, from the typical 1–2K in 2000 to 4K, 8K, or beyond. I believe that the next generation of cinema—*broadband cinema, or macrocinema*—will add multiple windows to its language. When this happens, the tradition of spatial narrative that twentieth-century cinema suppressed will reemerge.

Modern visual culture and art offer us many ideas for how spatial narrative might be further developed in a computer; but what about spatial montage? In other words, what will happen if we combine two different cultural traditions—the informationally dense visual narratives of Renaissance and Baroque painters with the "attention demanding" shot juxtapositions of twentieth-century film directors? *My boyfriend came back from war!,* a Web-based work by the young Moscow artist Olga Lialina, can be read as an exploration in this direction.[47] Using the capability of HTML to create frames within frames, Lialina leads us through a narrative that begins with a single screen. This screen becomes progressively divided into more and more frames as we follow different links. Throughout, an image of a human

---

47. http://www.telepolis.de/tp/deutsch/kunst/3040?1.html. Liliana's other net.art projects can be found at http://www.teleportacia.org.

couple and a constantly blinking window remain on the left part of the screen. These two images enter into new combinations with texts and images on the right that keep changing as the user interacts with the work. As the narrative activates different parts of the screen, montage in time gives way to montage in space. Put differently, we can say that montage acquires a new spatial dimension. In addition to montage dimensions already explored by cinema (differences in images' content, composition, and movement), we now have a new dimension—the position of images in space in relation to each other. In addition, as images do not replace each other (as in cinema) but remain on the screen throughout the movie, each new image is juxtaposed not just with the image that preceded it but with all the other images present on the screen.

The logic of replacement, characteristic of cinema, gives way to the logic of addition and coexistence. Time becomes spatialized, distributed over the surface of the screen. In spatial montage, nothing need be forgotten, nothing is erased. Just as we use computers to accumulate endless texts, messages, notes, and data, and just as a person, going through life, accumulates more and more memories, with the past slowly acquiring more weight than the future, spatial montage can accumulate events and images as it progresses through its narrative. In contrast to the cinema's screen, which primarily functions as a record of perception, here the computer screen functions as a record of memory.

As I have already noted, spatial montage can also be seen as an aesthetics appropriate to the user experience of multitasking and multiple windows of GUI. In the text of his lecture "Of other spaces," Michel Foucault writes: "We are now in the epoch of simultaneity: we are in the epoch of juxtaposition, the epoch of near and far, of the side-by-side, of the dispersed . . . our experience of the world is less of a long life developing through time that that of a network that connects points and intersects with its own skein. . . ."[48] Writing this in the early 1970s, Foucault appears to prefigure not only the network society, exemplified by the Internet ("a network which connects points"), but also GUI ("epoch of simultaneity . . . of the side-by-side"). GUI allows users to run a number of software applications at the same time,

48. Michel Foucault, *Dits et ecrits: Selections, vol. 1* (New York: New Press, 1997).

and it uses the convention of multiple overlapping windows to present both data and controls. The construct of the desktop, which presents the user with multiple icons all of which are simultaneously and continuously "active" (since all of them can be clicked at any time), follows the same logic of "simultaneity" and the "side-by-side." On the level of computer programming, this logic corresponds to object-oriented programming. Instead of a single program that, like Ford's assembly line, is executed one statement at a time, the object-oriented paradigm features a number of objects that send messages to each other. These objects are all active simultaneously. The Object-oriented paradigm and multiple windows of GUI work together; the object-oriented approach, in fact, was used to program the original Macintosh GUI that substituted the "one command at a time" logic of DOS with the logic of simultaneity of multiple windows and icons.

The spatial montage of *My boyfriend came back from war!* follows the logic of simultaneity of the modern GUI. The multiple and simultaneously active icons and windows of GUI become the multiple and simultaneously active frames and hyperlinks of this Web artwork. Just as the GUI user can click on any icon at any time, thereby changing the overall "state" of the computer environment, the user of Lialina's site can activate different hyperlinks that are all simultaneously present. Every action changes either the contents of a single frame or creates a new frame or frames. In either case, the "state" of the screen as a whole is affected. The result is a new cinema in which the diacronic dimension is no longer privileged over the syncronic dimension, time is no longer privileged over space, sequence is no longer privileged over simultaneity, montage in time is no longer privileged over montage within a shot.

Cinema as an Information Space

As I discussed earlier, cinema language, which originally was an interface to narrative taking place in 3-D space, is now becoming an interface to all types of computer data and media. I demonstrated how such elements of this language as rectangular framing, the mobile camera, image transitions, montage in time, and montage within an image reappear in the general purpose HCI, the interfaces of software applications, and cultural interfaces.

Yet another way to think about new media interfaces in relation to cinema is to interpret the latter as information space. *If HCI is an interface to computer data, and a book is an interface to text, cinema can be thought of as an interface to events taking place in 3-D space.* Just as painting before it, cinema presents us with familiar images of visible reality—interiors, landscapes, human characters—arranged within a rectangular frame. The aesthetics of these arrangements ranges from extreme scarcity to extreme density. Examples of the former are paintings by Morandi and shots in *Late Spring* (Yasujiro Ozu, 1949); examples of the latter are paintings by Bosch and Bruegel (and much of Northern Renaissance painting in general), and many shots in *Man with a Movie Camera.*[49] It would take only a small leap to relate this density of "pictorial displays" to the density of contemporary information displays such as Web portals, which may contain a few dozen hyperlinked elements, or the interfaces of popular software packages, which similarly present the user with dozens of commands at once. Can contemporary information designers learn from information displays of the past—particular films, paintings, and other visual forms that follow the aesthetics of density?

In making such a connection, I rely once again on the work of art historian Svetlana Alpers, who claims that Italian Renaissance painting is primarily concerned with narration, whereas Dutch painting of the seventeenth century is focused on description.[50] The Italians subordinated details to narrative action, urging the viewer to focus on a main event; in Dutch paintings, particular details and, consequently, the viewer's attention, are more evenly distributed throughout the whole image. While functioning as a window into an illusionary space, the Dutch painting is also a loving catalog of different objects, material surfaces, and light effects painted in minute detail (works by Vermeer, for instance.) The dense surfaces of these paintings can easily be related to contemporary interfaces; in addition, they can also be related to the future aesthetics of the macrocinema when digital displays will move far beyond the resolution of analog television and film.

---

49. Anne Hollander's *Moving Pictures* presents parallel compositional and scenographic strategies in painting and cinema, and it can be a useful source for further thinking about them as precursors to contemporary information design. Anne Hollander, *Moving Pictures,* reprint edition (Cambridge, Mass.: Harvard University Press, 1991). Another useful study that also systematically draws comparisons between the compositional and scenographic strategies of the two media is Jacques Aumont, *The Image,* trans. Claire Pajackowska (London: British Film Institute, 1997).

50. Alpers, *The Art of Describing.*

The trilogy of computer films by Paris-based filmmaker Christian Boustani (graphics and computer effects by Alain Escale) develops such an aesthetics of density. Taking his inspiration from Renaissance Dutch painting as well as classical Japanese art, Boustani uses digital compositing to achieve an information density unprecedented in film. Although this density is typical for the traditions on which he draws, it has never before been achieved in cinema. In *Brugge* (1995), Boustani recreates the images typical of the winter landscape scenes in Dutch seventeenth-century painting. His next film *A Viagem* (The Voyage, 1998) achieves even higher information density; some shots of the film use as many as one thousand six hundred separate layers.

This new cinematic aesthetics of density seems to be highly appropriate for our age. If we are surrounded by highly dense information surfaces, from city streets to Web pages, it is appropriate to expect from cinema a similar logic. In similar fashion, we may think of spatial montage as reflecting another contemporary daily experience—working with a number of different applications on a computer at once. If we are now used to switching our attention rapidly from one program to another, from one set of windows and commands to another, we may find multiple streams of audio-visual information presented simultaneously more satisfying than the single stream of traditional cinema.

It is appropriate that some of the densest shots of *A Viagem* recreate a Renaissance marketplace, a symbol of the emerging capitalism that was probably responsible for the new density of Renaissance painting. (Think, for instance, of Dutch still lifes that function like store display-windows to overwhelm the viewer and seduce her into making a purchase.) In the same way, the commercialization of the Internet in the 1990s was responsible for the new density of Web pages. By the end of the decade, all the home pages of big companies and Internet portals had become indexes containing dozens of entries in small type. If every small area of the screen can potentially contain a lucrative ad or a link to a page with one, this leaves no place for an aesthetics of emptiness and minimalism. Thus it is not surprising that the commercialized Web shares the same aesthetic of information density and competing signs and images that characterizes visual culture in a capitalist society in general.

If Lialina's spatial montage relies on HTML frames and actions of the user to activate images appearing in these frames, Boustani's spatial montage is more purely cinematic and painterly. He combines the mobility of the camera and the movement of objects characteristic of cinema with the "hyperrealism" of old Dutch painting, which presented everything "in focus." In analog cinema, the inevitable "depth of field" artifact acts as a limit to the information density of an image. The achievement of Boustani is to create images where every detail is in focus and yet the overall image is easily readable. This could only be done through digital compositing. By reducing visible reality to numbers, the computer makes it possible for us to literally see in a new way. If, according to Benjamin, early twentieth-century cinema used the close-up "to bring things 'closer' spatially and humanly," "to get hold of an object at very close range," and, as a result, destroyed their aura, the digital composites of Boustani can be said to bring objects close to a viewer without "extracting" them from their places in the world. (Of course an opposite interpretation is also possible: We can say that Boustani's digital eye is superhuman. His vision can be interpreted as the gaze of a cyborg or a computer vision system that can see things equally well at any distance.)

Scrutinizing the prototypical perceptual spaces of modernity—the factory, the movie theater, the shopping arcade—Walter Benjamin insisted on the contiguity between perceptual experiences in the workplace and those outside it:

Whereas Poe's passers-by cast glances in all directions which still appeared to be aimless, today's pedestrians are obliged to do so in order to keep abreast of traffic signals. Thus technology has subjected the human sensorium to a complex kind of training. There came a day when a new and urgent need for stimuli was met by the film. In a film, perception in the form of shocks was established as a formal principle. That which determines the rhythm of production on a conveyer belt is the basis of the rhythm of reception in the film.[51]

For Benjamin, the modern regime of perceptual labor, where the eye is constantly asked to process stimuli, manifests itself equally in work and leisure. The eye is trained to keep pace with the rhythm of industrial production at the factory and to navigate through the complex visual semiosphere beyond the factory gates. It is appropriate to expect that the computer age will follow the same logic, presenting users with similarly structured perceptual experiences at work and home, on computer screens and off. Indeed, as I have already noted, we now use the same interfaces for work and leisure, a condition exemplified most dramatically by Web browsers. Another example is the use of the same interfaces in flight and military simulators, in computer

---

51. Walter Benjamin, "On Some Motives in Baudelaire," in *Illuminations*, 175.

games modeled after these simulators, and in the actual controls of planes and other vehicles (recall the popular perception of the Gulf War as a "video game war"). But if Benjamin appears to regret that the subjects of industrial society lost their premodern freedom of perception, now regimented by the factory, the modern city, and film, we may instead think of the information density of our own workspaces as a new aesthetic challenge, something to explore rather than condemn. Similarly, we should explore the aesthetic possibilities of all aspects of the user's experience with a computer, this key experience of modern life—the dynamic windows of GUI, multitasking, search engines, databases, navigable space, and others.

Cinema as a Code

When radically new cultural forms appropriate for the age of wireless telecommunication, multitasking operating systems, and information appliances arrive, what will they look like? How will we even know that they are here? Will future films look like a "data shower" from the movie *The Matrix*? Does the famous Xerox PARC fountain, whose water stream reflects the strength or weakness of the stock market, with stock data arriving in real time over the Internet, represent the future of public sculpture?

We do not yet know the answers to these questions. However, what artists and critics can do is point out the radically new nature of new media by staging—as opposed to hiding—its new properties. As my last example, I will discuss Vuk Cosic's ASCII films, which effectively stage one characteristic of computer-based moving images—their identity as computer code.[52]

It is worthwhile to relate Cosic's films to both Zuse's "found footage movies" from the 1930s, which I invoked in the beginning of this book, and to the first all-digital feature-length movie made sixty years later—Lucas's *Stars Wars: Episode 1—The Phantom Menace*.[53] Zuse superimposes digital code over the film images. Lucas follows the opposite logic: In his film, digital

---

52. http://www.vuk.org/ascii.

53. The reason that I refer to *Stars Wars: Episode 1—The Phantom Menace* as the first all-digital film, as opposed to reserving this title for *Toy Story,* the first feature-length animation by Pixar (1995), is that the former relies on human actors and real sets, supplementing them with computer animation. It is, in other words, a traditional live-action film simulated on computers, in contrast to *Toy Story,* whose reference is cartoons and the tradition of computer animation.

code "lies under" his images; that is, most images in the film were put together on computer workstations; during the postproduction process, they were pure digital data. The frames were made from numbers rather than bodies, faces, and landscapes. *The Phantom Menace,* therefore, can be called the first feature-length commercial abstract film—two hours worth of frames made from a matrix of numbers. But this is hidden from the audience.

What Lucas hides, Cosic reveals. His ASCII films "perform" the new status of media as digital data. The ASCII code that results when an image is digitized is displayed on the screen. The result is as satisfying poetically as it is conceptually—for what we get is a double image—a recognizable film image and an abstract code together. Both are visible at once. Thus rather than erasing the image in favor of the code as in Zuse's film, or hiding the code from us as in Lucas's film, code and image coexist.

Like the VinylVideo project by Gebhard Sengmüller, which records TV programs and films on old vinyl disks,[54] Cosic's ASCII initiative[55] is a systematic program of translating media content from one obsolete format into another. These projects remind us that *since at least the 1960s the operation of media translation has been at the core of our culture.* Films transferred to video, video transferred from one video format to another, video transferred to digital data, digital data transferred from one format to another—from floppy disks to Jaz drives, from CD-ROMs to DVDs, and so on, indefinitely. Artists noticed this new logic of culture early on: By the 1960s, Roy Lichtenstein and Andy Warhol had already made media translation the basis of their art. Sengmüller and Cosic understand that the only way to deal with the built-in media obsolescence of a modern society is by ironically resurrecting dead media. Sengmüller translates old TV programs into vinyl disks; Cosic translates old films into ASCII images.[56]

Why do I call ASCII images an obsolete media format? Before the printers capable of outputting raster digital images became widely available toward the end of the 1980s, it was commonplace to make printouts of images on dot matrix printers by converting the images into ASCII code. In

---

54. http://www.onlineloop.com/pub/VinulVideo.

55. www.vuk.org/ascii/aae.html

56. See also Bruce Sterling's Dead Media Project http://eff.bilkent.edu.tr/pub/Net_culture/Folklore/Dead_Media_Project/.

1999 I was surprised to still find the appropriate program on my UNIX system. Called simply "toascii," the command, according to the UNIX system manual page for the program, "prints textual characters that represent the black and white image used as input."

The reference to the early days of computing is not unique to Cosic, but is shared by other net.artists. Jodi.org, the famous net.art project created by the artistic team of Joan Heemskerk and Dirk Paesmans, often evokes DOS commands and the characteristic green color of computer terminals from the 1980s;[57] Russian net.artist Alexei Shulgin has performed music in the late 1990s using an old 386PC.[58] But in the case of ASCII code, its use evokes not only a peculiar episode in the history of computer culture but a number of earlier forms of media and communication technologies as well. ASCII is the acronym of "American Standard Code for Information Interchange." The code was originally developed for teleprinters and was only later adopted for computers in the 1960s. A teleprinter was a twentieth-century telegraph system that translated the input from a typewriter keyboard into a series of coded electric impulses, that were then transmitted over communications lines to a receiving system that decoded the pulses and printed the message onto a paper tape or other medium. Teleprinters were introduced in the 1920s and were widely used until the 1980s (Telex being the most popular system), when they were gradually replaced by fax and computer networks.[59]

ASCII code was itself an extension of an earlier code invented by Jean-Maurice-Emile Baudot in 1874. In Baudot code, each letter of an alphabet is represented by a five-unit combination of current-on or current-off signals of equal duration. ASCII code extends Baudot code by using eight-unit combinations (that is, eight "bits" or one "byte") to represent 256 different symbols. Baudot code itself was an improvement over the Morse code invented for early electric telegraph systems in the 1830s.

The history of ASCII code thus compresses a number of technological and conceptual developments that lead to (but I am sure will not stop at) mod-

---

57. www.jodi.org.

58. www.easylife.org/386dx.

59. "teleprinter," *Encyclopædia Britannica Online,* http://www.eb.com:180/bol/topic?thes_id= 378047.

ern digital computers—cryptography, real-time communication, communication network technology, coding systems. By juxtaposing ASCII code with the history of cinema, Cosic accomplishes what can be called an "artistic compression"; that is, along with staging the new status of moving images as a computer code, he also "encodes" many key issues of computer culture and new media art in these images.

As this book has argued, in a computer age, cinema, along with other established cultural forms, indeed becomes precisely a code. It is now used to communicate all types of data and experiences, and its language is encoded in the interfaces and defaults of software programs and in the hardware itself. Yet while new media strengthens existing cultural forms and languages, including the language of cinema, it simultaneously opens them up for redefinition. Elements of their interfaces become separated from the types of data to which they were traditionally connected. Further, cultural possibilities that were previously in the background, on the periphery, come into the center. For instance, animation comes to challenge live cinema; spatial montage comes to challenge temporal montage; database comes to challenge narrative; the search engine comes to challenge the encyclopedia; and, last but not least, online distribution of culture challenges traditional "off-line" formats. To use a metaphor from computer culture, new media transforms all culture and cultural theory into an "open source." This opening up of cultural techniques, conventions, forms, and concepts is ultimately the most promising cultural effect of computerization—an opportunity to see the world and the human being anew, in ways that were not available to "a man with a movie camera."

Index

development of screen, 95–103

overview, 94–95

representation versus simulation,
111–115

3-D and, 80–84

VRML, 83

window, 97–98

International Business Machines Corporation (IBM), 24

"International style" of modern visual
culture, 56

Internet. *See* World Wide Web

Interpellation, 61

Interpretation of Dreams, The (Freud),
59

Introduction to Poetics (Todorov), 12–13

Invisible Shape of Things Past, The
(ART+COM), 87, 88–89

Ippolito, Jon, 42–43

Jacquard, J. M., 22

Jacquard loom, 22, 42, 48

Jakobson, Roman, 77, 206

Jameson, Fredric, 131, 229–230, 252

Jay, Martin, 105, 175

Johnny Mnemonic (1995), 216, 313, 318

Johnson, Paul, 147–148

Johnson-Laird, Philip, 60

JPEG format, 54, 290

Jurassic Park (1993), 138, 142, 152,
200–204

"Just in time" delivery, 36

Juxtaposition of elements, 158–159

Kabakov, Ilya, 266–268

Kaufman, Mikhail, 240

Kepler's camera obscura, 104, 106

Keying, 150, 152

Kiefer, Anselm, 265

Kinetoscope, 23, 40, 298, 313, 315

Kino-brush, 307–308

Kino cheturekh izmereneii ("The Filmic
Fourth Dimension"), 156

Kino-eye, xxviii, 243, 273–281, 307–308

Kino-Pravda ("Cinema-Truth"), 149

Kleiser-Wolczak Construction Company, 194

Kodak, 137, 197

Komar, Vitaly, 203

Koolhaas, Rem, 115, 281

Krauss, Rosalind, 234–235

Kruger, Barbara, 142

Kuhn, Thomas, 285, 314

Laboratory experimentation, 15

Lacan, Jacques, 174–175

Lakoff, George, 60

Language

C, 117

of cinema, 309–333

avant-garde versus mainstream, xxvi

cinegratography, 309–314

code and, 330–333

information space and, 326–330

macrocinema, 322–326

"primitive" to "classical," 107

spatial montage, 322–326

temporality, 314–322

term of, 7

understanding, xv

COBOL, 117

computer media, 7

concept of, 7, 12–13

of cultural interfaces, 69–93

cinema, 10, 78–88

Human Computer Interface, 10,
88–93

overview, 69–73

printed word, 10, 73–78

effects and, xxviii

FORTRAN, 117

VRML, 250